ROMANS

Theological Masterpiece

Volume 1
Romans 1 - 8

JOSEPH R. HOLDER

Sovereign Grace Publications
Cullman, Alabama

Romans: Theological Masterpiece
Published by Sovereign Grace Publications
Post Office Box 1061
Cullman, Alabama 35056
www.sovgrace.net
sovgracepublications@gmail.com

Copyright © 2014 by Joseph R. Holder
All rights reserved. No portion of this book may be reproduced, stored in a retrieval system, or transmitted in any form or by any means, except brief quotations in printed reviews, without written permission from the publisher.

ISBN 978-1-929635-19-1

Scripture quotations, unless otherwise noted, are from the *King James Version* of the Bible.

Printed in the United States of America.

Volume 1 Contents

1 Introduction (1:1-7)	1
2 Theology with a Loving, Pastoral Touch (1:8-17)	5
3 Wrath Revealed (1:18-23)	11
4 Sinful Man's Moral Bottomless Pit (1:24-32)	17
5 Romans 2: What Was Paul's Intent (2)	21
6 Inexcusable! (2:1-12)	25
7 Godly Faith-Walk versus Superficial Pretense (2:13-27)	31
8 God's Definition of a Jew (2:28-29)	37
9 What Advantage to the Jews? (3:1-2)	41
10 Does God Need Our Unrighteousness? (3:3-8)	47
11 What is the State of Man with God? (3:9-18)	55
12 Man's Condition After the Fall (3:9-18)	61
13 Man's Deficiency: Ability and Motive (3:9-18)	65
14 God's Righteousness: With and Without the Law (3:19-23)	69
15 God's Solution for Sin—and for Sinners (3:24-26)	75
16 The Law of Faith (3:27-31)	79
17 Justification by Faith: What Does it Mean? (4:1-5)	83
18 Justification by Faith: Old Testament Perspective (4:3,6-10)	87
19 God's Promised Blessings to Abraham… (4:11-17)	93
20 Abraham and Hope (4:17-22)	99
21 Abraham's Example Urges Us to the Same Faith (4:23-25)	103
22 Glorious Peace (5:1-2)	109
23 How Does Justification by Faith Work? (5:3-5)	113
24 From the Lesser to the Greater (5:6-11)	117
25 Man's Hope: God! (5:6)	121
26 A Saving God (5:6)	127
27 For Whom Did Christ Die? (5:6)	133
28 For Whom Did Christ Die? For Sinners or Good People? (5:7-8)	139
29 Super-Abounding Grace: Secure Salvation in Christ (5:9-10)	145
30 Eternal Blessings: A Present Reality (5:11)	151
31 All of Grace: Why? (5:12, 18-19)	155
32 Why Must God Alone Save Sinners? (5:12-17)	161
33 The Universal Reign of Death (5:13-14)	167
34 Adam and Jesus: Comparison or Contrast? (5:15-17)	173
35 The Threefold State of Man (5:18-19)	179

36 Grace Reigns! (5:20-21)	183
37 The Ethics of Grace (6:1-2)	187
38 Baptism or Baptism? Biblical Ecclesiology (6:3-10)	191
39 A Christian Self-Image (6:11)	201
40 Christian Ethics (6:12-14)	207
41 Christian Service (6:14-16)	213
42 Whom Do You Serve? (6:17-18)	219
43 A Servant: Christian Ethics (6:19-22)	225
44 Wages and a Gift (6:23)	231
45 The Death of Legalism (7:1-4)	237
46 How Do You Serve God? The Old or New Way (7:4-6)	247
47 Intense Conflict: A Characteristic of Grace (7:7-13)	251
48 The Dynamics of Spiritual Conflict (7:14-21)	255
49 Two Laws in Conflict (7:22-25)	261
50 Another Law: No Condemnation (8:1-4)	267
51 Nature vs. Conduct (8:5-9)	275
52 A Matter of Life and Death (8:10-11)	281
53 Christian Ethics and Life in Christ (8:12-14)	287
54 The Spirit of Adoption (8:15-16)	295
55 Joint-Heirs with Christ (8:17-18)	301
56 Final Things: What do you expect? (8:19-23)	305
57 Hope: The Interface Between the Temporal... (8:24-25)	309
58 The Holy Spirit: Our Holy Helper (8:26-27)	313
59 Who? What? How? Things that Work for Good... (8:28)	323
60 God's Five-Step Plan: Eternity to Eternity (8:29-30)	351
61 All Things or All Things? (8:31-34)	365
62 Who's Behind the Who? (8:35-39)	373
63 No Separation: God's Commitment (8:35-39)	379

1
Introduction

> PAUL, a servant of Jesus Christ, called to be an apostle, separated unto the gospel of God, (Which he had promised afore by his prophets in the holy scriptures,) Concerning his Son Jesus Christ our Lord, which was made of the seed of David according to the flesh; And declared to be the Son of God with power, according to the spirit of holiness, by the resurrection from the dead: By whom we have received grace and apostleship, for obedience to the faith among all nations, for his name: Among whom are ye also the called of Jesus Christ: To all that be in Rome, beloved of God, called to be saints: Grace to you and peace from God our Father, and the Lord Jesus Christ. (Romans 1:1–7)

Paul's letter to the Romans has been described as the only inspired "Systematic theology" text in existence. Theologians frequently write a thesis of their cardinal beliefs, more or less arranged in their view of a systematic arrangement of these beliefs. I have a shelf full of these texts in my library. Some of them are commendable reading; some are questionable at best. The more I read them, and the more I read Paul's inspired writings, the more I want to read Paul.

At its heart, any worthy book that claims the "Systematic Theology" category must look behind a list of doctrinal ideas, "Systematically" arranged to the "Systematic Arranger." When Paul wrote the words, "Concerning his Son Jesus Christ our Lord..." he made the point. If we become so focused on the various doctrinal ideas that we find in Romans that we forget the Person of the Lord Jesus Christ, in particular his incarnation, death, burial, resurrection, and victorious ascension, we lose the value of our study. Without him and his finished work at the heart of our message, any doctrinal statement becomes a nice philosophical idea, but little more.

Of all the New Testament letters appearing under his name, Romans is likely the only letter that Paul wrote to a church to which he did not personally first preach the gospel and convert them to the faith of Christ. Paul's letter to the Romans anticipates a visit, but he has not at the time of writing this letter ever visited Rome.

Although I treasure the convenience of the Bible's present physical arrangement, divided into chapters and verses, sometimes this arrangement hinders cohesive reading and interpretation more than it helps. If you plan to study a particular book of the Bible, in particular one of the New Testament letters, you should first read that letter from beginning to end several times over. Try to get a clear and cohesive sense of the letter's purpose and contents. Where possible, look for a title or a brief sentence—never an endless rambling sentence—that captures the letter's message. One of my favorite examples of this thematic title is my title for the Book of Jonah, "I won't go; I will go; I wish I hadn't gone." Although I haven't found a similarly catchy title for the Roman letter, my inclination would be something in the category of "Get your act together." Clearly from the content of the Roman letter, there were major Jew-Gentile tensions in Rome, and very likely in the church there as well. We find an interesting hint at such a problem in the Book of Acts.

> *And found a certain Jew named Aquila, born in Pontus, lately come from Italy, with his wife Priscilla; (because that Claudius had commanded all Jews to depart from Rome:) and came unto them* (Acts 18:2).

Notice the parenthetic statement: the Roman emperor Claudius had commanded all Jews to depart from Rome. We find a supportive statement in the historical writings of the Roman historian Suetonius, referring to a heated controversy in Rome among various sects of the Jews because they disagreed regarding a certain notable person named "Crestus." Given the clear point of Acts 18:2, it would appear that believing and unbelieving Jews in Rome became quite heated in their disagreement regarding the Person of the Lord Jesus Christ. Rather than bother himself with any attempt to settle this private cultural and religious problem, Claudius simply expelled all Jews from the city.

Imagine the specific setting of the church in Rome. They consist of a mixture of both Jews and Gentiles, but they all agree on the Person of Jesus. However, they are expelled from the city under Claudius' edict. At some future time, they are presumably allowed to return to the city. The members of the Roman Church return to their church, expecting to find things as they left them, but they may have been unhappily surprised to discover a changed church that had become all too "Gentile" for their liking. We have no specific historical knowledge of this situation, but it seems to explain a lot of the pervasive emphasis that Paul places on the question in his Roman letter.

If you make a habit of reading Paul's letters from beginning to end in one setting, you will discover that Paul typically identifies his major theme in writing somewhere near the beginning of his letters, and he then closes the idea-parenthesis by repeating that idea near the end of his letter. Paul quickly notifies the Romans at the beginning of this letter that he intends to visit them, and that he hopes they will support him in his desire to travel from them into what we know today as Western Europe after he leaves Rome. The Roman Church can't provide support of any kind, prayer or financial, if they are engaged in a bitter internal schism between Jewish believers and Gentile believers. In Romans 15:23-24, we see the closing parenthesis of Paul's point regarding his travel plans and his desire for the Roman Church's support in this work. Thus, I reach my suggested thematic title of "Get your act together."

Concerning his Son Jesus Christ our Lord.... Whatever the doctrinal theme we find in Romans, we must anchor that doctrine in Paul's opening foundational truth. Everything he intends to write in this letter he here reminds us that his objective is to show its clear link to the person and work of the Lord Jesus Christ.

By whom we have received grace and apostleship, for obedience to the faith among all nations, for his name: Among whom are ye also the called of Jesus Christ.... Paul in no way indicates that he views the Roman Church as any different from any other church that he has written or to whom he has preached. The slow rise of the Roman Church from one of many churches the Lord raised up and blessed into the corrupted idea of the "Mother Church" is a sad chapter in the history of the Christian faith. The history of this church serves as a powerful reminder that is briefly stated in the cliché, "Absolute power corrupts absolutely."

Whether we worship in a New Testament church in Rome or in a small community near our home, we can only claim the title of church based on the simple formula that Paul here states. The Lord calls us in grace to strive toward a common goal, "…obedience to the faith…." God in Scripture has set the mark of what is and what is not legitimately classified as "…the faith." He did not give the Roman Church, nor any other church or church pastor, license to revise or in any way alter "…the faith…" that he personally gave. Notice this principle in Jude's letter.

> *Beloved, when I gave all diligence to write unto you of the common salvation, it was needful for me to write unto you, and exhort you that ye should earnestly contend for the faith which was once delivered unto the saints.* (Jude 1:3)

Jude identifies that this faith was "...once delivered..." not that it is constantly revised. And Jude further identifies that the faith was delivered to the saints, not to the Church at Rome. Paul underscores the same point.

> *But if I tarry long, that thou mayest know how thou oughtest to behave thyself in the house of God, which is the church of the living God, the pillar and ground of the truth.* (1 Timothy 3:15)

The institution of the Lord's church, not any particular local church, is the "...pillar and ground of the truth...."

"Faith" appears in our King James Bible some two hundred thirty-one times in its various forms. In most appearances, we find the simple reference to the principle of faith. In a number of New Testament passages, we find the word in conjunction with the definite article, the, as in "...the faith." It is my belief that these specific appearances of "the faith" refer to a body of commonly believed truths that united all of the apostles, and faithful ministers and churches of the first century. Our objective as twenty-first century believers is to study to discover that "faith" and to obey it. Paul reminds us that we have been called to "...obedience to the faith."

2
Theology with a Loving, Personal Touch

First, I thank my God through Jesus Christ for you all, that your faith is spoken of throughout the whole world. For God is my witness, whom I serve with my spirit in the gospel of his Son, that without ceasing I make mention of you always in my prayers; Making request, if by any means now at length I might have a prosperous journey by the will of God to come unto you. For I long to see you, that I may impart unto you some spiritual gift, to the end you may be established; That is, that I may be comforted together with you by the mutual faith both of you and me. Now I would not have you ignorant, brethren, that oftentimes I purposed to come unto you, (but was let hitherto,) that I might have some fruit among you also, even as among other Gentiles. I am debtor both to the Greeks, and to the Barbarians; both to the wise, and to the unwise. So, as much as in me is, I am ready to preach the gospel to you that are at Rome also. For I am not ashamed of the gospel of Christ: for it is the power of God unto salvation to every one that believeth; to the Jew first, and also to the Greek. For therein is the righteousness of God revealed from faith to faith: as it is written, The just shall live by faith. (Romans 1:8–17)

Continuing our thought that Paul's Roman letter is our only inspired systematic theology text, we need not add one additional compliment to his theme. Many—perhaps most—systematic theology texts avoid any kind of warm or personal touch. They are wholly impersonal, dealing with various Bible doctrines in a highly technical way. In Romans, though Paul deals with most of the major doctrines that define sound Biblical doctrine, he always does so in a warm, almost pastoral, and personal manner. He supremely cares for God, and he is uncompromising on questions of significant Bible Doctrines (A quick read of Galatians makes that point beyond doubt). But, through all the doctrines and in all of his primary emphasis on God, Paul never forgets that he is writing to a truly human, flesh and bones human audience, and he loves them dearly. His primary objective is to lead them to the same understanding of God and of sound Bible doctrine that the Lord has given to him.

Even though Paul had never visited the church in Rome at the time of his letter, he still sounds sincerely pastoral and caring for the people in this church. He thanks the Lord for them and for their sound Christian witness. He prays for them and for their special needs. He even prays for the Lord to remove the obstacles that have so far hindered his visit to them. He longs to finally see them and to preach the gospel to them so as to enrich them in the faith, even as he expects to be comforted in the faith as he comforts them. He seeks to establish them in this mutual faith.

...to the end you may be established; That is, that I may be comforted together with you by the mutual faith both of you and me. For Paul, relativism was not an acceptable belief system. Further, for Paul, a wide, highly inclusive and highly tolerant acceptance of various beliefs was also not acceptable. His objective and prayer is that the Romans be established, settled and grounded in the mutual faith, a belief system that both the Romans and Paul believed in common. A common faith, a uniform belief system anchored in the revelation of God in Scripture, was always Paul's goal, and he was not the least bashful to confront anyone who contradicted that common belief.

Students of the New Testament sometimes refer to the New Testament letters, the books that begin with Romans (perhaps the whole New Testament), as being "occasional" letters. The meaning is that each writer of these letters became aware of a need or a problem that should be corrected in the life of his recipient, be that recipient an individual, a whole church, or a whole region of churches. Not a single New Testament letter was written as a friendly "How are you? I am fine," generic, "Howdy, friend" letter. Each letter reveals a need in the recipient audience that the letter addresses and corrects. Simply stated, each letter in the New Testament surfaces problems and needs in the original audience, and sets forth the corrective action or doctrine that, if believed and applied, will establish the recipients in the common faith of the New Testament.

I am debtor both to the Greeks, and to the Barbarians; both to the wise, and to the unwise. So, as much as in me is, I am ready to preach the gospel to you that are at Rome also. Occasionally people who do not understand the doctrines of grace properly will hurl insulting, derogatory, and often untrue accusations against these believers. While I do not believe that Scripture teaches that God uses the gospel in any way to bring about the new birth, I believe quite strongly that the Lord commanded us to preach the gospel where ever and whenever we have opportunity.

In Paul's words in this verse, we owe a debt to the Lord's people where ever we find them, and with no regard for the dialect they speak or the color of their skin. We can only pay that debt by preaching the gospel to them. God obligates us to do so.

Occasionally critics of those who hold to the doctrines of grace will falsely accuse us of downplaying the importance of the gospel or of not being as ready as Scripture requires us to preach the gospel. They err. Some of the most self-sacrificing preachers I've ever known believed the doctrines of grace and made incredible sacrifices to preach anywhere the door of opportunity opened for them. This self-sacrificing devotion to preaching the gospel stands in rather vivid contrast to modern preachers who require a minimum financial guarantee before they will agree to preach at a certain place.

A friend and pastor of a contemporary church told me many years ago of an occasion when the church that he served invited a well-known and highly-esteemed seminary professor to speak to their church. The man required a minimum "contribution" to his ministry before he agreed. And, to my friend's great disappointment, within three or four days of the speaking engagement, this professor started phoning the church treasurer, asking where his money was. Godly men who believe in grace will go anywhere they can and preach the gospel without guarantees or assurance of personal enrichment. So who is the more willing and obedient preacher? We are ready to pay the debt that the Lord lays on us, and we do not seek debt owed to us in the process.

For I am not ashamed of the gospel of Christ: for it is the power of God unto salvation to every one that believeth; to the Jew first, and also to the Greek. A simple review of the grammar of this sentence will dismiss much bad doctrine that is sometimes imposed onto it. Who is the recipient audience of the gospel, according to Paul? He makes the point quite clearly. The gospel is God's power, indeed saving power, to those who believe. The verb "…believeth…" is present tense. Paul did not teach that the gospel was God's saving power to people who presently do not believe, but who might at some future time believe the good news of the gospel. Paul reinforced this point as he began a sermon that we find recorded in Acts.

> *Men and brethren, children of the stock of Abraham, and whosoever among you feareth God, to you is the word of this salvation sent* (Acts 13:26).

The Lord doesn't send his gospel to all humanity. He sends this good news message to a particular class of people, a class that Scripture repeatedly and clearly identifies. Aside from their being natural or cultural Jews, children of the stock of Abraham, Paul addressed his gospel to anyone in his present audience who feared God. Just as Paul defined his recipient audience in Romans 1:16 as believers, he qualified his audience in Acts 13:26 as God-fearers.

How do we know the spiritual state of people to whom we might preach? We do not always know, nor can we know. Our objective in preaching is not to pre-inspect and pre-qualify our audience. Our divine assignment, or divinely assigned debt, is to preach to any and all who will hear us. Let the message of God—and the God of the message—qualify the audience and apply the message to their hearts.

The word "salvation" in any of its various forms that appear in Scripture is a broad term. It does not always refer to the same thing. This sequence of questions is occasionally used by R. C. Sproul to accurately make the point that I here make. When we see this work in Scripture, we need to ask a number of questions to learn what the passage is teaching.

1. Saved from what?
2. Saved to what?
3. Who does the saving?

Scripture uses the term to identify a wide variety of "salvations" or deliverances.

1. Deliverance from natural disaster. Only by abiding in the ship could Paul's fellow-travelers ensure their safety during shipwreck (Acts 27:31).
2. In Acts 2:40, Peter commanded his repentant hearers to "...save yourselves from this untoward generation." In this case Peter's hearers did the "saving." And Peter answered the question, Saved from what? He was not telling these people what they needed to do for their eternal salvation, but he rather was teaching them what to do to save themselves from a wicked generation of people who, though claiming to be the custodians and teachers of God's true way, were in fact suffering from

moral and spiritual scoliosis. The Greek word translated "untoward" or "crooked" in this verse is the root for our English word, *scoliosis*.
3. In 1 Timothy 4:16, Paul urged Timothy to be faithful in his ministry. In so doing, Timothy would both save himself and his hearers. In terms of their possessing eternal life, or eternal salvation, both Timothy and his hearers already possessed it. However, in terms of this particular need, Timothy would become the savior, and his faithful ministry would save him and his hearers from many pitfalls.
4. When we examine the word "salvation" from a truly spiritual perspective, Scripture abundantly makes the point that it uses the word in more than one way. Every appearance of the word does not deal with going to heaven when we die. *"Therefore I endure all things for the elect's sakes that they may also obtain the salvation which is in Christ Jesus with eternal glory"* (2 Timothy 2:10). In this verse, Paul identifies a salvation that is "...in Christ Jesus..." but he also distinguishes this particular salvation from the salvation that relates to "...eternal glory." Dr. Tom Constable makes the point of this passage quite clearly: "*Here then are **saved people in need of salvation**! The salvation in view is necessarily sanctification or, perhaps, more precisely, victorious perseverance through trials (1:8; 2:3, 9)*"[1] [emphasis added]. The people of whom Paul writes are saved; they are heirs of "eternal glory." However, they distinctly need a present salvation that relates to the gospel in the here and now.
5. We cannot miss the point that Scripture also uses the term specifically at times related to God's eternal purpose to save his elect, his beloved and chosen people, from their sins. Matthew 1:21 clearly and simply makes that point, and Jesus alone is God's appointed Savior in that function.

By describing his gospel as God's power to save believers, Paul makes his point for us. We need not add anything to that point. Based on 1 John 5:1, a believer in Christ already possesses eternal life; is already born again. So Paul's objective is not to preach to people to contribute in some way to

---

[1] Tom Constable, *Tom Constable's Expository Notes on the Bible*, 2 Ti 2:10 (Galaxie Software, 2003; 2003).

their new birth, but he rather preaches to born-again people to save them to a productive, God-glorifying life in the here and now.

For therein is the righteousness of God revealed from faith to faith: as it is written, The just shall live by faith. Paul reinforces the points we've already made. In the gospel, God reveals his righteousness from faith to faith.

Two major views of the "...faith to faith..." term are to be considered. One view holds that God sends the gospel to his born-again children who have faith, but their hearing, believing, and obeying the gospel shall grow their faith. The gospel then becomes God's method of growing our faith from one degree to a greater degree of fruitfulness, a Bible truth, whether this verse makes that point or not.

The second view is that both the preacher and the hearer must possess faith for the gospel to be communicated so as to produce the results described in this lesson. This is also a Biblical truth. The person who has no faith has no way to hear, understand, believe, or implement the teachings of the gospel. *"But the natural man receiveth not the things of the Spirit of God: for they are foolishness unto him: neither can he know them, because they are spiritually discerned"* (1 Corinthians 2:14).

Thus, according to Paul's systematic theology model, our gospel message begins with a God-centric declaration that, though not in any way contributing to the new birth, provides a highly beneficial blessing to those who hear it and believe it.

3
Wrath Revealed

For the wrath of God is revealed from heaven against all ungodliness and unrighteousness of men, who hold the truth in unrighteousness; Because that which may be known of God is manifest in them; for God hath shewed it unto them. For the invisible things of him from the creation of the world are clearly seen, being understood by the things that are made, even his eternal power and Godhead; so that they are without excuse: Because that, when they knew God, they glorified him not as God, neither were thankful; but became vain in their imaginations, and their foolish heart was darkened. Professing themselves to be wise, they became fools, And changed the glory of the uncorruptible God into an image made like to corruptible man, and to birds, and fourfooted beasts, and creeping things (Romans 1:18–23).

Paul juxtaposes God's wrath in our study verses to God's righteousness that appears in the verses preceding. While God reveals his righteousness in the good news of the gospel, he reveals his wrath from heaven. Perhaps more damage to the Christian faith has been wrought by preachers who presume that they must reveal both God's righteousness and his wrath in their preaching, giving rise to the derogatory use of "fire and brimstone" preaching. While Paul quite clearly establishes the point of God's righteousness in his wrath against sin, he distinguishes the source of information regarding this righteous wrath.

All too often Bible students who study this lesson become unprofitably sidetracked by a pointless pursuit of the question, "Are these recipients of God's wrath born again or not?" Paul does not make a point either way on this question, so neither should we. His purpose seems to further affirm God's righteousness that he has declared in the gospel; even in righteous wrath against sin—and sinners—God remains wholly righteous. The recipients of divine wrath justly deserve that wrath. The utter unprofitable question misses Paul's whole intent. Whether a person is born again or not, God is righteous, and he declares his wrath against "…all ungodliness and unrighteousness of men.…" He doesn't give a free pass to his children who sin. He doesn't cause them to sin, and he doesn't passively allow them to sin so that he may then orchestrate their sin for a greater good. He reveals his wrath from heaven against all sin. Period; end of story. Isn't that the point of the passage?

As Paul unfolds this teaching, he doesn't delve into profound salvific doctrines. He anchors his points on the basic moral character of God and his moral commandments that relate to his righteous character. As sinful people choose to reject God's moral code, they follow a predictable course, a point that Paul will trace through the remainder of this chapter. The utter moral rebellion of these people appears in the general description, "...who hold the truth in unrighteousness." To "hold" indicates a choking, stifling suppression of truth, in this context, a reference to God's moral truth.

Because that which may be known of God is manifest in them; for God hath showed it unto them. A certain tension surfaces as we examine this sentence. Paul and other inspired writers make the point repeatedly and clearly that the unregenerate not only do not have any desire toward God and his righteousness, but they cannot do so (Romans 8:5-8; 1 Corinthians 2:14 – do not overlook both the absence of a desire for good in these verses, and also a comprehensive inability that appears in the use of "...cannot..." or "...neither can he...")

So what is it that "...may be known of God..."? Contextually, Paul repeatedly makes the point that, however, incapable fallen man may be of desiring or performing right deeds as believers think of this conduct, even fallen humans have a basic sense of morality, albeit a sense that they consistently defy and ignore. In fact, Scripture indicates that fallen man is perversely bent to hate and defy God's moral law. However, Scripture does not teach that fallen man is ignorant of its moral content.

Fallen man has the ability to know that certain behaviors are inherently and morally wrong. They are utterly void of any spiritual ability, the point of the two passages cited, but they are not so void of the ability to know the difference between moral rightness and wrongness. That "...which may be known of God..." relates to his moral character, not to his spiritual dealings with his people. Paul's contextual point has to do with moral character, not with going to heaven when you die, and he affirms that God has made his moral character known to fallen man.

Consider a primary example. When God gave Adam his Garden-law, he warned Adam of the penalty for violation. In the same day that Adam ate the forbidden fruit, he would die. Since Adam lived to be over nine hundred years after the Garden incident, the primary death indicated in the penalty is clearly not physical death, though physical death certainly follows that violation as the ultimate outcome. As we read the account of the fall and of God's confrontation of Adam and Eve in the Garden (Genesis 3), the point that Paul here makes is clear. Immediately upon eating the forbidden fruit, Adam and Eve were aware of their changed condition. They knew that their actions violated God's law, and they knew that God's wrath was sure to fall upon them. They have now fallen, no less so than after God drove them from the Garden. Yet they are keenly aware of their sin and of God's reaction to their sin.

When God confronts Adam and Eve, they immediately reveal the fallen, broken character that has defined sinful humanity from that day to this. They try to hide themselves from God, a foolish and futile effort. Then, when God confronts them, they reveal the fallen, broken, "blame game" that we see in sinful humans to this day. Never accept responsibility for your sins; find a way to twist the facts and blame someone else for the sins that you committed. And who better to blame than God? "The woman whom thou gavest to be with me, she gave me of the tree, and I ate it" (Genesis 3:12). "The serpent beguiled me, and I did eat" (Genesis 3:13). True to fallen man's character, what better culprit to blame for one's sin than God himself? Man continues to seek creative ways to blame God for his sins.

We cannot doubt from the Genesis 3 narrative that, however fallen they were, Adam and Eve clearly knew that they had crossed the line of God's moral law to them. That is precisely the point that Paul makes in our study passage. Fallen man still knows that he has broken God's moral law; he simply doesn't care.

In making this point, Paul asserts a fundamental worldview that Scripture consistently affirms. In the philosophical challenges that wrestle with the question of evil, no worldview wholly avoids some degree of difficulty. Invariably, when some tragic event occurs, people of various philosophical or religious persuasions will question, "Why?" Even among Christians, you will hear, "If God is all-powerful and all-good, why/how could God allow such a thing?" The questions themselves reveal a preconception that fails to grasp the Biblical worldview. Some who profess Christian faith will hold to the historical deist idea that God created the material world, set certain physical or natural laws in motion, and withdrew, wholly becoming the observer. Others will embrace the mirror opposite view and claim that God literally causes every event that occurs. And often advocates of one or the other of these two radical views will play the

Excluded Middle (or the older "Horns of Dilemma") logical fallacy by claiming that no other view exists. You must embrace one or the other of these extreme views.

Factually, many other views exist, and Scripture rejects both of these views in favor of the ignored middle ground. From Genesis to Revelation, Scripture affirms that God created the material universe, and that he remains intimately involved, but Scripture also affirms with equal clarity the nature of his involvement. God never causes, or for that matter, even passively "allows" wicked people to do wicked things. How can we say this? Simple. The passage before us makes the point. God shows man his moral character, and he commands man to obey that moral code. He holds man fully and individually responsible and accountable for his own conduct. Adolph Hitler was not a pawn on the strings of a cosmic puppeteer. Hitler made moral—utterly immoral—choices for which Hitler was alone responsible and accountable to God. The Biblical middle ground holds that God created a moral universe, not an impersonal machine universe that simply runs on its own, or a robotic universe in which every event unfolds according to the cosmic puppeteer's string-pulling.

For God shall bring every work into judgment, with every secret thing, whether it be good, or whether it be evil (Ecclesiastes 12:14).

Just as God held Adam and Eve personally responsible for their actions, he continues to hold individual humans personally responsible and accountable to him for their actions. Either in this life by means of chastening his own children, or in the Day of Judgment when he shall judge and righteously sentence the wicked, God rules this universe as its Moral Governor. This Biblical worldview maintains the moral high ground in defense of God and of his moral governance over all.

Professing themselves to be wise, they became fools, And changed the glory of the uncorruptible God into an image made like to corruptible man, and to birds, and fourfooted beasts, and creeping things. The words behind this English translation are interesting. The Greek word translated "wise" is *sophos*, and the Greek word translated "fools" is *moraino*, the Greek root for our English "moron." God-hating, God-rejecting humans view themselves as wise, as so very "sophisticated," but in fact God views those same humans as being moral morons. Thus, they are in fact "sophisticated morons." And not so sophisticated at that, when God shines his moral spotlight on them. Simply stated, sinful, depraved man's problem is not an intellectual, but a moral problem.

While actively rejecting God's moral compass and conduct, sinful humans consciously and actively dishonor God. They habitually corrupt the moral image of God that he has revealed of himself in nature, by changing that image into their own corrupted image. Chuck Swindoll has made an interesting observation from this passage. Consider modern man's near-worship of the automobile, and you get just one glimpse of this degenerative process. Notice Paul's description of the path that man follows, and observe its application in just one of the major automobile manufacturers. In full defense of Ford, we could choose almost any other auto maker and see similar results.

1. The first step of degeneration appears as sinful humans change the image of the uncorruptible God into an image made like to corruptible man. The first few generations of Ford automobiles were named after notable humans, e. g. "Ford," "Lincoln."
2. The next step in the downward path creates a corruptible image of God in the image of birds. And soon Ford followed the pattern. We see "Thunderbird," and Ford's lowly "Falcon," a model they'd like to forget.
3. The third step degenerates to four-footed beasts. And the good folks at Ford lived up to the human flaw with such auto models as "Cougar" and "Mustang."
4. And the final downward step depicts God in terms of creeping things. Are we surprised to find the appearance of "Cobra" in the noted auto models?

Lest you think that I unfairly picked on the Ford folks, I confess to owning a Ford that I dearly love, but I do not worship my truck, nor do I in any way compare it to my God.

As we study the following lessons from Paul, we shall see his development of God, the Moral Governor of his world, and the Moral Judge of those—all of them—who choose to ignore and to break his moral Law.

4
Sinful Man's Moral Bottomless Pit

Wherefore God also gave them up to uncleanness through the lusts of their own hearts, to dishonour their own bodies between themselves… For this cause God gave them up unto vile affections: for even their women did change the natural use into that which is against nature…And even as they did not like to retain God in their knowledge, God gave them over to a reprobate mind, to do those things which are not convenient; Being filled with all unrighteousness, fornication, wickedness, covetousness, maliciousness; full of envy, murder, debate, deceit, malignity; whisperers, Backbiters, haters of God, despiteful, proud, boasters, inventors of evil things, disobedient to parents, Without understanding, covenantbreakers, without natural affection, implacable, unmerciful: Who knowing the judgment of God, that they which commit such things are worthy of death, not only do the same, but have pleasure in them that do them. (Romans 1:24–32)

In Romans 1:18, Paul stated that God reveals His wrath from heaven against all ungodliness and unrighteousness of men. As we read the verses following, we see two major points. First, we see the full depths of man's sin that fully deserves divine wrath. Secondly, we see three specific stages of man's digression into deeper sin. Man in sin without God never improves. He only grows worse, plunging himself deeper into his sins than he was before. It is instructive to see the various manifestations of man's sin in each of these stages.

1. First stage. *Because that, when they knew God, they glorified him not as God, neither were thankful; but became vain in their imaginations, and their foolish heart was darkened. Professing themselves to be wise, they became fools, And changed the glory of the uncorruptible God into an image made like to corruptible man, and to birds, and fourfooted beasts, and creeping things. Wherefore God also gave them up to uncleanness through the lusts of their own hearts, to dishonour their own bodies between themselves: Who changed the truth of God into a lie, and worshipped and served the creature more than the Creator, who is blessed for ever. Amen.*
2. Second Stage. *For this cause God gave them up unto vile affections: for even their women did change the natural use into that which is against nature: And likewise also the men, leaving the natural use of the woman, burned in their*

lust one toward another; men with men working that which is unseemly, and receiving in themselves that recompence of their error which was meet.

3. Third Stage. *And even as they did not like to retain God in their knowledge, God gave them over to a reprobate mind, to do those things which are not convenient; Being filled with all unrighteousness, fornication, wickedness, covetousness, maliciousness; full of envy, murder, debate, deceit, malignity; whisperers, Backbiters, haters of God, despiteful, proud, boasters, inventors of evil things, disobedient to parents, Without understanding, covenantbreakers, without natural affection, implacable, unmerciful: Who knowing the judgment of God, that they which commit such things are worthy of death, not only do the same, but have pleasure in them that do them.*" (Romans 1:21–32)

The deeper sinful man plunges himself into this moral black hole the more he becomes wholly self-destructive, as well as destructive of any good thing around him.

While Scripture teaches that God shall eventually call every thought, word, and deed to account before Himself and His righteous Law, the question arises. How does God react now to this pattern of human sin? Three times in this context, we read the rather unusual language that in one way or another states the answer to this question, "…God gave them up…" "…God gave them up…" and "…God gave them over…."

By these three stages, punctuated by the "God gave them up/over" divine reaction, we discover that God maintains His moral government of this world. He rules, not by irresistible coercion, but by moral commandment. It is said that a famous artist always subtly imbedded a representation of himself into each of his paintings. Psalm 8, Psalm 19, and many other Scriptures, including this lesson from the first chapter of Romans, reminds us that God has stamped His signature onto His creation. Fallen man cannot evolve himself into a spiritual relationship with God, but he has the moral quality of knowing right from wrong, though, as noted in our last study, man's dominant problem is not a matter of intellect, but of moral collapse. Many years ago I subscribed for several years to a monthly journal published by a group of people, many of whom had respectable natural science credentials, but they also believed in the Bible account of creation, not in evolution. In one month's journal, the publication featured an article that reported on a gathering of scientists in Great Britain. These scientists were atheistic scientists who rejected the Biblical record. The keynote speaker shocked the gathering with his speech. He clearly stated that he was not a Christian or a believer in God, but, based on scientific evidence and reasoning, he had come to reject the idea of evolution. He then used a fascinating analogy. To believe in evolution as a scientist is equivalent to believing that a whirlwind can sweep through a junk yard and assemble a Boeing 707, flight ready. This scientist didn't try to explain beginnings or origins. He simply confronted the idea of evolution as a scientist and concluded that it was untenable.

If I were walking along a shoreline that man had never walked before and happened to see a watch lying on the sand, picked it up, and, upon observation and study, learned that this device is synchronized precisely with the earth's time system, my first logical conclusion would be to wonder who its creator was, not ponder how such a magnificent machine could have evolved.

God imprints His creative signature onto His created universe so that, from the constellations that we only see through the Hubel telescope all the way to submicroscopic cells, the order and intelligence of nature cries out for an intelligent Creator. The conclusion of God's observation of His creation (first chapter of Genesis) is that "...God saw that it was good." (Genesis 1:25) Along with a sense of pleasure and accomplishment, this word "Good" also carries a certain moral quality. God endowed a moral compass into His natural creation, including the man and woman that He made. God's dominion over His creation as its moral Governor is such that, at the final Judgment, He can righteously declare that sinful man is "...without excuse..." for all the sins that he committed. (Romans 1:20)

The three-fold appearance of the "...God gave them up..." point also reminds us that God, as moral Governor of the universe, exercises a certain restraining influence on this world. However, the three stages of man's response to divine morality provide evidence that God does not irresistibly cause or manipulate human behavior. He commands the good, publishes the righteous penalty for violation, and the blessing for obedience, and intervenes in natural ways that encourage right thinking and acting. As sinful, fallen humans consciously choose to ignore these revelations and commandments, choosing rather to dig deeper into the black hole of sin, God reacts in the only way that He as a righteous moral Governor can react. He "...gives them up..." to their depraved appetites. He withdraws a measure of His divine restraint. Rather than feel alarm at the divine withdrawal, wicked, fallen humans hungrily plunge deeper into the self-satisfying pursuit of their sinful appetites.

Who knowing the judgment of God, that they which commit such things are worthy of death, not only do the same, but have pleasure in them that do them. Notice that these wicked people sin specifically against their own knowledge. Despite knowing God's judgment against such wickedness, these people indulge in these sins with abandoned pleasure nonetheless.

We need occasionally to review this passage to remind ourselves of how utterly disinclined wicked people are toward God and anything that bears the divine moral imprint. The idea that a person with this disposition would have any interest in salvation is absurd, a point that Scripture makes, along with the point that such people have no ability whatever to transform themselves into a person of moral and of spiritual integrity. For such a person, the only thing more hellish than his conduct would be to live in the moral constraints of such a God-centered faith-walk. Fallen, depraved man has neither the will nor the ability to so live. If we were to choose to ignore the many Scriptures that teach the truth of salvation all of God and all of His grace, a careful study of man's moral blackness would demand a belief in salvation by grace alone and all of God alone, for sinful man lacks both the desire and the ability to alter his essential nature. This wicked disposition is embedded in his very nature (Jeremiah 13:23).

5
Romans 2: What Was Paul's Intent?

> What then? are we better than they? No, in no wise: for we have before proved both Jews and Gentiles, that they are all under sin.... (Romans 3:9)

I am supremely thankful for the chapter and verse division of the Bible. It facilitates our location of various verses that enrich our studies and our godly faith-walk. However, the very blessing of this structure may lend itself to an excessive and superficial division of Scripture into isolated sentences or thoughts that tend to ignore the flowing context of the lesson. The first two chapters of Romans are often abused by this piecemeal view.

The New Testament letters were written as one flowing message to first century recipients. The human author had a specific purpose or objective in mind for his letter. Some problem or need existed in his recipient audience that needed attention and/or correction, the point of the letter. One doesn't read long in Romans to clearly realize that major tensions existed within the worshipping community of believers in Rome between Jews and Gentiles. We find this thread throughout the Roman letter. A wise foundation for in depth study of any New Testament letter is to read the letter from beginning to end at one setting, and to repeat the reading several times before going back over the letter for a more comprehensive study of its content.

If we approach the Roman letter in this way, we will notice a significant contrast between the content of the first chapter, following Paul's introduction, and the second chapter. While Paul deals with unacceptable sin in both chapters, the character of the sins exposed and condemned in each section is quite different. In the first chapter, Paul traces the utter depravity of sinful man. We see hints that these sinners worshipped their own sinful appetites, but we also see a calculated refusal in them to submit to God's moral laws. In the second chapter, we see highly religious people who use their religion to magnify themselves and to put down others who do not share their religious perspective. However, Paul is no less opposed to their sins than to the sins that he condemns in the first chapter.

If we pause at the end of the second chapter and ask the simple question, "What was Paul's objective in writing these two chapters at the beginning of the Roman letter?" Why open one of the most theological letters in the New Testament with these two moral indictments? Our study verse answers the question. Before Paul can develop a sound and comprehensive—and "systematic"—statement of God's saving grace for sinners, he must sweep away the superficial and establish that, Jew or Gentile, religious or not, fallen humans are sinners, hopeless and helpless in their state, and in need of a Savior who can save them from their sins, regardless of the shape their sins may take.

Simply stated, Paul tells us in this verse that he "...before proved...." It is generally accepted that Paul had never visited Rome prior to writing the Roman letter. For this reason, the Roman letter is somewhat unique in that Paul's other letters were written to people whom he had taught, many of whom were first converted under his preaching. No doubt, the believers in Rome knew of Paul, but he had never visited the city prior to writing this letter. For this reason, Paul's prior proof that he mentions cannot be some past sermon that he may have preached in Rome. We must look inside the Roman letter for the proof of which he writes. We need only examine the first two chapters to discover that proof.

In the second half of the first chapter, Paul focuses on the base sins of Gentiles who have no knowledge of the Ten Commandments or of Jewish interpretation of those Commandments. In Paul's own words, he proves that Gentiles are "...all under sin...." In the second chapter, Paul clearly turns his focus to highly religious Jews who are quite comfortable to moralize human behavior and to tell people around them how wrong certain behaviors are, though they are equally comfortable ignoring their own personal practice of many of those same sins.

> *Thou therefore which teachest another, teachest thou not thyself? thou that preachest a man should not steal, dost thou steal? Thou that sayest a man should not commit adultery, dost thou commit adultery? thou that abhorrest idols, dost thou commit sacrilege? Thou that makest thy boast of the law, through breaking the law dishonourest thou God?* (Romans 2:21-23)

In his commentary on Romans 2, John Gill quotes from a first century Jewish writer who made a corroborating observation of Jewish attitudes and behavior in the first century. The writer observed that the Jews no longer enforced the Mosaic Law against adultery, particularly the penalty for adultery, stoning of the guilty parties. The writer complained that adultery was so commonly practiced among Jewish peoples of the first century that, if the penalty of stoning the guilty were to be enforced, the executioners would run out of stones before they stoned all the guilty sinners who broke that law. Paul is fierce in his rejection of the double-standard immorality of the Jewish people to whom he addresses this second chapter of the Roman letter.

When we examine the details of the second chapter, we will look further into this question of Paul's intent in these two chapters. Suffice for the moment to make a simple observation. Paul's intent in the first chapter and his dealing with God's wrath revealed from heaven against the black sins of irreligious Gentiles is not to show them how they may obtain eternal life or eternal salvation.

Likewise, Paul's point in the second chapter is not to tell errant religious Jews how they may obtain eternal life or eternal salvation. He states his purpose in our study verse. His aim is to prove that neither Jew nor Gentile can approach the cross of Christ with any form of personal superiority or merit. One is as fully "…all under sin" as the other. One is as wholly in need of a Savior as the other. When Gentile sinners are weighed in the moral scales of right and wrong that God has revealed to them in His natural creation, they are without excuse for their sinful lifestyles. When Jewish sinners are weighed in the moral scales of God's Moral Law that He gave to them by Moses, they, too, are without excuse for their sinful ways. They had an inherent advantage in that God gave them His Law through Moses, but they squandered that advantage and now stand guilty and righteously condemned by that very Law.

6
Inexcusable!

> Therefore thou art inexcusable, O man, whosoever thou art that judgest: for wherein thou judgest another, thou condemnest thyself; for thou that judgest doest the same things. But we are sure that the judgment of God is according to truth against them which commit such things. And thinkest thou this, O man, that judgest them which do such things, and doest the same, that thou shalt escape the judgment of God? Or despisest thou the riches of his goodness and forbearance and longsuffering; not knowing that the goodness of God leadeth thee to repentance? But after thy hardness and impenitent heart treasurest up unto thyself wrath against the day of wrath and revelation of the righteous judgment of God; Who will render to every man according to his deeds: To them who by patient continuance in well doing seek for glory and honour and immortality, eternal life: But unto them that are contentious, and do not obey the truth, but obey unrighteousness, indignation and wrath, Tribulation and anguish, upon every soul of man that doeth evil, of the Jew first, and also of the Gentile; But glory, honour, and peace, to every man that worketh good, to the Jew first, and also to the Gentile: For there is no respect of persons with God. For as many as have sinned without law shall also perish without law: and as many as have sinned in the law shall be judged by the law. (Romans 2:1–12)

Often discussions of the first two chapters of Romans become derailed by the irrelevant question; were the people whom Paul described in Romans 1:18-32 children of God? Paul doesn't address this question, so why should we?

Although Paul doesn't use the word "inexcusable" in the first chapter, he makes the point quite directly. Sinful humans have no moral rationale for their wicked conduct. It is inexcusable! Therefore, God's judgment against sinners is right, just, and righteous.

One might think that, if God's judgment is so consistent against wicked Gentiles, perhaps He might go easier on religious Jews. By the time we leave the second chapter of Romans that idea wholly dissolves. God's judgment is righteous against any sinner, pagan Gentile (first chapter) or religious Jew (second chapter). While Paul in principle documented that pagan Gentiles who pursue sin with a hearty appetite are inexcusable, he begins the second chapter by making the point with emphasis. A thin and inconsistent façade of religion may deceive other humans into thinking someone is deeply religious, but God knows the deepest, darkest secrets of the human heart, every human heart. (John 2:24)

...for wherein thou judgest another, thou condemnest thyself; for thou that judgest doest the same things. Human judgments are often compromised by values—or lack of values—or by other variables that have no bearing on the sinful behavior of the sinner.

A few years ago a friend and I were talking about a man whom we both knew who had departed from Biblical faith. I tried to explain to my friend that I continued to pray for this man, that I had talked with him at length, but to no avail, so I felt that the only right thing for me to do was to put a conspicuous distance between him and me. My friend surprised and disappointed me with his reply, "He has been such a good friend to me that I will not walk away from him, no matter what he believes or does." My friend chose to ignore God's model of righteous judgment in favor of compromised human judgment based on personal favors and friendship, not based on righteous principles. Jesus fully understood our human frame when He defined the requirements of faithful discipleship.

> *If any man come to me, and hate not his father, and mother, and wife, and children, and brethren, and sisters, yea, and his own life also, he cannot be my disciple.* (Luke 14:26)[2]

Jesus did not command the disciples, or us, to mistreat or to disrespect our families, a violation of the Fifth Commandment. The point deals with priorities. If we elevate anything or anyone to a position that competes or supplants our faithful service to God, that person or thing becomes our idol, a false god. Jesus did not say that this compromise makes being a disciple difficult. He said compromise makes discipleship impossible; we **cannot be** His disciple. Sadly, anytime we put either Biblical morality or Biblical doctrine on the sliding scale of relativism, we shall eventually discover the slippery slope that slowly leads us lower and lower into the swamp of human sin with no fixed boundary.

Paul's charge against the religious Jews of his day in this chapter clearly identifies their problem. They were quite accurate and fierce in their

---

[2] The Geneva Bible footnote to this verse captures the point clearly: "If anything stands between God and him, as Theophylact says: and therefore these words are spoken in a comparative way, and not by themselves."

opposition to Gentiles and to the sinful idolatries and immoral actions of Gentiles in their day. However, their opposition seems to have related more to the racial or cultural differences than to the moral, for Paul rebukes the religious Jews with the reminder that they actually practiced many of the same sins for which they condemned Gentiles. If their judgment were based on God's fixed moral commandments, and not on relativistic human judgments, they would oppose the sin because God's moral Law opposed it, regardless of who practiced the sin. Paul reminds these folks that they have no moral basis whatever to condemn Gentiles for sin that they themselves routinely practiced.

But we are sure that the judgment of God is according to truth against them which commit such things. Notice that Paul builds his moral assessment of right and wrong on God's judgment, not on the race, the culture, or past friendships with these people. If God condemns a behavior, it is wrong, and God-fearing people must stand with God and not try to ignore or to rationalize such sinful conduct. Sinful humans occasionally complain that God's judgment against sin—and against sinners—is simply too severe. Paul confronts this attitude and affirms, with no exception, that God's judgment is right and true.

And thinkest thou this, O man, that judgest them which do such things, and doest the same, that thou shalt escape the judgment of God? Or despisest thou the riches of his goodness and forbearance and longsuffering; not knowing that the goodness of God leadeth thee to repentance? Throughout Scripture, God clearly defines two lifestyles, righteous and sinful. With equal clarity, He consistently teaches us in Scripture that He always disapproves and shall righteously condemn those who practice sin, and he shall bless those who practice true righteousness.

These verses reveal a gem of truth regarding the principle of repentance. Many years ago, a friend who held to somewhat different beliefs than I described his view of preaching and influencing people to the Christian life. "You must preach Moses to them before you preach Christ to them. Take them to Sinai before you take them to Calvary." This attitude is wholly legalistic and ungrounded in Scripture. Where in the New Testament do we ever read that Moses takes priority over Christ or that the Law is essential to faith in Christ?

We have a written, inspired record of several sermons that the apostles and first preachers preached in the Book of Acts. In every case, the preacher went straight to Calvary and to the resurrection of Jesus. When these preachers did go to Moses, it was not to put their hearers under a legalistic yoke that no one could bear (Acts 15:10 – This whole chapter deals with the first generation of believers wholly rejecting this Moses first—then Christ error). Rather than affirming the Moses—then Christ— New Testament preachers and writers reject it. They didn't preach Moses and Jesus; they preached "...Jesus Christ, and him crucified" (1 Corinthians 2:2).

We need to anchor our minds in Paul's teachings on repentance in this passage. It is not fear of Moses or of the Law that leads people to repentance. It is the goodness of God. Moses does not compete with Jesus in the repentance continuum. The most powerful motivation available to repentance is an abiding sense of God's incredible goodness.

But after thy hardness and impenitent heart treasurest up unto thyself wrath against the day of wrath and revelation of the righteous judgment of God; Who will render to every man according to his deeds: To them who by patient continuance in well doing seek for glory and honour and immortality, eternal life: But unto them that are contentious, and do not obey the truth, but obey unrighteousness, indignation and wrath, Tribulation and anguish, upon every soul of man that doeth evil, of the Jew first, and also of the Gentile; But glory, honour, and peace, to every man that worketh good, to the Jew first, and also to the Gentile: For there is no respect of persons with God. For as many as have sinned without law shall also perish without law: and as many as have sinned in the law shall be judged by the law. Frequently, New Testament writers remind us of the rules that we invent and adopt to evaluate our behavior. Any rule that we create, or for that matter any Biblical rule that we misconstrue for wrong motives or purposes is liable to judge us just as severely as we try to wrest the rule to judge others.

The religious Jews of Paul's day held to a firm view of salvation by works. In these verses, Paul does two things. First, he never mentions a different measure for Gentiles than for Jews. God judges all humans and their behavior based on one rule, His righteous, just, and moral character and Law. Secondly, after exposing the hypocrisy of the Jews' unrighteous judgment against Gentiles, Paul holds them to the fixed righteous principles of God's moral law. The proverbial bottom line would have shocked Paul's Jewish readers. They didn't measure up to God's moral code, so they had no claim to God's blessings based on their actual behavior. They were just as undeserving as the Gentiles whom they so harshly condemned.

Occasionally, folks who believe, similar to first century Jewish belief that their salvation depends on their works will cite these verses to prove that their belief is correct. Perhaps these verses say too much for these folks.

"...according to..." defines a precise proportion. If salvation is by human works, no one, not a single human being, has any claim on eternal salvation with God apart from "...patient continuance in well doing...." This simple statement doesn't indicate that God judges on any kind of relative scale. It is absolute. If someone invests ninety percent of his life in "...patient continuance in well doing..." but slips a mere ten percent of the time, that person has no basis to claim eternal life with God. He failed to live up to the rule.

Often Paul and other New Testament writers will say (write) the same thing more than once in different words. If we don't catch their intended meaning in one form, perhaps we'll get it from the alternate form. Paul observes this practice in our study verses. Put the two descriptions side by side and notice the parallels.

The character of these people: Righteous people "...by patient continuance in well doing...."	These are the same people described by "...every man that worketh good...."
What they shall receive: "...eternal life."	"...glory, honour, and peace...."

The parallel in Paul's two descriptions of these people's character is clear. Why should we confuse the same parallel in his description of what they receive? Often we become rather myopic in our interpretation of Biblical terms. The simple appearance of the word prompts us to think one and only one thing about it because of our preconceptions. Without question, the New Testament uses the word "Eternal" to refer to things that transcend time; they are endless. However, we overlook that Scripture typically associates various elements of quality along with that measure of timelessness. Think about it. If we think only of timeless existence with God, wholly apart from any sense of quality, we end up with a superficial view of heaven as one endless boring existence. Heaven with God, aside from its endless quality, only inspires the believer when we add the element of quality.

By considering both of these qualities in the word "eternal," we gain valuable insights into many Scriptures that associate eternity with godly things that we experience in the here and now. When Paul instructed Timothy to "Lay hold on eternal life..." (1 Timothy 6:12), he was writing to a godly, faithful minister of the gospel, not to an unsaved man. Timothy could not consistently strive to gain what he already possessed. However, Timothy needed to grasp the eternal quality of God and of God's life to enrich his own discipleship and his ministry to others. Just a few short verses later, Paul uses this same term relative to rich believers being cautious not to trust in their uncertain riches, and to use their wealth in godly ways so as to bless those around them in time to come. (1 Timothy 6:19) If we interpret this lesson as wealthy believers using their money to gain entrance into heaven, we end up implying that they buy heaven with money, hardly an acceptable Biblical principle.

In our study passage, I suggest that Paul's use of "…eternal life…" in the first instance is further explained and clarified by the words that he uses in the second instance, "glory, honour, and peace." He is dealing with a godly quality of life in the here and now, not implying that salvation and eternity with God is to be gained by our works. Scripture never contradicts itself, so if we accept the clear and repeated statements of Scripture that eternal salvation is "Not of works…" (Titus 3:5), we should not impose an interpretation onto other passages such as the one we now study that contradict those Scriptures.

Paul's contextual point in Romans 2 deals with inconsistent, hypocritical Jews who falsely judged others harshly for the same sins that they regularly practiced themselves. This context does not teach us about going to heaven when we die, but how we live now, especially if we live in critical and unrighteous judgments against others.

7
Godly Faith-Walk versus Superficial Pretense

(For not the hearers of the law are just before God, but the doers of the law shall be justified. For when the Gentiles, which have not the law, do by nature the things contained in the law, these, having not the law, are a law unto themselves: Which shew the work of the law written in their hearts, their conscience also bearing witness, and their thoughts the mean while accusing or else excusing one another;) In the day when God shall judge the secrets of men by Jesus Christ according to my gospel. Behold, thou art called a Jew, and restest in the law, and makest thy boast of God, And knowest his will, and approvest the things that are more excellent, being instructed out of the law; And art confident that thou thyself art a guide of the blind, a light of them which are in darkness, An instructor of the foolish, a teacher of babes, which hast the form of knowledge and of the truth in the law. Thou therefore which teachest another, teachest thou not thyself? thou that preachest a man should not steal, dost thou steal? Thou that sayest a man should not commit adultery, dost thou commit adultery? thou that abhorrest idols, dost thou commit sacrilege? Thou that makest thy boast of the law, through breaking the law dishonourest thou God? For the name of God is blasphemed among the Gentiles through you, as it is written. For circumcision verily profiteth, if thou keep the law: but if thou be a breaker of the law, thy circumcision is made uncircumcision. Therefore if the uncircumcision keep the righteousness of the law, shall not his uncircumcision be counted for circumcision? And shall not uncircumcision which is by nature, if it fulfil the law, judge thee, who by the letter and circumcision dost transgress the law? (Romans 2:13–27)

How many people have you known who made a great pretense of being a Christian, but their lifestyle simply did not measure up to their words? Our study passage reveals Paul's response to first century Jews who suffered from this deficit. They freely talked up the moral tenets of the Mosaic Law, but they didn't practice it.

Jesus repeatedly confronted the religious leaders of Judaism for their hypocritical attitudes and actions. The many such episodes that we read in the gospels indicates a prevailing pattern of immorality among the leaders of Judaism in the first century. They had memorized the Mosaic Law and their hundreds of added rules. They could split the proverbial ideological hairs when asked to define a sin or to point it out in someone else's conduct, but they were conspicuously blind to their own practice of the same sins.

For not the hearers of the law are just before God, but the doers of the law shall be justified. Paul reminds the Jewish people in Rome that God knows and judges our thoughts and actions without the blind limitations of superficial human observation. Contextually, justification in this passage does not relate to our eternal justification from our sins and our eternal, legal standing before God. The passage emphasizes personal conduct. God judges right living, innocence or justification[1] of right conduct in terms of what a person does, not what he hears or says.

For when the Gentiles, which have not the law, do by nature the things contained in the law, these, having not the law, are a law unto themselves: Which shew the work of the law written in their hearts, their conscience also bearing witness, and their thoughts the mean while accusing or else excusing one another. No greater rebuke could be imagined against the arrogant Jewish religious people of the first century than Paul's words here.

Non-Jews, Gentiles, whom God has touched by grace have God's Law written in their hearts. They may have never heard a rabbi expound on Moses' Law, but the God who wrote that Law first on tables of stone for Moses in Mount Sinai has written a higher and more personal expression of that Law in the hearts of every one of His chosen and regenerated (born again) children. They may not know the external fineries of Judaism's rigid legalism, but they know the true moral character of their God and of His Law by its abiding presence in their hearts. They live with its convictions. Its testimony reshapes their conscience and conviction. It alters their conduct.

At times, commentaries will explain this passage as referring to "Common grace," a term they use to refer to some semblance of God and of His moral character that every human being supposedly possesses. This idea of "Common grace" will not stand the light of Scripture that describes every unregenerate sinner as wholly depraved. Try harmonizing this idea

---

[1] The word translated justified in the New Testament can refer to the act of making the unjust just, or it can refer to the legal verdict of a judge declaring the accused in a trial to be "Not guilty" of the crime accused. Given the context of this passage, we have no basis for imposing one's final, eternal justification onto the passage. Paul is simply stating that right conduct as measured by God has to do with what one does, not with what goes in the ears or out the mouth.

with Paul's description of the wicked in Romans 3:10-18. Scripture teaches that fallen man is without a moral excuse for his sins, but it does not teach that some element of God resides in every human. God shall indeed accuse and sentence wicked humans to a just moral penalty at the Second Coming for their refusal to obey His moral Law. However, the idea of common grace tends to compromise and to contradict Scripture's clear teaching that fallen man is wholly depraved, or, the more familiar term, "totally depraved." The term historically refers to the corrupting and eroding quality of the fall that touched every aspect of man's being. Originally, this term aimed to refute the Arminian view that a "spark" of divinity resides in every human, which, if the person will encourage it into a flame, he may save himself from his sins.

Where ever Scripture refers to God's Law written in the heart, it describes God's grace that changes a person in the new birth, not to a universal or common-to-all-humanity trait (consider as examples Jeremiah 31:31-34; 2 Corinthians 3:3; Hebrews 8:10; Hebrews 10:16). Paul's contextual emphasis in our study passage confronts the double-minded attitude of first century Jewish religious leaders. They pretended to be the elite and informed custodians of God's higher moral law, but they lived as if no such law existed. In contrast, the despised Gentiles whom God's grace had touched and changed, lived with that law in their hearts, and their personal conduct was far more honoring to God than the religious elite among Judaism.

In the day when God shall judge the secrets of men by Jesus Christ according to my gospel. No doubt God shall judge all of man's actions, secret or public, at the Second Coming, but Scripture often refers to His judgments that occur throughout time. God has not resigned His moral governance of humanity till the Second Coming. He constantly convicts and judges our conduct throughout our lives. These judgments occur in keeping with the gospel, Paul's description of the judgment of which he writes in this passage. Though the gospel in no way contradicts God's moral Law or of His final judgment of the wicked on Judgment Day, Scripture typically refers to the basis of His judgment at the Second Coming as being according to His Law applied to and judging fallen humans' sins, not as being "…according to my gospel."

Behold, thou art called a Jew, and restest in the law, and makest thy boast of God, And knowest his will, and approvest the things that are more excellent, being instructed out of the law; And art confident that thou thyself art a guide of the blind, a light of them which are in darkness, An instructor of the foolish, a teacher of babes, which hast the form of knowledge and of the truth in the law. Thou therefore which teachest another, teachest thou not thyself? thou that preachest a man should not steal, dost thou steal? Thou that sayest a man should not commit adultery, dost thou commit adultery? thou that abhorrest idols, dost thou commit sacrilege? Thou that makest thy boast of the law, through breaking the law dishonourest thou God? The recipients of Paul's letter, the people he here charges with hypocritical sin, could not hide their sins behind ignorance. They not only knew the will of God as it related to moral conduct, but they even approved of those judgments. They simply chose to ignore the application of that Moral Law to their own conduct.

Periodically people will naively claim that all sin is the same, that we should not in any way discriminate against various sins as being greater or lesser than other sins. Scripture contains no such teaching. Consider Jesus' own words:

> *Woe unto you, scribes and Pharisees, hypocrites! for ye devour widows' houses, and for a pretence make long prayer: therefore ye shall receive the greater damnation.* (Matthew 23:14)

> *Which devour widows' houses, and for a pretence make long prayers: these shall receive greater damnation.* (Mark 12:40)

> *Which devour widows' houses, and for a shew make long prayers: the same shall receive greater damnation.* (Luke 20:47)

> *Jesus answered, Thou couldest have no power at all against me, except it were given thee from above: therefore he that delivered me unto thee hath the greater sin.* (John 19:11).

If no sin is greater than any other sin, these verses confront us with a colossal miscarriage of divine judgment and justice, for the condemnation against a crime must righteously relate to the crime itself. Greater condemnation or judgment demands the fact of a greater sin that requires the greater condemnation.

For the name of God is blasphemed among the Gentiles through you, as it is written. For circumcision verily profiteth, if thou keep the law: but if thou be a breaker of the law, thy circumcision is made uncircumcision. Therefore if the uncircumcision keep the righteousness of the law, shall not his uncircumcision be counted for circumcision? And shall not uncircumcision which is by nature, if it fulfil the law, judge thee, who by the letter and circumcision dost transgress the law? Paul here neutralizes all the false and superficial judgments of these people. God commanded circumcision, but He commanded it with a moral intent. His people were to submit to circumcision as an external sign that they lived to God and under His moral government, not to man's lack of moral judgments. If those who accepted the sign of God's moral covenant failed to live up to its teachings, their circumcision became one of many witnesses against them and not a basis for these people to claim favored status with God.

When Samuel confronted Saul for his failure to obey the Lord's command, Saul, typical of a sinner's rationalization of his sins, tried to justify his conduct, even to indirectly claim that he intended to honor God by the very act of his sin against God's commandments. The most bizarre of sinful human conduct appears when the sinner tries to blame God, either directly or indirectly for his sins (1 Samuel 15:22ff). Adam tried it. "And the man said, The woman whom thou gavest *to be* with me, she gave me of the tree, and I did eat" (Genesis 3:12). Eve tried it. "And the LORD God said unto the woman, What *is* this *that* thou hast done? And the woman said, The serpent beguiled me, and I did eat" (Genesis 3:13).

Eve's faulty reasoning is no less an attempt to blame God than Adam's. Who made the serpent? Eve's faulty reasoning tries to shift the moral responsibility off her shoulders to the serpent, and, since God made the serpent, she tries to reason that God in some way either caused or "Orchestrated" (a favorite word in some circles for trying to make God cause sin without appearing to do so) her sin. Guilty sinners, when confronted, typically demonstrate their sinfulness by shifting the responsibility away from themselves and onto someone else. In the minds of perverse sinners, God seems to be a favorite target for causing sin. There is one insurmountable problem with this blame-shifting strategy. God refuses to buy it!

Let no man say when he is tempted, I am tempted of God: for God cannot be tempted with evil, neither tempteth he any man: But every man is tempted, when he is drawn away of his own lust, and enticed. Then when lust hath conceived, it bringeth forth sin: and sin, when it is finished, bringeth forth death. Do not err, my beloved brethren. Every good gift and every perfect gift is from above, and cometh down from the Father of lights, with whom is no variableness, neither shadow of turning (James 1:13-17).

When sin appears, God is never responsible. The only things that He gives are "...good and perfect" gifts. James rightly attributes the origin of sin to sinful human hearts, and Scripture steadfastly refuses to accept the idea that God in any way, either directly or indirectly, causes sin. The true origin of sin lies in the enticing lust that grows in the fertile soil of sinful human hearts, never in the heart of God.

8
God's Definition of a Jew

> For he is not a Jew, which is one outwardly; neither is that circumcision, which is outward in the flesh: But he is a Jew, which is one inwardly; and circumcision is that of the heart, in the spirit, and not in the letter; whose praise is not of men, but of God. (Romans 2:28–29)

Since the appearance of radical dispensationalism, beginning with J. N. Darby in 1827-30, Christians who accept these teachings impose an excessive focus, at times almost an obsession, on the Jews. They tend to believe that the Jewish people remain God's chosen and favored people just as they were in the Old Testament.

A common belief in this school of thought holds that, as the Second Coming approaches, Jewish people in large numbers shall recognize that Jesus is their Messiah and shall fully embrace the faith. Paul's Roman letter knows nothing of this idea, and our present study verses wholly redefine what a Jew is and is not, so that national, racial, cultural, or ritual identity means nothing. God recognizes as a true "Jew" that person whose heart He has "circumcised" and in whose heart He has written His Law. From that point forward in the Roman letter, any favorable reference to a Jew should be viewed through this definition.

God's distribution of the land of Canaan to the twelve tribes was to be a fixed assignment, not a fluid real estate investment as in our culture. Several years ago, a statewide statistic was published in the State of California where I live that indicated on average, Californians move every seven years. Land in ancient Israel was to be passed down to family heirs through successive generations in keeping with God's original assignment of the land to the tribes.

When King Solomon died, his successor, Rehoboam, threatened severe taxation and near-despotic policies toward the people. His harshness prompted a rebellion, led by Jeroboam. In the end the majority of ten of the twelve tribes broke from the nation and became the Northern Kingdom. The Northern Kingdom retained the name "Israel," and the Southern Kingdom adopted the name "Judah." (2 Kings 17:6) The fall of Israel, the Northern Kingdom, to Assyria occurred around 720 B. C. The Assyrians routinely practiced dispersing captured peoples throughout

Assyria, effectively forcing them to intermarry and to lose their nationalism and their native culture. Although Judah, the Southern Kingdom, displays an inconsistent pattern of submission to God, the reason for their seventy year captivity to Babylon, around 597 B. C.

Subsequent to the fall of the Northern Kingdom, the Old Testament slowly shifts its focus to Judah, the Southern Kingdom. "Israel" as a separate and identifiable people, no longer existed. The few Jews who remained in the Northern Kingdom after the Assyrian conquest soon acquiesced and intermarried, becoming the Samaritan peoples of subsequent generations. In the first century, the Jews despised the Samaritans as a fallen, corrupted, half-breed race of disgraced people to the memory of the Jews' ancient greatness. Although Scripture occasionally refers to "Israel and Judah" after the fall of Israel, given the demise of Israel as an identifiable people, it is quite likely that we should interpret the identity of the people to whom this name is given in some way different from the ten northern tribes that followed Jeroboam.

Between the historical demise of the ten tribes, known as "Israel," and Paul's redefinition of the term "Jew," Scripture clearly urges us to adopt a new perspective on both of these names. "Israel" no longer exists as a separate or identifiable people, and the only "Jew" of significance to God is one who has been made a "Jew" by God's saving grace. The external, racial, or cultural identity of both names, and the people associated with those names, no longer exists.

Given the strict rules of real estate in Old Testament Israel/Judah (i.e. the twelve tribes of Israel before Assyrian conquest, and Judah, the two remaining tribes, along with remnants from the northern tribes after the Assyrian conquest), Jews were required to register their family identity and births in an official registry that was kept in the temple in Jerusalem. If someone were required to prove his Jewish heritage, he had to link himself to his Jewish family in those archives.

When the Romans destroyed the temple in 70 A. D., this record was destroyed. Based on New Testament era requirements, no one living today can technically prove that he/she is a Jew. And, further, based on Paul's new definition of a "Jew" in our study passage, it doesn't matter. The only true Jew of significance is the person whom God has changed by writing His Law in their hearts and circumcising their hearts, cutting their hearts off from their former depraved self and touching them by grace.

The whole radical dispensational idea of a Jewish restoration to the faith near the Second Coming cannot be proved convincingly at all by Scripture. In Ephesians 2:14 and context, Paul affirms that the segregating wall that kept Jews and converted Gentiles separate in temple worship has been broken down in the Lord Jesus Christ. Now all of God's children whose hearts God has touched and changed by grace stand on equal footing beneath the cross. The only way to make a Scriptural case for a Jewish restoration is to make a Scriptural case that God has—or shall—reinstate the middle wall of partition, something that Scripture never asserts.

As a student of the Bible, and as a respecter of those ancient people, I am thankful that a remnant of Jewish people was able to reclaim some of their ancient land in 1947. However, this regaining of real estate in no way fulfills any Biblical prophecy. Jesus defined the only valid basis for a restoration of blessings to those ancient people who rejected their God and His Messiah (Matthew 23:39), and the basis of blessings restored in that passage has to do with their acknowledging of Jesus as the Messiah who came in the name of the Lord, in no way related to a regaining of real estate.

If I were to witness a significant number of Jews embracing a truly Biblical faith in the Lord Jesus Christ, I would rejoice, but my joy would be no different than if I observed a large number of Gentiles embracing the faith. The New Testament model of the faith ignores race, culture, ancient history, skin color, or any other of the endless list of superficial factors that sinful humans use to segregate themselves and to mistreat others.

> *There is neither Jew nor Greek, there is neither bond nor free, there is neither male nor female: for ye are all one in Christ Jesus. And if ye be Christ's, then are ye Abraham's seed, and heirs according to the promise* (Galatians 3:28-29).

The amazing miracle of sound New Testament, God-honoring faith embraces that race, language, culture, skin color, or other such factors mean nothing. Regardless of skin color, language, or any other superficial variable, God in mercy finds a sinner whose heart is black with sin, washes it in the blood of His darling Son, and it becomes white as snow.

9
What Advantage to the Jews?

What advantage then hath the Jew? or what profit is there of circumcision? Much every way: chiefly, because that unto them were committed the oracles of God. (Romans 3:1–2)

Having put both Gentiles and Jews under intense scrutiny and finding both deficient in different ways, Paul must now deal with the obvious question, the proverbial "elephant in the room" issue. Did the Jews gain any benefit from being God's chosen people in the Old Testament era? If not, what was the point? And if so, why subject them to such intense criticism now? And, if they enjoyed an advantage at one time, but lost it, why did they lose it? Who was responsible for their loss? These are significant questions today, but they were far more so in the first century.

From a human, sinful perspective, many times through human history, the people who attain great stature in a given era adopt arrogant personal attitudes and beliefs regarding their status. In their prime, the ancient Jews believed that they were formed of dust just like other humans, but they believed that the "gods" formed them of Greek dust which was superior to the dust found in other regions of the world, so they thought themselves therefore superior to others.

First century Jews embraced similar attitudes regarding their separate status. They seemed to interpret their separateness at God's hand to some form of superiority. It may have been racial or cultural, or some of both. When the Syrophoenecian woman requested that Jesus cast the devil out of her daughter, Jesus noted that she was a Greek, non-Jew, and therefore, in the eye of first century Jews, a Gentile "dog." (Matthew 15:22-28; Mark 7:25-30) Her insistent appeal for a mere crumb of blessing from Jesus prompted His gracious response.

We tend to pick up the origin of the Jewish people with Abraham and trace their history carefully forward, but we may overlook Abraham's status prior to God's call. Abraham was a Chaldean, not from a distinct race or culture. Ancient Jewish tradition held that his family made their livelihood by making and selling idols, so he may well have been involved in Chaldean paganism when the Lord first appeared to him. God didn't choose a superior specimen of humanity to build the Jewish people. He chose an ordinary man and transformed him and his offspring into a special people. When Abraham sought the Lord's confirmation and assurance of His promise, God met Abraham where Abraham had lived for most of his life, Chaldea. The form of the covenant that God made with Abraham in Genesis 15:8-21 was the exact form of an ancient Chaldean contract. God found Abraham in Chaldea, but He forged a new people out of this former pagan Chaldean. Ezekiel confronts his fellow-Jews in the midst of the Babylonian captivity with this fact.

Thou art thy mother's daughter, that lotheth her husband and her children; and thou art the sister of thy sisters, which lothed their husbands and their children: your mother was an Hittite, and your father an Amorite (Ezekiel 16:45).

These thoughts take us full circle back to the same questions that Paul asks in Romans 3:1. The Jewish people had no racial advantage over any other people. There is no Biblical basis for a racist claim of superiority to be made by anyone of any race. The Bible will not support anyone's shameful claim of racist bigotry. Paul rejects this notion in Acts 17:26, in Galatians 3:28, Colossians 3:11, to cite only a few of many passages that wholly refute any form of racist superiority.

What then was the advantage that the Jewish people enjoyed, but lost? Paul answers the question as directly as he asks it. Although there were many benefits to God's call of the Jewish people to Himself, the primary and chief advantage was that God gave these people the custody and knowledge of His Law, expanded and enriched by all of the holy writings of the Old Testament. An "Oracle" is normally considered to be an utterance, something spoken. In the case of the Jewish heritage, God spoke to His chosen messengers among the Jews of the Old Testament, and they committed God's words to writing for the knowledge and benefit—advantage—of the whole nation.

While the surrounding nations to Israel were cultivating the most heinous of atrocities in the name of their pagan gods, Israel worshipped God with grace and joyful mercy. Instead of sacrificing their children to pagan gods in the fire, Israel heard God's command to nurture their children with constant reminders of the Law of God. While the surrounding nations pursued one bloody ritual after another to appease their imaginary pagan gods, Israel respectfully observed their priests each year making a sacrifice that reminded them that God had provided a substitute sacrifice for their sins, the theme and message of the whole Levitical priesthood, fulfilled in the Person of the Lord Jesus Christ and fully explained in the New Testament Book of Hebrews.

When God delivered His people from Egyptian slavery, He reminded them that His Law would bless them in ways they could not imagine.

And said, If thou wilt diligently hearken to the voice of the LORD thy God, and wilt do that which is right in his sight, and wilt give ear to his commandments, and keep all his statutes, I will put none of these diseases upon thee, which I have brought upon the Egyptians: for I am the LORD that healeth thee. (Exodus 15:26)

In recent years, two physicians researched the health aspects of the Mosaic Law and wrote many of their discoveries.[1] They anchor their research on the above verse. Obedience to God's commandments and Law would prevent the common diseases of the Egyptians from plaguing the Jewish people who obeyed. As we read many of the lifestyle mandates of the Mosaic Law, we may be liable to missing the points that these men make. Every tenet of Mosaic Law is not moral; much of it deals with a holistic lifestyle. These physicians examine one Mosaic teaching after another that dealt with daily behaviors and lifestyle. Consistently, every mandate that we discover in Moses' Law related to human health and hygiene has been proved by medical research to be correct. Medical research stumbled onto many of these truths as late as the twentieth century, but simple obedience to God's Law by the Jewish people some fifteen hundred years BC gave them a healthy advantage over any other nation that existed in their time. Just a few examples will make the point.

1. God commanded that all human waste be collected, taken a safe distance outside the camp and buried. Failure to follow this practice almost destroyed human life with the Black Plague in Medieval Europe.

---

[1] McMillen, S. I., M.D., Stern, David E., M.D., **None of These Diseases**. This book is published by Revell, A division of Baker Book House Publishers, ISBN 978-0-8007-5719-9.

2. A woman who gave birth to a baby was to be quarantined for a stated time. Her "uncleanness" did not indicate sin, but served as a safe insulation for her and her newborn baby from exposure to disease and infection.
3. Mosaic Law lays great emphasis on the dangers of exposure to human blood. Again, the "uncleanness" referenced in Moses' Law protected healthy people from any number of diseases that were transmitted by contact with the blood or other bodily fluids of a diseased person.
4. Late in the nineteenth century western medical science struggled with the mystery that a midwife could go to the home of a woman in labor and deliver a healthy baby, while a pregnant mother with complications would go to a hospital where a trained physician would deliver the baby, but frighteningly often, both mother and baby died. Why? Doctors and nurses did not understand the danger of blood-carried infection and disease. A doctor would attend to a patient with a severe infection or an infectious disease, and go immediately into the delivery room to deliver a baby, but the doctor would not wash or change his outer garments, thus infecting the mother and newborn baby with the disease of his former patient. When a physician first suggested that Mosaic Law might be based on something more scientific than any doctor of the day learned in medical school, he was ridiculed and eventually driven out of his practice. However, when the medical community eventually discovered the insidious powers of communicable infections and diseases, they implemented various practices that effectively prevented their conveying these diseases to other patients, they in fact started practicing what God commanded His people to practice in fifteen hundred BC.

What advantage did the Jews have as God's chosen people? Paul's words ring loud and true. "Much every way." And that advantage lies in their having God's spoken message to them, committed to writing and preserved for centuries so that every succeeding generation of the Jewish people had that same holy writing, that same advantage.

We could put the many teachings of Moses' Law—of God's Law given to Moses—to the test and discover with each one of them that God spoke the truth to His people and thus gave them a holy advantage in His holy "oracles." While we have illustrated this truth from the perspective of God's moral and lifestyle commandments, the most important advantage that God gave to these people was a true knowledge of Him and of His holy, righteous, and merciful character. With the changing tides of human history and culture, any number of new and unusual situations might occur not specifically mentioned in Mosaic Law, but the overarching and comprehensive revelation of God in the whole body of Old Testament writings, those holy "oracles," establishes a perspective of God that translates into any culture and that is competent to put any human attitude, culture, or philosophy to the test of God and of His Law. In this revelation, God gave the Jews of the Old Testament an incredible advantage over any other nation or culture that existed during their long existence.

What happened to this special people? Despite such an advantage, why did they go so very wrong? In the first century when Paul writes these words, Jesus, God Incarnate appeared, fulfilled literally hundreds of prophetic utterances, "oracles," from those Old Testament writings, and yet the very people who entered this era with an advantage ended up losing it all. How could they lose their favored and blessed standing with God? In the verses that follow, Paul will answer these questions as clearly as he defined the advantage in the first two verses of the chapter.

10
Does God Need Our Unrighteousness?

For what if some did not believe? shall their unbelief make the faith of God without effect? God forbid: yea, let God be true, but every man a liar; as it is written, That thou mightest be justified in thy sayings, and mightest overcome when thou art judged. But if our unrighteousness commend the righteousness of God, what shall we say? Is God unrighteous who taketh vengeance? (I speak as a man) God forbid: for then how shall God judge the world? For if the truth of God hath more abounded through my lie unto his glory; why yet am I also judged as a sinner? And not rather, (as we be slanderously reported, and as some affirm that we say,) Let us do evil, that good may come? whose damnation is just. (Romans 3:3–8)

For years, I pondered these verses and couldn't get past the sense of doublespeak, a conclusion that I knew to be wrong, but I failed to grasp the point. Paul writes, by the Holy Spirit's direction, with amazing logical flow. He reasons through difficult points with precision and accuracy. Many twenty-first century readers have trained their minds to skim what they read, but you'll miss Paul's points if you skim. His writings require focused concentration.

During my business career, I often enjoyed studying people in various business situations. I learned that some people speak in long, rambling paragraphs. I learned to listen to these people in "paragraphs." I watched their leading thoughts and caught their focus, but not every word. Other people spoke with brevity and precision. I had to listen to every word they spoke. When you read Scripture anywhere, but especially Paul's writings, avoid "paragraph" skimming. Weigh every word.

Paul introduces this chapter with a question. Given his sharp criticism of the Jews in the second chapter, has Paul given up on the Jews? Is there any advantage to being a Jew versus a member of some other race or culture? Paul affirms an advantage, but he puts that advantage in the past tense, "...were committed...." As this chapter unfolds, Paul will affirm that the advantage once enjoyed by the Jews no longer exists. In the New Testament age, grace, not race, is the one factor that makes any difference in people.

To further this point, in our present study verses, Paul asks yet another set of questions. The Jews received holy writings from God that propelled them centuries ahead of the people around them, both morally and culturally. If the Jews squandered those blessings, as the second chapter affirms, does their failure mean that God has in some way failed, that His purpose for them has fallen to the ground in vain?

As abruptly as Paul askes the question, he answers it. "God forbid" is one of the strongest possible forms of a verbal negative. Paul then develops the point of our lesson. Man's failure does not defeat or frustrate God's faithfulness. You will find the Old Testament passage referred to by "...as it is written..." in the fifty-first Psalm. Based on the language of the passage in that Psalm, fallen, broken, corrupt humans judge God, but God is always right, justified, in what He says, and He overcomes when depraved mortals dare to judge Him.

This idea goes to the heart of the question before us in Romans 3. Paul redirects the emphasis from man's vain accusations against God to God's faithfulness. Because humans, even God's chosen people in the Old Testament, the Jews, fail, does their failure defeat God or reflect badly on Him? Did God fail? And Paul's answer, as well as David's, rejects the idea. When David failed his moral responsibility by sinning with Bathsheba and then murdering her husband, David in this Psalm confesses his personal failure, not God's, "Against thee, thee only, have I sinned...." David didn't blame God for his sin, neither directly nor indirectly.

The whole absurd notion that fallen, depraved sinners can shift the responsibility for their sins off to God comes to the forefront in our study passage. Paul plays the devil's advocate at this point. If in fact our sins in some way are caused by God, either directly or indirectly, or if in some way God "orchestrates" them to commend or benefit Himself, what must we conclude? The first moral dilemma is obvious. If God is dependent on our moral failures, i.e. our sins, to make His righteousness prevail or appear the better, God has no moral basis on which to judge sinners and impose righteous wrath against them in judgment. If God needs our sins, and thus in some way relies on them to further His work, He becomes an accessory to the sin. He therefore loses His moral high ground on which He claims to judge sinners righteously and justly. On this particular point, a number of major errors have appeared, and, thank the Lord, most of them have soon died of their own immoral weight.

Believe it or not, a few people who claim to be Bible believing Christians claim that God actually causes sin, one aspect of the moral absurdity that

Paul refutes in our study lesson. Years ago, I was researching one of the groups that advocates this idea, and I found an internet site in which an advocate of this view quoted part of Romans 6:17, "But God be thanked that ye were the servants of sin...." The man actually interpreted this partial sentence to mean that Paul thanked God that the Romans had at one time been slaves to sin. He alleged that God caused them to sin, so Paul thanked God that He had made these people to sin. The man failed to read the remainder of the verse that explains Paul's thanksgiving, beginning with the next word in the verse, "...but...."

More often people who flirt with this upside down, immoral belief will twist words and try to evade the idea by one or another form of word games. For example, some folks in this school of belief will say that they do not believe that God causes sin, but they do believe that He has decreed either to "Orchestrate" every sin that occurs for some greater good in the end, or else He decreed to prevent the event from occurring at all. Thus, they actually believe that God is in some way instrumental, causatively so, in the wicked event, but it is supposedly acceptable because of the greater good that they believe God decreed to come of the sinful events.

If a man were to so entwine himself in a criminal act in our culture, or in any moral culture, and were to be discovered, he would be rightly charged as an accessory to the crime, and he would be righteously punished for his culpability. Consider a historical event of some note.

President Richard Nixon did not break into the Watergate offices, but he was involved in "orchestrating" the burglary. Did the country praise him for his integrity? No, in fact the country, including the leaders of the President's own political party, denounced his conduct, and he was forced to resign from the presidency in moral disgrace. His crime was` that he was involved in the "orchestration" of the crime.

How then can anyone morally reason that God could do likewise and maintain His moral integrity, much less preside in righteous judgment over depraved man's sins? It is this point that Paul addresses and refutes in our study passage. If our sin, our "unrighteousness," commends, in some way is "orchestrated" to benefit God, how can God righteously judge the sinner whose sin He in some way He involved Himself, even indirectly, as with the disgraced president? In Paul's words, "...why yet am I also judged as a sinner?" If Paul's sin assisted God in doing what God wanted to do, on what moral basis would God judge Paul's contribution to divine purpose?

If Paul in fact did something that God either caused or manipulated for His purpose, God should reward Paul, not judge him as a sinner.

Paul concludes this lesson with a direct and categorical rejection of this whole immoral line of reasoning. For anyone to reason as he has just represented, and to claim that Paul agreed, according to Paul, constitutes slander. It wholly misrepresents everything Paul believed and taught. In the moral and logocal conclusion of such perverse reasoning, fallen, sinful man shifts the responsibility from himself to God, "Let us do evil that good may come." A person with such an upside down moral view of God might logically decide that the more he sins the more glory God gets for his conduct. If any perverse belief deserves the descriptive classification of blasphemy, this belief deserves to be placed at the head of this category.

Given the intensity of Paul's rejection of this line of immoral reasoning, we should not at any point in any of Paul's inspired writings interpret him to revert to this idea in that context. For example, when Paul reasons in Romans 8:28 that "...all things work together for good to them that love God..." we should not interpret "all things" in that passage to include the immoral and sinful acts of humans, the precise idea that Paul rejects in our study passage. Scripture affirms that some things do not work, that some things do not work together (e. g. 2 Corinthians 6:14-17), and that many things occur that are not good.

A more instructive interpretation of "...all things..." in Romans 8:28 unfolds if we allow Paul in that context to define his intended meaning of the term. In Romans 8:32, four short verses later, Paul uses this same exact term with unquestionable precision, "He that spared not his own Son, but delivered him up for us all, how shall he not with him freely give us all things?" How should we define "...all things..." in this verse? We can rightly interpret the term only to refer to "things" that we receive specifically through the sacrificial death of the Lord Jesus Christ. And we may conclude with all comfort and safety that "all things" that we receive because God lovingly "...spared not his own Son..." unequivocally work together, and they work for our good.

Another tactic that advocates of the error which Paul rejects in our study passage attempt is to say that everything that occurs, including the most heinous and sinful acts of fallen humans, unfold "according to the will of God." Shortly after the shooting in Tucson, Arizona in early 2011, I heard a sermon by a man who holds to this view in which the man repeatedly stated his belief that everything that occurred in Tucson that day, including the murder of the nine year old girl, unfolded precisely according to the will of God. Every moral being's morality is anchored in that being's will. To state that such heinous sins harmonize with God's will is to say that God morally approves of them. Paul utterly rejects such an idea when he defines behavior that harmonizes with God's will.

> *For this is the will of God, even your sanctification, that ye should abstain from fornication: That every one of you should know how to possess his vessel in sanctification and honour; Not in the lust of concupiscence, even as the Gentiles which know not God: That no man go beyond and defraud his brother in any matter: because that the Lord is the avenger of all such, as we also have forewarned you and testified. For God hath not called us unto uncleanness, but holiness.* (1 Thessalonians 4:3-7)

God's will never approves of man's sins, so man's sins are never "according to the will of God." The Lord avenges such attitudes and behaviors; they are never "according to His will."

One more favorite word game that advocates of this abominable idea will often practice plays out a "Red Herring" logical fallacy. The "Red Herring" logical fallacy attempts to side-track the focus of discussion away from the point to something different. Take the spotlight off the problem idea, and you evade its exposure. When you object to the idea of God causing sin, and someone responds, "Well, don't you believe that God sometimes uses occasions when we sin for a greater good?", two major "Red Herring" steps appear in this response.

First of all, when this question appears, often in a discussion of Romans 8:28 and "...all things..." in that verse, the point wholly evades the wording of the passage. Paul did not reason that God sometimes intervenes in the sinful conduct of human beings; the passage unequivocally embraces "...all things..." not just some things occasionally.

Secondly, and more blatantly, this question wholly misrepresents the argument, as well as Scripture. If you disagree with this idea, its defender will accuse you of being a "virtual deist." Those of us who oppose this doctrine are not deists. We wholly reject that God remains aloof and uninvolved in our lives.

The claim that denial of this errant idea leaves the person denying the idea in the position of being a "virtual deist" is itself a classical example of the "Excluded Middle," or in older terminology, the "Horns of the Dilemma" logical fallacy. You must either agree with the errant idea , or you supposedly hold the only alternative, the mirror opposite view. In fact, more than two opposite and extreme ideas exist regarding this question, and the truth appears in the "Excluded Middle" of the two points, not in either of the two stated extremes.

Further, this misrepresentation of God's intervention implies that God in some way causes the human sin in which He intervenes. It wholly ignores that every occasion in Scripture in which God does intervene in human sinful experience is to condemn that sin, and to intervene so as to prevent its grievous consequences upon His beloved children, never to cause it. Unless the advocate of this dreadful idea can prove by Scripture that God caused the sin in which He intervenes, his claim fails to prove his point. And if he claims that God caused the sin, he effectively pleads guilty of the very error that Paul examines and refutes in our study passage.

For example, God intervened when a wicked pagan king threw three of His faithful children into a burning furnace. Praise God! But for this or any other such lesson to make the point implied by the question, we must find the passage that states that God caused the pagan king to throw those godly men into the fire (James 1:13-15 correctly attributes the cause of sin to the perversity of the sinner's own lust, and James 1:16-17 affirms that every act of God in intervention in our lives is "...good and perfect...", not sinful. With our moral and righteous God, we need not fear so much as a "...shadow of turning..." from this wholly righteous character). Whenever God intervenes in the lives of His children, His intervention is always on the side of loving care and protection of His child, and never in the act of causing the sinful act that threatened His child.

For a god to cause grievous danger to his followers, only to step in at the last minute to deliver them from that danger is immoral, illogical, and absurd. It would be as if this god sent a drunk driver to run into you and your family who are driving to church. Then the same god stands by till you are at the point of death. At the last possible moment, that dreadful god sends his ambulance with his paramedics to the scene, picks you up and takes you to his hospital where his doctors treat your wounds, and, while you are recovering in his hospital, this perverse deity pays you a visit and asks, "Don't you think I'm a good god to take such good care of you?"

This analogy is not original with me, but it underscores the moral dilemma of all who hold to this errant view. Such a deity resembles the many fatalistic pagan gods of history, but the god of this idea in no way resembles the moral and merciful God of the Bible.

11
What is the State of Man with God?

> What then? are we better than they? No, in no wise: for we have before proved both Jews and Gentiles, that they are all under sin; As it is written, There is none righteous, no, not one: There is none that understandeth, there is none that seeketh after God. They are all gone out of the way, they are together become unprofitable; there is none that doeth good, no, not one. Their throat is an open sepulchre; with their tongues they have used deceit; the poison of asps is under their lips: Whose mouth is full of cursing and bitterness: Their feet are swift to shed blood: Destruction and misery are in their ways: And the way of peace have they not known: There is no fear of God before their eyes. (Romans 3:9-18)

In these verses, Paul summarizes his thoughts through the first two chapters. If the Jews failed in their calling and God opened the door of blessing to the Gentiles, can the Gentiles now claim an advantage just as the Jews possessed an advantage in the Old Testament era? As quickly as Paul raises this idea, he rejects it. God's premise of blessings in the New Testament is not Gentiles over Jews or Jews over Gentiles. If the Romans think that this is Paul's point, they've missed his reasoning through the first two chapters of his letter to them.

...for we have before proved both Jews and Gentiles, that they are all under sin. Where did Paul "...before prove..." these points? Think about the first two chapters of Romans. In the first chapter, after his greeting and introduction, Paul focused his thoughts on typical sinful behaviors that characterized Gentiles. In the second chapter, he specifically addressed the sinful behaviors of the Jews. In the first chapter, Paul proved that pagan Gentile behavior, especially worshipping the creature more than the Creator, was sinful. In the second chapter, he begins by addressing Jews and proving that their hypocritical judgments against non-Jews, while they failed to live up to the law that God gave to them, was sinful.

What are the consequences of proving that all humans, according to nature, Jew or Gentile, are sinners? What does this mean? Paul follows his summary of the first two chapters with a detailed list of quotes from the Old Testament, each of which explains and demonstrates the impact of sin on all humanity.

1. *There is none righteous, no, not one.* In their own sinful minds, both Jews and Gentiles, the very people whom Paul described according to God's moral values, may have thought of themselves as righteous, but they all failed God's assessment of true righteousness. As one example, the Greeks who in so many ways were among the most enlightened of Gentile cultures, believed in many gods. They even taught that the gods formed man of the dust of the ground. However, they also believed that the gods formed them of special dust from Greece. Since Greek soil was superior to any other soil, according to their ideas, they were naturally superior to all other humans.
2. *There is none that understandeth.* In the New Testament, Paul will elsewhere affirm that it is impossible for fallen, unregenerate humans to understand or to grasp the things of God. (1 Corinthians 2:14)
3. *There is none that seeketh after God.* This simple statement refutes most teaching among all denominational Christian groups in that it categorically states that none in this fallen state seek after God. Most of these good folks teach that man must in some way seek after God before God will save (In the sense of the new birth or eternal salvation) them. Unknowingly, they teach that fallen man must do what Scripture teaches that he cannot do.
4. *They are all gone out of the way.* If we accept Scripture's consistent identification of the right way that pleases God, no fallen human follows that way. They've all left it.
5. *They are together become unprofitable.* Bible words are precise. Do not overlook the word "together" in this point. This idea traces the fallen human condition back to its original source. Scripture teaches (As Paul will teach in Romans 5) that all of humanity was associated with Adam in the Garden of Eden. Adam served as their federal head. He represented them no less than Jesus represented all of His elect in His atoning

death. When Adam sinned, all humanity inherited the consequences of that sin.

6. *There is none that doeth good, no, not one.* Sinful humans worship themselves (Philippians 3:19), but that self-worship is idolatry. None in the number of sinful man deserves worship. None consistently do good..

7. *Their throat is an open sepulchre.* Watch how people act and listen to their words. If you listen attentively, you will hear what goes on in the person's deepest thoughts. And man apart from God, in his unchanged sinful state, has only one condition to reveal. However enlightened he may think himself to be, God views him as he is, an open and occupied grave.

8. *With their tongues they have used deceit.* Sinful man congratulates himself when he thinks that he has successfully deceived someone, especially when the deceit results in personal gain.

9. *The poison of asps is under their lips.* Paul puts a lot of emphasis on the tongue and its link to human depravity. Not only do we learn that the throat of the wicked is an open grave and full of deceit, but now Paul adds to the blackness. The words of the wicked are loaded with deadly poison, and, like a deadly snake, they look for people to bite.

10. *Whose mouth is full of cursing and bitterness.* He hasn't finished with the tongue. Wicked people despise the successes of others. They look for ways to curse or belittle any worthy accomplishment of others, and they react to another person's success with their own bitterness because they did not likewise succeed.

11. *Their feet are swift to shed blood.* Not only do the wicked reveal their black, sinful nature with their speech, but they also willingly manifest it with their actions. Get in their way, in any way interfere with their self-worshipping pursuits, and they will take you out with no regret or reservation.

12. *Destruction and misery are in their ways.* Consider the results of their conduct. While the wicked strive without reservation to gain for themselves, they could care less if the heap destruction and misery onto you--onto anyone who interferes with the selfish pursuits.

13. *And the way of peace they have not known.* Peace, what is that? The wicked would probably consider peace to be boring, something that the weak and unworthy might pursue.
14. *There is no fear of God before their eyes.* The term "Fear of God" in Scripture typically refers to a sense of respect or reverence toward God that evokes a deep-seated desire to obey Him. The wicked know nothing of such fear. If the wicked ever have any thoughts of God, they are thoughts of hatred and resentment. They work to avoid God rather than seek to please Him. (Job 21:14; "...Depart from us...we desire not the knowledge of thy ways.")

Following the Protestant Reformation, Arminius sought to compromise the teachings of the Reformers by striving to popularize ideas similar to the teachings of Pelagius. He taught that fallen, sinful man retains a certain core of Adam's unfallen nature. If fallen man will simply follow and cultivate that unfallen component, typically associated with the will, fallen man may save himself, regain a favored, spiritual standing with God. The early children of the Reformers soundly rejected this idea. In their effort to clearly distinguish their beliefs from both Pelagius and Arminius, they coined the term "total depravity."

For the originators of this term, total depravity does not mean that every wicked person is as wicked, and behaves as wickedly as he possible can. They rather focused this term against the "free will" idea of Arminius, teaching that the fall destroyed all the moral faculties of man, his will included. The passage before us clearly describes fallen man's "total depravity."

In coming chapters we will more fully address the point, but, in this examination of man's utter sinful condition, we need to address a vital point of Biblical truth. In their zeal to emphasize man's sinful state, some folks will assert that, even after the new birth, the child of God remains "totally depraved." Clearly the language of our study passage will not allow such a conclusion. If the regenerate child of God remains totally depraved after the new birth, how do we account for his hunger and thirst for God and for righteousness? Others, sensing this problem and trying to avoid it, will carve the regenerate person into isolated pieces and claim that the residual sinful nature that a child of God retains, even after the new birth, is totally depraved, though they do affirm that the "regenerated part" is not so depraved.

Both of these ideas ignore the origin of the term, and both miss the teaching of Scripture on the profound and permanent change that God effects in each of His children in the new birth. Total depravity, as depicted in our study passage, accurately, though admittedly dreadfully, describes fallen, unregenerated, sinful man. To suggest that a born-again person in any way continues to be totally depraved dishonors God and God's saving work in His children. Scripture does not teach this idea.

Think about the detailed description that Paul gives of the wicked in our study passage. If none seek after God, even after regeneration, how do you explain a born-again person's deep hunger for God? The profound change that God in grace makes in the new birth should never be so minimized or dishonored.

12
Man's Condition after the Fall

What then? are we better than they? No, in no wise: for we have before proved both Jews and Gentiles, that they are all under sin; As it is written, There is none righteous, no, not one: There is none that understandeth, there is none that seeketh after God. They are all gone out of the way, they are together become unprofitable; there is none that doeth good, no, not one. Their throat is an open sepulchre; with their tongues they have used deceit; the poison of asps is under their lips: Whose mouth is full of cursing and bitterness: Their feet are swift to shed blood: Destruction and misery are in their ways: And the way of peace have they not known: There is no fear of God before their eyes. (Romans 3:9-18)

Given Paul's emphasis throughout the Roman letter on "Jews and Gentiles," one could likely safely conclude that a significant tension existed between these two classes of people in the church at Rome, prompting Paul to write them in an effort to relieve the tension and get the church back on the right course. The Roman historian Suetonius mentioned an episode during the reign of Claudius Caesar in which Claudius expelled all Jews from the city of Rome because of a heated dispute among them regarding a man named "Crestus." Most Christian commentators who mention this episode believe it refers to the intense disagreement between Christian and non-Christian Jews regarding our Lord. Acts 18:2 mentions this episode to explain why Aquila and Priscilla were in Corinth, not their home in Rome.

After his introduction to the Roman letter in the first chapter, Paul focuses his thoughts on the wrath of God revealed against all ungodliness and unrighteousness of men who suppress the truth. The cultural focus of the sins that Paul mentions in this context might lead us to think that Paul primarily had reference to Gentiles. Then in the second chapter Paul specifically addresses Jews and their sins. Thus by the time Paul gets to the third chapter he has fully confronted the fact of human sin, both among Jews and Gentiles. "…we have before proved both Jews and Gentiles, that they are all under sin" seems to refer us to the first two chapters of this letter.

At this point Paul gives us a rather intimate view of sin, but he does not focus his thoughts on culturally unique sins. He confronts the universal dominance of sin among humanity regardless of culture. Sin is a greater problem that the culture in which a person lives! The dominant culture may well predispose a person to certain sins, but the sin problem transcends culture and indicts every human being.

Paul begins the tenth verse of Romans 3 with "As it is written." The rather vivid description of man's pervasive sinful condition is a series of quotations from Old Testament Scriptures. Paul used Old Testament Scripture exclusively to assault human pride and to pronounce both Jews and Gentiles alike as hardened criminals in all-out rebellion against our holy God.

Notice the universality of Paul's terms; "none," "They are all...", "They are together...", "There is none...." Culture, age, race, philosophy; nothing exempts fallen man from this sinful state. Other than those who are influenced by the teachings of Pelagius or others who hold to similar views, Christians have historically referred to this pervasive state of sin as "total depravity."

Those who embrace Pelagius' ideas or similar beliefs will strongly object to the term and the idea of inherent and pervasive sin. Often they quip that the word "depravity" is never found in the Bible. However, notice Strong's definition of the word "wickedness" in Romans 1:29.

> **1** depravity, iniquity, wickedness. **2** malice. **3** evil purposes and desires.[1]

The first term used to define this word is *depravity*. While the word may not appear in the Bible, clearly the idea does find solid support in Scripture.

Why do we need to study the depths of man's sinful state? Often people complain that this subject is depressing. It is never comfortable to look into one's personal closet and see what has been hidden safely away out of sight! When the prophet exhorted the people to "...look

---

[1] James Strong, *The Exhaustive Concordance of the Bible : Showing Every Word of the Test of the Common English Version of the Canonical Books, and Every Occurrence of Each Word in Regular Order.*, electronic ed. (Ontario: Woodside Bible Fellowship., 1996), G4189.

unto…the hole of the pit whence ye are digged" (Isaiah 51:1), he was referring to the origin of the Jewish nation in Abraham, a pagan Chaldean!

The intent of the term "total depravity" is not to convey that wicked people are as evil and sinful as they possibly can be, but rather than unsaved humans are alienated from God and fallen in every component of their being. Nothing in fallen man escaped the impact of the fall, including man's will, as we examined in the last chapter. Paul's intent in our study passage seems to be an illustration of the conduct that pervasive human depravity causes.

Whether we consider Andrew Fuller's quasi-Arminian "duty faith" idea that unsaved humans have a duty to believe the gospel and exercise faith in Christ, or the wholly Arminian view that man, not God, must accomplish salvation, we create an impossibility for unsaved man. It should be noted that Fuller repeatedly and emphatically taught that man's salvation was conditional on belief of the gospel, making his views truly quasi-Arminian. Whether one holds that belief of and obedience to the gospel is the direct cause of salvation or simply the instrument of salvation, both two views run headlong into the problem of man's depravity in his unsaved state. How can a person whose state of being matches Paul's description in our study verses possibly "believe" the gospel and exercise faith in Jesus as his/her Savior? Paul repeatedly emphasized that unsaved, depraved humans do not, will not and—in other passages such as 1 Corinthians 2:9-16—*cannot* embrace or believe the spiritual realities of God's grace. To require unsaved humans to respond in faith to the gospel prior to their new birth, or regeneration, is to demand the impossible of them.

Jesus corroborated this truth in His dialogue with Nicodemus (John 3:1-10) by telling Nicodemus that a man must first be born again, literally born from above—of God—*before* he has the ability either to see or to enter the kingdom of God. The logical point that Jesus made in this lesson affirms that, prior to the new birth, a person lacks the ability to either see or to enter God's kingdom, to function in any way spiritually pleasing to God. For any system of theology to require any condition of unregenerate humans creates an impossible condition. They cannot perform it; they lack the ability, not to mention the inclination, to do so.

The prevailing view of man's fallen and unsaved state, and the prevailing view of the action necessary for man to correct his problem is that God gives man a "fresh start," a "new beginning," the opportunity to start over and do better. Thus these views utterly ignore and reject the profound depth of man's fallen state. Sinful man's condition requires far more than a fresh start to resolve his sin problem. Adam had a "new beginning" in the Garden of Eden in a perfect world. What did he do with his opportunity? If Adam failed in such an ideal state, what makes anyone think they can truly remedy their fallen and sinful condition in the present world?

What are the implications of man's depravity to our theological beliefs? To our view of how a man is saved? We cannot frame a Biblical and correct view of salvation until we have first come to terms with the profound and pervasive impact that sin has on all of humanity. Once we come to terms with man's true condition after the fall, we clearly see that man's only hope for salvation lies in God alone. Man lacks both the ability and the inclination to do anything, mental or physical, to reverse his condition.

Paul dealt with this impossibility when he described our unsaved state as being "dead in trespasses and sins" (Ephesians 2:1-10). Requiring a dead person to do something is as sensible and logical as requiring an unregenerate person to do something either to complete or to accomplish his/her salvation. Paul could have described us in our unsaved state as being asleep, as being out of touch with our spiritual reality, or any number of other less severe conditions. However, he chose the analogy of "*dead* in trespasses and sins" by the direction and inspiration of the Holy Spirit for good cause.

The person whose moral and spiritual state matches Paul's description in our study verses is a spiritually dead person! He is quite active and alive in terms of human life, and most definitely alive to sinful human passions and conduct, but he is dead to spiritual reality and to any ability or inclination toward God. He views God and spiritual matters as "foolishness," not as something to be believed and embraced as good and true.

Thus our eternal salvation must be by God's grace alone. Nothing else can save!

13
Man's Deficiency: Ability and Motive

What then? are we better than they? No, in no wise: for we have before proved both Jews and Gentiles, that they are all under sin; As it is written, There is none righteous, no, not one: There is none that understandeth, there is none that seeketh after God. They are all gone out of the way, they are together become unprofitable; there is none that doeth good, no, not one. Their throat is an open sepulchre; with their tongues they have used deceit; the poison of asps is under their lips: Whose mouth is full of cursing and bitterness: Their feet are swift to shed blood: Destruction and misery are in their ways: And the way of peace have they not known: There is no fear of God before their eyes. (Romans 3:9-18)

So then they that are in the flesh cannot please God. (Romans 8:8)

But the natural man receiveth not the things of the Spirit of God: for they are foolishness unto him: neither can he know them, because they are spiritually discerned. (1 Corinthians 2:14)

What is the real problem with fallen, unregenerate humanity? Is it ability or is it motive? Those who follow more or less the Pelagian/Arminian view of theology will assert that man retains the ability to please God, so they view their primary mission in preaching as motivating fallen man to do the right thing. As we have learned in our study of the impact the fall had on Adam and all of subsequent humanity, man lost the ability *and* the motive to do good.

These verses, Romans 3:9-18, emphasize fallen sinful man's actual conduct, but in so doing they speak both to man's ability and his motive. Perhaps man's motive leads this description of man's fallen sinfulness, for motive drives conduct. To further make the point add Romans 8:8, a verse which concludes a tightly reasoned lesson from Paul in the Roman letter regarding sinful fallen man's lack of spiritual ability: "…they that are in the flesh *cannot* please God." To these verses, add 1st Corinthians 2:14, another summary conclusion that follows Paul's consistently reasoned teaching regarding fallen man's nature and sinful disposition. This verse speaks directly to sinful man's lack of ability to "receive the things of the Spirit of God."

All of these verses confront the popular notion of unsaved man's ability. If an unregenerate (not born again, not saved from sin) person possesses an inherent ability to do as much of spiritually righteous acts as a regenerate person—thus his only saved-unsaved distinctive is his motivation—these verses mean nothing at all, for they categorically address the unsaved person's lack of ability to perform acceptable spiritual actions, physical or mental.

The word translated *cannot* in Romans 8:8 is a combination of two words in the Greek text of the verse. The first word is a strong negative. The second word has the following meaning:

> **1** to be able, have power whether by virtue of one's own ability and resources, or of a state of mind, or through favourable circumstances, or by permission of law or custom. **2** to be able to do something. **3** to be capable, strong and powerful.[1]

Thus the linking of the two words emphasizes fallen man's (Paul's term "they that are in the flesh") lack of ability to please God. Interestingly the same two words appear in 1st Corinthians 2:14, "...*neither can.*" Both of these verses reject the idea that fallen unsaved humans possess the ability to 1) please God, 2) receive the things of the Spirit of God, or 3) know such things.

In combination these three passages describe unsaved humans quite clearly. They actively practice sin, and they lack the desire and the ability to pursue God and godliness—anything spiritual in the sense of things that relate to God from a truly spiritual perspective.

Isaiah focuses on the desires, motives, or will of the wicked in terms of spiritual matters.

> *Let favour be shewed to the wicked, yet will he not learn righteousness: in the land of uprightness will he deal unjustly, and will not behold the majesty of the LORD.* (Isaiah 26:10)

---

[1] James Strong, *The Exhaustive Concordance of the Bible : Showing Every Word of the Test of the Common English Version of the Canonical Books, and Every Occurence of Each Word in Regular Order.*, electronic ed. (Ontario: Woodside Bible Fellowship., 1996), G1410.

The word "will" speaks to the wicked person's conduct, but it also addresses his/her natural inclination, the will itself. Thus both fallen humanity's will, motives, or desires, and abilities are alien to any action or attitude that can possibly please God.

What are the theological implications of this inherent lack of ability and motive? Clearly they are significant. Any view of regeneration that requires any form or degree of participation from the unregenerate person imposes an impossible task upon him. Such a view of the new birth demands that the person think or do what he/she utterly lacks both the ability and desire to do. In effect it demands the impossible, leaving us with the senseless conclusion that in the end no one could possibly gain his/her salvation; the logic of such a view of salvation leaves heaven empty and hell with a population explosion!

In a rather futile attempt to avoid the problems of this theological view some folks view the human means that they continue to insist on requiring for a person to be saved as a "means" or "instrument" and not the actual cause of salvation itself. However, this view gives no relief from the implications of these passages. Is fallen man any more capable of exercising "means" or "instrumentality" than of performing actual works to accomplish his/her personal salvation?

Paul's view of the unregenerate person's utter lack of ability to do anything spiritually acceptable to God explains his analogy in Ephesians 2:1; prior to God's saving grace and work in the unregenerate sinner, we all were "dead in trespasses and sins." There is a world of difference between a sick person and a dead person. The sick person may suffer various degrees of deficiency, but they inherently possess life and with it certain residual abilities. The dead person has no ability and no cognizance of anything. There are no functional degrees of death. Dead is dead!

The Old Testament prophet Jeremiah acknowledged this same inherent lack of desire and ability.

Can the Ethiopian change his skin, or the leopard his spots? then may ye also do good, that are accustomed to do evil. (Jeremiah 13:23)

In the analogy there is nothing inherently wrong with the Ethiopian's skin color any more than there is anything wrong with the leopard's spots. Jeremiah's point deals with ability. What the Ethiopian and the leopard are by nature they cannot change.

However, when we go from the analogy to the lesson, both Jeremiah and Paul confront sinful and fallen humanity with the fact that there *is* something profoundly wrong with depraved humanity, but such a person is as wholly lacking in ability to alter his/her condition as the Ethiopian or the leopard. To tell a person whom we consider to be unregenerate that they must do something to alter their spiritual nature or state would be as futile and senseless as going to the cemetery and telling the dead in their graves that they need to do something to remedy their death—or telling the Ethiopian or the leopard that they need to think, wish, or do something to change their basic nature. It is demanding the impossible of the incapable!

There are no degrees of ability in any of these passages. There is no residual or dormant ability that needs merely to be encouraged and energized. There is no hidden talent that merely needs to be developed. The young man who approached Jesus with the preconception that he could do something to save himself—and errantly thought he had already done it all—was no doubt disappointed when Jesus reminded him that, despite all he had claimed to have done, he yet was deficient (Luke 18:18-30).

Fallen, depraved humanity as a consequence of the fall and demonstrated every moment of their lives thus lacks both the desire and the ability to do anything of a spiritual quality or nature that honors God, much less anything that merits divine favor or salvation.

The implications are tremendous. Left to their own abilities and/or desires and will, all of fallen humanity cannot—and do not—desire any form of fellowship with God. Based on the array of Old Testament citations that Paul gives us in the passage from the third chapter of Romans, they are rather hostile to God than neutral toward Him. The remedy for man's sin problem does not therefore lie in man but in God—necessarily so.

14
God's Righteousness: With and Without the Law

> Now we know that what things soever the law saith, it saith to them who are under the law: that every mouth may be stopped, and all the world may become guilty before God. Therefore by the deeds of the law there shall no flesh be justified in his sight: for by the law is the knowledge of sin. But now the righteousness of God without the law is manifested, being witnessed by the law and the prophets; Even the righteousness of God which is by faith of Jesus Christ unto all and upon all them that believe: for there is no difference: For all have sinned, and come short of the glory of God. (Romans 3:19-23)

Before moving forward, Paul will once again remind his readers of the major points that he made in the first two chapters and summarized in 3:9. In terms of God's righteous judgment of man, being a Jew or a Gentile makes no difference with Him. God's moral law applies to every human, and the result of His righteous judgment of every human's conduct is the same. Every mouth of every human is stopped. None can claim that he has attained to God's moral commandments. None can protest God's judgment against him as being unfair or as not considering all the evidence of his conduct. Every mouth is stopped. Every protest against God's righteous judgment is silenced. Defiant, sinful man may well complain against God before other humans, but on Judgment Day when God shines the spotlight of righteous judgment on every detail of his conduct, the same voices that protest so loudly before men will be silenced. God's righteous law shall prevail, and sinful man shall stand before the Righteous Judge, convicted by undeniable evidence of his sins.

In the New Testament, two words appear that deal with the formal legal sentence of a judge: justification and condemnation. Justification is the equivalent to our "Not guilty," and condemnation is the equivalent to our "Guilty as charged." Thus, Paul's point stands firm. Given man's unquestioned guilt based on his actual sins, no human, past, present, or future, can claim justification, "Not guilty as charged," before God.

If any human stands before God, the righteous Judge, and hears the final sentence, "Justified," the sentence shall be based on something other than that person's conduct. God's law performs flawlessly in its function of identifying what is sin, "...*by the law is the knowledge of sin.*" Sinful man loves to redefine sin into something other than what it is—sin. But, when sinful man stands before God, the righteous Judge, his pretentious word games and redefinitions shall fail. God's law shall shine the light of reality onto one sin after another, and all shall see that sin for what it is, sin.

What is this idea, "...*the righteousness of God without the law*"? What other source do we have to know God's righteousness beside His law? Twice Jeremiah answers our question, both in Jeremiah 23:6 and in 33:16.

Notice in 23:6 the reference is to "...*his name...THE LORD OUR RIGHTEOUSNESS,*" and in 33:16, the reference is to "...*the name wherewith she shall be called, The Lord our righteousness.*" In these two passages, Jeremiah anticipates the central truth of our eternal salvation. God takes away the guilt of our sins by charging them to the Lord Jesus Christ, who fully and legally satisfied God's justice for them, and He then charges to our account the spotless righteousness of our Lord Jesus Christ. It is His righteousness, but by grace abounding, He now calls us by the name, and therefore identifies us in His love as having His righteousness.

Jeremiah prophetically anticipated Paul's words in our study passage. If you want to know what God's righteousness means as He intended it, lived out in actual conduct, your desire is easily satisfied. Simply look through the lens of Scripture at the life and Person of the Lord Jesus Christ. He lived God's righteous law in every finite detail. He never broke it in any way. He is God's "*righteousness...without the law....*" Throughout the New Testament, whenever you read about something or someone who was "...*witnessed by the law and the prophets...*" you always see the Person of the Lord Jesus Christ.

...*by faith of Jesus Christ....* Somewhat understandably, many sincere believers struggle with the idea of Jesus, or of God, having faith. If we define faith as grasping what we cannot clearly see, as in "...*we walk by faith, not sight...*" the point is clear. However, the point of 2 Corinthians 5:7 specifically refers to our exercise of faith, not God's. In Romans 3:3, Paul has already categorically associated faith with God, "...*make the faith of God without effect.*" However, a contemporary use of this word *faith* will make the point of such Scriptures that no thinking, believing

Christian should oppose. Every legal contract of any significance contains a "Boilerplate" provision that the agreeing parties sign and agree to, that they enter into this contract with honest intentions of fulfilling its requirements. They sign this contract "...in good faith." They do not sign with any reservation of guile or deceit. They truly agree to fulfill the terms of the contract. If we view the passages that use terms such as we find in this verse, *"...faith of Jesus Christ..."* in the same way as we use the term in a legal contract, any objection to the term dissolves.

God never tells us something in Scripture with duplicity, with any element of deceit. He is always faithful to His word and to His covenant. Every promise God makes He makes "In good faith." And quite often, God's "Good faith" promise is wrapped up in the Person and work of the Lord Jesus Christ.

...unto all and upon all that believe.... In this point, believing is not a demand put on us, but a term that describes those who understand and rejoice in the righteousness of God that He has manifested without the law. The distinguishing point of faith has nothing to do with Jews and Gentiles. It has to do with the condition of the heart where God's grace has worked a gracious and miraculous change. If we look at believers apart from their faith in Christ, we will see one consistent pattern: *"For all have sinned, and come short of the glory of God."* But focusing on the human behavior alone and not on God who changes the hearts will not reveal the final solution. God knew before He created the first molecule of creation that we would sin and come short of His glory. For that reason, He provided grace and justification for His elect in the Person and work of the Lord Jesus Christ. And that is the point that Paul here makes.

Two errant points that are commonly held in our times need examination. First, even among many who teach strongly on the grace of God, belief is preached as a condition to the new birth. Only those who hear and believe the gospel can experience the new birth. Two Biblical truths refute this idea. The first truth appears in the context that we now study.

Carefully examine Paul's description of the man without God in this chapter. If this description is correct, and it is, how likely is the man who doesn't seek after God—and God is not in all his thoughts—to believe the message of the gospel? Not only will he not believe the gospel, Paul taught that he cannot do so. First John 5:1 further affirms the proper corollary between the new birth and believing in Jesus.

> *Whosoever believeth that Jesus is the Christ is born of God: and every one that loveth him that begat loveth him also that is begotten of him.* (1 John 5:1).

The person who believes the core message of the gospel, that Jesus is the Christ, has already been born of God. Therefore belief cannot be made into a condition to become born again.

The second errant idea is that believing the gospel or generally an act of faith is not a work. According to this view, requiring that a person believe in Jesus as a condition to the new birth is not really requiring that person to work, so this idea is not really salvation by works. Jesus Himself refutes this idea as clearly as John refutes the first errant idea.

> *Then said they unto him, What shall we do that we might work the works of God? Jesus answered and said unto them, This is the work of God, that ye believe on him whom he hath sent.* (John 6:28-29).

This passage is quite clear. The Jews asked Jesus a simple question. They wanted to know what they could do that would please God. All of God's children should seek God's will so directly. Jesus didn't delve into a mystical theological treatise. He answered their question. If they wanted to work a work that God would accept and honor, they should believe in Him Whom God had sent. If in fact believing is not a work, why did Jesus teach that it is a work?

Believing in Jesus is the noble objective of gospel preaching. He embodied all truth that in any way is associated with us and our relationship to God. He is the one Mediator between God and men. We shall all believe in Him in heaven (2 Thessalonians 1:10). When Jesus was preparing the disciples for His departure, He used these words, "...*ye believe in God, believe also in me.*" (John 14:1) A. T. Robertson, a highly respected twentieth century New Testament Greek scholar, wrote of this verse.

Ye believe ... believe also (*pisteuete ... kai pisteuete*). So translated as present active indicative plural second person and present active imperative of *pisteuō*. The form is the same. Both may be indicative (ye believe ... and ye believe), both may be imperative (believe ... and believe or believe also), the first may be indicative (ye believe) and the second imperative (believe also)....[1]

After more than three years of personal time with Jesus, these men still struggled to believe everything they needed to believe about Him. Do not overlook Robertson's point. They did truly believe in God. They needed to believe in Jesus in the same way that they already believed in God. Simply stated, they needed to believe that He was God Incarnate, God come in human flesh. They needed to believe in this way. So do we.

---

[1] Robertson, A. T., *Word Pictures in the New Testament*, quoted from SwordSearcher Bible study software; John 14:1.

15
God's Solution for Sin—and for Sinners

Being justified freely by his grace through the redemption that is in Christ Jesus: Whom God hath set forth to be a propitiation through faith in his blood, to declare his righteousness for the remission of sins that are past, through the forbearance of God; To declare, I say, at this time his righteousness: that he might be just, and the justifier of him which believeth in Jesus. (Romans 3:24-26).

Our passage flows freely through the panorama of God's eternal purpose in the Person and work of the Lord Jesus Christ. Paul consistently reasons through this chapter from the hopeless and helpless state of sinners to the finished and successful work of the Lord Jesus Christ. What sinners cannot do—and do not want to do—to extricate themselves from the consequences of their sins God has accomplished fully through His Son. Our legal standing of innocence before God does not grow out of our purity, but out of what He did on our behalf.

Paul's first step in our present study addresses the quality of our legal standing, and he concludes that we have the blessed position before God of "not guilty," the equivalent in our legal terminology of "justified" in first century Greek and Roman culture. How can someone who is actually guilty be viewed before the law as innocent without a dreadful miscarriage of justice? In human legal justice, this cannot be. Even if we pay the penalty required by the law, the charge against us remains and testifies against our innocence. However, in God's amazing purpose, when Jesus died for our sins, the actual guilt of our sins became His, and His spotless innocence became ours. When Paul writes that we are freely justified by God's grace, he reminds us that God legally views us as innocent.

Paul further qualifies our justification by the term *freely*. The English word says everything that we need to know about our legal standing before God, but the Greek word translated *freely* adds even more emphasis to the point. We find another appearance of this Greek word that adds beautiful clarity to the point of the word in this passage.

But this cometh to pass, that the word might be fulfilled that is written in their law, They hated me without a cause. (John 15:25).

In this verse, *without a cause* was translated from the same Greek word as *freely* in our study passage. Just as fully as the wicked people of Jesus' day hated Him without anything in Him to justify their hatred, God justified His people in the Lord Jesus Christ without any merit or motivation whatever in them. There is nothing in you or me to explain God's justifying us. Everything that explains His legal sentence we find in the Person of the Lord Jesus Christ.

Justification in Scripture has to do with legal standing, the verdict of "Innocent." Justification is not an experiential principle, but a legal one. Our justification explains many of our spiritual experiences and reactions, but they all relate to the results of our justification. Justification itself is a matter of God and of His Law, not our experiences as children of God.

...through the redemption that is in Christ Jesus. We tend to compartmentalize the various words that appear in Scripture to describe God's amazing grace in the saving of sinners, but Scripture integrates them all, each word reminding us of what God required—and performed—to accomplish our eternal security through our successful Surety. While the various ideas of "redemption" in Roman first century culture contribute richly to our understanding of God's grace on our behalf, the Old Testament law of redemption likely serves as the best example.

When Israel finally possessed the land of Canaan, God assigned specific geographic areas to each tribe, further subdividing smaller portions to each family. Effectively, real estate was to belong to the same family and tribe in perpetuity. However, Moses' Law provided for the satisfaction of extraordinary debts by requiring the person who owed more than he could pay to serve his creditor up to forty-nine years. Regardless of the amount owed, at the end of the cycle, the man went free, and the debt was dismissed. This limitation would likely impose wise reservations on the amount of money a wealthy man would loan to his neighbor.

Based on the Law of Redemption, at any time a man was serving his creditor to settle his debt, a near family member could intervene, pay the creditor, and the indebted servant was set free. Moses' Law was quite specific that the person paying the debt on behalf of another must be a "near-kinsman." If we apply this principle to the word *redemption* in the New Testament, many sound truths appear clearly. Jesus didn't die for an unnamed and uncertain number of people whom He knew in advance would turn to Him and therefore not really need His payment of their debt. He paid the price of redemption for His family. He was their "near-kinsman" before Calvary. When the angel assured Joseph of Mary's supernatural pregnancy, he made the point, "...*he shall save his people from their sins*" (Matthew 1:21). His work was specifically done for His own family. Thus we learn that our legal standing of "not guilty" comes as the result of Jesus paying the legal debt that we rightly owed.

Now that Jesus has paid our debt, we no longer owe it. We do owe Him the debt of unspeakable gratitude for grace beyond imagination, but we do not owe Him that debt any longer. God didn't transfer our impossible debt from Himself to Jesus. If the debt was impossible for us to pay to God, it would be no less impossible for us to pay Jesus that same amount.

Whom God hath set forth to be a propitiation through faith in his blood..... We likely would never hear the word *propitiation* in our daily activities. It is a unique word. The best and simplest definition is "satisfaction." We find it used in reference to the "mercy seat" in the Book of Hebrews. Some Bible scholars will actually translate the word as "mercy seat." In that case, they would translate our verse as "*Whom God hath set forth to be a mercy seat...*"

The corollary is valid. The high priest sprinkled the blood of the annual goat sacrifice on the "mercy seat" in the Holy of holies. In symbolic form, the eyes of the cherubim that were carved into the "mercy seat," the lid that covered the Ark of the Covenant, looked down toward the tablets of stone on which God's Ten Commandments were carved, a reminder that sin existed and called for the life of the sinner. However, after the priest sprinkled the blood of the substitute sacrifice, the cherubim saw a covering of blood over the tablets of the Law. What a vivid image of God's *propitiation*, His satisfaction for our sins.

...*to declare*... The declaration here is God's, not ours. By all that Jesus did during the Incarnation, and specifically what He did in suffering for our sins, God declares that His righteousness, not ours, and His Son's work, not our own, is the only acceptable satisfaction for our sin problem. Only by this incredible legal substitution can Paul write that through this specific work, God is both just and the justifier of His people.

As pointed out in the last chapter, belief in this context is descriptive, not a prerequisite for eternal salvation. The Bible teacher who appeals to such passages as this and "invites" or "urges" lost, hell-bound sinners to believe so that they may escape eternal judgment misuses the passage. It describes the child of God; it does not add a human condition, in Jesus' own words (John 6:28-29) a human "work" as a prerequisite to the benefits of Jesus' work.

We should distinguish the actual work the Lord Jesus Christ performed for the propitiation of our sins from God's "declaration" of His acceptance of that work. The work was performed at Calvary, and God "declared" His satisfaction with the work three days later when Jesus arose from the dead. Our belief of that glorious truth puts us in harmony with God's declaration. It establishes fellowship between God and us. Our belief does not put away our sins, nor does it function as a condition that we must perform to gain participation in the finished work of Christ.

God gives us eternal life in the new birth based on what Jesus did on our behalf, and that work needs no supplement or added contribution from us. It is complete. Once we receive the life of God in the new birth we need to learn the truth of what God has done to accomplish our eternal life with Him. In believing in Jesus, just as the Father effectively believed (good faith in advance of His work that He would fully perform it) in Him, we put ourselves in fellowship with God. Remember 1 John 5:1, as well as John 5:24; the believer has already been born again, has already passed from death to life. Belief doesn't cause it or contribute to it. Belief enables us to peacefully understand the incredible miracle that God accomplished out of His grace alone for us. In that way, our belief becomes the basis of our fellowship with God, for in true belief we view the work of Jesus as gloriously accomplished and successful, just as the Father views it. Therein, our belief establishes our fellowship with God.

16
The Law of Faith

> Where is boasting then? It is excluded. By what law? of works? Nay: but by the law of faith. Therefore we conclude that a man is justified by faith without the deeds of the law. Is he the God of the Jews only? is he not also of the Gentiles? Yes, of the Gentiles also: Seeing it is one God, which shall justify the circumcision by faith, and uncircumcision through faith. Do we then make void the law through faith? God forbid: yea, we establish the law. (Romans 3:27-31).

When Paul wrote that God set Jesus Christ "...*forth to be a propitiation...for the remission of sins that are past, through the forbearance of God*," he specifically identified a truth that many Christians do not understand to this day. Ask most Christians today how God saved (put away the sins of) His people in the Old Testament, and they will tell you that people before Jesus had to obey Moses' Law. They never consider that Jesus atoned for past sins no less than for future sins of His chosen people.

The atoning death of the Lord Jesus Christ satisfied God's righteous demands for the sins of Old Testament elect people no less than for your sins and mine. This context, affirmed by Galatians 3:21, specifically teaches that the Law of Moses had no more ability to atone for sins in the Old Testament era than it has today. God's forbearance applied the work of Jesus to His people throughout the Old Testament era, because He knew perfectly the results of Jesus' work. God didn't give the Law to put away sins; He gave it to remind His worshipping people in that time of the coming Savior, and to show them in surprising details how He would accomplish their redemption. You see this point in the context of Galatians 3:21, as well as throughout the Book of Hebrews.

A superficial reading of this context might conclude that in some way Moses' Law and faith are at cross purposes. This faulty conclusion is the point that Paul addresses in our study verses. We do not think of faith in terms of it being a "law" or of it functioning as a "law." I here use the term "law" as a scientist might use the word in reference to a fixed principle of science or nature. An electrician might know the relationship of "Ohm's Law" to his electrical business, for example. Paul here affirms that faith as a principle of our interaction with God is quite specific in its function and work, like a "law" of science. Thus Paul rightly speaks of two "laws," Moses' Law and the "law" of faith. Moses' Law functioned based on how the people obeyed it or not; it was the "...*law of works*."

I deeply respect the accomplishments of the Protestant Reformers and the religious liberty that we enjoy today because of their labors. They did much to shift the emphasis of Western Europe and North America away from salvation by works as taught by the Roman Church. That significant contribution fully appreciated, we should not deify them. One point of terminology I here specifically address. When the Reformers coined the term "Justification by faith," they intended to distinguish their belief from the Roman Church's view of salvation by works. However, when the New Testament uses the term, "Justified by faith," the context is always related to discipleship, not new birth or eternal salvation.

Neither Moses' Law nor faith, *per se*, was designed by God to put away sins. As Moses' Law served as an instructive guide to direct Old Testament worshippers to the coming Christ, so faith in similar fashion instructively directs us to that same Christ. In this way, both the Law of Moses and faith have one and the same object, the Person and work of the Lord Jesus Christ. This is Paul's point as he rejects the idea that the law and faith are in some way contradictory. For Paul, they both point to Christ. However, what the Law did imperfectly and indirectly in the Old Testament era, faith does perfectly and directly in the New Testament era. You will notice that Paul in Galatians 3 writes of the law in the past tense, "...*the law was our schoolmaster*...." However, when Paul here writes of the correct workings of faith, he shifts to the present tense, "...*we conclude that a man is justified by faith without the deeds of the law*."

The whole dynamic of faith as our guidepost to direct us to the Lord Jesus Christ sets the stage for Paul's next point. Under the leadership of faith, being a Jew or being a Gentile is wholly irrelevant. It doesn't matter. Whether we are Jew or Gentile, we attain fellowship with God, justification by faith, in exactly the same way.

Occasionally I have read or heard Bible students attempt to make a distinction between "...*by faith*..." and "...*through faith*..." in this lesson.

However, Paul's primary objective in this context is to emphasize that there is no difference, not to explain that there is a difference in the way people from different races or cultures learn of Jesus and frame their lives in fellowship with their God.

Paul's final point before going into significant details regarding exactly how this thing called "Justification by faith" works in the fourth chapter is to underscore his point yet one more time. Faith and Moses' Law are not contradictory, nor are they exclusive of the other. God called on His people under Moses' Law to look to Him by faith, to view the work of their priests through faith, and to see through the lens of Moses' Law the coming Messiah, God Incarnate, God in human flesh, who would fulfill, not void or contradict all the indicators that He had invested in Moses' Law.

The conclusion is that the law served a useful though temporary function. Faith, however, is a permanent principle that directs us, and assists us in living our lives in fellowship, peaceful, joyful fellowship with God (Romans 5:1-5). We shall study this beautiful truth more fully through the fourth chapter.

17
Justification by Faith: What does it Mean?

What shall we say then that Abraham our father, as pertaining to the flesh, hath found? For if Abraham were justified by works, he hath whereof to glory; but not before God. For what saith the scripture? Abraham believed God, and it was counted unto him for righteousness. Now to him that worketh is the reward not reckoned of grace, but of debt. But to him that worketh not, but believeth on him that justifieth the ungodly, his faith is counted for righteousness. (Romans 4:1-5).

Throughout the New Testament, and especially in Paul's writings, Abraham frequently appears as the timeless model of faith--and godly works. Paul asks what Abraham found, but, as he develops his thought, he teaches us to find the same thing in our pursuit of the faith-walk. For Paul, Abraham is not merely a philosophical idea; he is a real man who had a real experience with God that is reported in Old Testament Scripture, and his life serves as an instructive example of true faith to us.

Paul closes the third chapter with a reference to justification by faith; he opens the fifth chapter with that same topic, so we should prepare to learn much about justification by faith in the fourth chapter. A correct reading of the fourth chapter will validate that expectation.

In the last study, I noted that the New Testament uses this term, "justified by faith," consistently in reference to the faith-walk, to our discipleship, not to our new birth. The fourth chapter of Romans emphatically affirms this truth.

For if Abraham were justified by works, he hath whereof to glory; but not before God. Given the topic introduced in the closing verses of the third chapter, we would expect to see "*...justified by faith...*" in this verse, but instead we see "*...justified by works....*" Why? What is Paul's point? He will explain his point clearly.

Notice first that Paul says that Abraham "*...hath whereof to glory, but not before God.*" Sometimes, either in false humility or as an expression of a bad understanding of Biblical teaching on the dynamics of the godly faith-walk, you will hear people say, "If I do something good,

God gets all the credit, and I get none." There is a subtle shift from the Bible basis of doing good, "glory," to the human basis, "credit," in this expression. Why? Secondly, the attitude expressed wholly contradicts Paul's stated point in our study passage. Abraham had reason to glory. He did the right thing. He followed the leading of the Holy Spirit to believe what God said, and to act on that belief. He could joyfully and peacefully live with his actions. *"...But not before God"* puts this attitude into the right perspective. Abraham could not adopt an independent or arrogant attitude toward God because of his right conduct. His actions didn't earn his eternal life, but Scripture affirms a balanced attitude of moral responsibility that rightly honors God, even in the attitude of glorying.

This verse emphasizes that our good works are not in some selfish way competitive with God. They are, rather, our faithful, obedient acts of cooperation with God in our obedience (2 Corinthians 6:1). When Abraham lied in a sinful act of self-preservation about Sarah being his sister, not his wife, he had no reason to glory, but he had abundant reason to bow in shame at his actions.

A second reason for someone to make this unbiblical and unbalanced comment is that they might hold to an errant belief regarding God's governance of His people and of His universe. If you believed that God caused every thought, word, and deed, then you would assign all "credit" for your conduct to God. However, regardless of the word games that people who hold to this fatalistic, pagan idea of God may play, they cannot escape that their belief inevitably makes God responsible, either directly or indirectly, for their sins, something that contradicts Scripture and egregiously violates the righteous character of God.

Adam and Eve wanted to give God "...one hundred percent of the credit" for their sin. *"The woman thou gavest to be with me, she gave me of the tree, and I did eat"* (Genesis 3:12). *"The serpent (whom God had created, so He must be at fault) beguiled me, and I did eat"* (Genesis 3:13). Beware the attitude that attempts either to credit God or to blame God for everything. It started in the Garden of Eden after the fall, and it continues to this day to grow in the soil of human sin.

How was Abraham justified by works? We might leap to James and learn a necessary truth of godly faith. It will eventually translate its trust in God into personal conduct. That is indeed a Biblical truth, but it is the truth that James will teach us; it is not the truth that Paul teaches in our present study. After stating that Abraham was justified by works, Paul's next point is to quote Genesis 15:6, "*Abraham believed God, and it was counted unto him for righteousness.*" Paul's point in his *"...to him that worketh..."* and *"...to him that worketh not, but believeth..."* is not to praise slothful passivity in our lives. It is rather to establish a foundational attitude for every act of godly conduct that we shall ever do.

As we face life and its difficulties, do we primarily trust in our own power and genius, or do we trust in God? Before we get to Genesis 15 in Abraham's life, we have already followed him in his sad detour into Egypt. He has learned the painful truth that sin never honors God and therefore sin never gives us reason to glory. Abraham tried working and not believing in God while in Egypt, and we know the sad outcome of that choice. Neither God nor Abraham gloried in Abraham's sinful action.

In contrast, Abraham's response to God in Genesis 15 gave Abraham reason to glory in that he believed God. Why would Paul describe Abraham's act of believing as "*...justified by works*"? Consider the situation. God called Abraham to leave his family and become a nomad when Abraham was around seventy years old. This event appears in the closing verses of Genesis 11. By the time we get to Genesis 15, some ten to fifteen years have lapsed. From the beginning, God promised Abraham that he and Sarah would have a son who would prove to be a blessing to all the families of the earth.

Before you ho-hum this point, consider the reality that Abraham faced. When God called him to leave Ur, Abraham was seventy years old. By the time we get to Genesis 15, Abraham is eighty to eighty-five years old, but he and Sarah have not yet seen that promised son. If God told you at age 80-85 that you would become the father or mother of a child, how would you react? To say the least; accepting that idea would not be easy to believe. In fact, you just might have to "work" at believing that God's promise was literal and literally true. And if God told you that the actual event was still some time in the future, your challenge, your "work," would be all the more challenging.

I'm seventy years old, so I can appreciate in a minor way the dilemma that Abraham faced. Do you still struggle with the idea that believing in God is described in Scripture as a "work"? Aside from this passage, study John 6:28-29. In response to the Jews' question to Jesus regarding what they might do to "...*work the works of God*," Jesus gave them a very simple answer, to "...*believe on him whom he hath sent.*" Jesus described believing in Him as a work. If Jesus described belief as a work, I am quite satisfied to accept His word on the question. Aren't you?

Frequently, contemporary Christians will quote Genesis 15:6, the verse that Paul here quotes, and interpret the verse as defining Abraham's moment of salvation, and their meaning for "salvation" is that this is Abraham's first moment of eternal salvation. This populist interpretation, however, will not stand the test of Scripture.

If in fact this moment of belief was Abraham's moment of "saving faith," advocates of this idea must explain Abraham's previous ten to fifteen years of walking by faith. With the exception of his detour into Egypt, Abraham left Ur (see the closing verses of Genesis 11) by faith, and he has been walking by faith for well over a decade. Genesis 15:6 cannot disclose Abraham's first faith event.

This simple truth is again confirmed in Hebrews 11:8 where we read that Abraham's leaving Ur was an act of exemplary, Hebrews 11 kind of faith. I have talked with a few advocates of this populist view who actually say that, although Abraham walked by faith from his exit from Ur, his faith from that time till Genesis 15:6 was of an inferior quality that did not rise to the "...quality of saving faith." If this idea is true, we must resolve the dilemma that Hebrews 11 gives us one example after the other of "inferior faith." No thanks! I'll believe what Hebrews 11:8 simply states. There was nothing inferior about Abraham's faith through those long, lonely nomadic years, and Hebrews 11:8 removes any possible doubt about the fact. Therefore, Genesis 15:6 identifies an exemplary moment in the long faith-path that Abraham has been travelling for over a decade already.

This simple Bible truth wholly rejects the idea that Genesis 15:6 reports Abraham's moment of eternal salvation. That event occurred long years prior. Genesis 15:6 records a moment of spiritual growth in Abraham's faith that holds him up before us as a noble example. Believe God as fully as Abraham believed Him, and you, like Abraham, will "...*have whereof to glory, but not before God.*"

18
Justification by Faith: Old Testament Perspective of a Timeless Truth

> For what saith the scripture? Abraham believed God, and it was counted unto him for righteousness....Even as David describeth the blessedness of the man, unto whom God imputeth righteousness without works, saying Blessed are they whose iniquities are forgiven, and whose sins are covered. Blessed is the man to whom the Lord will not impute sin. Cometh this blessedness then upon the circumcision only, or upon the uncircumcision also? for we say that faith was reckoned to Abraham for righteousness. How was it then reckoned? when he was in circumcision, or in uncircumcision? Not in circumcision, but in uncircumcision. (Romans 4:3, 6-10)

To anchor his justification by faith (and works through the function of faith in us: Romans 4:2; John 6:28-29) teaching in Old Testament Scripture, Paul quotes two key passages at the beginning of this chapter-long lesson. First he quotes from Genesis 15:6 regarding Abraham finally more fully believing God's longstanding and oft-repeated promise. Then he quotes from the thirty-second Psalm. A full and careful study of these two Old Testament lessons will prepare our minds to fully appreciate Paul's teaching in this chapter on justification by faith.

Genesis 15:6

As mentioned earlier, many teachers read Genesis 15:6 without its context and history and errantly interpret the verse as Abraham's initial act of faith. Since they believe that the sinner must respond in faith to the gospel, they extrapolate their errant interpretation to teach that Genesis 15:6 records Abraham's experience of eternal salvation. In their teaching, prior to this event, Abraham was lost, in their view of the term, eternally so. The context of Paul' citation in this chapter should urge us to take a different view of that verse.

In the history of Abraham's life, from the closing verses of Genesis 11 to this point, we see a man whom God calls, speaks to him, and leads him for ten to fifteen years before we reach this verse. Except for his disgraceful time in Egypt, every time that Abraham stops for any length of time, he erects an altar and worships God. This lifestyle hardly depicts an unsaved man. The single most important point to the correct understanding of Genesis 15:6 appears in Hebrews 11.

> *By faith Abraham, when he was called to go out into a place which he should after receive for an inheritance, obeyed; and he went out, not knowing whither he went.* (Hebrews 11:8).

In a chapter devoted to exemplary and powerful faith in Old Testament saints, Paul specifically identifies that Abraham was living by faith from the time he left Ur of the Chaldees, an event recorded in the closing verses of Genesis 11, ten to fifteen years prior to Genesis 15:6. Paul quite clearly did not believe that Genesis 15:6 was Abraham's first act of faith or his moment of eternal salvation.

When confronted with this passage, some Bible teachers who hold more to the errant view of justification by faith than the Biblical view will actually say that Abraham did have faith and walk by it prior to Genesis 15:6, but, prior to Genesis 15:6, Abraham's faith was inferior, not rising to the quality of their view of "saving faith." A very well-known Bible teacher actually gave this answer to a question after one of his public sessions. If Abraham's faith prior to Genesis 15:6 was "inferior faith," then these teachers need to explain to us how Paul devoted an entire chapter, Hebrews 11, to Old Testament saints whose examples only rise to the level of "inferior faith."

The Biblical truth of these verses shines beautifully and clearly against the obtuse ideas of "inferior faith." Hebrews 11 comes to us from the Holy Spirit to remind us that countless (Hebrews 11:32) Old Testament saints whose faith shines across centuries to remind us of the power of God in the lives of His servants who truly serve Him by exemplary faith. Factually, Hebrews 11 knows nothing of "Inferior faith." Rather it sets before us the noble power of godly model faith, including Abraham's life from Genesis 11, not beginning over a decade later in Genesis 15.

What does Genesis 15:6 actually teach us? It teaches us that a godly, faithful servant encountered a season of life in which he struggled with the Lord's promises, and, godly, faithful man that he was, he asked the Lord for assurance of the promise. Our faithful God abundantly gave His servant the reassurance that he sought, and that servant believed God. When we examine Genesis 15:6 from the perspective of Scripture and not from non-Scriptural philosophical ideas, we begin to see the pattern of Scripture regarding the term in question, "Justification by faith." Precisely as Romans 5:1 states, the New Testament term, "Justified by faith," relates to our peaceful fellowship with God, not with lost sinners gaining eternal life.

Psalm 32

Paul quotes two verses from this Psalm as a foundation for his teaching in this chapter on justification by faith.

> *Saying, Blessed are they whose iniquities are forgiven, and whose sins are covered. Blessed is the man to whom the Lord will not impute sin.*

You will find these words in Psalm 32:1-2, with the interesting observation that David's words in the second verse add an additional thought, *"...and in whose spirit there is no guile."* As you read the complete psalm, it becomes apparent that the writer, presumably David, since the Psalm is identified as *"A Psalm of David. Maschil,"* is writing of a season of intense conviction because of a sin that he committed. At first, he focuses on the deep conviction that he felt because of the sin. *"...my bones waxed old through my roaring all the day long."* Nighttime gave him no relief, *"...For day and night thy hand was heavy upon me."*

Then the Psalm changes its tone. *"I acknowledged my sin unto thee, and mine iniquity have I not hid. I said, I will confess my transgressions unto the Lord; and thou forgavest the iniquity of my sin. Selah."* I suggest that David likely wrote this Psalm many years after his Bathsheba episode. The scenario fits perfectly. David kept his sin hidden from public view until Nathan the prophet confronted him. Then David confessed his sin, and Psalm 51 records his prayer of confession to the Lord. Repentance after the Bathsheba incident was a major event in David's spiritual life and growth, but it was not his initial act of eternal salvation or new birth. David exhibits admirable faith in God from his early youth. It was the young David who walked onto the field with Goliath in greater trust in his God than in his king's armor. Further, the next verse in Psalm 32 affirms the point in our context of study, *"For this shall every one that is godly pray unto thee in a time when thou mayest be found: surely in the floods of great waters they shall not come nigh unto thee."* David himself tells us that the prayer of confession and forgiveness that he prayed is a prayer of the godly, not a prayer of a lost sinner. When a child of God faces his/her sins and confesses them to the Lord, praying for forgiveness, He is always found. He never hides from His repentant child. Never!

In the context of Romans 4, interpreted by that context, the "Imputation" of righteousness without works, forgiven iniquities, covered sins, and sin not imputed all relate to a repentant and believing child of God, not to the lost. David was as surely already born again (Yes, new birth is a timeless principle of God's saving work in his people, not a unique New Testament act; Jesus questioned Nicodemus for not knowing the principle of the new birth from his Old Testament knowledge in John 3) when he wrote this psalm as Abraham was when Genesis 15:6 describes him as believing in God, and his belief was counted for righteousness. In Romans 4:6, Paul associates the principle of Psalm 32 with Genesis 15:6 in the words *"...the blessedness of the man, unto whom God imputeth righteousness without works."*

In both Old Testament lessons, we have children of God taking specific steps, steps of the heart and mind, not yet of the feet, that brought them to closer fellowship with God. This is the principle that Paul has been working toward from the beginning of this letter. He affirms the point.

> *Cometh this blessedness then upon the circumcision only, or upon the uncircumcision also? for we say that faith was reckoned to Abraham for righteousness. How was it then reckoned? when he was in circumcision, or in uncircumcision? Not in circumcision, but in uncircumcision.* (Romans 4:9-10)

Here Paul takes us back to his point in the closing verses of the third chapter. Justification by faith in the sense of present fellowship with God, the New Testament's use of that term, is race-blind and culture-blind. It matters not whether the child of God grew up in a devoted Jewish home, as Timothy did, or in a wholly pagan Gentile home. When God touches the heart in new birth, and that born-again child begins to seek righteousness and fellowship with God by believing

God and by repenting of his former sins, the combined action of the two Old Testament lessons to which Paul appeals, blessedness surely follows.

As he unpacks these life-changing truths to Jews and Gentiles alike, Paul is reaching a bedrock principle of the grace of God and of the New Testament principle of walking by faith. Think back to the historical background of the Roman Church that we examined in the beginning. A church came to exist that included both Jewish and Gentile believers. These faithful believers apparently engaged unbelieving Jews in the Roman synagogues. The debate grew in intensity till it came to the emperor's attention and he ordered all Jews expelled from the city. (Acts 18:2) Sometime later the believing Jews started returning to the city and to their church. Likely the culture of the church had changed somewhat in their absence, and understandable tension developed between Jewish believers and Gentile believers in the church. This is a logical reconstruction, not a historically documented one, but the construct matches what we do know of the historical background of this church from Scripture and from what we read in the Roman letter. Clearly in the Roman letter, Paul hopes to heal a Jew-Gentile schism within the Roman Church, and to motivate the united church to prepare for his visit and to prepare to assist him when he hopes to leave them and travel into Europe to preach the gospel there.

As predominately Gentile believers in the world today, we thank the Lord for the rich truths that Paul was directed by the Holy Spirit to write in the Roman letter, truths that, based on his teachings, are as available to us as to any other believer in God in any age or of any race, culture, or background. Both God's saving grace and temporal blessings are based on grace, not race, and they are equally available to all children of God who walk the faith-walk that Paul here teaches and describes. What a blessing!

19
God's Promised Blessings to Abraham:
A Promise to us as well

> And he received the sign of circumcision, a seal of the righteousness of the faith which he had yet being uncircumcised: that he might be the father of all them that believe, though they be not circumcised; that righteousness might be imputed unto them also: And the father of circumcision to them who are not of the circumcision only, but who also walk in the steps of that faith of our father Abraham, which he had being yet uncircumcised.. For the promise that he should be the heir of the world, was not to Abraham, or to his seed, through the law, but through the righteousness of faith. For if they which are of the law be heirs, faith is made void, and the promise made of none effect: Because the law worketh wrath: for where no law is, there is no transgression. Therefore it is of faith, that it might be by grace; to the end the promise might be sure to all the seed; not to that only which is of the law, but to that also which is of the faith of Abraham; who is the father of us all, (As it is written, I have made thee a father of many nations,) before him whom he believed, even God, who quickeneth the dead and calleth those things which be not as though they were. (Romans 4:11-17)

When any religious perspective begins to lose its legitimate anchors, it drifts into fierce devotion of the superficial. First century Jews exhibited this behavior in their strong emphasis on circumcision. Instead of an outward mark of their deep devotion to God, circumcision for them became a requirement for one to gain access to God (Acts 15:1).

Paul anchors his gospel in the Old Testament Scriptures, and God's original intent for circumcision. It is doubtful that many, if any at all, first century Jews ever thought of the fact that Abraham received the promise of God's blessing for him and for his offspring prior to being circumcised. Paul makes this fact a pivotal point in his teaching.

Based on Paul's teaching, what was God's intent in circumcision? *"...a seal of the righteousness of the faith which he had yet being uncircumcised..."* Prior to his circumcision, Abraham had already believed God's promise (Genesis 15:6), and God had already counted Abraham's faith as a righteous work. Circumcision was not necessary for that blessed state in Abraham; it served only as an outward sign of his blessedness.

Paul introduces a term that he will use frequently in the remainder of the Roman letter, *"righteousness of faith"* or similar terms. His use and explanation of the term as it related to Abraham in this chapter is the key to understanding his intent and use of the term throughout the balance of the letter. The term links us directly to inspired Scripture's description of God's response to Abraham's belief in Genesis 15:6, "Abraham believed God, and it was counted unto him for righteousness." Whatever we make of the term, we must anchor our thoughts in this episode in Abraham's life.

Consider the setting. God called Abraham to leave his native Ur of the Chaldees. Abraham first moves to Haran where he stays for an unknown time, perhaps as long as five years. Then he begins his faith-pilgrimage. Each time he stops for any length of time, Abraham erects an altar and worships God. Hebrews 11:8 tells us that Abraham's faith walk began with his exit from Ur. By the time we arrive at Genesis chapter fifteen, ten to fifteen years have passed.

As you read the Genesis record through this experience (closing verses of Genesis 11 through Genesis 15), notice how often the Scripture indicates Abraham's age at the time. By the time we walk with Abraham into Genesis 15, he is a seasoned follower of God. To apply Paul's term to this season of Abraham's life, he has been a "faith walker" for well over a decade already.

Only after Abraham's belief and God's response in Genesis 15:6 do we read of Abraham circumcising himself and the men in his company. Contrary to the ideas of first century Judaism, circumcision could not account for Abraham's blessed condition. However, Paul rightly reminds us that one factor has been constant with Abraham from the day he left Ur. He has been walking by faith, and God has been blessing him along his pilgrimage. Abraham's confident acceptance of a supernatural blessing that lay still future years ahead was contingent on his believing God and trusting that God's promises would be fulfilled based on God's faithfulness to His word.

Paul reasons that if only the people who know and follow Moses' law are heirs of the promises that God gave to Abraham, the whole Genesis scenario is false, and faith, the one common link from Abraham's exit from Ur to Genesis 15, is invalidated. If circumcision, or the Law of Moses which first century Jews associated with circumcision, is the operative principle necessary for a people to enter into faith's blessings with God, the very faith on which those promises stand has been voided. It means nothing. Forget faith, just be circumcised and keep the law. Ah, but what about those who are circumcised and do not keep the law? Where do they stand with God? This question drives us to the heart of the error of legalism, for not a single Jew from Moses to Jesus every fully kept that law perfectly. Only Jesus fulfilled Moses' Law perfectly.

Therefore it is of faith, that it might be by grace; to the end the promise might be sure to all the seed; not to that only which is of the law, but to that also which is of the faith of Abraham; who is the father of us all. What is the "it" of which Paul writes in this verse? Contextually, Paul has been dealing with the righteousness of faith, the same blessing that Abraham received in Genesis 15:6, so we should not ignore this context and strive to make "it" something else.

Occasionally a few folks who believe in the doctrines of grace, including God's eternal election of a people whom He secures through the work of His assigned Surety, the Lord Jesus Christ, a people who shall all, none lost, spend eternity with Him in glory, will wholly ignore this passage and conclude that God has not only chosen His eternal family, but that he also just as effectually has chosen a specific people whom He shall enlighten and cause to believe His truth and obey Him here in time. Thus you have two equally effectual elections, not one. If you are not included in the second election, forget ever trying to know the truth or to find the rich blessings of faith. Unless you are included in this version of the charismatic "Second Blessing," you are excluded.

This whole notion not only ignores this verse; it contradicts it. Paul will have nothing to do with one philosophy of exclusivism that replaces another. The promise of blessings to those who believe God and who walk with Abraham along the path of the "righteousness of faith" is equally available to every born-again child of God. The promise of the Lord's rich blessings, God counting your faith for righteousness, is as broad as the born-again family of God. The conditions necessary to participate in those blessings are the same as they were when God gave them to Abraham. Regardless the rational ideas that make the outcome seem impossible, regardless the delay in fulfillment and the lapse of many years, when God gives you a promise, you believe Him.

While a true belief in God shall motivate us to godly conduct, never to moral or spiritual passivity, the foundation for every temporal blessing that we shall ever enjoy is anchored to this passage. The "righteousness of faith" of which Paul writes is not the conduct that genuine faith prompts, but the belief in God itself. This belief in God is not the cheap momentary response to an altar call or a superficial agreement with a sermon or testimony that you hear from a preacher. It is a profound, life-changing event that occurs between you and God alone. It follows the pattern of Abraham's experience with God in Genesis 15.

God doesn't look at your race or culture to see if you are eligible for this blessing. He doesn't look at your response to an altar call or to a preacher's sermon. He looks squarely into the depths of your heart. When He sees an honest struggle with the magnitude of what He promises, when He sees you confront your own weaknesses and doubts with honesty, and when He sees that you, despite all the resistance and conflict, truly believe Him and trust His promise to you, He opens the door to the "righteousness of faith" blessings, just as He did to Abraham.

As long as you play the superficial pretense game, you cannot expect the promised blessing. Our pretenses may well deceive other people, but we cannot hide ourselves from the Lord. The more honestly we bow before Him and fully acknowledge our own weakness and failures, but turn from self-reliance as the solution to an unqualified belief in Him and in His promise of blessings, the more we shall see those promises enrich and bless our lives.

Do not read Genesis 15:6 and jump away from that lesson. Read the full lesson. Despite those long years of his faith walk, Abraham confronts the reality of his present state and asks God for some form of reassurance, "Behold, to me thou hast given no seed: and, lo, one born in my house is mine heir." (Genesis 15:3) In Abraham's case, the promise would be fulfilled when he and Sarah had the promised son. But Abraham is now probably in his eighties. By nature, the promise is less likely—indeed, less possible—with each passing year.

It is this growing impossibility that drives Abraham to his knees in prayer to God for some indication that he understood God's promise correctly. And it is this honest appeal to God to which the Lord responds with the promise. Despite his age and all the apparent impossibilities associated with any kind of literal fulfillment, Abraham now believes God, and God honors His faithful servant's belief. That, my friends, is what justification by faith is all about.

For you and me, a similar faith does not tie itself to some self-set personal goal or desire. It ignores self and looks to God and to His promises for us, and it believes that God is serious about keeping His word to His beloved children. Here is one of God's most foundational promises. Do you believe it?

> *Let your conversation be without covetousness; and be content with such things as ye have: for he hath said, I will never leave thee, nor forsake thee. So that we may boldly say, The Lord is my helper, and I will not fear what man shall do unto me.* (Hebrews 13:5-6)

20
Abraham and Hope

(As it is written, I have made thee a father of many nations,) before him whom he believed, even God who quickeneth the dead, and calleth those things which be not as though they were. Who against hope believed in hope, that he might become the father of many nations, according to that which was spoken, So shall thy seed be. And being not weak in faith, he considered not his own body now dead, when he was about an hundred years old, neither yet the deadness of Sarah's womb: He staggered not at the promise of God through unbelief; but was strong in faith, giving glory to God; And being fully persuaded that, what he had promised, he was able also to perform. And therefore it was imputed to him for righteousness. (Romans 4:17-22)

In Romans 4:16, Paul emphasizes that the promise of blessings to the family of God is through faith, not race or culture, and therefore the promise extends to all children of God alike. Neither Jews nor Gentiles have any kind of advantage over the other.

Paul now adds emphasis to that point. When God changed Abram's name to Abraham, he said, "...for a father of many nations have I made thee." (Genesis 17:5) The name "Abram" means "Exalted father," and "Abraham" means "Father of a multitude." When faith dominates a person's life, he/she distinctly shifts away from self-exaltation and moves toward unselfish interest in others. Only if the promise of blessings by faith extend beyond one nation, Israel, however blessed that nation was in her day, does God's promise come to fulfillment. Thus, the point that Paul makes in the fourth chapter of Romans, however shocking it may have seemed to first century Jews, was the literal fulfillment of God's promise that He made to Abraham in Genesis.

I'm only seventy years old, but I can begin to appreciate the amazing miracle that God performed that would enable Abraham to father a son at age one hundred, as well as Sarah to bear that son when she was also well beyond natural child-bearing age. I can appreciate that Abraham may have faced some "work" to believe that God's promise was literal and faithfully true. For this miracle to occur, God must reverse the degenerative processes of age and restore both Abraham and Sarah to their prime.

If the Lord appeared to me and gave me a similar promise, I'd try to believe Him, but I must confess that I'd have to work at the effort. The only way that I could believe such a miraculous promise would be to ignore my own age and the age-related state of my physical body and to trust God explicitly to bring the miracle to pass.

Our study passage takes us through this very process with Abraham and helps us to realize the true character of the miracle that Abraham was to experience at the Lord's hand. Effectively, God must *"...quicken[eth] the dead..."*, i.e. the deadness of both Abraham's and Sarah's reproductive systems to bring about this miracle. This is precisely what Abraham was called on to believe, and he did. Praise God, he did!

Who against hope believed in hope. What does this unusual comment mean? Most commentaries observe that every natural factor was against the outcome that God promised to Abraham, but that he believed God anyway. His belief was contradictory to hope; yet he hoped.

This point is unquestionably true, but is that the point that Paul intends by the language here? The Greek word translated "against" is *para*. We find this word in our contemporary English language in such words as "paralegal," a person who works closely with an attorney, or "paramedic," a person who works closely with medical doctors. A "paralegal" does not work contradictory to the attorney with whom he works, nor does a "paramedic" work contradictory to the physician with whom he works. They work together, the attorney or physician directing and the "para" following instructions.

If we apply the obvious word meaning of "para" to Paul's language, what lesson do we draw from the passage? While all the factors that Abraham knew contradicted the promise, Abraham trusted God and His promise more than he trusted his own knowledge of his age and his deteriorating body. Abraham's posture did not contradict hope. Quite the opposite, Abraham relied on hope and took his instructions from hope. He was leaning against or upon this hope. For this reason, God honored Abraham's faith and accounted his faith for righteousness.

Notice all the terms that Paul stacks, one upon the other, to imbed in our minds the depth of Abraham's strong belief that God would actually fulfill the promise made.

1. He ...*believed in hope.* In fact, based on the word *para*, we could add "...against hope..." as one of these points.
2. He was ...*not weak in faith.*
3. He disregarded ...*his own body now dead....*
4. He disregarded ...*the deadness of Sarah's womb.*
5. He ...*staggered not at the promise of God through unbelief.*
6. He ...*was strong in faith, giving glory to God.*
7. He was ...*fully persuaded that, what he had promised, he was able also to perform.*

Each of these points opens up a floodgate of rich thoughts and blessings to our minds regarding God's faithfulness to His children. Paul's whole point is to remind the Romans, and us, that Abraham is not at all an isolated exception. He is the rule of faith! The same God who was faithful to His promise to Abraham is just as faithful to His promise to you and to me. What He promises, He is also able to perform.

At times, we observe people whom we have regarded as strong "faith-walkers," and marvel at their strong faith. At other times, people whom we have thought to be strong in faith disappoint us. One point in this list stands out as a key indicator of a truly strong faith. The believer who walks by the rule of faith in his life will consistently imitate Abraham in that he will seek to give glory to God, not gain it for himself. He will not ignore the needs of others or the teachings of Scripture to build a personal legacy for his name.

The inhabitants of Babel followed that rule (see Gen. 11:4). The consequences of their desire to make a name for themselves will follow anyone who turns from giving glory to God to gaining glory for himself. The more consistently a believer says and does things that consciously put self in the background and glorifies God the more his conduct affirms his faith.

Look over the major decisions or actions you have made in the last six to twelve months. How many of these actions can you honestly assess as fully intended to glorify God without any hint of self-gain?

21
Abraham's Example Urges Us to the Same Faith

Now it was not written for his sake alone, that it was imputed to him: But for us also, to whom it shall be imputed, if we believe on him that raised Jesus from the dead; who was delivered for our offences, and was raised again for our justification. (Romans 4:23-25)

We tend to read the Genesis record of Abraham's life and think of the miraculous birth of Issac as a nice, but impossible story, something of a benevolent hyperbole, not reality. But we forget that the whole nation of Israel began with Abraham and that "miracle child." If Isaac's birth was a fantasy, then the whole nation that came from him must also be a fantasy. The events are real. The God who created this whole universe is comfortably able to reverse the processes of aging in a couple and to give them a child in their old age.

Paul has reached his primary objective in reasoning through the dynamics of justification by faith. His point was never simply to tell a story about a man in the long ago. His purpose was quite immediate and specific. He wants the Romans, and us, to know that the same God who intervened by a true miracle in the life of Abraham is no less able to intervene in our lives with the miracle of mercy that we need.

Paul's model here does not set us up to make God our magic miracle worker to give us anything that we want. We should not forget that the idea of a child in Abraham's old age was God's, not Abraham's. An Abraham-like faith does not turn faith into a personal mantra, a magic potion by which we can obtain anything we wish. It weans us from such self-centered ideas and leads us to live in the shadow of our God and in all our lives to seek to glorify Him alone.

While I would not question that God on occasion may still reveal His will to His children in various ways, I would strongly suggest that God most often reveals His will to us through the teachings of Scripture and Biblical preaching. God never contradicts Himself, so beware the sincere, but sincerely mistaken souls who tell you that God has called them to do something, but the thing they are supposedly called to do contradicts Scripture.

Second Peter 1:21 affirms that the writing of Scripture occurred by the directing and moving of the Holy Spirit. The Holy Spirit is not confused. If He revealed certain truths and principles in Scripture, do not expect Him to have second thoughts, updated ideas, or in any way to contradict Himself as He has revealed His will in Scripture. When someone claims a Holy Spirit revelation that contradicts Scripture, you can rest assured that Scripture is true and that person is mistaken. He may have had a revelation, but the Holy Spirit was not the source.

The framework of faith that Paul establishes in his teachings on Abraham is wholly God-centric and God-glorifying. God appeared to Abraham and directed him to leave his native Chaldea and to travel to a land that God would later reveal to him, the land that his offspring, surely given to him by a miracle from God, would eventually inherit. Abraham obeyed and began his pilgrimage.

When the Lord first appeared to Abraham, he was around seventy years of age. He was around eighty to eighty-five when God reassured him and he believed God's word, Genesis 15:6. Isaac was born when Abraham was a hundred years of age. Probably Abraham would have been quite happy if God had brought Isaac into the world when he was seventy-one or seventy-two, and showed Abraham the Promised Land before Isaac was ten years old, but that was not to be. Abraham must be weaned from Chaldea. Indeed, Abraham must be weaned from himself. He must learn slowly over these long, tedious years of his pilgrimage to trust his God, however impossible the promise may have seemed. He must learn that the child shall come from God, not from his own ingenuity.

Abraham's detour to Egypt proves his need to grow and to learn. His painful Hagar-Ishmael experience further proves that Abraham needed to grow into that position where, when the promised child finally came, he would know that he came from God alone. Trusting God is not equivalent to trusting ourselves. We need to learn this painful lesson as fully as Abraham did. The path of faith, the work of faith (remember Romans 4:2; Abraham was justified by works in the act of believing God), is a long process of learning and growing, not an overnight miracle.

But for us also, to whom it shall be imputed, if we believe on him that raised Jesus from the dead. Do not leave the fact that Abraham's believing God, and his faith being counted to him for righteousness was not Abraham's new birth experience. It was rather a point in his spiritual growth at which he believed God more fully than he had for the prior ten to fifteen years. Our believing on God who raised Jesus from the dead does not mark our new birth experience any more than Abraham's Genesis 15:6 belief marked his new birth. Justification by faith in Scripture deals with our peaceful fellowship with God, not with our new birth. We should associate it with our discipleship, not with our new birth.

No less than the pleading father who cried, *"Lord, I believe; help thou mine unbelief,"* (Mark 9:24) each of us must face our brokenness and our frailty. We must learn the painful, but necessary lessons of personal limitations before we are fully ready or able to trust in God who knows no such limitations. We must learn to abandon, deny self before we can trust God as fully as the Abraham example requires. We must learn to grow beyond thinking of God as the indulgent grandfather who will give us anything we want if we just ask Him. We must learn that the end of faith comes from God no less than the commandment to believe Him.

For Abraham to actually believe that he and Sarah would have a son in their old age was truly a demanding challenge, if you will in Paul's words, a work that justified his faith. God does not reveal to us that we shall be parents in our old age. He actually reveals something far greater, the fact that His Son, the Lord Jesus Christ, actually died a cruel and ignominious death at the hands of wicked men, that His body was buried and sealed in a tomb in the outskirts of ancient Jerusalem, and that three days later, the tomb, though guarded by soldiers, broke open, and the same Jesus who died came out of that grave, alive and victorious. Does it take some "work" for you and me to believe this fact? Of course it does, but that is the point of the Abraham example.

At the heart of the gospel, we come face to face with a far greater miracle than Abraham and Sarah having a son in their old age. We must come to terms with the reality that God Incarnate, was nailed to a cross and that He died a literal, physical death. Faithful Christians have so strongly proved this point that the old favorite atheistic ploy that Jesus merely swooned, fell into a coma, is no longer raised by most atheists. Jesus was crucified by Roman soldiers who had crucified many people before. They knew the process they administered. They knew when the person on the cross died. They would not stop till they had fully confirmed that the victim was truly dead. Further, if the now abandoned "Swoon Theory" were true, how did such a depleted human break open a sealed tomb and walk out of it past an armed guard who were there to prevent the disciples from stealing His body?

Our path to the rich blessings of Abraham's faith does not take us to a hundred years of age and a miracle birth. It rather takes us to an ancient cross where a man was hung, where He died, was taken down, wrapped in various compounds and clothing, effectively forming a solid body cast around His body. It takes us to a moment in which this man, who was far more than just a man, returned to life, miraculously came out of the body cast so as to leave it in the tomb intact, where He took the time to neatly fold His face napkin and place it in another part of the cave-tomb.

It takes us to his side as He breaks the seal and moves a stone that weighed approximately a ton away from the tomb's opening. It takes us to the women who first visited the tomb the next morning and discovered it empty. It takes us to John and Peter who excitedly run to the tomb after hearing the women's report. It takes us to a mountain top fifty days later, where this same Jesus who died and arose took His exit from those disciples and returned to His glory in heaven. It calls on us to believe this report as a fact no less real and true than Isaac's birth.

Who was delivered for our offences, and was raised again for our justification. Paul will not only tell us what we must believe if we are to follow the Abraham example of faith, but he also tells us why Jesus did all this. He didn't face the Jewish court and the Roman executioners because He was a common criminal or a blasphemer of the Jews. He faced all this for you and me, so that you and I would not have to face its equivalent, just and eternal punishment for our sins.

We know His death was not because of His wrongs, but ours. But we must also come, fully so, to realize that His resurrection on the third day, as literal as His death, was because He had accomplished our ultimate justification before God and His righteous law. The justification of which Paul here writes is not our justification by faith, but the essential legal work that He accomplished on our behalf, the same justification of which Paul wrote in Romans 3:24-25. Because of what Jesus did for us, we can believe this amazing truth and enjoy peaceful fellowship with God rather than face His just wrath against our sins.

At its heart, the belief that results in our justification by faith calls on us to believe the true, literal account in the gospels of Jesus' life, death, resurrection, and glorious ascension. It is no less challenging for us to believe this truth than it was for Abraham to believe God's promise to Him. New Testament justification by faith is God's sharing this incredible good news with us, His children, and giving us access to the rich blessings of faith in action. In this process, and in this process alone, we are able to join with Abraham, to believe God, and for God to lovingly, graciously, and Fatherly account our faith in His Son as righteousness.

22
Glorious Peace

> Therefore being justified by faith, we have peace with God through our Lord Jesus Christ: By whom also we have access by faith into this grace wherein we stand, and rejoice in hope of the glory of God. (Romans 5:1-2)

Both Jesus and His chosen inspired writers of our New Testament associate God's initial work in the fallen sinner's heart as the imparting of life to the dead. Jesus used this analogy when He taught Nicodemus in John 3. He used the analogy in John 5:25 where He explained how that initial imparting of life takes place. He, not any human voice, speaks, and they that hear live. His voice possesses this unique and exclusive life-giving quality.

Paul picks up the point in Ephesians 2:1. However, when Paul describes the justification by faith that has now occupied in excess of a full chapter of his letter to the Romans, he does not tell us that justification by faith produces eternal life. He rather defines peace with God as the outcome.

In the first chapter of Colossians, Paul teaches us that we have redemption through Jesus' blood, His life freely given to the Father at Calvary, that He made peace, our eternal and secure peace with God, through the blood of His cross. Only after affirming the effects of the finished work of the Lord Jesus Christ does Paul shift from our legal and positional standing with God through the death of our Lord Jesus Christ to our state of mind. Despite having these benefits bestowed upon us and in us, Paul notes a grave mental problem in us.

> *And you, that were sometimes alienated and enemies in your mind by wicked works, yet now hath he reconciled In the body of his flesh through death, to present you holy and unblameable and unreproveable in his sight: If ye continue in the faith grounded and settled, and be not moved away from the hope of the gospel, which ye have heard, and which was preached to every creature which is under heaven.* (Colossians 1:21-23)

Notice the arena shift from God's work on our behalf that He freely bestows on and in us to our minds, "...in your mind...." And do not overlook the conditional "if..." of verse 23.

These verses deal with our state of mind; if you will our state of faith after the new birth. Paul's focus on our minds where we may continue an adversarial attitude toward God or we may apply all the truths of what Jesus did to our minds, to our thinking, and, thus, to our actions, "if..." we continue holding those truths sacred in our minds. The vital life-giving work in this context is completed by the time we arrive at verse 21, but our spiritual mindset needs to be brought into harmony with that work. Although Paul did not use the term, he effectively described the process of justification by faith in these three verses.

That justification by faith relates to the mindset of the already-born-again person is further confirmed in Romans 5:2. The believer who is justified by faith already "...stands..." in this grace and already rejoices in hope of the glory of God. Beloved children in a family have free access to the family cupboard when they are hungry, but someone who is not a family member has no privileges in that family resource. As born-again children of God, we "...*have access by faith into this grace...*" this family grace in which we presently stand.

In Philippians 4, Paul begins the closing of his letter to this church with a series of admonitions. He directs the Philippians to make these godly behaviors the habit of their lives, with a promise of blessings if they obey.

And the peace of God, which passeth all understanding, shall keep your hearts and minds through Christ Jesus. (Philippians 4:7)

This is the peace that grows out of justification by faith in the child who truly believes the truth of the gospel and experiences justification by faith. You see in them a spiritual depth and stability that is missing in other believers who have not matured to this point in their faith.

Paul repeats almost the same point to the Colossians. The third chapter of Colossians deals with our spiritual wardrobe. Paul directs us to put off some inappropriate spiritual clothes and to put on godly garments that glorify our Lord. Every wardrobe finally comes together into beautiful coordinated attire by that final touch. The same applies to our spiritual clothes.

And let the peace of God rule in your hearts, to the which also ye are called in one body; and be ye thankful. (Colossians 3:15)

We may "...let..." this peace rule our lives, in which case we find enduring peace in the heat of life's hottest fires, or we may neglect this peace and face the heat of those fires unprepared. Again, Paul describes our justification by faith through the common outcome, peace; specifically, the peace of God.

The fires of life attack believers with special fierceness, but the child of God has one, and only one, effective protection against that heat. When you face your life's deepest trial, its most shocking and disillusioning event, how will you deal with it? Will you turn all your attention to the trial and fall into its vice? Or will you look beyond the trial and keep your heart focused on your God who is greater than any trial? When our life experiences a spiritual World War III, we are able to face the ordeal with peace, but only so long as we keep our focus on our Lord and trust Him to stand beside us and to deliver us. That, my friends, is what justification by faith in Scripture is all about.

23
How Does Justification by Faith Work?

> And not only so, but we glory in tribulations also; knowing that tribulation worketh patience; And patience, experience; and experience hope; And hope maketh not ashamed; because the love of God is shed abroad in our hearts by the Holy Ghost which is given unto us. (Romans 5:3-5)

In human experience, people learn best when they observe a principle in action before they learn the way it works. In the fourth chapter of Romans, Paul used Abraham's life (David's as well in the background in that he cited from the thirty-second Psalm) as the living example of justification by faith. In the fifth chapter, he now explains the dynamics of justification by faith. How do we get from our moment of trial to faith that surmounts the trial?

Before we examine the four steps in this process, let's reflect on the fact that Paul introduces both Abraham and David as examples of justification by faith from the Old Testament. We've studied the life of Abraham in this area through the fourth chapter. The growth of faith in Abraham enabled him to overcome his doubts related to a thirty-year delay in fulfillment of the promise and related to his and Sarah's advancing age, far past normal child bearing age.

When we read the entire thirty-second Psalm, we encounter a believer in God who has sinned and who is struggling with a fierce conviction of conscience. As long as he tried to work out the problem of his sin and the conviction that it brought with it on his own, he was miserable. Only when he confessed his sin to the Lord did he find forgiveness and relief. Interesting, in the early scene of this Psalm, you see a man in deep turmoil. After his confession and the Lord's loving forgiveness, the man rejoices in the peace that came.

Isn't that how Paul described justification by faith in Romans 5:1? By these two examples, we learn that trusting in the Lord and taking our problems to Him, even our greatest sins and failures, is the only course that brings resolution of our problem and relief, sweet, peaceful relief from our doubts and from our convictions.

And not only so, but we glory in tribulations also; knowing that tribulation worketh patience.... Paul was not a warped person who enjoyed suffering. He saw the value of suffering for Jesus' sake because of the outcome that tribulation brings. If we confessed honestly to our deepest inclinations, we'd all likely need to confess to a significant amount of impatience. We want things to turn out the way we want them, and we aren't always the most understanding and resigned souls when things turn out badly, compared to our expectation. Some of us might be inclined to rather ugly attitudes and reactions when our desired expectations are disappointed, attitudes and actions that compromise our desire to live a godly life. When we realize that we behaved badly, we are far too inclined toward rationalizing and justifying our bad conduct instead of taking the necessary steps toward justification by faith.

How do you react when something bad or troublesome happens? You see, Paul doesn't start this process with a blank page. He begins with a child of God who has been walking by faith and has some years of experience in the faith walk, just like the Abraham example of the fourth chapter. If we do not face our tribulations through faith, we will never realize patience as an outcome of that tribulation. When the tribulation first strikes, if we look past the tribulation to our faithful God and seek His grace and counsel to deal with it, we just might come to realize that He is greater than the tribulation, and trust Him more than we fear the tribulation. Ah, faith is doing her noble work.

And patience, experience.... If we face our tribulations in our broken humanity, we'll react with anger and frustration, never experiencing patience. If we face our tribulations through faith, we'll trust the Lord to protect and guide us through the tribulation. That attitude will lead us through the tribulation to the next growth step in our path toward justification by faith.

Whether we react to our tribulations by faith or by our own angry frustrations, we shall experience something from them. However, if we face the tribulation with faith in the Lord to guide us through it, the outcome in us will be shaped by faith, not by the tribulation. Tribulation without faith in the Lord will produce angry bitterness. Tribulation with faith will produce a godly experience of the Lord's merciful help.

This lesson prepares us for the reality of life in a broken world, but it also shows us the outcome when we face this broken world with an unbroken faith. The faith-experience that grows out of tribulation is a polar opposite to the normal experience of tribulations. Instead of the tribulation shaping us into angry, bitter, disappointed people, the faith-experience of the tribulation shows us the goodness and greatness of our Lord through the tribulation.

Do not overlook the point that Paul makes here. Faith will not help you evade all the bad things in life. It will not lead you through a carefully threaded detour that avoids difficulties. It insulates and empowers you as you go through the "tribulations" of life. I can look back over a lifetime of experiences and tell you from the paths that I have walked that this passage is true. I've chosen the path of human response at times, and I was consistently disappointed in the outcome and in myself for choosing that path. I've also chosen the faith-path at times, and, regardless of the dark threats that I faced, the outcome was blessed. That is the point that Paul teaches us in this lesson.

And experience, hope.... Every experience does not produce hope. The non-faith path, chosen in the face of tribulation, will produce bitterness and disappointment. The faith-path shall surely result in hope.

Many contemporary Christians do not understand the Biblical principle of hope. For them, "hope" is wishful, and probably unrealistic, thinking. The principle of hope in Scripture contains at least two important components, joy and expectation. In Scripture, hope is consistently associated with joy, peaceful joy. Secondly, Scripture never associates hope with wishful thinking. In Scripture, hope signals a strong expectation of a good result. It would be fully accurate to say that Biblical hope is joyful expectation of something good, and something good from God.

Few things impart as much comfort and grow our faith like a completed experience in which we faced the difficulties and disappointments of life in faith and actually saw the Lord's hand in bringing us to a good place. We have followed Paul on a course, defined and directed by faith that always produces this result. Faith alters our focus and perspective. Without faith, we shape our attitudes by the things that happen to us. With faith, God shapes our attitudes by His grace that guides us through the trials. No faith; bad things in life shape us, and the shape they impose on us cannot be good. Faith-walk; God guides us to a "justified" faith, a valid faith in Him, and that faith, firmly anchored in our faithful God, shapes us.

And hope maketh not ashamed; because the love of God is shed abroad in our hearts by the Holy Ghost which is given unto us. Why does hope make us not ashamed? When we face life and whatever it throws at us with our faith firmly fixed in the Lord, we will walk through life's experiences, including its darkest trials, standing closely to our loving God. Faith doesn't avoid the trials, but it alters our experience in them. And God's abiding grace with us as we go through those trials will never disappoint us. We'll never cross the valley of the shadow of death and rise to the mountain peak on the other side of that valley disappointed in our God (Psalm 23:4). Instead of focusing on the tribulations of life and questioning God, an attitude of unbelief that inevitably produces disappointment, faith keeps us close to the Lord through our trials and, when we look back on the trial, we will always realize that our loving Father stood by us, watched over us, and protected us, even as we experienced the fiercest storms of life. His abiding Holy Spirit resides in us and shall always point us to Him who loves us and who stands by us through every trial.

What a God! What a Savior!

24
From the Lesser to the Greater

> For when we were yet without strength, in due time Christ died for the ungodly. For scarcely for a righteous man will one die: yet peradventure for a good man some would even dare to die. But God commendeth his love toward us, in that, while we were yet sinners, Christ died for us. Much more then, being now justified by his blood, we shall be saved from wrath through him. For if, when we were enemies, we were reconciled to God by the death of his Son, much more, being reconciled, we shall be saved by his life. And not only so, but we also joy in God through our Lord Jesus Christ, by whom we have now received the atonement. (Romans 5:6-11)

In the third chapter of Romans, Paul briefly deals with our legal standing in and through the person and work of the Lord Jesus Christ. He now returns to that truth. How does this legal process and work impact us? How did it take place? I find it interesting and instructive that Paul brackets our experiential justification by faith with powerful teaching on God's legal work and process that delivers us from the final and legal consequences of our sins. In our faith-walk, we interact with the indwelling Holy Spirit to grow through life's tribulations into strong believers in God. In God's legal work that removes the legal consequences of our sins and enables God to righteously treat us as beloved children and not as hardened criminals, God does all of the work. We were without strength to do anything in that work.

We need to understand the profound love of God in His work of putting away our sins and making us His beloved children to ever be able to trust Him as fully as we must in the faith-walk that we've studied in the fourth chapter of Romans. Knowing what God has done for us when we could do nothing for ourselves, constitutes the essential foundation for that supernatural faith that trusts God, despite every trial and dark valley that we may encounter in life.

If we fail to understand that all of our timely blessings in the faith-walk rely on a faithful God who loved us so unbelievably that He did for us what we could not do at a time when we didn't even know we needed to do anything, we shall hopelessly confuse the blessings of

God in our lives. I will illustrate this confusion with two rather extreme examples.

Many very devout and sincere Christian folk in our day fail to understand their own helpless state before God saved them. They confuse what God does in our eternal salvation with the things that Scripture commands us to do as God's children in our obedient faith-walk. The result of this confusion appears when they assign one or more conditions that they sincerely believe that they must perform to gain their eternal life. They mistakenly attribute the early steps of their faith-walk to the securing of their eternal life, rather than understanding that they were actually without any strength whatever to do anything in this process. Paul doesn't tell us that we had a little strength, though insufficient. He tells us that we were without strength. Period. We had none, nada. Our condition was such that we could not do anything whatever to obtain that life.

Some people who suffer this confusion assign very little activity to themselves as their role in this process; some impose an endless list of impossible requirements. Whether they think they must do one thing or an endless list of things, they fail to confront Paul's simple point in our study passage. In fact, they had no strength, none whatever, to perform any righteous condition.

The other confusing extreme is almost a mirror opposite of the first example. A few people believe in a near-fatalistic idea that God either directly causes or indirectly manipulates every event in their life. If they do something, it is because God decreed that they do it. This view utterly contradicts the teachings of Scripture regarding God's moral governance of His world, as well as His moral commandments to mankind.

While the first example of confusion requires man to do what Paul says we did not have the strength to do, this view makes our discipleship, our justification by faith, as wholly and exclusively God's work as our new birth. We do nothing, and God does everything.

People who hold to this view will deny that we have any responsibility to obey, actually teaching that God either directly causes or directly "orchestrates" every event in time, regardless of how black and sinful. As the first view imposes an impossible work onto an incompetent, void-of-strength sinner, this view imposes an immoral posture onto God. Many who hold to this view will say that they do not believe that God causes sin, but their language says otherwise. They effectively believe that God created a cosmic puppeteered universe in which He pulls every string to affect every action that unfolds. They utterly reject the Biblical truth that God created a moral universe, and that He governs His universe as its Moral Governor. From the beginning in the Garden of Eden, God gave man a rule of behavior, a law that contained both blessings for obedience and a curse for disobedience. God has never altered that moral government principle.

What we had no strength--Paul says that we were without strength--to accomplish, God through His Son accomplished. While you read occasionally of one human actually dying for those who are dear to him, even that experience is rare, but it is virtually unheard of for one human to give his life for a worthless scoundrel.

I was born in July, 1941. A young man, son of my parents' neighbor, suggested the name that my parents decided to give me. When World War II broke out later that year, he joined the army. He was involved in the Normandy invasion. While he and several of his fellow-soldiers were taking shelter in a foxhole, a German grenade was thrown into their foxhole. This noble young man immediately fell over the grenade. He knowingly died to save his buddies. Ah, the noble few who unselfishly give their lives for others deserve our respect.

Contrast this unusual and admirable human behavior with what Jesus did for us. When He died for us, we were not nice, godly people. We were wicked sinners. Despite that ugly fact, He willingly gave Himself for us. This amazing act is what Paul describes as God commending His love to us in the act of Jesus' death.

God's grace-miracle doesn't stop with Jesus dying for us. His death had purpose, design, and intent. A legal event unfolded in His death that is humanly impossible. By what Jesus did in His death, we who were in every way unquestionably guilty of every charge against us in heaven's righteous court, miraculously lose our guilt. It isn't that God merely overlooks our sins because He loves us so much. What happens in a courtroom definitely produces emotions and alters subsequent experiences of the accused person, but the actual verdict of the court is not itself a personal experience. Our legal standing before God that resulted from Jesus' death on our behalf is not part of our personal experience. It is ultimately a legal matter that God resolved through the death of His Son. He remains righteous, and yet He declares that those who were unquestionably guilty are declared by God, the righteous Judge righteously declares to be innocent, not based on their behavior, but based on His Son's sacrificial death, those for whom He died.

Occasionally I have heard or read preachers who lose their balanced and Biblical view of God in their effort to honor Jesus. They depict God as cold, unfeeling, and ready to drop the ax on every sinner's neck. Scripture utterly rejects this idea. Do not overlook in our study passage that the driving force of our legal justification is God Himself. In no way and at no time is God the Father and Jesus in conflict on anything, much less the essential work of our justification by Jesus blood, even God's grace.

Just as a human court's verdict imposes obvious consequences onto the person judged, Paul reminds us of the merciful consequences of Jesus' death on our behalf. Considering that God justified us, declared His righteous verdict of "Not Guilty," by His grace (Romans 3:24), based on Jesus' blood (Romans 5:9), Paul tells us the precise results of that legal verdict, *"...we shall be saved from wrath through him," "...we were reconciled to God by the death of his Son..." "we shall be saved by his life."*

25
Man's Hope: God!

For when we were yet without strength, in due time Christ died for the ungodly.
(Romans 5:6)

It has been said that the Book of Romans is the most "theological" book of the Bible. Perhaps so, but, unlike most intensely "theological" works, it is also one of the most practical letters of the New Testament.

There is an obvious benefit to reading and studying topical systematic theology works that intensely deal with the major doctrines of the Bible. The weakness of such books is that they obscure the Bible's common method of teaching, integrated and harmonized truth that is not delivered to us piecemeal in individual isolation chambers—*TV dinner style*. Scripture presents the whole fabric of Biblical truth harmoniously linked as a whole body of truth—*a spiritual gourmet meal.*

What is the Bible's response to the fallen condition of humanity? In the third chapter Paul surfaces the fact that unnamed critics had intensely criticized his teachings. They suggested that Paul's emphasis on God's saving grace in salvation meant that Paul magnified sin so much as to teach people that the more they sinned the more God's grace would be manifest. In today's theological climate no doubt these folks would have called Paul an antinomian (opposed to the law, amoral, and irresponsibly living in sin "because we are not under the law but under grace"), the favorite damning word used by contemporary neonomians (folks who create a new law which they teach people must obey to gain their salvation).

Paul intensely rejected their false accusation. *"And not rather, (as we be slanderously reported, and as some affirm that we say,) Let us do evil, that good may come? whose damnation is just"* (Romans 3:8). In the verses leading up to these words Paul reasoned that if God predestinated or ordained (Use the word you wish; the idea is that they were trying to say that Paul believed that God was either directly or indirectly responsible for man's sin) sin and then orchestrated it for His glory, God could not hold the sinner accountable for his sin.

In this amazing lesson Paul refutes both the fatalistic view that God some way orchestrates all events according to a secret purpose for His glory and the man-centric view that man is responsible for his own salvation. To thread the theological needle between these two errant views and to affirm the truth that lies distinctly between them demonstrates a true masterpiece of writing.

Given the intensity of this rejection of his critic's false accusation, I believe this errant accusation against Paul sets the stage for the greater part of teaching that Paul unfolds throughout the Roman letter. In terms of theological errors that surface from time to time Paul's Roman letter could have been written yesterday, not almost two thousand years ago; it maintains relevance throughout the history of Christian doctrine across the centuries.

The Roman letter is written in dialectical style, meaning that Paul wrote the letter reasoning with these unnamed critics, first considering their ideas or accusations and then showing the error of their teaching by affirming the truth of the gospel that he believed and taught everywhere. Along with Paul's response in the ninth chapter of Romans, Romans 3:8 displays one of the most intense rejections of error to be found in the New Testament. This style of writing labored to correctly depict the critics' ideas and then to interact with them so as to display the truth of the opposing viewpoint. For Paul to paint his critics with a false "straw man" view that misrepresented them would have been an egregious violation of his own integrity. He refused to follow such unethical tactics. He wants to win them, not pulverize, humiliate, and defeat them.

From this rejection of the false accusation in Romans 3, Paul immediately develops the fact of man's utter sinfulness, depravity, followed by a powerful affirmation of God's exclusive role in the salvation of sinners, both before and after the cross (Romans 3:25 affirms that Jesus' justifying, saving grace saved people who had sinned before Calvary just as He saves people after Calvary: "...for the remission of sins that are *past*.")

Next in a convincing argument that he in no way taught believers to live in sin so as to enlarge divine grace, in the fourth chapter Paul deals extensively and clearly with the walk of faith, using Abraham as his primary example of a transformed life. God didn't transform Abraham by the law—Moses didn't receive it till around five hundred years after Abraham. God transformed Abraham by His amazing grace, and Abraham responded to God's grace by walking according to the "rule of faith."

What a powerful antidote to the false accusation of Paul's critics. God saved Abraham while he lived in Ur and was practicing a life of paganism. How do we know this? Hebrews 11:8 affirms that Abraham was walking by faith from the time he left Ur of the Chaldees. *Thus Genesis 15:6, which is often interpreted as Abraham's moment of salvation, is literally decades too late to match the New Testament evidence of Abraham's salvation!*

Do those who teach that a person must "exercise saving faith" prior to the new birth and in order to receive the new birth, believe that a person must walk in this faith for decades before God saves him? No, they teach that a person's *first act* of faith is sufficient to produce the new birth, but their interpretation of Genesis 15:6 defies their belief, affirmed by Hebrews 11:8, one of many instances of exemplary faith in what has rightly been called the faith's "hall of fame" chapter in the Bible.

Romans the fourth chapter depicts Abraham, a saved man, walking by faith, not a saved man living in sin so as to enlarge divine grace. There is no evidence that Abraham looked for excuses to sin—though on a few occasions he did sin—so as to enlarge God's grace. Quite the contrary; these chapters from Abraham's life affirm that, even without the law Abraham lived an exemplary life of faith that demonstrated in his conduct his devotion to God in a fashion that is held up throughout Scripture as the model for the believer in Christ who seeks to live life to the honor of God.

New Testament use of Abraham as the premier example of the walk of faith depicts him—before and after Genesis 15—as walking according to the rule of faith. Paul could not possibly have chosen a better example to refute the false accusation of his critics than Abraham. God appeared to this man in his native land, called him to leave it for a better place that God would give to him and his offspring, promised him a large family despite his advancing age with no children, and Abraham progressively obeyed God based on faith that governed his conduct.

In today's theological isolation chambers where each Bible doctrine is carefully segregated from its partners, the dominant teaching regarding faith and works seeks to set them in diametrical opposition. Faith is depicted itself as a work that is someway not supposed to really be a work. Faith is further often identified as the saving grace of man rather than faith's object, the Lord Jesus Christ.

If Paul taught the abominable error that his critics accused him of teaching, how could they explain the life of Abraham, beginning from the time he left Ur, not beginning from Genesis 15:6?

Once Paul affirmed the amazing integration of God's grace that saves with the divine influence that God's saving grace brings to bear upon those whom he saves, he returned to the dynamics of salvation in the fifth chapter of Romans.

There is nothing in Scripture that suggests that everyone whom God saves will have the dramatic experience of Abraham, or for that matter that every one whom God saves will be as faithful as Abraham. Paul sets Abraham before us as an example to be followed, not as an absolute that God orchestrates in the life of everyone whom He saves. You don't exhort people to do what they have been invariably and absolutely orchestrated to do. You exhort people who face choices to follow the right example in the decisions they make when facing those daily choices in life. God didn't teach us in Scripture that the walk of faith is absolutely orchestrated so that you cannot do otherwise if you are "really saved." Rather He sets Abraham's life before us in three distinct New Testament letters as a model with exhortations that we should consciously order our lives according to faith in the same way that Abraham did. If we are divinely orchestrated to live the life of Abraham, why should Scripture include such intense exhortations for us to do so? Corroborating his argument in Romans 3:4-7, Paul refutes the accusation against him of being a fatalist by the dynamic exhortation for us to follow the example of Abraham's life and walk of faith.

How do we react when someone falsely accuses us? Some of us might slip into deceitful duplicity and obscure what we believe to avoid criticism, a sad and blatant example of fundamental dishonesty that no Christian should ever consider. Some of us might feel the sting of the accusation and shun teaching the very thing that is true, because of the accusation.

Were this the case with Paul he would have avoided teaching the amazing truth of God's saving grace to avoid giving his critics the tools with which they criticized him. Not Paul; he refused to be intimidated by false accusations, and affirmed the whole truth that he had been taught, so as to refute the critics' false depiction of his teachings, yet so as equally to give us the full account of the truth that God had revealed to him. We have much to learn from Paul—and from our God.

26
A Saving God

For when we were yet without strength, in due time Christ died for the ungodly.
(Romans 5:6)

In our last chapter we examined the chapters leading up to this verse, particularly the centrality of the false criticism aimed at Paul by unnamed critics in the third chapter. They accused Paul of teaching, "Let us do evil that good may come." Paul's intense rejection of this false charge—a "slanderous" report—as well as his equally intense objection to the criticism of his teaching on election in the ninth chapter, suggests that Paul was confronting a major objection to his essential theology. There a critic questioned Paul's conclusion regarding personal election with *"Thou wilt say then unto me, Why doth he yet find fault? For who hath resisted his will?"* (Romans 9:19). It is highly likely that the same critic raised both objections. Both objections deal with God's sovereignty in salvation; both question God's role in sin though from somewhat different perspectives.

These intense criticisms of Paul's essential theology set the stage for what we find logically and sequentially reasoned out in the whole Book of Romans. Immediately following the introduction Paul addresses God's righteousness and His judgment against sin. The second chapter extends the divine judgment against sin from primarily non-Jews (as in the first chapter) to Jews who pretended to be devoted to their faith, but who failed to live their faith. Sin, salvation, and discipleship frame the whole Roman letter and its core message.

Interestingly if you explain the doctrines of grace that Paul taught in the ninth chapter of Romans to a professing Christian who is not familiar with them, you will hear almost identical objections to the idea that you see in these two objections in the third and ninth chapter of Romans. God's truth is unchanging, and the critics' objections have remained rather the same for twenty centuries.

Does believing in divine and personal election make a person anti-evangelical or even neutral to evangelism? Does believing in God's sovereign grace for one's eternal salvation encourage a person go be antinomian, to think as if he/she is so not under moral obligation to

God as to encourage a lax view toward sin? Many of the people in our time who embrace the view of Paul's critics make these accusations.

George Ella, a writer from Europe who believes in the doctrines of grace, makes an interesting—and I believe—accurate point. Many of the folks who constantly charge "antinomianism" against any and all who hold to these doctrines fully have created their own "new law" that they added to the teachings of the Bible, a law which they impose upon people and use to threaten their hearers with eternal ruin unless they obey that law. This error includes the teachings of all who advocate any form or degree of synergistic salvation (In this context I use the word "salvation" to refer to how a sinner is saved from his/her sins and made an heir of eternal heaven, not to the various uses of the word "salvation" in Scripture that relate to the discipleship of God's regenerate elect in this life.).

What is "synergistic salvation"? It is the idea that God and you work together in accomplishing your salvation. "He does His part—you do your part." Others hold to a less obvious form of the same doctrine. They attempt to draw a fine line between man directly contributing to his salvation and God using human activity of some sort as an "agent" rather than as a cause in completing the salvation process. Common teachings in this category hold that God uses the gospel preached and believed by the unsaved (unregenerate, not born again) as an agent to accomplish the new birth. While holding to human agency, many folks in this school of thought firmly state—and apparently truly believe—that they do not believe man has any role in his salvation, all the while holding that apart from some activity on either the part of the preacher or the part of the hearing sinner no one can possibly be born again.

Ella's point is clear in his writings. "Neonomians" who have created a new law that man must obey in order to become born again are increasingly pointing the "antinomian" finger at any and all who do not join their new law—new gospel.

In this new paradigm of synergistic salvation faith is morphed into a work itself and made to be the centerpiece of this new law. This is not the teaching of Scripture regarding true Biblical faith, nor for that matter was it the view of the leading Reformers in the Protestant Reformation. W. G. T. Shedd, a highly respected Reformed leader of a few generations back, understood this point and advocated a clear view of the new birth as being accomplished first to last by God without human agency. (I would not endorse all of Shedd's views, but in this point he affirms a fundamental Bible truth.) Other men in the Reformation family tree could likewise be offered who held to this view and who rejected the synergistic quasi-Reformed view that dominates our theological landscape today.

In 1832 Primitive Baptists separated from their Baptist brothers and sisters who were teaching this neonomian view of salvation. Even then they were accused of being anti-evangelistic, antinomian, and in various ways opposed to the spread of the gospel. This was a false charge! One need only read Benjamin Griffin's *History of the Mississippi Baptists* or various other works from that era to understand the falsity of this charge. Our Primitive forefathers in the faith made it clear that they objected to the preaching of a new gospel instead of the old gospel of the New Testament. Is the gospel an instrument in the new birth, either by voluntary human will or by a divine and irresistible decree? Our forefathers rejected the idea in favor of the gospel as a proclamation of good news to God's regenerate elect.

Samuel Richardson (signed the London 1644 Confession of Faith) and William Kiffen (signed the London 1689 Confession of Faith), along with Tobias Crisp (1600-1643) all affirmed their belief and that of their ancient English Baptist fellowship that faith is an evidence, not an instrument or cause, of regeneration. So this belief is altogether historical, as well as Biblical. As with Paul, so today neonomians readily and irresponsibly hurl "antinomian" labels against Paul and those who preach what Paul preached. "Antinomian" is precisely the accusation these critics aimed against Paul in the third chapter of Romans.

Any form of synergistic salvation loads its advocates with a heavy weight of guilt for not doing more to reach more people or being more convincing when they talk with people to gain more followers of their view. In fact doubt becomes a centerpiece of this errant theology so much so that its followers often spend inordinate amounts of time questioning both their own salvation and the salvation of everyone whom they meet.

What did Paul believe—under the inspiration of the Holy Spirit—regarding our salvation?

1. *"When we were without strength...."* Paul knew nothing of any residual merit or strength in the unregenerate by which they might save themselves.
2. *"...Christ died for the ungodly."* Paul did not write that Christ died for reformed and formerly ungodly people. Nor did he write that Christ died only for good people. He wrote the only truth that sin-sick, regenerate sinners can believe that will give them comfort and peace. *"This is a faithful saying, and worthy of all acceptation, that Christ Jesus came into the world to save sinners; of whom I am chief."* (1 Timothy 1:15)

The verses in this immediate context follow Paul's tightly reasoned response to the critics' false charge of antinomianism in the third chapter. After God called Abraham to leave Ur, Abraham didn't practice a life of "antinomianism," despite the fact that he did not have the formality of the written law at that time. Rather Abraham immediately began a walk of faith, not of sin.

Paul sets Abraham before us in the fourth chapter of Romans as a noble example of the way we should live. He makes no allegation that either Abraham or we are divinely decreed to walk the walk of faith. (In regeneration, the new birth, God imparts the ability to walk the walk of faith, but He does not infallibly decree our walk. Rather He sends the Holy Spirit and guides us in that direction. We make the choice to follow the Holy Spirit or not.)

An example is not an irresistible decree. In these chapters Paul precisely balances God's sovereign saving grace and our *subsequent* obligation to obey God and walk the walk of faith. Consider the following words from Tobias Crisp, mentioned above.

> We do not perform Christian duties in order to our being delivered from wrath; but we perform them because we are delivered. A man will work for Christ who has tasted of Christ's loving-kindness: he stands ready to shew forth the praise of that glorious grace which hath so freely saved him. Such a man is as glad to work for Christ's sake, as if he was to work for his own salvation. There are many ingenious persons in the world, who will be more ready to serve a friend that has already raised them; than to serve a master, that they may be

raised. This is the true service of a believer. His eye is to the glory of Christ, in regard to what Christ hath already done for him: and not in expectation of anything Christ hath yet to do. He looks upon all, as perfectly done for him in the hand of Christ, and ready to be delivered out to him as his occasions may require. The work of salvation being thus completed by Christ and not to be mended by the creature; the believer having now nothing to do for himself, all he doth, he doth for Christ…Salvation itself, therefore, is not the end proposed in any good work we do. The ends of our good works are, the manifestation of our obedience and subjection; the setting forth the praise of God's grace and a view to *their* profit; and the meeting the Lord Jesus Christ in the performance of duty, where he will be found, according to his promise: these are some of the special ends, for which obedience is ordained, salvation being settled firm before.

To which all of God's children should say a loud and zealous "AMEN." This is no "new doctrine," nor is it "antinomianism." It is God's old truth!

27
For Whom Did Christ Die?

For when we were yet without strength, in due time Christ died for the ungodly.
(Romans 5:6)

A question that is sure to excite and to polarize any Christian discussion is this: "For whom did Christ die?" The dominant view of our time is that Jesus died potentially for every human being, but that His death accomplished nothing of significance unless each individual comes to believe that fact and to embrace it in faith, an act of the individual that makes it a reality. Otherwise it is mere theory or potential, not fact at all.

A variation of this idea is that Jesus died to put away all the sins of all humanity with a single exception. He did not die for the sin of unbelief. Therefore the only sin that will justly send anyone to hell at the final Day of Judgment is the sin of not believing in Jesus.

I find this idea interesting in that Jesus mentioned specifically what the wicked did and did not do in His last Judgment lesson in Matthew 25:31-46. I find it equally interesting that in this passage Jesus didn't say a word about belief or unbelief; rather He passed sentence against the wicked based on specific actions they committed or failed to practice.

I do not in any way diminish the gravity of unbelief. Nor do I question that unbelief is in fact a sin. Rather I raise the point to refute the claim that Jesus died for all sins with this one exception, and that thus the only sin that will send anyone to hell is this particular sin of unbelief.

The respected Puritan writer/theologian John Owen is credited with the following assessment of the question, "For whom did Christ die?"

The Father imposed His wrath due unto, and the Son
underwent punishment for, either:

1. All the sins of all men.
2. All the sins of some men, or

3. Some of the sins of all men.

In which case it may be said:

a. That if the last be true, all men have some sins to answer for, and so, none are saved.
b. That if the second be true, then Christ, in their stead suffered for all the sins of all the elect in the whole world, and this is the truth.
c. But if the first be the case, why are not all men free from the punishment due unto their sins?

You answer, *"Because of unbelief."*

I ask, Is this *unbelief* a sin, or is it not? If it be, then Christ suffered the punishment due unto it, or He did not. If He did, why must that hinder them more than their other sins for which He died? If He did not, He did not die for all their sins!"

I suggest that Owen raises a far more sound and Biblical case than the present day and often emotional case that Jesus died for everyone, though the contemporary case in effect acknowledges that His death for everyone actually accomplished nothing in fact. Unless the person for whom Christ supposedly died does something (The "something" will vary depending on the theological school of thought confronted with the question. It will range from simple acceptance or belief of the fact all the way to baptism in water and faithfulness in good works till death.), the person for whom Jesus died will spend eternity in hell despite Jesus' death for him/her. In other words Jesus did as much for the apostle Paul as He did for Nero, so each person's eternal destiny has nothing to do with what Jesus did, but with what one individual does and the other does not do.

So who will be praised in eternity for salvation? If this doctrine is true, not Jesus, for His work didn't actually save anyone; their decision and/or conduct is the actual saving event that is responsible for where they spend eternity.

In an effort to avoid the embarrassment of these deficient views when compared with Scripture, some folks in our time will assert that man must comply with various conditions, but then say that God orchestrates their compliance. I suggest that this view is an unstable compromise that, within a generation or less time, will revert either to its inherent Arminian view (from the salvation by works view of James Arminius) or will fall into full fatalism, making God cause every event that occurs, even sin.

It is fascinating that in the first eight verses of the third chapter of Romans Paul confronted and refuted both of these errant views, charging his unnamed critics with a slanderous misrepresentation of the truth that he taught. *Holding faithfully to the truth of Scripture while carefully and consistently avoiding both errant extremes is the high challenge of every Bible student who seeks to follow Scripture, not correct and revise its divinely inspired message.*

I raise another interesting point that Paul presents in this passage. *Christ died for the ungodly.* Invariably in the contemporary and populist views of salvation Jesus is depicted as dying fully for reformed—or reforming—sinners, but not simply for sinners! And those who teach what Paul taught in this verse are invariably accused of being "antinomian," not because they advocate a sinful lifestyle or because they advocate a low view of either moral integrity or of God's moral law, but merely because they believe as Paul did (and interestingly Paul was accused of the same straw man antinomian error in Romans the third chapter), the simple fact that Jesus died for sinners! They were chosen sinners. They were elected to be the objects of divine mercy. They receive the law of God written in their hearts in the new birth, an event that to some extent transforms their moral convictions and character from that moment forward. But when Jesus died for them, He did not view them as transformed sinners, as repentant sinners, but as wholly undeserving sinners with only one claim to His divine mercy, that they were the vessels of divine election and mercy in God's eternal covenant of salvation.

It is sad indeed that the trumpet sound from most modern pulpits strongly implies that Jesus' death is only beneficial to reformed sinners, to repentant sinners, to believing sinners, or to otherwise improving sinners, and that such mercy is directly contingent on their personal action, mental or moral. One must wonder; how much comfort might this doctrine have been to a vicious and persecuting Saul of Tarsus on the road to Damascus when divine grace struck him to the ground?

For that matter, how much comfort can such a message be to you and me since Paul specifically indicated that he is a pattern of salvation to all future believers in God (1 Timothy 1:16)? The decisive impetus in these systems of teaching is that the final decision is yours, not God's, and your action or lack thereof will determine whether you spend eternity with God in heaven or in hell separated from God.

The decisive issue in Scripture is God's decision, not yours or mine! And Paul in this verse sounds the clarion sound of God's truth, *"Christ died for the ungodly."* We cannot justify any other view from Scripture, nor can we add layers of conditions or qualifiers onto this description with any degree of Biblical authority. Paul did not say that Christ died for all ungodly; he did not advocate universalism. But he distinctly wrote by the inspiration of the Holy Spirit for all the family of God to read from that day forward, *Christ died for the ungodly.* "

Someone who hears this doctrine for the first time will invariably accuse its advocates of teaching a "new doctrine." Is this doctrine of Jesus dying for sinners a new doctrine? Is the idea that sinners are saved by God alone and not by a cooperative venture between Jesus and sinners really a new doctrine? I could offer quotes across the centuries to prove otherwise. Here I will offer only one.

We all recognize the name Augustus Toplady, the author of the beautiful hymn "Rock of Ages." Although a lifelong Anglican, Toplady consistently respected and fellowshipped with non-Anglican preachers who held to the same views of God's saving grace that he held. Here I quote from Toplady who in this instance is quoting (with his full agreement) the Baptist preacher John Ryland. The quote will lead off with an introductory paragraph from George Ella, one of many Toplady biographers.

> Ryland shared with Toplady and John Gill the glorious doctrine of election and justification from eternity, meaning that election and justification are not time-bound graces, secured by the response of a believer but eternal actions of God quite irrespective of time. Toplady records how Ryland told him on July 11, 1769:

> The souls of the elect were saved upon trust for four thousand years. The Father gave credit to Christ, and glorified his saints,

on the footing of a sacrifice not then offered up, and of a righteousness not then wrought. Christ also, in the days of his flesh, went on credit with his Father every time he said to a sinner, 'Thy sins are forgiven thee,' previous to his offering himself on the cross.[1]

Here Toplady cites Ryland approvingly regarding the divine prerogative of salvation prior to the cross, not based on people keeping the Law—an act that Scripture says they never did (Ecclesiastes 7:20)—or some other man-centered action, but rather on a "trust" and "credit" arrangement between the Father and the Son, based on the merit of Jesus' death alone *even before Calvary!*

On Page 33 of this book Ella states, "Toplady, argues on a number of occasions that God draws his elect from all sorts and conditions of men, whether they be Arminians, Stoics, or whatever." Is this a "new doctrine"? Hardly, not only did Toplady believe it in the eighteenth century, he presented it as the fundamental and proper view of the Anglican Church of that time, though he often complains against the church's growing laxity in doctrine, morals, and intellect. He further frequently fellowshipped with Baptists and other "Dissenters" who shared his theological beliefs regarding this important doctrine of salvation.

When we study regeneration or the new birth, we shall fully explore the moral and spiritual change that God effects when He bestows eternal life on one of His chosen vessels. The doctrines of grace do not teach or even imply that subsequent to salvation a person is as engaged in sin as before or as morally reprobate as before the new birth. Legalists incessantly try to quantify how much moral or spiritual change occurs after regeneration, something that they cannot do from Scripture. However, Scripture clearly affirms that the new birth alters a person's moral and spiritual nature and character.

Believers in the Bible doctrines of grace not only believe that God's grace is altogether exclusive in salvation; they believe that the same grace of God that saves also teaches those whom He saves (Titus 2:11-

---

[1] Ella, George M., *August Montague Toplady: A Debtor to Mercy Alone* (Durham, England: Go Publications, 2000) 147.

15). May we be found faithful, still believing what Paul taught by the direction of the Holy Spirit.

28
For Whom Did Christ Die: For Sinners or Good People?

For scarcely for a righteous man will one die: yet peradventure for a good man some would even dare to die. But God commendeth his love toward us, in that, while we were yet sinners, Christ died for us. (Romans 5:7-8)

When you analyze the prevailing contemporary views of salvation in its varied forms (from "easy decisionism" to "lordship salvation," from a simple act of consenting faith to full-blown salvation by works that includes baptism and a lifelong record of faithfulness), a central issue surfaces across all of these views. They challenge the fundamental premise of New Testament teaching that is clearly set forth in this passage.

> **The prevailing view asserts that Jesus only died for reformed sinners (or *reforming* sinners), for repenting sinners, or for sinners who decided to "accept" either Jesus or the truth of the gospel as they heard and received it.**

It thus adds limits and qualifications to the New Testament doctrine that Jesus died for sinners! It thus attempts to refute and to constrict the New Testament teaching. Further, advocates of these views rather commonly accuse those who embrace the New Testament truth set forth in this passage of being "antinomian" in their teachings, interestingly the precise accusation that Paul's unnamed critics raised against him in Romans 3:1-8. The only limit that the New Testament applies to the death of Jesus is the limit divinely set in Scripture; Jesus died for "...his people" (Matthew 1:21), for his elect or chosen people (specifically asserted in the various passages dealing with factual redemption, a specific price paid for a particular people, a price that in fact purchased those people, not merely made salvation possible for those who choose to comply with the terms and conditions of "neo-nomianism," adding a new law to Scripture by which to constrict the Biblical teaching of Jesus' certain and successful redemption of His particular and chosen people.

Commonly people who sense personal vulnerability will react in a highly assertive manner against their potential critics to avoid the spotlight. In this case those who foster these new laws that restrict and compromise Biblical redemption, making them "neo-nomians," will hurl the "antinomian" accusation freely against their potential critics. Name-calling apparently seems safer to them than following Paul and New Testament teaching.

If Paul was accused of being antinomian, as he was in Romans 3:1-8, and if Paul rejected that accusation, at the same time carefully rejecting any implication that God caused sin, as he also did in this passage, should those who believe New Testament doctrine not follow his example and avoid both errors in their own beliefs? And if we do not find our own modern critics hurling similar accusations at us, should we not question whether we are teaching the same doctrines that Paul taught by the direction and inspiration of the Holy Spirit?

Interestingly, when Augustus Toplady, the beloved author of "Rock of Ages," was confronting growing Arminianism in his "home" Church of England, he used the following point to confront the skeptical and insecure doctrine that a person could be "saved" today and lose his salvation tomorrow.

> Indeed there is nothing in heaven but joy. The peculiar presence of Deity most eminently manifested there, is an endless and ever-increasing source of blessedness, both to the spirits of the just, and to the seraphs that never fell. Where God is possessed; where Christ is seen; where the adorable Trinity pour forth their plenitude of glory unclouded on the delightful, undazzled view; where saints, the children of redemption, are the melodious songsters; and angels, the first fruits of creation, are the enraptured musicians; where the grand employ is praised, and Jehovah himself is the exceeding great reward; surely there the cup of joy must overflow; and only the blest inhabitants themselves can tell how blest the inhabitants are.
>
> Is there then any thing that can heighten the celestial triumph? That can add to the felicity of those who stand in the divine presence and enhance even their transcendent joy? There is: and we have just heard what it is. It is the regeneration

of a fallen soul. It is the renewal of a sinner below. As our Lord expresses it at the 10th verse, There is joy in the presence of the angels of God over one sinner that repenteth. No sooner is every fresh conversion made known on high than additional joy is there. The memorable day is, if I may so speak, marked as a festival in the calendar of heaven. Beatified saints exult, angels clap their wings, and the whole united choir raise their voices, and strike their golden harps for joy that a soul is born of God and made free for the Jerusalem which is above.

Such exalted hosannas would not resound, on those occasions, among the inhabitants of the skies, if the doctrine of final perseverance was untrue. Tell me, ye seraphs of light; tell me, ye souls of elect men made perfect in glory, why this exuberance of holy rapture at the real recovery of a single sinner to God? Because ye know assuredly that every true conversion is 1.) a certain proof that the person converted is one of your own elect number; and 2.) that he shall be infallibly preserved and brought to that very region of blessedness into which ye yourselves are entered. The contrary belief would silence your harps, and chill your praises. If it be uncertain whether the person who is regenerated to-day may ultimately reign with you in heaven, or take up his eternal abode among apostate spirits in hell; your rejoicings are too sanguine, and your praises are premature. You should suspend your songs until he actually arrives among you: and not give thanks for his conversion until he has persevered unto glorification.[1]

Two points are worth our added consideration in this quote from Toplady. First, Toplady clearly affirms the security of salvation in the death of Christ, something consistently affirmed in his poems and in his prose works that are preserved. Secondly, Toplady uses the term "perseverance" to refer to God's preserving of His elect so that they cannot finally and eternally fall from their saved state in Christ, not to refer to their abiding faithfulness in good works and faith. "…if the doctrine of final perseverance was untrue," is clearly explained by Toplady to refer to God's preserving, not to our abiding in the faith by

---

[1] Ella, ibid. 287-288.

his subsequent, "…he shall be infallibly preserved and brought to that very region of blessedness into which ye yourselves are entered." The contemporary interpretation of "perseverance" that focuses on the abiding—and presumably divinely orchestrated—faithfulness of every true elect in faith and manifest godliness fails the historical test of the use of this theological term by respected past theologians such as Toplady. Clearly Toplady viewed this doctrine as the final and certain efficacy of the redemption of Christ to "preserve" the elect so that they cannot lose their salvation and fall finally and eternally away from their standing as children of God and heirs of eternal blessings, not as a guarantee against stumbling or faltering in faith and obedience by a regenerate elect.

Paul's introduction of this point by the fact that on rare and noble occasions one human may actually give up his/her life to protect or preserve someone whom he/she loves deeply points us in the direction that he intends to go with the spiritual point of this lesson. In the case of Jesus' death we cannot look to worth, merit, or inherent goodness in the elect as motives for either God's love or for Jesus' death. When Jesus died for us, we possessed none of these qualities. We were in every meaningful sense "sinners"! ... *while we were yet sinners, Christ died for us.* I appropriately close this chapter with a few lines from one of my favorite Toplady poems.

> The work that his goodness began,
> The arm of his strength will complete;
> His promise is, Yea and Amen,
> And never was forfeited yet:
> Things future, nor things that are now,
> Not all things below or above
> Can make him his purpose forgo,
> Or sever my soul from his love
>
> My name from the palms of his hands
> Eternity will not erase;
> Impress'd on his heart it remains
> In marks of indelible grace:
> Yes, I to the end shall endure,
> As sure as the earnest is giv'n;

More happy but not more secure,
The glorified spirits in heav'n.

My Christian friend, your eternal security stands fast with God, not based on your faithfulness, but based on the value of the divine earnest that God has bestowed upon you. It affirms your eternal secure standing in the redemption of our Lord Jesus Christ. Jesus really is the Savior and "friend of sinners"!

29
Super-Abounding Grace: Secure Salvation in Christ

> Much more then, being now justified by his blood, we shall be saved from wrath through him. For if, when we were enemies, we were reconciled to God by the death of his Son, much more, being reconciled, we shall be saved by his life. (Romans 5:9-10)

Go back through this context and look at the various phrases that convey essentially the same truth, what God has accomplished for His elect in the death of Christ.

1. *Christ died for the ungodly*, Verse 6.
2. *Christ died for us*, Verse 8.
3. We are *now justified by his blood*, Verse 9.
4. We *shall be saved from wrath through him*, Verse 9.
5. *We were reconciled to God by the death of his Son*, Verse 10.
6. We *shall be saved by his life*, Verse 10.
7. *We have now received the atonement*, Verse 11.

Seven distinct notes communicate and emphasize one common truth. In light of the generally accepted interpretational tool, the "perspicuity of Scripture," the clarity of Scripture (The idea is that the more important God thinks something is the more clearly He states it in Scripture, and the more frequently He repeats it in Scripture.), this passage distinctly intends to convey strong emphasis on a central truth of our salvation in Christ. Reconciliation, atonement, justification, and salvation (a varied term, but in similar contexts as this) all distinctly refer to what God did for His elect in the Lord Jesus Christ, not to what we do.

Given the idea of the critics' false accusation of Paul, it seems bold and altogether fitting for him to drive the point home that they falsely represented his teachings. What better way to make that point than by presenting a thorough, balanced, and concise statement of his beliefs for all to read directly from his own pen. Then all could read for themselves both Paul's true beliefs and the straw man misrepresentations of his critics.

In these verses we see clearly the doctrine of substitutionary atonement. That is, that the Lord Jesus Christ died for a specific people, not simply to bring salvation within reach of all. Paul does not leave the death of Christ clouded with any uncertainty whatever. Paul repeats in each of these terms a reference to a specific people for whom Christ died, as well as a specific price paid to secure that benefit for those people. For whom did Christ die? For 1) *the ungodly*, 2) for *us*, 3) for those who are *now justified by his blood*, 4) for those who *shall be saved from wrath through him* (not through their own works or through a cooperative effort by both Him and them), 5) for those who *were* (factually, not merely potentially) *reconciled to God by the death of his Son*, 6) for those who *shall be saved* (a note of certainty regarding their salvation, not a mere statement of potential or possibility based on something they might or might not do) *by his life*, and finally 7) for those who have *now received the atonement* (literally, the reconciliation). In none of these terms did Paul leave any doubt or uncertainty as to the fact that Jesus' death clearly secured the salvation of those for whom He died.

It is my belief that Paul's unnamed critics were in fact two warring groups of people inside the Roman Church, people who had allowed pride and the party spirit to become stronger than their faith in Christ. I reach this conclusion because throughout the letter Paul specifically rebukes both Gentile and Jewish pride. He confronts Jewish pride in the second chapter and Gentile pride in the eleventh, though these two contexts are by no means the only sections where this pattern appears in the letter.

What was the actual belief of these people? In what specific details did they disagree with Paul? It may be more difficult to deal with specifics in this point, but it seems clear that much of the disagreement in Rome was at least similar to what Paul repeatedly encountered where ever he preached and established new churches. The most concise statement of this disagreement appears in the fifteenth chapter of Acts. If we read the opening verses regarding the initial disagreement in Antioch between Paul and Barnabas and those who taught a different gospel than they, it appears that the disagreement was over how God saves sinners in the ultimate or eternal sense. If we read the Jerusalem Church's actual letter (Acts 15:22-29), it seems quite likely that they were teaching that a non-Jew must become a practicing Jew before he/she can possibly become a "true" Christian. If we observe that the letter seems to have been written by the authority of the Jerusalem Church, we may reasonably conclude that the people who were teaching this error and creating the problem in Antioch, as well as likely the churches in Galatia (likely the churches that Paul established during his "First Missionary Journey" in the fourteenth chapter of Acts) were in fact members of the Jerusalem Church. Although we could not make dogmatic conclusions to this whole scenario, it pulls together a wide variety of facts that do appear in the context of Acts the fourteenth and fifteenth chapters.

The idea that a contingent of Christians in the Jerusalem Church was behind this error is—to say the least—intriguing. It goes a long way to explain why Paul repeatedly emphasized the true nature of both our eternal salvation as well as our discipleship in all of his letters.

Through this possible scenario we may focus the likely problem, both between Antioch and Jerusalem and between warring factions within the church in Rome, to one of two possibilities.

1. Despite all that Jesus did during the Incarnation, He merely made salvation possible. True and final salvation in fact depends on a person's belief and good works. Perhaps it even depends on his/her becoming a practicing Jew as an intermediate step to becoming a truly good Christian.
2. Salvation is by grace, but a believer in Christ may only gain spiritual maturity in the faith by embracing Judaism and growing through Judaism into "true" Christianity."

It matters little which of these two views we adopt; either view helps us to understand the dynamic with which Paul was confronted where ever he traveled and where ever he preached. We get the distinct impression that these errant believers "shadowed" him everywhere and lurked in the shadows till he left. Then they would begin sowing their false ideas, likely claiming superior knowledge and authority because they were respected members of the "mother church" in Jerusalem.

Factually Paul and Barnabas preached the same gospel truth that Peter, James, and others in Jerusalem preached. As the Jerusalem Church's letter in Acts 15 affirms, the problem was not at all a theological disagreement between these men; it was rather a dissenting contingency within the Jerusalem Church who disagreed with their own church and its pastor or pastors.

Based on a scenario that roughly approximates this situation, Paul's reasoning in Romans is logical and reasonable. He must cover every detail of his beliefs so as to remove any doubt from the minds of the at-large-membership in the church in Rome regarding his faith and apostleship. In order to accomplish this objective he must confront and refute the errors of both sides in the contention that was tearing at the very fabric of the Roman Church.

Ah, how typical of human nature. A few egotistical and pride-driven people strive for supremacy while large numbers of hungry sheep go hungry seeking sound and balanced spiritual meat. Rather than conclude that this problem was inevitable, Paul devoted his whole Roman letter to healing the breach, to breaking the egotistical pride of the schismatic leaders in both Jewish and Gentile parties within the church, so that all of the church in Rome would reunite in the faith and in their respectful fellowship, viewing the Lord Jesus Christ and His truth as more important that their ego or pride.

Nothing softens sinful human pride as fully as being brought face to face with the reality of one's own sinful condition and utter dependence on God for salvation and for everything good. Prior to our salvation, none of us was deserving and good in the eyes of God! We were alike—Jew or Gentile made no difference whatever—fallen in our sins and not only undeserving, but also wholly incapable of doing anything at all to remedy our plight. The change that transformed us from darkness into light, from "children of wrath even as others" to "children of the King" was brought about by God alone through the Lord Jesus Christ, not by anything we did or even thought to do. It is no coincidence that Paul goes immediately from this powerful teaching on what we have through the death of Christ to what we inherently possessed in our native human existence in Adam. Our utterly hopeless and helpless condition in Adam is the reason that our salvation must be wholly—beginning to end—by God alone and not by anything in us.

We have a secure hope of salvation with God throughout eternity, based on what Jesus did on our behalf, not based on what we did. No single passage in the Bible more clearly teaches this truth that the verses we have been studying in Romans fifth chapter. May we anchor our faith in these verses and in the profound truths that they affirm. We have the potential right now for joy in these truths as we melt the demands of personal ego and sinful pride. Praise to God alone for salvation and all things good.

30
Eternal Blessings: A Present Reality

> And not only so, but we also joy in God through our Lord Jesus Christ, by whom we have now received the atonement. (Romans 5:11)

Our study of Romans fifth chapter has focused on the work of Christ and its securing of eternal blessings for us. That focus on eternal blessings follows Paul's line of reasoning in these verses. But what about the "here and now" someone might ask. In our study verse Paul bridges the gap between eternity and the temporal world in which we live. He affirms that we may live in supreme joy based on God's present blessing and our realization of the blessings we have in God through the Lord Jesus Christ, indeed "our" Lord Jesus Christ.

We don't hear the word "atonement" very often in our contemporary culture. What does it mean? Here are several definitions of the word.

> "Atonement" (the explanation of this English word as being "at-onement" is entirely fanciful) is frequently found in the OT. See, for instance, Leviticus, chapters 16 and 17. The corresponding NT words are *hilasmos*, "propitiation," 1 John 2:2; 4:10, and *hilasterion*, Rom. 3:25; Heb. 9:5, "mercy-seat," the covering of the ark of the covenant. These describe the means (in and through the person and work of the Lord Jesus Christ, in His death on the cross by the shedding of His blood in His vicarious sacrifice for sin) by which God shows mercy to sinners.[1]

The *Friberg New Testament Greek Lexicon* defines the word as "**15188 katallagh,**, literally *exchange, profit from exchange*; figuratively in the NT, as the reestablishing of personal relations *reconciliation, change from enmity to friendship* (2C 5.18, 19)."

---

[1] W. E. Vine, Merrill F. Unger and William White, *Vine's Complete Expository Dictionary of Old and New Testament Words* (Nashville: T. Nelson, 1996), 2:44.

Four occurrences; AV translates as "reconciliation" twice, "atonement" one **1** exchange. 1A of the business of money changers, exchanging equivalent values. **2** adjustment of a difference, reconciliation, restoration to favour.[2]

to reconcile. Reconciliation, restoration, exchange. A change or reconciliation from a state of enmity between persons to one of friendship. Between God and man it is the result of the *apolútrōsis* (629), redemption, the divine act of salvation, the ceasing of God's wrath. In the NT, it means reconciliation, i.e., restoration ling the world to God.[3]

Despite various emphases, all of these definitions focus on the central work accomplished by God to bring us into peace and favor with Him. Our reconciliation, our atonement, did not occur because of something we did, but because of something that God did.

The distinctive "we" makes the obvious point that what Jesus did was not done for a vague and unknown group. It was for a specific "we." This verse rejects the notion that Jesus died to merely make salvation—or in the words of the verse, the atonement—available for everyone, but effective only for people who meet various conditions to obtain it. Jesus died for a specific people who "now" are blessed with the benefits earned by His death. Notice the emphasis in the definitions of this word on the idea of a literal exchange, not dissimilar to an exchange of currency. In His death Jesus took our sins onto Himself. In His resurrection He affirmed that His righteousness, the "atonement," now belongs to us. He didn't merely open the currency exchange bank and invite us to trade our sin-money for his righteousness-money. The exchange has already occurred. By using this verse as a summary of what he has been teaching in the prior verses, Paul specifically identifies our present atonement, our peaceful

---

AV Authorized Version
[2] James Strong, *The Exhaustive Concordance of the Bible : Showing Every Word of the Test of the Common English Version of the Canonical Books, and Every Occurence of Each Word in Regular Order.*, electronic ed. (Ontario: Woodside Bible Fellowship., 1996), G2643.
NT (New Testament)
[3] Spiros Zodhiates, *The Complete Word Study Dictionary : New Testament*, electronic ed. (Chattanooga, TN: AMG Publishers, 2000, c1992, c1993), G2643.

and secure relationship with God, to the death of Christ. Our joy is based on the knowledge of what Jesus accomplished for us, not on what we did to gain access to that atonement.

The agency by which we "now" receive the atonement is not what man says or does, but "…through our Lord Jesus Christ." Occasionally critics of the doctrines of grace object that we believe in salvation apart from conditions. They err in this accusation. We indeed believe that our eternal security is based on conditions. Further we believe that all the conditions imposed by Almighty God were met by and in the person of the Lord Jesus Christ. Not only did He meet the conditions of our salvation, but He also now serves as the agent by which those conditions and blessings flow from God to us. The idea that the gospel is in some way instrumental in a person's salvation actually seeks to supplant the instrumentality of the Lord Jesus Christ with a fallible human instrument. Consider this fundamental flaw in the idea that the gospel is instrumental in a person's salvation. Short of the Lord Jesus Christ and the apostles when speaking or writing under the inspiration of the Holy Spirit, there has never been a sermon preached that was without flaw in some way or another. Paul asserts, "…we have this treasure in earthen vessels…" (2 Corinthians 4:7). If God in fact uses preaching in any form as His agent to reach and regenerate the lost, how much error may a given sermon contain and still be used by God in this work? Where is the divine line in the sand? And if a person comes to believe that God used a specific sermon for his/her regeneration, despite its flawed content, is this person not highly susceptible to magnifying the content of that sermon as if it were all true rather than perceiving it as part true and part error? How effective will a teacher be later in convincing this person that a particular point in that sermon was in fact error?

God indeed uses the gospel to reveal Christ in His regenerate elect and to bring them to the joy of knowing His blessings in and for them. Herein is the Biblical instrumentality of the gospel. Prior to the new birth, Scripture describes a person as being "dead" in trespasses and in sins (Ephesians 2:1). Scripture further affirms that the person in this unregenerate state is wholly incapable of knowing spiritual truths. In fact Scripture affirms that spiritual things appear as foolishness to the "natural man." (1 Corinthians 2:14) Thus the popular view that an unregenerate person has the ability to perceive the truth of the gospel, to believe it, and to embrace it flies in the face of Paul's clear teaching in these lessons. In fact such teaching builds its whole notion on an impossible premise. Reason with a person who is "dead" and wholly alienated from God. Convince a person to embrace and truly believe in something that he perceives as altogether foolish and absurd.

Further Paul affirms that "...they that are in the flesh cannot please God." (Romans 8:8) This passage further compounds the impossible situation already affirmed in the above passages. From the contextual perspective of spiritual conduct, conduct that pleases and honors God from a distinctly spiritual perspective, the person who is not born of God can do nothing that pleases God. Thus the popular notion of the unregenerate person doing something to bring his/her regeneration into being presumes that the person does something that does not—in fact "cannot"—please God. Are we then to believe that such a person does something that is repugnant to God in order to in some mystical way reverse God, please Him, and gain access to the saving work of the Lord Jesus Christ?

Paul rejects all such double-speak in favor of the profoundly simple truth of the New Testament gospel. In the atoning, reconciling work of the Lord Jesus Christ God accepted that work as satisfaction for our sins and "through our Lord Jesus Christ" completed the exchange once and for all. The death of Jesus didn't place a divine offer of exchange on the table. It didn't merely post a rate of exchange that we must evaluate and either accept or reject. Paul affirms that the exchange has already occurred and we "...have now received" it, the atonement. The atonement of which Paul writes is not merely a potential event to be decided in the future. It is a factual event that has already occurred.

What is our response to this glorious event? Do we complain because God didn't give us a role in its success? No—a thousand times no—we "joy in God" because of the grand event. To Him alone be the glory!

31
All of Grace: Why?

> Wherefore, as by one man sin entered into the world, and death by sin; and so death passed upon all men, for that all have sinned: Therefore as by the offence of one judgment came upon all men to condemnation; even so by the righteousness of one the free gift came upon all men unto justification of life. For as by one man's disobedience many were made sinners, so by the obedience of one shall many be made righteous. (Romans 5:12, 18-19)

In the preceding verses Paul made one of his strongest arguments that our eternal salvation is all of God to be found in the New Testament. In making this argument he asserted precisely the truth that caused his critics to misrepresent his teachings as appears in the first eight verses of the third chapter of Romans. Although he dealt with the ethical issues of the doctrines of grace in the fourth chapter—and will do so emphatically in the sixth chapter—Paul here refuses to allow the critics and their straw man exaggerated misrepresentations of his teachings to drive him away from the truth of the gospel that he taught. What is the necessity of holding so rigidly to the idea of grace alone for both the power and the agency or instrument of eternal salvation? From Romans 5:12 to the end of the fifth chapter Paul will deal with this question quite specifically. Can't man have just a little role to play in his salvation? Even if God orchestrates his response so that God gets all the credit, can't man do something in the process of causing or bringing about his new birth? Paul emphatically says no. Our question is why. In the lesson before us he gives the reasons.

Verses thirteen through seventeen in this chapter are set off by parenthesis. A parenthetical expression is added in literary works to clarify or to provide added details or explanations to what has been said. In this parenthesis Paul reasons with incredible emphasis and logical argumentation. I intentionally quoted the lesson without the parenthesis. As quoted, the lesson states the point that Paul intended.

Theologians sometimes refer to the features of this lesson under the term "federal headship." What does this mean? What is the theological significance of this idea? Let's examine the lesson and see what Paul has in mind.

1. *...by one man sin entered into the world....* No great mystery here; the first three chapters of Genesis cover this historical event quite clearly. I emphasize that these chapters cover historical events, not symbolic or figurative events. Did God really create the material universe, or is the first chapter of Genesis a mere myth not to be taken either literally or seriously? Hebrews 11:3 affirms that true Biblical faith embraces that God created the material universe. This simple verse categorically rejects the ancient Gnostic and contemporary New Age philosophies that God despises all things material. How could He despise them? He created them with the repeated *moral and aesthetic conclusion,* "It was good." Periodically well meaning Bible students will attempt to compromise the Bible account of origins in a futile effort to evade the criticism of atheistic evolutionary claims by asserting that human beings existed for untold centuries before the first chapter of Genesis. In this failed effort to satisfy unbelievers they deny—if not factually at least by implication and by a loose allegorical interpretation—the whole Bible account of origins. In this allegorical view Adam and Eve were not real human beings at all, but merely mythical representations of human history. Others will acknowledge them as real human beings, but never offer rational and reasonable explanations of the impact of Adam's and Eve's sin on humans prior to their existence.

    In this lesson Paul builds his whole theological lesson on the fact that Adam was as truly a real historical being as Jesus was. He further makes the case that it was Adam's sin that introduced sin into the human race and, with it, the dreadful consequences of sin. Adam becomes the true representative of all humanity in this lesson.

2. *...and death by sin....* One wonders; in the case of the view that humans existed prior to Adam and Eve—were they sinless? The inevitable consequence of sin is death. In the parenthetical portion of this lesson Paul will expand this point to indicate that death reigned in the human race from Adam to Moses and the giving of the Law. We normally associate

death with the penalty for breaking God's Law, so how could death reign for centuries prior to the giving of the Law to Moses? Paul here associates death with Adam and his sin, not with Mosaic law. Around the fourth century an English monk, Pelagius, advocated that there was no inherent or "federal headship" impact from Adam's sin on subsequent humanity. Logically he argued that the only impact of Adam's sin in the Garden of Eden was that he set a bad example for his offspring. Are we then to conclude that the only impact of Jesus' Incarnation is that He set a good example for us? Some of Pelagius' followers seem to have embraced this idea; perhaps Pelagius himself embraced it. Paul's reasoning in this chapter categorically rejects such an idea. The ratio of deaths to births universally from Adam's creation to our time has been a solid and uncompromising one hundred percent, a true one-to-one ratio. Not a single human has evaded the logical implications of Adam's sin, death. Death may come late as with many of the patriarchs in Genesis. It may come early as with infants who die in infancy or—God forbid—who are killed by their parents prior to birth by abortion. (If you doubt that abortion kills a real human being, I urge you to read Psalm 139 carefully.) Why is death universal to the human family? Paul asserts that it is so because sin is universal; we inherited it from Adam. Adam's basic nature was altered by his decision to sin and walk away from God, and that corrupted DNA/moral nature was passed along to every single one of his offspring.

3. *...so death passed upon all men, for that all have sinned.* Paul emphasizes the universality of sin by the observable fact of universal death. I do not believe in childhood innocence in terms of the nature possessed by infants. If childhood innocence were true, based on Paul's reasoning in this lesson, infant death would be impossible. Scripture clearly affirms a degree of behavioral innocence in infants, but it never affirms innocence of the nature possessed. We are born with the same nature that we manifest in adulthood, including our moral fallenness and our inherent proclivity toward sin. *...all have sinned* likely refers to the inherited quality of sin that

we derive from Adam, an inherent trait that eventually manifests itself in actual sinful conduct.

4. *Therefore as by the offence of one judgment came upon all men to condemnation....* "Therefore" indicates that Paul is here reviewing and further explaining what he has already stated. One man's sin, Adam's, brought judgment and the sentence of "Guilty as charged," the equivalent in the New Testament to the word "condemnation." All subsequent humanity to Adam were specifically and directly impacted by what Adam did. How could we read this lesson and reach any other conclusion?

5. *...even so by the righteousness of one the free gift came upon all men unto justification of life.* So far Paul has focused tightly on Adam and the consequences of his sin. Now he shifts from the implications of Adam's sin to Jesus and the implications of His Incarnation and righteousness. And here we see the clear implications of this term "federal headship." It is actually two distinct "federal headships," one in Adam and the other in Jesus. The implications of Adam's headship bring the consequences of Adam's sin upon all of his offspring, all humanity. There is no option. There is no choice to be made. It occurs in every single instance. Every child born into "Adam's family" inherits the moral and spiritual state that Adam brought upon himself in his sin. Not a single child born into the human family was given a choice as to whether or not he/she wished to embrace the Adam-condition. They inherited it. Adam's federal headship made it as certain as the child's human nature itself. It became an integral part of our human nature when Adam chose to eat the forbidden fruit in the third chapter of Genesis.

But now let's shift our focus from Adam to Jesus. Paul introduces Jesus and the implications of His "federal headship" with the simple "even so" comparison. The rules by which we become members of Jesus' family and children of God who shall spend eternity with Him in heaven have an "even so" corollary with the implications of Adam's sin.

We become members of God's family in the Lord Jesus Christ by a "genetic" event no less than we became members of

Adam's family by a similar natural genetic event. We didn't volunteer to become a member of Adam's family. Neither do we "volunteer" to become members of Jesus' family! This point goes to the heart of Paul's teaching in Romans 5:6-11.

6. *For as by one man's disobedience many were made sinners, so by the obedience of one shall many be made righteous.* "For as by…so by…." Paul's comparison between Adam and Jesus are so emphatic as to defy misunderstanding. This teaching confronts the whole paradigm of "decisional" salvation that prevails in contemporary Christianity. Unless advocates of this view can make a compelling case that Scripture teaches that every human being at some time personally chooses to become a member of the human race, of Adam's family, they cannot harmonize their salvation teaching with their idea that the new birth, the beginning of eternal life in an individual, occurs because of a decision that they make. The Greek word translated "made" in this verse (both instances) means to "constitute." It refers to the essential constitution of a being, not to a mere peripheral feature. What Adam did altered the essential "constitution," the essential nature of his offspring, of those whom he represented in federal headship. Likewise, according to Paul, what Jesus did alters the essential constitution, the essential nature of those for whom He died. It is not their decision or works that saves them; it is what Jesus did as their Savior, their new and spiritual "federal head."

So why must our salvation in Christ be all of grace and not in some degree by anything that we do? Paul's reasoning concludes that our fallen and sinful standing in Adam renders any acceptable action on our part wholly impossible. If we are ever to be moved from our identity in Adam's family to a new identity in Jesus' family, it must be by an act of God that bestows that familial relationship on us no less than our birth into the human family.

This truth gives powerful logical significance to the analogy of spiritual life that Jesus introduced in the third chapter of John's gospel during His conversation with Nicodemus, an analogy repeated several times throughout the New Testament by other inspired writers.

Two major deviations from this bedrock spiritual truth are rather common in theological circles in our time. The first deviation openly advocates salvation by works, by some form of human effort or another. You either perform these works, or you will not be saved.

The second deviation is more subtle, but also more insidious because it presents itself as advocating that salvation is all of God. It asserts that salvation is all of God, but it then asserts that unless a person clearly exhibits a certain degree of behavioral change in his conduct he isn't really saved at all. Although advocates of this view are reluctant to assign a specific degree of behavioral change to reach their conclusion that a person is saved (I find it absurdly egotistical that they consider themselves judges of a person's eternal state with God, a point that Scripture will not permit.), *they tend to assign the same behavioral characteristics to their conclusion regarding a person's being saved or not that advocates of salvation by works assign to their theological system.* The rather ironic result is that both errant systems of salvation end up with exactly the same number of folks being saved! Perhaps, despite a convincing amount of window dressing, both systems are far more similar than advocates of either system care to acknowledge.

Advocates of this second errant system typically obsess about "assurance of salvation." Followers of this theological error are constantly reminded that they must seek perpetual assurances of their salvation, or perhaps they are not really saved at all. Christianity degenerates into a monstrous and self-serving "It is all about me and my assurance of my salvation" humanistic philosophy. *Biblical assurance of salvation builds on self-denial, not self-obsession!* The more we deny self and make our Christian life about serving God by serving others the more spiritual blessings we realize, including assurance of our salvation. The more we are willing to make our faith all about ourselves and our self-assurance the less assured we are. Thus advocates of this error constantly doubt both their own salvation as well as the salvation of everyone else! Dreadful!

We have barely introduced this vital theme. We must linger with these verses and with their spiritual implications.

32
Why Must God Alone Save Sinners?

> Wherefore, as by one man sin entered into the world, and death by sin; and so death passed upon all men, for that all have sinned: (For until the law sin was in the world: but sin is not imputed when there is no law. Nevertheless death reigned from Adam to Moses, even over them that had not sinned after the similitude of Adam's transgression, who is the figure of him that was to come. But not as the offence, so also is the free gift. For if through the offence of one many be dead, much more the grace of God, and the gift by grace, which is by one man, Jesus Christ, hath abounded unto many. And not as it was by one that sinned, so is the gift: for the judgment was by one to condemnation, but the free gift is of many offences unto justification. For if by one man's offence death reigned by one; much more they which receive abundance of grace and of the gift of righteousness shall reign in life by one, Jesus Christ.) (Romans 5:12-17)

According to Scripture, what is the condition of man in his natural state before God saves him? He does not exist as God created Adam and Eve in the Garden of Eden. He certainly doesn't act the part of a creature of a moral and righteous God.

In the third chapter of Romans, as well as in the verses leading up to our study passage, Paul has explained our justification by grace and by the blood of Christ from God's perspective. He now will take us to the "other side" of the problem and explain why God must do all the work necessary for our final justification.

Historical theology uses a term that it draws from this passage, "federal headship." The intent of this term is explained in Paul's words in our study passage. When Adam sinned, he brought consequences, not only upon himself, but upon all of his offspring. None escape. In this way, Adam became all of humanity's "federal head," or legal representative in his sinful action in the Garden.

However, Paul goes on to teach us that the Lord Jesus Christ also came as the "federal head" of His elect, of all for whom He died. And just as universally as Adam's offspring suffered the consequences of Adam's sin, so all of God's elect actually benefit from the righteous work of the Lord Jesus Christ.

You will notice that Paul in our study passage uses the term, *"...gift of righteousness...."* Righteousness is right conduct, right action. How can one person actually receive the right conduct of another? By human action and perception, it cannot be. We may observe a righteous person's conduct and benefit from his good example, but we cannot actually receive his righteousness. We can only receive the *"...gift of righteousness..."* by the work of God through the Lord Jesus Christ. Paul explains this process in our study passage.

...as by one man sin entered into the world.... God didn't bring sin into the world. Man is the guilty party. We have examined the principle already, but we need to repeat it for emphasis. God didn't create a robotic or puppeteer universe. He created a moral universe, and He governs His universe as its moral Governor. He didn't make Adam in the Garden as a robot, programmed or dangled on cosmic strings to do only what he dictated by pulling the strings. He created Adam as a moral creature. He gave Adam one commandment, one behavior that Adam was responsible to obey. He explained quite clearly to Adam that this law contained both a blessing if he obeyed it and a curse if he broke it.

In the simplest and most literal sense, Adam possessed free will. He could choose to obey, or he could choose to disobey. He knew the consequences of both choices. He had the ability to obey, and he had the ability to disobey. His choice was a moral choice. Do what God, his Creator, commanded, the morally right thing to do, and enjoy the Garden and its blessings. Break God's commandment, the morally wrong thing to do, and face God's certain moral judgment, expulsion from the Garden and its blessings for himself and for his offspring after him.

Superstitions abound regarding the actual sin that drove Adam and Eve from the Garden. Don't chase superstitions. Genesis 3 tells us precisely what the sin was; eating the forbidden fruit of the tree of knowledge of good and evil. Adam and Eve's intimate relationship had nothing to do with their expulsion. When God made Eve and gave her to Adam, He joined them as husband and wife, and He commanded them to procreate, to multiply and replenish the earth, so their doing so was an act of obedience to God, not a sin.

...and death by sin.... God quite directly warned Adam that the consequences, the judgment against him for eating the forbidden fruit,

would be death, *"...in the day that thou eatest thereof...."* (Genesis 2:17). God also warned Adam that his death would occur "...in the day..." that he ate the forbidden fruit.

According to Genesis 5:5, Adam lived to the ripe old age of 930 years. The obvious question begs to be answered. Did Adam die *"...in the day..."* that he ate the forbidden fruit, or did he die nine hundred thirty years later?

My first answer is "Yes." Yes, he died in the very moment that he ate the fruit. From that moment, Adam and Eve displayed a fearful attitude toward God, an attitude wholly absent during their time of obedience in the Garden. As the third chapter of Genesis records, both Adam and Eve immediately exhibited the attitude of fallen sinfulness, even to the extent of trying to shift the responsibility for their sin off to God. The death that occurred on that day also started a degenerative process that was apparently absent in the Garden, a process that reached its completion nine hundred thirty years after God had created Adam.

Nevertheless death reigned from Adam to Moses.... We cannot precisely know the time lapse from Adam to Moses, though I respect Bishop Ussher's calculations based on the ages at death of the various people named in Scripture during that era. Paul's point is simple. God didn't give His full Law until He gave it to Moses on Mt. Sinai, literally centuries after Adam and Eve were driven from the Garden. Death is the penalty for the violation of God's Edenic Law, or of His moral law. There is no record of a specific law from God to man during this time. So why did people die during that time? That is Paul's reasoning in this verse. And his explanation takes us back to that term "federal headship."

God created Adam in His image and likeness. Humanity retains some of that image and likeness (Psalm 8; Hebrews 2:6-8, where Paul refers to this passage. "...A little lower than the angels..." at the least implies man's original creation. It is likely that Psalm 8 also explains the specific way in which God created man in His image and likeness. As God rightly held dominion over His creation, He passed that oversight to man), clearly some of it was lost in the fall. Paul appeals to the fact that humans who lived during this time inherited Adam's fallenness. They did not inherit Adam's Garden purity. A careful reading of the Scriptures that deal with this era will strongly suggest that God did in fact reveal His moral character and commandments in some way, though not as clearly or as formally as to Moses on Mt. Sinai.

...who is the figure of him that was to come.... How was Adam a "figure" of Christ? How could he be, given the polar opposite behavior and consequences of the two? The answer appears in their mutual representation. Adam in his sin represented all of his offspring; when he sinned, he brought the consequences of his sin onto all of his offspring who would ever follow. Likewise, in the "figure," when Jesus came into the world, He represented all of God's elect; when Jesus lived a sinless, righteous life, He lived it on behalf of all whom he represented. When He faced suffering and death, He did not face it for wrongs that He had done, but for His elect. By His suffering the equivalent penalty for the sins of those for whom He died, He could righteously bestow His righteousness, "...the gift of righteousness..." onto all of His elect whom He represented in His Incarnation.

The *"...not as...so also"* dynamic that appears in verses 15-17 further develops this representation. We live in a world that testifies to the impact of sin. We see it everywhere we look all around us. Paul anchors his teaching on that obvious observation, but he catapults his teaching into a world that stretches every fiber of our comprehension to grasp. In fact, human comprehension simply cannot possibly grasp his point. We only get a sense of its grand outcome by the indwelling testimony of the Holy Spirit.

We are born with a nature that is distinctly and consistently inclined to sin. We cannot claim any superiority to Adam, for, so long as we possess only his nature, we imitate him every time we face a decision that requires a moral choice. We twist God's moral law and rationalize a sinful action that we think will enhance our personal pleasure. And we even follow Adam's example when we face the consequences of our sinful behavior by passing the responsibility for our sinful choices off to someone else. And sinful man's favorite recipient remains God. When all else fails, blame God. How fallen is this once noble creature?

Consider a few logical and Biblical points relative to Adam's sin and the consequences that resulted.

Prior to the fall:
1. Adam had no knowledge of evil or sin.
2. Adam had knowledge of good as God had revealed it in the Garden.
3. Adam had free will. He had the ability and the mental capability to reason and to anticipate the consequences of his actions. He could freely choose to obey God, or he could freely choose to eat the fruit. He could not, however, choose to do either without facing the blessings or the consequences that God imposed on his actions.

After the fall:
1. Man has knowledge of both good and evil.
2. Man now possesses a broken, fallen will. He has lost the ability to freely and fully choose to obey God's moral law. Fallen man's deepest problem lies deep within his mind and appears in the abilities that he lost in the fall.
3. Man has lost the ability to fully and freely obey God. His will refuses to consider obeying God; he cannot obey. He does not have that ability. (John 8:43; *"...even because ye **cannot** hear my word."* 1 Corinthians 2:14; *"...neither **can** he know them, because they are spiritually discerned."* The words "cannot" and "can" denote ability. In both verses, the Biblical point deals specifically with sinful man's utter lack of ability, ***what he cannot do***, because he lacks the ability)

In taking us from God's grace (*"...justified freely by his grace..."* Romans 3:24) to man's fallen inability in our present study verses, Paul has fully explained the true necessity of God's "gracious" (motivated and enacted based on God's grace) process for saving His chosen people from their sins and securing for them the "...gift of righteousness..." in the Person and work of His Son and our Savior, the Lord Jesus Christ. He has shown us that we could not possibly have cooperated or in any way contributed to any other scheme of salvation from our sins. Hallelujah! What a Savior!

33
The Universal Reign of Death

> For until the law sin was in the world: but sin is not imputed when there is no law. Nevertheless death reigned from Adam to Moses, even over them that had not sinned after the similitude of Adam's transgression, who is the figure of him that was to come. (Romans 5:13-14)

We now turn from the primary sentence of Paul's discussion of federal headship—both of Adam and of Christ—to the parenthetical explanation that Paul gives in this chapter. If we accept the essential point that Paul makes—that death is the penalty for sin—we put ourselves on a course that avoids countless theological errors when we arrive at our study of salvation, how a person is moved from the federal headship of Adam to the federal headship of Christ. However, we also raise other questions that must be addressed. Many well meaning Christians fiercely advocate and defend the idea of the "age of accountability," a point in a child's maturation at which he/she becomes responsible and accountable to God for personal sins committed. Normally advocates of this idea will set an age around twelve or thirteen as the "age of accountability." If asked to defend their view, they appeal to Jesus' appearance in the temple at the age of twelve (Luke 2:42). Such an explanation of this passage represents a rather glaring misuse of Scripture, for in no way does this passage or any adjacent verses in any way discuss anyone's moral state or accountability for sins. It rather provides us with the sole narrative of Jesus' inherent righteousness between His birth and the beginning of His public ministry. Interestingly, when God actually imposed judgment against rebellious Israel in the wilderness, His judgment was against all people age twenty or above (Numbers 14:29), not thirteen or fourteen.

I do not advocate either age as presenting a Biblical basis for this well-meaning but ill-founded teaching. The fundamental principle of Biblical interpretation, the "perspicuity of Scripture," the clarity of Scripture, that asserts that God devotes both volume and clarity in Scripture to all doctrines that He views as important for our spiritual health, inherently puts the age of accountability idea under serious doubt.

Based on Numbers 14:29, God considers age as He pronounces punishment or judgment against people. We should acknowledge that fact without abandoning Biblical teaching that ignores—rather than teaches—a formal doctrine of the age of accountability.

What does this question have to do with our study verses? I suggest that it has everything to do with them. What is the "similitude of Adam's transgression"? Is it not the sin of an adult human being committing an informed act of sinful rebellion against God and His known moral code? So who were those from Adam to Moses who died, though they had not committed such a sin? I offer the words of Augustus Toplady in a brief treatise that he wrote, "A Short Essay on Original Sin," giving his explanation of this specific verse.

> Infants are here designated by the apostle: who have not sinned actually and in their own persons as Adam did, and yet are liable to temporal death. Wherefore, then, do they die? Is not death the wages of sin? Most certainly. And seeing it is incontestibly [sic] clear that not any individual among the numberless millions who have died in infancy was capable of committing actual sin; it follows that they sinned representatively and implicitly in Adam. Else they would not be entitled to that death which is the wages of sin, and to those diseases by which their death is occasioned, and to that pain which most of them experience in dying. ...This is the doctrine of the Church of England....Original sin is the fault and corruption of the nature of every man.[1]

Notice that Toplady, a devoted and respected minister in the Church of England throughout his lifetime, affirms his view of our study passage, as well as affirming that his view represented the teaching and belief of the Church of England at the time of his

---

[1] Ibid. *Augustus Montague Toplady: A Debtor to Mercy Alone* by George Ella, p. 640. (Some contemporary theologians will affirm the sentence of death due to federal headship, but reject the idea of a fallen nature. It is my belief that the two go hand in hand. Death, the sentence of God against sin, follows sins committed or—in the case of dying infants—a fallen nature. I do not believe that a person can hold to a common nature possessed by humans before and after the fall. The fall corrupted man's most basic nature, and all subsequent humans inherit that nature at conception.)

writing. It should be further noted that in this essay Toplady repeatedly and emphatically affirmed that the responsibility for sin's entrance into humanity was attributable to Adam, not to God or to a mysterious divine decree.

Toplady's view of this passage is that those who *"had not sinned after the similitude of Adam's transgression"* refers to infants who, though they committed not a single act of informed and conscious rebellious sin against God, nevertheless died from Adam's banishment from Eden till the Mosaic law was given. By focusing so specifically on this era and on the nature of death during this time, it is obvious that Paul had a rather specific point to make, a point that I believe Toplady correctly uncovers.

What is Paul's primary point? The disease of sin is as universal as the human family! Not even death at a tender age avoids the disease—in fact the disease explains even the question of death at a tender age, not by asserting that infants sin so as to personally bring the sentence of suffering and death upon themselves, but rather that they are conceived and born into the world with the disease of sin already in them and thus its consequences upon them. Those who advocate infant purity (that infants do not inherit Adam's fallen nature or death due to his sin through federal headship) have a far greater problem to explain than those who hold to Paul's teaching in this lesson. How do they explain death, the sentence of sin, being forced upon an "innocent" infant who has not so sinned? They must in effect explain the justice of God in passing an undeserved and unearned sentence upon a supposedly innocent being!

The question of "original sin" and its impact on infants has been debated from earliest Christian history. Most historical accounts of early efforts within the Church of Rome to defend the practice of infant baptism (infant sprinkling) assert that infants are born with some form of inherited sin that—in this aberrant view of baptism is washed away by baptism. Thus Roman attacks against those who rejected their view of infant baptism focus on the false assertion that their critics held to some form of infant damnation by their denial of the rite of baptism to infants.

Many critics of Primitive Baptists historically accused our faith-ancestors of believing in infant damnation because they denied infant purity. Our historical writings clearly document the falsity of the charge. Although not a Primitive Baptist by any stretch, Charles Spurgeon preached a whole sermon affirming his belief in divine mercy in electing and saving dying infants. Our faith-ancestors did not believe in infant damnation; rather they believed that God saves infants in the same way that He saves adults. It should be added here that the strong majority view historically among Primitive Baptists was—and I believe is—that God elects all dying infants, not just some of them, to salvation. However, the basis of their salvation, according to their teaching, is divine mercy, eternal divine election, and the blood of Christ, not infant innocence.

The question of the dying infant's eternal destiny should not be confused with the truth of Paul's teaching here. Clearly the salvation of the infant cannot stand on grounds of purity in light of Paul's teaching in this lesson. I believe that Scripture teaches that infants who die in their infancy are saved, not by personal purity but by divine mercy and divine election. Later in the Roman letter when dealing specifically with God's election (the ninth chapter) Paul will note that God endures "with much longsuffering" the "vessels of wrath" who by sin are fitted for destruction. Although not dealing specifically with the question of infant election—but with the general truth of election—in this context, Paul's careful and inspired choice of words deals with the whole doctrine of election, including the infant. Those who teach that some infants will spend eternity in hell (typically explained by advocates of this idea on the basis of Adam's sin, not the infant's personal sin) must explain how an infant who dies in infancy—especially an infant who was killed by his/her parents prior to birth—tests divine "longsuffering." *Advocates of this doctrine of infant damnation cannot claim Paul—or any other inspired writer for that matter—as their friend!*

I find it enlightening that every instance in which Scripture assigns specific grounds on which the wicked shall be judged and sentenced to eternal separation from God, bases that sentence on personal sins committed, not on mere nature possessed. I do not question that the corruption of Adam's nature is sufficient to justify a righteous sentence of eternal separation, but I do question the point of an infant being in hell based on specific eschatological passages that deal with eternal judgment, passages that without exception base the final sentence of separation on personal sins committed that deserve the sentence. As just one example, the language of Matthew 25:31-46—"I was hungry, and ye gave me no meat…I was a stranger, and ye took me not in…naked and ye clothed me not, sick, and in prison, and ye visited me not…"—is the language of personal conduct, not the language of federal headship and original sin.

I further observe that the various passages and Biblical analogies dealing with redemption and its eternal blessings affirm that God saves people in one exclusive way, not many. The idea of multiple ways of final salvation is wholly foreign to Scripture. "…so is *every one* that is born of the Spirit." (John 3:8; emphasis added) God does not teach us in Scripture that He engaged multiple means or grounds of salvation depending on the dispensation in which the person lived, their exposure to knowledge of Him in the gospel, or on their age at the time of their death. Every one who is born of God—every one who becomes a member of Jesus' spiritual "federal headship," does so in one and the same way, by divine election, mercy, and the redemptive blood of Christ—never on any other basis. If all who die in infancy are saved, as I believe the Scriptures to teach, it is because of God's sovereign choice, based on His electing love, His inexplicable mercy, and the redemptive work of our Lord Jesus Christ, not on any other basis whatever.

34
Adam and Jesus: Comparison or Contrast?

> But not as the offence, so also is the free gift. For if through the offence of one many be dead, much more the grace of God, and the gift by grace, which is by one man, Jesus Christ, hath abounded unto many. And not as it was by one that sinned, so is the gift: for the judgment was by one to condemnation, but the free gift is of many offences unto justification. For if by one man's offence death reigned by one; much more they which receive abundance of grace and of the gift of righteousness shall reign in life by one, Jesus Christ. (Romans 5:15-17)

Often folks who study these verses tend to draw multiple comparisons between Adam and Jesus. Scripture indeed draws certain comparisons between them. For example, we have just completed our study of federal headship; both Adam and Jesus appear in this chapter from Paul's Roman letter as federal heads, as representative of all people whom they individually represent. Adam is the federal head of the human family—no exceptions. Jesus is the federal head of God's chosen family—no exceptions here either. However, a study of the language that Paul uses in this lesson indicates that he had contrast more in mind than comparison. Consider such words as "but" and "not as" in the passage. These are words of contrast. Consider the consequences of each federal head's actions on their representative "family." Adam's conduct brought negative consequences on all of his representative family, while Jesus' actions bring amazing positive consequences on all of His representative family. I will not argue the point with good brothers who choose to focus their thoughts of this lesson on the comparative features between Adam and Jesus, for their intent and theological soundness is not in question, at least among those with whom I have discussed this question. However, as I survey the passage and assess my own interpretation of the lesson, I am inclined to focus more on the contrast than the comparison. For example, the third chapter of Genesis clearly indicates that Eve ate the forbidden fruit first, and that Adam immediately followed her in eating it. He ate it knowingly. Since Moses in Genesis does not mention Adam's motive, we have no way of knowing from Scripture what Adam's motive was. Any conclusion as to his motive must stand on our personal speculation. However, when we get to the New Testament and begin to study Jesus' work on behalf of His chosen people, we find abundant Scriptural testimony to identify His motive in suffering, dying, and rising again for His people. His work was an act of love for His people and profound obedience to the will of the Father—to His will. His and the Father's will are in no way at conflict.

In terms of federal headship—the fact that what each federal head did had and has material impact on the individuals they represented—the two are similar. However, Paul introduces our thought with a straightforward "But not as...so also" assessment. The free gift bestowed on God's elect because of Jesus' work is in some material sense "not as" the impact of Adam's sin and its impact on humanity.

Do not overlook the basic terms that Paul chooses to describe each event. In assessing Adam's action and its impact on humanity Paul uses the term "offence." When he refers to Jesus' work and its impact on God's elect, Paul uses the term "free gift" and "the gift by grace."

In no point does Paul more emphatically draw contrast than in his description of results or consequences. In the case of Adam one act by one man brought "condemnation" onto all of his offspring. By his sinful act (not described here by Paul as a noble act or even as a loving act), Adam brought judgment, a legal verdict of guilty, onto all humanity. In contrast by his perfect obedience Jesus transformed the legal sentence for all of His elect, despite a just verdict of "Guilty as charged," from many offences into "justification of life," an official verdict from heaven's court of "Not guilty"! Despite their guilty participation in Adam's sin and sentence, and exclusively because of what He did, Jesus transforms His elect into the mirror opposite so that they now "reign *in life* by one." Adam's sin carried with it the sentence of death. Paul has already reasoned from this fact that death reigned from Adam to Moses over all humanity, even over those who did not sin as conscious adults. He clearly in this reasoning affirms that the death sentence did not originate against humanity in Moses' law, but in the Edenic law given to Adam.

We should further note Paul's emphasis in this federal headship line of reasoning that as he attributes the fact of sin and death in all humanity to Adam and his sin, he also credits the whole of our righteous standing and life with God to Jesus. If each individual must at some point in life choose to identify with Adam, we might have reason to make a parallel point that each individual must also at some point in life make a conscious choice to identify with Jesus. Absent this pivotal point, the accepted teaching in many pulpits that an individual's eternal destiny is contingent on a personal decision or choice to be made by that individual must fail for lack of Biblical support. Decisional salvation can claim no support in Paul's teaching here. In fact his teaching renders it an impossible theology, one in which all of humanity would universally face condemnation and death.

"…shall reign in life by one;" here Paul carefully uses a future tense verb. Although writing to Roman Christians who were already born again, already saved in terms of their present spiritual standing with God, Paul distinctly anticipates a future salvation or life yet to be experienced by them.

The idea that Jesus died provisionally for all humanity, but factually for none finds no basis whatever in this passage. Nor does the idea that Jesus died for all the sins of all humanity, except for the sin of rejecting Him or effectively choosing not to believe in Him, find support in this lesson. In contrast to either of these populist ideas Paul affirms that Jesus' work is as "unilateral" as Adam's. The impact of His work on behalf of His people is as involuntary and as specific as the impact of Adam's actions on his offspring.

The contrast between Adam and Jesus appears in no point more in contrast than in the consequences of their actions. We sometimes hear people refer to something they consider to be highly important as being a matter of "life or death." In the case of our lesson the term holds special significance. Adam becomes synonymous with the sentence of death, both physical death and spiritual death, while Jesus becomes synonymous with the sentence of life, both natural life in terms of the final resurrection of the body and in terms of spiritual life.

The prevalent teaching of our age—not essentially different from past ages other than the greater creativity with which advocates of human-centered salvation attempt to describe their ideas—that salvation in its final and decisive point depends on some action or decision by the sinner contradicts Paul's teaching in this passage. To one degree or another Pelagius and his successors taught that Adam's sin had no inherent impact on anyone else other than setting a bad example. Functionally the prevalent teachings of decisional salvation in our time must build their foundational premise on this error. According to their teaching, Adam made a bad decision and faced the consequences of his sin. At some point in their lifetime, according to advocates of this idea, each individual must make a decision either for or against God. Each individual must face his own serpent in his own Garden of Eden. Thus in the final analysis each individual becomes his own personal judge and jury. Each individual becomes either his own executioner or his own savior!

If we follow Paul's teaching in this lesson, whatever impact we receive from Adam's action becomes the basis for whatever impact we receive from Jesus' actions. If the impact of Adam's sin on us is nothing more than a bad example, we must conclude that the impact of Jesus' actions on us is nothing more than a good example! This teaching leads us to the dreadful conclusion that every individual person must become his or her own savior, or they shall have no salvation. If this were the case, why does Scripture so carefully and consistently present Jesus to us as the one and only Savior of sinners?

Is this a "new doctrine"? The answer echoes off the canyon walls of centuries, but the first and primary echo comes from the mouth of inspired Scripture. Consider these words from Augustus Toplady, the author of the favorite hymn "Rock of Ages."

From whence this fear and unbelief?
Did not the Father put to grief
His spotless Son for me?
And will the righteous judge of men,
Condemn me for that debt of sin,
Which Lord was charg'd on thee?

Complete atonement thou hast made,
And to the utmost farthing paid,
Whate'er thy people ow'd:
Nor can his wrath on me take place,
If shelter'd in thy righteousness,
And ransomed by thy blood.

If thou hast my discharge procur'd,

And in the sinner's room endur'd,
The whole of wrath divine:
Payment he cannot twice demand,
First at my bleeding surety's hand,
And then again at mine.

If thou for me hast purchas'd faith
By thy obedience unto death,
He must the grace bestow:
Would Israel's God a price receive,
And not the purchas'd blessing give?
His justice answers, No!

Turn then, my soul, unto thy rest;
The merits of thy great High Priest,
Have bought thy liberty:
Trust to his efficacious blood,
Nor fear thy banishment from God,
Since Jesus dy'd for thee.

Hallelujah, what a Savior!

35
The Threefold State of Man

> Therefore as by the offence of one judgment came upon all men to condemnation; even so by the righteousness of one the free gift came upon all men unto justification of life. ¹⁹ For as by one man's disobedience many were made sinners, so by the obedience of one shall many be made righteous. (Romans 5:18-19)

"It isn't fair." "Why would a righteous and all-powerful God allow such a thing to happen?" These complaints surface often, at times even among professing Christians in the midst of intense trial or pain. They build on a presumption that God either caused or orchestrated the event for some mysterious "greater good" that no one ever seems able to define or identify.

This question of "gratuitous" evil as it is called in philosophical circles, evil that is so heinous that it has no rational or moral basis to exist, challenges all world views, not just historical Christianity. For example, it equally presents a nearly insurmountable dilemma to the proponents of godless evolution. If, as they allege, man has evolved into such a refined state, how do they explain the occasional acts of utter depravity that one human commits against another?

The focused question for us deals with the existence of God and such acts of utter depravity. Did God either cause or orchestrate the event for a mysterious "greater good"? Unacceptable answers to the dilemma include the following:

1. *God caused, orchestrated, decreed, or "allowed" it for a greater good not known to us.* Occasionally theologians will banter these terms, as well as others, in a futile attempt to avoid the obvious problem with this view; ultimately God is in fact responsible for the event either directly or indirectly. The Old Testament prophet Jeremiah encountered what was apparently an overt claim that God caused the depraved idolatry and other sins of his day, but he categorically rejected and refused it. He certainly didn't acquiesce to it. Earlier in Romans (third chapter first ten verses) Paul also confronted this idea and equally rejected it in

quite direct language. In Paul's reasoning a claim that God causes or otherwise relies on our sins to accomplish His glory makes God the ultimate cause of the atrocity and removes Him from the moral high ground from which Scripture consistently presents Him as the final Judge of the universe. In other words, if God causes sin either directly or indirectly He cannot then judge guilty humans for their sins. He becomes a sinner Himself by His involvement in the sins that He is supposed to judge. If He is thus involved in the guilt of human sin, He cannot righteously judge anyone else for their sins. Here Paul rejects all forms of error that in any manner whatever implicate God in the sins of humanity.

2. *God operates according to the views of common deists.* He created the universe, set it in motion, and effectively became an absentee landlord, having nothing whatever to do with anything or anyone in the universe. This view is foreign to Scripture and thus cannot claim Biblical grounds for its support. Throughout the Bible we see one record after another that contradicts the deist's claims of divine non-involvement. From the flood to the Law on Mt. Sinai to Jonah and the city of Ninevah to the greatest of all contradictions of deism, the Incarnation, God demonstrates His involvement in the affairs of humanity. For our discussion the question relates to the manner and degree of divine involvement. A cursory reading of Thomas Jefferson's Bible reveals the deist's strategy; deny all miracles that illustrate God's involvement with mankind.

Those who embrace the first premise—that God in some way is directly or indirectly and ultimately causatively involved in every event of human conduct—occasionally hurl the straw man objection to their objectors that any view other than their own is functionally deism. They attempt to play the "horns of the dilemma" false logical argument against their objectors, denying altogether that any alternative view exists. In their errant view God either must cause everything that occurs, or He must cause nothing. Further, advocates of this errant view commonly build their false ideas on another logical fallacy, the "parts to the whole" fallacy. This error confuses one part of the whole of any logical entity to its whole. If my Toyota Camry is brown, this error presumes that all Toyota Camrys are brown. If God caused one birth defect (Gospel of John ninth chapter), He must cause every birth defect. Aside from building on multiple logical errors, this error also violates the basic character of God. It builds on eastern New Age, Star Wars pagan error; the "force," deity, consists equally of two wholly contradictory personalities, the good side and the "dark side." Thus in this view of God, Satan is merely God's "dark side," a view of God that is abominable to the consistent and plain teachings of Scripture.

In his opening thoughts James clearly rejects the capricious attitude of sinful humanity to blame God for either sin or the enticement to sin. "*Let no man say when he is tempted, I am tempted of God: for God cannot be tempted with evil, neither tempteth he any man: But every man is tempted, when he is drawn away of his own lust, and enticed. Then when lust hath conceived, it bringeth forth sin: and sin, when it is finished, bringeth forth death. Do not err, my beloved brethren. Every good gift and every perfect gift is from above, and cometh down from the Father of lights, with whom is no variableness, neither shadow of turning.*" (James 1:13-17) Fausset and a number of other respected theologians make an emphatic point from this passage that man cannot blame God *either directly or indirectly* for his sin.

Our study passage, along with a rather large number of other Scriptures, consistently attributes sin, either in its origin or in its routine practice to man, not to God. In Ecclesiastes 7:29 Solomon equally rejects this errant view, "Lo, this only have I found, that God hath made man upright; but *they have sought out* many inventions."

The Biblical view of God and His involvement with man is relatively straightforward and logical compared with the errant views that compromise His moral character and His deservedly righteous basis for judging all sins at the last day. God created man in a moral universe, a universe to be governed and judged by His moral law, but man violated his charge and brought divine judgment upon himself, his offspring, and all of the natural creation.

Both Solomon in the Old Testament and Paul in the New Testament clearly lay the responsibility for all kinds of evil at the feet of mankind, not at the feet of God. *Man, not God, is responsible for the existence of gratuitous evil, as well as all other forms of sin.* For all such acts of sin God shall judge and punish sinful humanity at the last Judgment. Could God have intervened and prevented any particular act of sin?

Of course He could have done so. But if divine intervention prevented every act of sin, there would be nothing for which God could or would judge mankind.

Further this view transforms the universe into a robotic universe wholly orchestrated by God, altogether eliminating any sense of moral responsibility or accountability on man's part. In the heat of trial and pain from sin, committed by ourselves or by others against us, we might think such a world would be an improvement.

Whatever variety of similarities we may rightly attribute to man created in God's image, moral consciousness and accountability for his conduct are clearly established in Scripture. The very fact of a final Day of divine Judgment affirms that God holds man accountable for his sins, something that God could not do according to Paul in Romans 3:1-10 if He is in any way responsible for man's sins.

36
Grace Reigns!

> Moreover the law entered, that the offence might abound. But where sin abounded, grace did much more abound: That as sin hath reigned unto death, even so might grace reign through righteousness unto eternal life by Jesus Christ our Lord. (Romans 5:20-21)

At least for most Bible readers, the fifth chapter of Romans is not the easiest chapter in the Bible to read and to understand. However, the two closing verses are delightfully clear and understandable. While I find many passages in the Bible that challenge and far exceed my ability to understand, I am often gratified to discover a pattern in Scripture that appears in this chapter. After a difficult passage, the inspired writers often punctuate the passage with a summary statement that is simply stated and thus easy to understand. I believe that is the case with this lesson. The two verses before us merely restate the content of the chapter in simple and comforting terms.

Often in contemporary pulpits people are told that God has many ways of saving people. Often those in teaching leadership will defend this statement by alleging that God saved people before the cross by their keeping the Law of Moses. According to Paul in Galatians (2:21 and 3:21 as just two concise statements that specifically refute such a claim), no one was ever saved by keeping the law. In fact in the two referenced verses Paul affirms that salvation by keeping the Law was—and is—impossible!

What did the Law of Moses accomplish? What was its divine purpose? Based on Paul's writings as well as other Scripture, God never designed the Law to give spiritual or eternal life. Here Paul affirms that a primary objective of the Law was to manifest sin in humanity. I believe that Scripture teaches that even fallen humanity retains some sense of right and wrong. However, without God's Law revealed and given to humanity, man would reveal his pride and deny his sinfulness altogether. Thus Paul affirms, *Moreover the law entered, that the offence might abound.* He affirmed in Romans 3:20 that *by the law is the knowledge of sin.*

In other passages in the Galatian letter Paul affirmed that the Law of Moses served as a "school master," an instructor to teach young children and grow them to maturity. I believe Paul in this analogy taught that Moses' Law pointed God's Old Testament people to a sinless Messiah. In terms of the priestly tenets of Moses' Law it also pointed the Old Testament people of God to the coming eternal priest who would eliminate those multiple animal sacrifices by accomplishing in a single sacrifice what all of the sacrifices under the Law failed to accomplish.

Paul reminds us of the Law's presence and function, but our study passage directs us to God's true remedy for sin. Bible respecting Christians have the information available to them, if they would use it, to know that God provided a remedy for sin in the Lord Jesus Christ, not in Moses' Law or in any other institution given to humanity. *But where sin abounded, grace did much more abound...."*

Occasionally those who hold to universal salvation, the belief that eventually all of humanity shall be saved, will appeal to this passage as supposedly supporting their doctrine. In the greater context of Romans fifth chapter they wrest the passage out of its setting and pour an errant meaning into it that cannot be supported by Scripture.

In these verses Paul specifically affirms that the reign of grace will only culminate in victory, in *...eternal life by Jesus Christ our Lord.* We may then ask a logical question. What kind of death does Paul have in mind in this chapter? In Verse twenty one Paul sets "eternal life" that is caused by God's grace through Jesus Christ in contrast with death that inevitably follows the reign of sin. Logically it follows that if he is dealing with spiritual and eternal life, he is also dealing with spiritual and eternal death. Someone might ask, "But doesn't sin cause physical death?" Of course it does, and Paul specifically deals with that aspect of sin in First Corinthians fifteenth chapter. Here he seems to be dealing with the spiritual, eternal implications of sin, although in Romans 5:14 he does address physical death. Clearly the two consequences of sin are linked; it produces both physical and spiritual death.

When Paul deals specifically with our salvation by God's grace alone in the second chapter of Ephesians, he uses the analogy of spiritual death as the beginning point, *And you hath he quickened, who were dead in trespasses and sins....* (Ephesians 2:1)

To what extent does the grace of God in Jesus go? Does His saving grace apply to all humanity? Does it apply only provisionally, leaving the final salvation decision up to the individual person? Or does it apply efficiently and effectually only to the elect? Considering Paul's extensive discussion of federal headship in this chapter, I believe that Paul is affirming the following:

1. *Grace reigns victoriously.* God's grace doesn't merely leave salvation open and possible to humanity. Grace doesn't propose to reign with the permission of fallen humanity. Grace reigns! And its reign is not defeated by human decisions or actions. Its reign only ends in success, *eternal life by Jesus Christ our Lord.*
2. *Grace reigns decisively.* Its culmination shall surely end only with eternal life.
3. *Grace reigns by God's power, not by man's.* Grace's reign is not by man's decision or will, but by Jesus Christ our Lord.
4. *Grace reigns exclusively.* Paul does not place human decisions or good works on the throne with grace. Grace sits on the throne alone.
5. *Grace reigns apart from human agency.* Paul does not tell us that we must coronate grace. Grace reigns apart from human assistance.

Below is a quote from the pen of the respected Puritan preacher/author John Owen, taken from his book entitled *The Death of Death in the Death of Christ* (Book One. This quote appears at the end of the third chapter.).

To which I may add this dilemma to our Universalists:--God imposed his wrath due unto, and Christ underwent the pains of hell for, either all the sins of all men, or all the sins of some men, or some sins of all men. If the last, some sins of all men, then have all men some sins to answer for, and so shall no man be saved; for if God enter into judgment with us, though it were with all mankind for one sin, no flesh should be justified in his sight: "If the LORD should mark iniquities, who should stand?" Ps.130:3. We might all go to cast all that we have "to the moles and to the bats, to go into the clefts of the rocks, and into the tops of the ragged rocks, for fear of the LORD, and for the glory of his majesty," Isa. 2:20, 21. If the second, that is it which we affirm, that Christ in their stead and room suffered for all the sins of all the elect in the world. If the first, why, then, are not all freed from the punishment of all their sins? You will say, "Because of their unbelief, they will not believe." But this unbelief, is it a sin or not? If not, why should they be punished for it? If it be, then Christ underwent the punishment due to it, or not. If so, then why must that hinder them more than their other sins for which he died from partaking of the fruit of his death? If he did not, then did he not die for all their sins. Let them choose which part they will.

Owen's logic is compelling, not to mention based on solid Biblical footing.

1. If Jesus died for all the sins of all humanity, we cannot logically deny universalism. There is no sin remaining to justify the sentence of eternal separation against anyone.
2. If Jesus died for some of the sins of all humanity, we remain in our sins, despite all that Jesus did. This view denies every passage in the Bible that affirms Jesus' substitutionary sacrifice on behalf of the elect.
3. If Jesus died for all the sins of the elect, nothing can separate the elect from the love of God and the joys of heaven.

It has not been an easy task to follow through the maze of man's tangled web of sin, but Paul has held our hand and given us the clear message that sin cannot destroy one of God's chosen vessels of mercy.

While dealing with this comforting truth, Paul has also confronted the blasphemous error of those who accused him of teaching that we are to sin all the more so as to bring more grace. He denies that heresy and affirms that God's grace does not shine in man's sin but in God's saving purpose. We celebrate our salvation, not based on the degree of our sins, but on the amazing degree of God's merciful grace. Having affirmed our secure position in Christ, Paul will now take us through the ethics of grace in succeeding chapters.

37
The Ethics of Grace

What shall we say then? Shall we continue in sin, that grace may abound? God forbid. How shall we, that are dead to sin, live any longer therein? (Romans 6:1-2)

Paul's critics (first eight verses of the third chapter of Romans) accused him of teaching, "Let us do evil, that good may come," a charge that he categorically rejected. If Paul had in any way believed this false charge, he would not have asked this question in the first place. In the second place he would not have answered it as he did in our study verses.

At its heart the errant belief of Paul's critics so intertwined the doctrines of justification and sanctification as to make one's justification depend on his sanctification. In this point I use the term "justification" to refer to our eternal justification by the grace of God through the agency of Jesus' sacrificial offering of Himself for us. I use "sanctification" to refer to the godly life of a believer who orders his/her life according to the will of God as revealed in Scripture.[1] Much teaching in our time confuses these aspects of justification and sanctification, errantly concluding that at least in principle many professing Christians in our time have far more in common with Paul's critics than with Paul!

A similar clash of beliefs between Paul and his critics will surface in the ninth chapter of Romans where Paul's critics again impute sinful

---

[1] It should be noted that both terms appear in various specific contexts of Scripture with various uses other than those I list above. For example, Paul's discussion of faith in the fourth chapter of Romans is not dealing with our eternal justification, but with the way we live our life according to the rule of faith. While Paul uses sanctification in First Thessalonians 4:1-7 to refer to our godly walk, we find a distinct use of the word in reference to our eternal standing in God's will in Hebrews 10:10. However, the clear teaching of Scripture affirms that our eternal justification by divine grace through Jesus' sacrificial offering of Himself to the Father accomplishes our eternal sanctification before God. Our justification by faith and our sanctification in time is contingent on our choosing to walk by faith in obedience to God's teaching in Scripture. When theologians confuse these two aspects of both justification and sanctification, they will eventually and inevitably end up believing much as Paul's critics appear to have believed as set forth in the third chapter of Romans, not as Paul believed and wrote by the inspiration of the Holy Spirit for our instruction and godliness.

consequences both to God and to Paul's teaching—in that chapter on divine election.

Paul's inspired teaching always balances the doctrine of saving grace with godliness. The grace of God that saves is also the grace of God that teaches a regenerate elect the difference between sin and righteousness and convicts a regenerate person to turn from sin and to live according to righteousness (Titus 2:11-14). Inspired Scripture does not know the idea of a person who has experienced the grace of God in the new birth not also having a quickened conscience that is sensitive to God and to God's righteous will. Many years ago a young woman who had grown up in a Christian home and had attended church with her parents departed from her teaching and conscience in a rather significant manner. Later when conviction became so heavy on her as to drive her to repentance, she protested, "When I was going to church, no one ever told me that x (the sin she had practiced) was wrong." I responded, "Didn't your conscience tell you clearly that it was wrong?" She didn't even pause to respond, "Yes, it did." A major characteristic of sinful habits imitates Adam's response to his sin in the Garden of Eden. When caught in the sin, try to blame someone else, even if you have to try to blame God. Do anything other than accept personal responsibility for your sin, an act that requires confession and repentance.

We may not always be able to observe a person's conviction or repentance. Nor may we always be able to observe their beliefs. Sadly, far too many professing Christians in our time think if they don't personally see evidences of a person's beliefs and/or repentance and faith, the person is not really born again. God does not reveal in Scripture that we will always witness the spiritual state of another person, but He does reveal in Scripture that His grace makes a moral change in every one whom He touches with divine and saving grace.

If the same grace of God that saves us also teaches us to depart from sin and to honor God with our lives, we may readily conclude that Paul's critics were wrong, joining Paul in his view of both justification and sanctification. God sovereignly accomplishes our eternal justification by grace alone through the agency of the sacrificial offering of our Lord Jesus Christ. In the new birth He applies the benefits of that justification to the individual, a work that alters the moral compass and the spiritual awareness of the regenerate elect.

Now the resident grace of God in the individual begins to teach and to lead that person. This is the manner of grace's operation as set forth in Scripture. We may rely safely and securely on this fact, not based on a legalistic scrutiny of each individual whom we meet, but rather based on the fact of the matter as revealed in Scripture. "…The Lord knoweth them that are his." (2 Timothy 2:19)

> Paul did not say that **we** always know them that are His.

In that same verse Paul added the point that he affirms in our study verses, "And let every one that nameth the name of Christ depart from iniquity."

The slippery slope of self-righteous judgmental scrutiny (justifying self and finding fault with others) inevitably leads a person to a legalistic view of salvation, not to mention a prideful attitude that narrows the scope of God's saving grace to the limits of human observation. If I must see convincing evidence of a person's saved state for that person to be really saved, then I must constrict the scope of God's saving grace to my field of vision. This idea flies in the face of Scripture. When Jesus taught Nicodemus regarding the new birth (first ten verses of the third chapter of John's gospel), he concluded his teaching with these words,

> *The wind bloweth where it listeth, and thou hearest the sound thereof, but canst not tell whence it cometh, and whither it goeth: so is every one that is born of the Spirit.* (John 3:8)

While one aspect of the work of the Holy Spirit[2] is perceptible by us—thou hearest the sound thereof—Jesus clearly tells us that we cannot tell where He came from or where He will go next.

---

[2] In the New Testament the word translated into our English for "wind" and "spirit" is the same word. Jesus' use of the analogy of "wind" is not a casual choice. He is saying that the Holy Spirit, working in accomplishing our new birth, blows—or works—where He pleases. He takes the new birth to whom He chooses, not to those who choose it. It is God's will, not man's that is operative in regeneration, a point that Paul will make emphatically in the ninth chapter of Romans as he teaches on divine and personal election.

How does the "ethic of grace" manifest itself in the life of a regenerate elect? We may not be able to discern the work, but Scripture assures us of the effect nonetheless. Often in building a case for the positive aspects of his teaching Paul will first deal with the negative, as he does in this instance. The whole of the sixth chapter of Romans develops the ethics of grace, but in our study verses that introduce us to this feature Paul first tells us what grace doesn't teach.

Shall we continue in sin that grace may abound? Since divine grace always conquers sin in His elect, shall we sin all the more so as to give grace more reason to shine? This idea precisely mirrors what Paul's critics accused him of teaching. As in the third chapter of Romans, again here Paul categorically rejects this blasphemous idea that surgically separates saving grace from its impact on the conscience.

God forbid. How shall we, that are dead to sin, live any longer therein? If divine grace has killed us to the eternal damning effects of sin, we can claim no reasonable basis on which to continue living in it now.

Martin Lloyd-Jones (introduction to his commentary on Romans) makes the case that Romans chapters six and seven form a topical parenthesis to the Roman letter, a parenthesis in which Paul specifically responds to the critics' accusation in the third chapter. While I respect his teaching and insights, I rather believe the whole Roman letter deals with these critics and their insidious impact on the Roman Church. The whole Roman letter is written in a dialectical form of reasoning in which Paul interacts throughout the letter with the error that surfaced in the third chapter, along with other errors that likely grew out of this problem. Thus I believe that the sixth chapter of Romans naturally and logically flows from Paul's reasoning in the fifth chapter. Saving grace is not "cheap grace," nor is it "immoral grace." It is ethical grace! It not only saves, but it also teaches the individual the "ethics of grace."

38
Baptism or Baptism? Biblical Ecclesiology

> Know ye not, that so many of us as were baptized into Jesus Christ were baptized into his death? Therefore we are buried with him by baptism into death: that like as Christ was raised up from the dead by the glory of the Father, even so we also should walk in newness of life. For if we have been planted together in the likeness of his death, we shall be also in the likeness of his resurrection: Knowing this, that our old man is crucified with him, that the body of sin might be destroyed, that henceforth we should not serve sin. For he that is dead is freed from sin. Now if we be dead with Christ, we believe that we shall also live with him: Knowing that Christ being raised from the dead dieth no more; death hath no more dominion over him. For in that he died, he died unto sin once: but in that he liveth, he liveth unto God. (Romans 6:3-10)

Bible commentaries and Bible students alike engage in lively dialogue about this passage. Does it refer to water baptism, or does it refer to the antecedent immersion (by the direct and immediate work of the Holy Spirit) of the child of God into the covenant benefits of Jesus' sacrificial atonement of which water baptism serves as an "external sign of the internal blessing"? Valid and sound points can be made for both views. Likewise both views can be loaded with unsound and unbiblical ideas, so we need to give the passage careful attention.

Regardless the view we embrace of the question, we should affirm that every believer in Christ who sincerely desires to serve and honor God should consider water baptism an important duty to be performed. Every person who submits to baptism should likewise engage his/her life with the implications of that baptism prominent in their choices and actions.

One of the most neglected New Testament doctrines among contemporary Christians and churches in our culture is the doctrine of "ecclesiology," the doctrine of the church. The word "church" appears twice in the gospels (Matthew 16:18 where Jesus indicates that He will build His church on the "rock," and Matthew 18:17 where believers who have disagreements with each other are directed to first attempt to work out their personal problems privately, but if that effort fails they are to appeal to the church for mediation). It is likely that the whole of the New Testament was either written to individuals or to local churches or groups of local churches. The word appears with increasing regularity in the New Testament letters that follow the gospels.

Contemporary Christians have all but lost the New Testament concept of the church. The New Testament uses this word in only two ways; 1) first and most commonly in reference to an individual local assembly and 2) secondly and rarely in reference to the whole of the redeemed family of God assembled in heaven at or after the last day. Never—not even once—does the New Testament refer to "the church" in the singular with reference to the collected body of all churches and denominations of Christians. The sadly common practice among contemporary Christians when faced with Matthew 18 interpersonal issues is not to follow this passage, but rather to "church-hop" and to find a different denominational church where they can ignore this passage and start over with a new group of believers. Typically since these people refuse to confront their personal failure to follow Scripture, they frequently discover the same kind of problems in their new church that they faced in their old church. Is it any wonder since the real problem is their personal pride and their refusal to follow the clear teaching of Jesus in Matthew eighteenth chapter?

On occasion in our world of increasingly diluted Christianity whole churches or whole denominations will veer off the course of their historical faith, leaving those who believed in their church's historical faith and practice with little option but to leave that church for a local body of believers whose beliefs and practices are more historical than the church that lost its way.

Until recent history and the entrance of "churches" that pride themselves more in being "seeker-sensitive" than in being Biblical, the generally accepted view of water baptism was that it served as the initial rite of a person's attachment—membership—in a local church assembly. Baptism is never presented in Scripture as a private or generic rite that gives one global affiliation with any and all local churches; in the New Testament it served to identify the individual with a specific local body of believers, a body of believers to whom this person lived in fellowship and to whom this person was held accountable and responsible for their Christian conduct. As just two specific examples, in the fifth chapter of First Corinthians Paul raised the question of immoral conduct in a man who had a public affair with his step-mother, a sin for which Paul directed the church to "…put away from among yourselves that wicked person." (1 Corinthians 5:13) The second example appears in First Corinthians 12:28.

And God hath set some in the church, first apostles, secondarily prophets, thirdly teachers, after that miracles, then gifts of healings, helps, governments, diversities of tongues.

Here Paul identified that every spiritual gift is "set…in the church," even the apostles. No man who occupies the ministry has any Biblical authority to view himself as aloof from the church of his membership, including specific accountability and responsibility to the church of his membership. Paul tells us in this verse that even the apostles were "set…in the church," not above it. Paul's affiliation with the Church in Antioch clearly affirms that he viewed the church of his membership in this way. Although he engaged some folks from the Jerusalem Church in a rather heated theological debate at Antioch, rather than claiming aloof apostolic authority, he and the church at Antioch took the matter of this conduct directly to the church in Jerusalem where that church corrected the matter and sent an official letter of record to the church in Antioch, even requesting that it be communicated to other churches where her members had possibly contributed to similar confusion by their false teaching and errant conduct.

A certificate of ordination is not like a degree from a college that you frame and hang on the wall as a personal accomplishment. It is a "conditional" affirmation of the man's role, valid and legitimate only so long as the man remains in faithful fellowship with the church of his membership and remains faithful to the doctrine and practice of his home church. Every Primitive Baptist certificate of ordination that I have examined through my fifty years plus includes a conditional statement indicating that if the man named in the certificate departs from the principles of faith and practice of his home church, the certificate becomes invalid. Although most churches do not issue certificates of ordination to deacons, the same principle should apply to them as well. A man should be honored for his office only so long as he remains faithful to his vows of fidelity to the presbytery that ordained him and to the church of his membership. Thus a preacher who departs from the doctrine of his home church should be removed from his office by his home church. Likewise a man who fails to maintain a clear and regular accountability to his home church should be removed from office. If Paul as a called and inspired apostle viewed himself as being "set...in the church," no man in either office in our time has any Biblical basis on which to claim exemption from that same accountability. Perhaps at some future time we will examine the doctrine of ecclesiology in more depth, but these principles seem clearly set forth in the New Testament.

Many years ago a man who claimed to be a preacher, but who interestingly never convinced a church of his calling, made this statement to me, "My ordination came from God, not from a church." Unfortunately this man had no Biblical claim whatever to being a New Testament minister of the gospel. If Paul affirmed that even he as an apostle was "set...in the church," and neither he nor any other inspired New Testament writer even once used the word "church" to refer to the whole of the Christian culture or to all collective New Testament churches in his time, no one in our time has any Biblical basis for such a prideful claim.

The same principle should apply to an individual member of a church who consciously avoids regular attendance and accountability to the church of his/her membership. To the extent a person fails to maintain public attendance and submission to the church of his/her membership, he/she should be denied the privileges of membership. Never in the New Testament does the idea of church membership or the use of the word "church" convey the idea of a global identity in which one is mystically a member of any and every church they choose to attend. We see this errant concept in a number of contemporary churches who consider you to be a "member" of their church simply by your presence in their auditorium on a given Sunday. This modern and errant concept gives rise to the unbiblical idea of church as little more than a "club" or a "voluntary service organization." It wholly violates the New Testament description of one of the Lord's local churches.

Given the full context of the sixth chapter of Romans, should we view baptism as set forth in this lesson to be the rite of water baptism or the antecedent work of the Holy Spirit, immersing every elect person into a personal and eternal relationship with God in the covenant of grace?

Baptism or Baptism?

The New Testament uses the word "baptize" in several distinct ways. Most often the word refers to a person's immersion into water, "baptism" as we commonly refer to it in the church ordinance. Once the word refers to the "immersion" of Old Testament Israel to Moses (1 Corinthians 10:2). On occasion New Testament writers use the word of a more personal and immediate act of God, as in First Corinthians 12:13, in which the person being baptized is wholly passive in the act. In the Book of Acts the word occasionally refers to the extraordinary outpouring of the Holy Spirit on people as at the Day of Pentecost (second chapter of Acts).

In the case of our study passage I have heard and read explanations of the word that interpret it as either water baptism or as the immediate work of the Holy Spirit immersing a person into a permanent and eternal identity with Christ and the blessings of His redeeming work. Both explanations have merit and both as typically explained express a Biblical truth. However, it is my settled belief that the work here described by Paul refers to the work of the Holy Spirit rather than to water baptism. I will provide some of the reasons for this belief in this chapter.

First the words in our English Bible (KJV) are presented in the state of being verb form ("are baptized"). In the underlying Greek syntax the verb is passive, not active. In the passages that refer to water baptism active voice verbs are rather consistently used, "…be baptized."

Secondly, Paul draws a "like as" corollary between this baptism and the resurrection of Jesus that is too emphatic and certain to refer to water baptism. In water baptism the person baptized is commanded to repent before baptism (not that it should not equally punctuate their lives after water baptism) and to live as active "apprentices," students and followers of the Lord Jesus Christ after baptism. However, Scripture as well as personal observation affirms that many who profess faith in Christ and submit to water baptism fail to follow through with active and consistent discipleship after their baptism. Paul's "like as...even so" comparison of the baptism of which he writes here with Jesus' resurrection seems to express more than a loose analogy. The word translated *likeness* in these verses is defined as follows:

> ...that which has been made after the likeness of something. 1A a figure, image, likeness, representation. 1B likeness i.e. resemblance, **such as amounts almost to equality or identity.**[1] (my bold for emphasis)

Further Paul argues that as we have been planted in the *likeness* of Jesus' death we *shall be* in resurrection. This verb identifies future tense, something that has not yet occurred but is certain to occur. If Paul were writing of water baptism, it seems that he would have spoken of a state of conduct that the Romans had already realized. It also seems that, if Paul intended water baptism here, he would have used a word that refers to duty or obligation, not to a certain future state. Notice in this fifth verse that the words *in the likeness of his* are italicized, meaning that the King James translators added the words. Effectively without these added words we read that our being *planted together with* Christ shall surely result in our being *like Him in resurrection*. As he was raised from the dead on the third day, we shall also be raised from the dead at the Second Coming (clear indication of a future, literal, bodily resurrection). The security of our resurrection depends, not on our personal merit, but on His immersing us into the benefits of Jesus death.

Paul further identifies other changes that God accomplished in this divine act of immersing His elect into a permanent identity with Jesus.

1. Our *old man is crucified with him*. Again, he asserts this result as a certain fact, not as an ethical obligation. He doesn't say that

---

[1] James Strong, *The Exhaustive Concordance of the Bible : Showing Every Word of the Test of the Common English Version of the Canonical Books, and Every Occurence of Each Word in Regular Order.*, electronic ed. (Ontario: Woodside Bible Fellowship., 1996), G3667.

our old man should be crucified with Him, but that it in fact is crucified with Him.

2. This crucifixion of our *old man* results in the destruction of *the body of sin* in such a way that from this point forward we *should not serve sin*. Regeneration which puts us wholly into the merits of Jesus' life and death makes us children of God and frees us from sin so that we should now serve God, not sin. Paul will expand this thought extensively in the verses following this passage. Here Paul develops the ethical implications of the new birth.

3. *...he that is dead is freed from sin*. Dead people do not continue sinning! Paul is not here suggesting sinless perfection in this life, but rather he is developing the profound implications of Jesus' immersion of His elect into identity with Him. He develops this point further in the next three verses. Our immersion into the benefits of Jesus' death frees us from the legal consequences of our sins.

4. (Verse 8) Those who are so identified with Jesus in His death *shall also live with him*. Here Paul again develops essential results, not duty. He expresses the outcome of our immersion into and with Christ in terms of certain future results. *...we shall also live with him*.

The certain consequences of our being "baptized" into Jesus' death leave no possibility for any other outcome, a point that could not be made in teaching relative to water baptism. It is altogether possible that a person whom God has not saved might for carnal reasons seek and receive water baptism. For example, when I was a child growing up in north Mississippi, every time local elections came around the local citizens who wanted to run for political office would start campaigning for the people to vote for them. On more than one occasion I recall a political candidate attending church and at the close of the service making a brief announcement of his candidacy and asking for the people's vote. Many of these men never darkened any church door for the next four years! It is possible that a man of this character might decide that being a member of a local church would be "good politics" for his ambition to political office, so he would join a church and be baptized, though he would never change his lifestyle to reflect New Testament Christianity. It is sadly the case that on occasion people sincerely join a church and are baptized in water, but subsequently allow the pressures and clutter of life to choke out their spiritual vision so that they do not manifest and live out New Testament Christianity as they should. Do any of us do so fully? However, in this passage Paul consistently presents a certain result from the baptism of which he writes. *...shall be* refers to more than one's ethical obligation.

In subsequent verses Paul will use this permanent relationship with Christ as the foundation on which to build his exhortation to the Romans to yield themselves to God as servants of God. Notice in these following verses that Paul uses words of obligation or exhortation, not words of certainty; "*Let* not sin…" "…yield…" "ye have obeyed…" (active voice, not passive voice) "…ye became…" The ethical obligations of the second half of the chapter rest on the theological foundation of the first half of the chapter.

Sadly a large segment of professing Christians fails to understand this logical relationship between their theological perspective and their conduct. They view their conduct as in some way contributing to their eternal security. Some literally believe that the more good works they perform in this life the more rewards they will have in heaven; consider the hymn with that theme, "Will There be any Stars in my Crown?" The idea of living a godly and consistent Christian life with no other motive than to obey and to glorify God is beyond their grasp. Thus a life that, according to Scripture, should be characterized by self-denial is in fact based on self-aggrandizement and self-gain. All of Scripture categorically rejects such a self-serving motive and attitude.

Excessive topical study of the Bible leads far too many sincere professing Christians to surgically dissect theology from Christian living. In their mind passage "A" deals with our salvation in Christ while passage "B" deals with our discipleship. However, they seldom make any attempt to integrate the two so as to understand the relationship between the two passages. The Biblical model integrates the fact of our salvation with our obligation to serve God. We do not live the Christian life from the motive of stars in our crown or for other potential self-gain. We live it with one single objective in mind, to glorify God. A clear example of this truth appears in First

Corinthians 6:20, "For ye are bought with a price: therefore glorify God in your body, and in your spirit, which are God's."

It is altogether possible—if not likely—that the error that Paul confronted (back to the first eight verses of the third chapter of Romans) was quite similar to the error that he and Barnabas confronted in Antioch (Acts fifteenth chapter). This error, not at all unlike the contemporary "stars in my crown" error, based discipleship on a motive of self gain; only by being circumcised and keeping the law could a person be "saved" in whatever sense advocates of this error viewed the idea of salvation. The idea of serving God for His glory alone escaped them.

Whether we engage in Christian conduct with the idea that we can thereby gain our salvation or with the idea that we can thereby gain assurance of our salvation (a common motive in contemporary Reformed theological circles), the motive of self-gain is never blessed in New Testament teaching. Never! Our obligation to serve God in Scripture always grows out of God's prior work of grace in us and for us, with the motive of glorifying Him, not gaining anything for self.

We have secure standing with Jesus in the eternal benefits of His atoning sacrifice. How well do our lives manifest profound gratitude to Him for His blessed work for us and in us?

39
A Christian Self-Image

Likewise reckon ye also yourselves to be dead indeed unto sin, but alive unto God through Jesus Christ our Lord. (Romans 6:11)

Many folks in our culture, including Christians, seem almost obsessed with self-image. On one side we are told that parents need to create any form of illusion or artificial environment possible to give their child a "positive self-image." The downside to failure is predicted to be lifetime scarring of the child. However, in typical knee-jerk fashion many folks, among them many Christians, embrace a mirror opposite attitude and seem to think the worse a person can imagine themselves to be the better. Not only balance, but Biblical truth finds itself firmly established between these two errant and unhealthy extremes. One extreme tends to turn a person into an incorrigible egotist while the other turns the person into a "depraved disciple," a true oxymoron.

I have long objected to the idea of evolution, not only on the basis of scientific evidence pro or con, but also on the basis of its impact on a person's thinking. Consider this wise observation from Solomon.

> *Eat thou not the bread of him that hath an evil eye, neither desire thou his dainty meats: For as he thinketh in his heart, so is he: Eat and drink, saith he to thee; but his heart is not with thee. The morsel which thou hast eaten shalt thou vomit up, and lose thy sweet words.* (Proverbs 23:6-8)

Solomon affirms that a person's way of thinking will weave its way into his/her conduct. If you think of yourself in a certain way, you will eventually act according to your dominant thought. If a person believes that he/she evolved from lower animals, eventually he/she will submit to the inclination to act like a lower animal!

Applying this observation from Solomon to our theme, a person who has only positive self-thoughts increasingly becomes convinced that he/she is invincible and never learns how to deal with frustrations and defeats that inevitably touch every life. Equally the person who views himself/herself as a "depraved disciple" will eventually manifest that attitude in actions.

Scripture is by no means deficient in terms of instructing us regarding how we should view ourselves as children of God. In our study verse Paul has just completed building the truth of our integral union with the Lord Jesus Christ in His Incarnation and in His substitutionary death for our sins. He arose from the grave, victorious over sin and death—"death hath no more dominion over him" (Romans 6:9). He is now alive to God and free from the sentence of sin against His elect, the reason for His Incarnation. Thus when Paul introduces the thought of our study verse with "Likewise..." he is directing us to look at our Lord's present relationship to sin and to embrace that attitude—that incredible victory—into our own mindset as "a child of the King."

Scripture uses such terms as "children" (both minor children and adult children), "little children," "friends," and "new creatures" to name only a few descriptions of those to whom God has given His eternal life.

This Biblical view rejects the egotistical and man-centric view of "positive self-image" in that it builds the case for our view of self on our relationship with the Lord Jesus Christ, not on any inherent merit in us.

This Biblical view equally rejects the "depraved disciple" mindset that can at times become so focused on a person's lack of merit that it engages in a context of worthlessness! Advocates of this view will appeal to passages, particularly in the New Testament and Paul's writings that refer to believers in Christ, even Paul and other apostles, as being the Lord's "servants," a word that in New Testament times was a near equivalent to the word "slave." However, this word as used in the New Testament seems more related to our attitude toward God in terms of our loyalty or obedience than to our vital standing with God. For example, notice the balance that Paul applies to the term in the following passage, along with his specific application of the word to a man's calling and service, not to his essential relationship with God.

> *Let every man abide in the same calling wherein he was called. Art thou called being a servant? care not for it: but if thou mayest be made free, use it*

rather. For he that is called in the Lord, being a servant, is the Lord's freeman: likewise also he that is called, being free, is Christ's servant. Ye are bought with a price; be not ye the servants of men. Brethren, let every man, wherein he is called, therein abide with God. (1 Corinthians 7:20-24)

According to Paul in this lesson, the term "servant" should be applied to our calling and our service to God. Simply stated, Paul rejects the dominant self-serving notion in our contemporary Christian culture that every Christian has a divine "right" to do anything he/she pleases so long as he/she does it sincerely. Any professing Christian who attempts to follow this idolatrous path should carefully consider that the Old Testament Book of Judges closes with an insightful commentary that summarizes the dreadful record of the whole book in one verse.

In those days there was no king in Israel: every man did that which was right in his own eyes. (Judges 21:25)

If we want to "do our own thing" and claim to be Christians, we need to understand that our self-serving, self-defined, and self-centered version of "Christianity" will produce precisely the same abominable results that we read repeatedly in the Book of Judges.

Biblical Christianity is not about every person doing what he/she wants to do, but about our coming to terms with the fact that, in terms of our role as disciples of Jesus, we are servants, not lords!

Paul insightfully reminds us in First Corinthians 7:20-24 that our only true freedom comes when we view ourselves and our service to God in the role of a servant, not a master. Only to the extent to which we regard ourselves as our Lord's apprentices and servants do we find the true freedom of Biblical Christianity.

Neither this passage nor any other passage where the term "servant" is used to describe a faithful disciple—justifies the attitude in us that we are nothing more than incarcerated criminals in a benevolent jail!

A simple question; is it correct either factually or theologically (There is no difference.) for us to regard ourselves or any regenerate elect person to be "totally depraved" after God's incredible work of regeneration? Given the many passages that clearly affirm and even describe the profound change that regeneration makes in the individual, it is both factually errant and bad theology for us to regard any regenerate elect as "totally depraved." The regenerate elect who believes himself/herself to be yet totally depraved is quite likely in the end to embrace conduct that honors depravity more than God; *"...as he thinketh in his heart...."*

Any concept of the new birth that fails to give proper regard to the specific impact of divine grace on the individual's personal character builds on errant theology and false interpretations of Biblical truth. A number of errant views deny the divine impact of saving grace on the individual.

The fundamental error of these ideas lies in their failure to regard the integration of God's work in regeneration—its impact on the individual. Both errors must build their basis on the idea that a regenerate elect consists of two separate and wholly segregated individuals living in one body. Contrary to this notion, Scripture affirms that in regeneration God puts "...my law **in** their inward parts, and write it **in** their hearts...." (Jeremiah 31:33 and context) God did not state that He would merely put His law in their bodies as an autonomous component, but He rather said that He would put His law "**in**" (I put this word in bold type in the quote for emphasis.) something already existent in them.

> **God does not write His law in our inward parts and in our hearts and leave us unchanged by that work.**

This passage confronts and refutes the notion that the Spirit of God dwells temporarily and without impact in a regenerate elect. Rather *at regeneration He dwells permanently in us,* and that permanent indwelling alters our conscience (specifically affirmed by Paul in Romans 2:15 and context, along with Romans 8:16). God's work of grace in His elect at regeneration doesn't merely add a second "man" to the existing person. It rather produces a "new creature" whose nature is effectively changed. The work of grace does not remove all appetite for sin, or all sinful activities from the regenerate elect, but it distinctly does far more than add an autonomous personality to the existing person. Paul affirms that the same grace of God that saves a person also teaches that person, a clear affirmation of the new covenant mentioned by Jeremiah in the above reference. (See also Titus 2:11-15; the same grace of God that saves also teaches us.).

So how does Paul instruct us to regard ourselves? Are we to view ourselves as useless and worthless worms or incarcerated criminals? If so where do we integrate the Biblical teaching on repentance and life-transformation into our lives? Are we to view ourselves as totally depraved hollow shells, only capable of doing good when God chooses to temporarily send the Holy Spirit to indwell us and orchestrate good deeds in us for a season? Or are we to regard ourselves as being dead to sin and alive to God through our Lord Jesus Christ? Our ability to so regard ourselves in this manner Paul specifically relates to the Lord Jesus Christ, not to our personal merit. However, Paul clearly intended for us to alter our life conduct based on this exhortation.

The word translated "reckon" was used in first century culture in reference to accounting or similar business activities. When I first studied accounting in my youth, it was not uncommon for old accountants to refer to their monthly task of posting and balancing their ledgers as "reckoning up the books." This word refers to a fact that we should consciously embrace and "post to the ledger" of our minds, a perpetual way of thinking that requires a permanent attitude both toward God and toward ourselves. An accountant who posts a fictitious entry to his ledger is guilty of fraud. An accountant who fails to post a relevant transaction to his ledger is guilty of unprofessional neglect. If our view of ourselves were to be measured by this word, would we find ourselves guilty either of fraud or of unprofessional neglect? May we embrace and "post to the ledger" of our minds and lives the profound and life-changing truth of Paul in this passage. It will change the way we live!

40
Christian Ethics

> Let not sin therefore reign in your mortal body, that ye should obey it in the lusts thereof. Neither yield ye your members as instruments of unrighteousness unto sin: but yield yourselves unto God, as those that are alive from the dead, and your members as instruments of righteousness unto God. For sin shall not have dominion over you: for ye are not under the law, but under grace. (Romans 6:12-14)

What are the moral or ethical implications of the doctrines of grace? If God has saved us all of His grace—and in no way contingent on what we think or do—are we then logically free to live in sin? This abominable idea seems to lie at the heart of Paul's critics who falsely charged him with believing "Let us do evil that good may come." (Romans 3:8) No doubt Paul is confronting that acrimonious charge in the sixth chapter of Romans. Instead of agreeing with the criticism—he rejected it as a slanderous misrepresentation of his teachings in that verse—Paul here affirms the true implications of grace in the life of one whom God has so saved, the only way anyone can be saved.

Rather than viewing himself and the Romans as being passive robots in the hands of a puppeteer deity, Paul urges the Romans to specific action. "Let not..." is not a passive phrase, but rather an imperative, a command. In the language of the New Testament the verb appears in the present tense. The action called for requires present immediate response from the Romans. It is in the active voice, meaning that Paul expects the Romans to do something, not merely sit by passively while God or outside forces orchestrate them to action. Finally the verb is in the imperative mood. Paul is commanding the Romans to do something. The analogy that he draws through the subsequent verses exemplifies the active role that he expects—commands—the Romans to pursue as a result of his teaching. He draws the dual analogies of soldier and servant. A soldier equips himself with armor and presents himself to his commanding officer, ready to follow commands and to actively engage the enemy on the field of battle. A servant doesn't ignore the instructions of his master, merely choosing to do as he pleases, when and how he pleases. He "submits" his will and energy to his master and applies all of his efforts and energy to the task assigned by the master.

Paul applies this dual analogy to the Romans in a focused and convicting manner. When a soldier "yields" his life and armor to his commanding officer, he pledges loyalty to that officer as the army engages the enemy in combat. First century warfare was not nearly so remote and impersonal as much of twenty first century warfare is. Essentially all the major activities of warfare involved some form of person to person, hand to hand combat. Thus Paul applies his teaching to the Romans to this "down-and-dirty" personal, in-the-trenches kind of strategy. In keeping with Paul's analogy, it would be as logical for a Christian to equivocate between righteousness and sin as for a first century soldier to change sides in the midst of a hand to hand battle with the enemy. The moment you submit to the authority of your commanding officer you commit to his army and pledge faithful service—life and limb—to him in battle. Can you imagine the utter chaos involved in a first century military campaign if the soldiers were constantly moving back and forth between sides, one moment fighting for one army and the next minute fighting for the opposing army? For Paul such chaos is the equivalent of a child of God one moment yielding his life and body to sin and the next moment submitting to righteousness.

The service of the faithful Christian is a voluntary and willing—joyfully willing—service, not a reluctant, compelled, or manipulated service. "Yield" repeatedly appears in this context in the form of a command, not merely a passive or involuntary act. Paul's critics seemingly failed to understand his teachings on the sovereignty of God in salvation. Based on Paul's interaction with them leading up to his rejection of their charge as slanderous in Romans the third chapter, it appears that they charged Paul with believing that he was a mere puppet in God's hands, merely doing what God programmed him to do. Paul's analogies in the sixth chapter of Romans follow his logical rejection of their charge in the third chapter.

From the first chapter of Genesis, Scripture consistently affirms that God's creation of humanity was wholly unique and distinct from His creation of all other forms matter or of life for that matter.

Inorganic matter was created under divinely instituted laws of physics and chemistry. It consistently responds to various environmental factors in ways wholly consistent with the natural laws that control and govern it. Based on the laws of gravity, if you release a coin from your hand, it will fall to the ground. Inorganic matter has no intelligence and no moral conscience.

God also made man—Adam and Eve initially—altogether different in quality and character from other forms of life. Neither plant life nor animal life possesses a moral conscience. What does Scripture intend by the various statements that God made mankind in his image and after his likeness? Some Christian scholars will appeal to the Trinity and affirm that God made humans in His likeness in that He made mankind with a tri-unity of essential constitution; body, soul, and spirit, while some equally respected Christian scholars reject this view, holding that mankind is essential dichotomous, consisting of two components, material and immaterial. Those who embrace the human constitution as something of a "trinity" often appeal to this similarity in man as the image and likeness of God.

Christian scholars offer various similarities between God and human composition as the basis for the Biblical idea that man is the uniquely and sole "life form" made in the divine image and likeness. As God rules over the universe, so He appointed mankind to rule over Planet Earth as His steward, a point that is reasonably supported by such passages as Psalm Eight.

It is my belief that the quality of moral discernment is one of the major points in which humans are made in the image of God. Other forms of life operate in quasi-moral ways (for example, a mother animal instinctively protecting her young), but their conduct seems more based on instinct than on moral conscience. Aside from angels—God's immaterial created life form—humans stand alone in their possession of a conscious moral conscience.

This moral quality of humanity—created in us by our Creator God—sets us apart from all of God's creation as made in His image. If we build our view of God's spiritual family, His new creation in Christ Jesus, on similar logic, we may logically conclude that those who are born of God possess a unique sense of God's moral nature and character that sets them apart from other humans. Various passages that draw analogies between the new birth and God's law written in and on the immaterial part of our being are one example of this point. Paul's analogy of circumcision of the heart (Romans 2:28-29) even more specifically affirms that in the new birth God not only adds a new life principle to us, but that He also in some significant way alters the life principle that existed in us prior to regeneration. The idea that a regenerate (born again) individual retains his/her old depraved nature, effectively untouched and unchanged by the new birth cannot stand in the face of the various Scriptures that describe the effects of the new birth such as those mentioned above.

The moral nature of man, especially the higher moral nature of a regenerate elect, forms the basis for the consistent Biblical exhortations to God's regenerate elect to actively, consciously, and willingly engage Christian actions—soldiers in the King's army and servants in the Master's house.

In our conscious, willing, and active commitment of service to God, Paul in these dual analogies affirms that we effectively place our lives in the hands of God as prepared and efficient weapons to be used by Him as He directs in the Christian warfare against Satan and sin. The analogy of warfare and servants is divinely chosen and inspired of God. Both soldiers in an army and servants in a wealthy household must actively, consciously, and willingly engage their duties, but they must do so under the direction and supervision of the commanding officer or the master of the house.

...as those that are alive from the dead. Paul advances the analogy. We are not mere inorganic and passive bricks in God's building, or inorganic swords or spears in God's hands. We are "living weapons" whose spirits and bodies are jointly committed to God and to His cause in the battle—or service—of life under His banner. The moral character that God created in humanity precludes any deterministic view that man acts out his life apart from a willing, conscious, and voluntary perspective. Paul urges us to live responsibly, consistently, and faithfully, as soldiers and servants who are accountable to their commanding officer or to their master.

For Paul there is no logical or moral basis for the believer in Christ to continue living in sin. The dominion of sin was not only legally broken at Calvary, but it was experientially and effectively broken in us at regeneration. We live with two conflicting natures, a conflict that Paul will develop in the next chapter of his Roman letter, but the dominant moral and spiritual factor in our lives now is God, so Paul urges—commands—us to live out our lives in harmony with that life principle. In the sixth chapter of Romans Paul lays the foundation for the seventh, but he does so in a carefully crafted form that will not allow any rationalization of sin and its ethical breach of God's moral law and character.

41
Christian Service

> For sin shall not have dominion over you: for ye are not under the law, but under grace. What then? shall we sin, because we are not under the law, but under grace? God forbid. Know ye not, that to whom ye yield yourselves servants to obey, his servants ye are to whom ye obey; whether of sin unto death, or of obedience unto righteousness? (Romans 6:14-16)

Are Christians today under the Ten Commandments? This question is sure to get an interesting discussion going just about anytime it comes up. It raises a valid challenge. Inherently God's moral character never changes, and the Ten Commandments clearly represent His moral character as well as His moral code for humanity. Yet Paul affirms in this lesson that we are not under the law. What did he mean? Without question Paul did not intend or imply that a Christian may lie, steal, or commit sacrilege and feel liberty in so doing.

Our "me-first" culture nurtures the idea that the final judge in all matters is one's personal conscience. If a person does just about anything they wish, it is perfectly acceptable so long as they do it "sincerely." In this worldview personal conscience and sincerity become the final authority for right and wrong. Occasionally Christians become infected with this hedonistic worldview and think that God respects our motives, sincerity in this case, more than He respects His moral character and commandments. How wrong can we be? Clearly sincerity and transparency are to characterize the Christian's conduct and motives in all things that we do, but the final deciding factor of the correctness—the right and the wrong of it—is not our conscience or our sincerity, but God's moral code and commandments.

What then? shall we sin, because we are not under the law, but under grace? Paul once again takes us right back to the slanderous charge his critics hurled at him in the third chapter of Romans. This cavalier attitude toward sin is precisely what they were saying that Paul taught.

Two major errors challenge this correct Biblical basis for obedience in the Christian. The first is legalism. Our basic human nature needs rules and regulations to keep it in check, so each of us has a built-in affinity for more rules and regulations. This human inclination appears in the Jewish culture of the first century. God gave them Ten Commandments, which He interestingly simplified and summarized into two global principles, loving (a Biblical word for conduct, not emotions) God and loving our neighbor. What did the Jews do with those Ten simple and understandable rules of conduct? First they expanded them to around six hundred technical rules. As if that were not enough, they further expanded them to well over a thousand different and even more technical rules. With so many rules layered over you, you'd have to check the rule book every morning before you woke up and told your spouse good morning! It is practically and humanly impossible for anyone to keep all of these rules.

What is the most basic rule of Christian discipleship? Is it legalism, in competition with the attitude of the Jews and their hundreds of rules and regulations? Or is there a better way to inform and motivate our service to God? Writing to a group of young churches that had been deceived into the legalistic trap, Paul answered these questions.

For in Jesus Christ neither circumcision availeth any thing, nor uncircumcision; but faith which worketh by love. (Galatians 5:6)

The fundamental problem with legalism is simple. The legalist simply does not trust the dominant and correct principle of Christian discipleship, faith working by love. "This might lead to…" is a favorite quip of the legalist. The legalist will reveal his/her distrust of faith working by love with such objections.

Faith is the fundamental practical link between God and His people. It appears as an attitude, not only of trust in God, but of obedience to God and to His teachings in Scripture. The application of Biblical faith in discipleship then becomes this faith translating God's Law into conduct that may be described as the action of love. Again, Biblical love does not refer to sentiment or emotion, but to how we act.

In 1st Corinthians 13:4-7 Paul specifically defined the action of Biblical love. When a Christian treats another Christian with harshness and defends his/her action with "I call them as I see them," or other such self-rationalizing terms, he/she is violating the spirit of Biblical discipleship. Notice Paul's caution and exhortation regarding the attitude of our words.

Let your speech be alway with grace, seasoned with salt, that ye may know how ye ought to answer every man. (Colossians 4:6)

According to Paul, the embedded seasoning that flavors every word we speak should be characterized by the same principle of grace that God displayed when He saved us. This principle is life changing when we implement it! It for ever eliminates the critical, acrimonious words and attitudes of the legalist who inherently judges others as beneath him/her and uses this judgment to magnify self.

The other adversary to Biblical discipleship is determinism. This "God does it all" attitude flies under the banner of giving glory to God, but reduces acts of discipleship to an irresistible response in us to a divine decree. In determinism neither faith nor love work; we merely respond irresistibly and without any motive to a divine decree, much as the divine laws of nature apply to a falling rock.

Know ye not, that to whom ye yield yourselves servants to obey, his servants ye are to whom ye obey; whether of sin unto death, or of obedience unto righteousness? The context of Romans sixth chapter deals with our service to God. Paul is not telling the Romans how to become children of God, but rather how to become *faithful servants* of God. In the language of the New Testament the verb yield appears in the present tense. It identifies something that is going on—or should be going on—right now. It is in the active voice, referring to something that we are instructed to do, not to something that will be done in us by another, even by God. It is in the indicative mood, referring to specific action, not merely to pleasant thoughts about the actions commanded.

Paul's instructions to the Romans in no way implies a passive or inactive "yielding," but rather it identifies an active, willing, and conscious decision to live in the service of God and not in the service of God's enemy. Paul makes his point very personal and direct. "Know ye not…" is the equivalent to "What? Don't you know…?" The ethical weight of Paul's teaching here makes a powerful point for our instruction. We can't serve sin and claim to be God's servants. To the extent that we actively choose sin in any form in our conduct to that same extent we have sold out to God's archenemy, Satan.

Suppose that you are working for a firm that builds its business on highly sophisticated patents and trade secrets. How do you suppose your firm would react if they discovered that you occasionally had dinner with the research leader of your firm's chief competitor and that you freely talked to this person about your firm's patents and trade secrets? Do you suppose that you'd be given a promotion or that you'd be fired for violating the trust of your employer? Paul is applying similar logic to our discipleship. He is asking such questions as "Where is your loyalty?" Where are you exerting the efforts and intelligent energy of your life?"

According to Paul, the moment you consciously "yield" your time, mind, or energy in action to something, you become its slave, its servant. For Paul both discipleship and disobedience are conscious and willing choices made by us, choices that carry consequences with which we must reckon. The comedian Flip Wilson made a fortune with his quip, "The devil made me do it." Paul would not have accepted Wilson's excuse. He would have responded to Wilson with, "If you chose to do it, you are responsible, and you must answer for it."

...*whether of sin unto death, or of obedience unto righteousness.* Paul also clearly presents the specific consequences of our choices and actions. If we choose sin and anesthetize our conscience into a sleepy state of denial of the sinful character of what we choose to do, God does not go to sleep with our tortured conscience. He will still respond with the chastening consequences of our choices. Death wears many faces. God warned Adam that he would die on the very day that he ate the forbidden fruit. Although Adam lived over nine hundred years after that even, he died instantly upon eating the forbidden fruit, just as God warned that he would. He died to fellowship with his Creator. He died to innocence and to the enjoyment of the Garden in which God had placed him. Later in this letter Paul will warn the Roman believers (not lost sinners),

> *For if ye live after the flesh, ye shall die: but if ye through the Spirit do mortify the deeds of the body, ye shall live.* (Romans 8:13)

A child of God may choose sin and die in some integral way. This death does not separate him/her from the love of God or from heaven, but it shall surely separate him/her from incredible fellowship and joy in a life of serving God. Child of God, never minimize this death! If you find yourself enticed to follow a course of sin, take a long reflective study of Psalm the thirty second chapter. It tells you what you shall surely face; sleepless nights with a nagging conscience, a pillow wet with tears of regret, a sense of guilt that pierces all the way to the marrow of your bones, and an incredible sense of emptiness where sweet fellowship with God should reside.

As Paul in our study passage shows us both sides of the question, he does the same thing in this verse from the eighth chapter of Romans. When we choose to obey God as faithful servants, yielding every aspect of our lives to Him for His use, not ours, we will discover a passionate pursuit of righteousness, life and joy that Peter describe as "…joy unspeakable and full of glory." (1 Peter 1:8)

When Joshua told Israel to "…Choose you this day whom ye will serve…" (Joshua 24:15), he was not telling godly people that they have a choice altogether dependent on their sincerity. He distinctly told them that he and his family had no choice! They had already chosen to serve God. The choice that he gave the people was based on their prior choice not to serve God. Joshua's warning to them, and his choice to them, was simple. Once you choose not to serve God, no other choice will give you joy or satisfaction. All such choices will prove to be fruitless and miserable, a life of endless wind but never any refreshing showers of rain!

42
Whom do you Serve?

But God be thanked, that ye were the servants of sin, but ye have obeyed from the heart that form of doctrine which was delivered you. Being then made free from sin, ye became the servants of righteousness. (Romans 6:17-18)

Only the most irresponsible of theologians would dare to imply that Paul thanked God because the Romans—or anyone for that matter—was a slave to sin. Paul's thankfulness rather related to the present fact. No longer were the Romans serving sin as its slaves, but now they had escaped that slavery and were the servants of righteousness, the reason for Paul's thanksgiving to God.

In his commentary on this verse John Gill draws an analogy. A soldier may for a time become a prisoner of war, held by hostile forces in a prison camp. Eventually the prisoner escapes, returns to friendly territory and rejoins his own forces. At that time he has every reason to be thankful for his escape and for his present situation.

Paul's emphasis in this section of the Roman letter focuses on Christian service, discipleship not the transformation from death to life. He thanks God that the Romans are now "servants of righteousness," not children but servants. We do not become children of God by our faithful service, but by birth, a birth effected by God immediately and sovereignly without our works or other contributions. However, we become servants of God by a conscious, willing, and altogether voluntary decision to serve God, not sin.

...ye have obeyed from the heart.... Christian obedience cannot be coerced or reluctant obedience. God only accepts and blesses obedience that grows out of a joyful and willing obedience, obedience from the heart. On occasion I have listened to very sincere people describe their initial experience of turning from sin to serve God in terms that contradict this passage altogether. They describe convictions and conflict, often acknowledging their reluctant decision to serve God more out of fear of consequences than out of joyful willingness. A reluctant decision to serve God based more on fear of consequences than on a conviction of rightness falls distinctly short of

the obedience that Paul describes in this passage. Scripture rejects superficial, external, and legalistic obedience. Consider this passage from Paul's letter to a group of churches that had learned the gospel from him, but rather quickly fell prey to legalistic teaching that lead them away from Paul's gospel to "another gospel" (Galatians 1:6).

> *For in Jesus Christ neither circumcision availeth any thing, nor uncircumcision; but faith which worketh by love.* (Galatians 5:6)

To get a vivid sense of this passage consider the wording if you were to express the mirror opposite to it. What word might you substitute for "faith"? In the Galatian letter Paul repeatedly draws a contrast between faith and law, or, to put it in simple terms for us, legalism. What word might express the opposite to "love" in this sentence? Perhaps the most significant word might be "fear." Let's restate the sentence in its opposite form. "For in Christ Jesus neither circumcision availeth any thing, nor uncircumcision, but legalism which worketh by fear." To observe and listen to many Christians describe their view of discipleship, they have embraced this mirror opposite interpretation of the passage!

When discussing the fundamental concepts of the doctrines of grace with Christians who hold to salvation by some form of cooperation between God and man, you often hear the protest, "Well, if I believed that doctrine, I'd just go out and live my fill of sin." In making such statements people reveal their own motives far more than they realize. Do they practice righteousness only because they think they will gain heaven or something else of great value to them by such practice? In other words is their practice of righteousness exclusively for self-gain? Or do they practice righteousness based on the simple fact that it is right? If something is right to do, should we not practice it regardless of whether it means gain for us personally or not? If we expect our criticism—our just criticism—of the health and wealth heresy to be credibly accepted, we need to practice our righteousness solely because such conduct is right, whether we gain by it or not.

I sometimes wonder. Do folks who practice righteousness out of a legalistic motive not trust the Biblical concept of faith working by love? Did Paul trust it? He must have trusted it fully since he summarized his whole Galatian letter with this principle of right

Christian conduct. Perhaps the person who appears to distrust the principle of faith working by love actually doesn't trust him/herself or God.

...*that form of doctrine*.... The word form is translated from a Greek word whose primary meaning is a mold. Dr. Tom Constable describes this verse—I believe—correctly.

> The form of teaching Paul had in mind was the teaching that the Lord Jesus Himself gave during His earthly ministry and then through His apostles (cf. Gal. 6:2) in contrast to the Mosaic Law. God had not forced Paul's readers to yield to it as to law. They had willingly embraced it as law for themselves. They had committed themselves to it from their hearts. Paul was not stressing the fact that the Lord had committed His teachings to his readers, as the AV translation implies, but that they had committed themselves to it.[1]

Notice especially Constable's closing thought, "Paul was not stressing the fact that the Lord had committed His teachings to his readers...but that they had committed themselves to it." Men build forms in the desired shape before they begin to pour cement. Women used molds to make Jello desserts, and then pour the liquid Jello into them. Paul here describes the fixed mold of truth to which a faithful believer commits his/her service to God.

Constable further describes this concept of Christian obedience.

> The slavery of the readers to righteousness was therefore voluntary. It seems that because of his very nature man must be the slave of something. "Righteousness" here is the result of following Christian teaching, and it is the equivalent of godly living. It is righteous character and conduct.
> Paul did not say that every believer takes advantage of his or her freedom from sin's tyranny to become a slave of God. He said his readers had done so, and in this he rejoiced. Dedication to God is voluntary, not automatic for the Christian (cf. v. 13;

---

[1] Tom Constable, *Tom Constable's Expository Notes on the Bible* (Galaxie Software, 2003; 2003), Ro 6:17.

12:1). If a believer does not truly dedicate himself or herself to God, he or she will continue to practice sin (v. 16).

6:19 Paul had put his teaching in human terms. He had compared the believer's situation to that of a free person on the one hand and to a slave on the other. He did this to help his readers grasp his point but evidently also to make a strong impact on them. Paul felt constrained to be very graphic and direct in view of their past. They had formerly deliberately yielded to sin. Now they needed to deliberately present (offer) themselves as slaves to God (cf. vv. 13, 16). This would result in their progressive sanctification. Note again that progressive sanctification is not totally passive or automatic. It requires some human action.[2]

Notice Constable's point that our Christian service—literally our slavery—to righteousness is wholly voluntary, not coerced. Also notice that it is not universal to the family of God. Only those regenerate elect who consciously make the voluntary choice to serve righteousness discover and enjoy the blessing of this noble service.

Paul reasons that in exactly the same way we consciously and voluntarily chose sin prior to our relationship with God, now we are commanded to make a similar conscious and voluntary choice to serve God and righteousness.

...that form of doctrine.... We should also pay special attention to the point that Paul makes in this simple expression. The doctrine of true Christianity is not a form of doctrine that we choose. It is not "our own truth," New Age relativism style. It is a fixed mold or form of doctrine. We do not reform or mold the doctrine to fit our ideas. Rather we mold our lives to fit the mold of Biblical doctrine or teaching. If some of our thoughts or actions fall outside the mold of doctrine set forth in Scripture, we are not to redesign the mold, but we are commanded to redesign our lives so that our conduct fits the fixed mold of Christian truth set forth in Scripture.

Being then made free from sin, ye became the servants of righteousness. Paul emphasizes the point already made in the prior verse and underscored

---

[2] Tom Constable, *Tom Constable's Expository Notes on the Bible* (Galaxie Software, 2003; 2003), Ro 6:18-19.

by Constable's comments. We were legally freed from the eternal and damning consequences of sin by the substitutionary sacrifice of our Lord Jesus Christ. We personally received the benefit of this work at the new birth. However, we gain the sense of personal freedom from sin only to the extent that we choose to walk away from slavery to sin and commit ourselves to the service of righteousness. Acceptable service to God cannot be a coerced or involuntary obedience. It must be a conscious obedience voluntarily chosen by us. In these thoughts Paul is repeating the same point that he made in 6:11, "Likewise reckon ye also yourselves to be dead indeed unto sin, but alive unto God through Jesus Christ our Lord."

The army of Christian soldiers is a "voluntary" army, not a conscripted collection of rebellious and reluctant soldiers who serve because they were drafted and had no choice other than serve or go to jail! They serve because they believe in the principle of faith working by love. They serve because they believe in the cause for which their army does battle. It is right! Whether they end their tour of service with medals and a hero's welcome home or they die a tortured death as a result of injuries sustained in faithful service, they serve because they believe their service is right. They do not serve for reward, though reward or blessing is promised to faithful service (1 Corinthians 9:17).

Let us serve our tour of duty faithfully, joyfully, loyally, and willingly—because it is right and without any motive for personal gain or any sense of divine conscription or coercion.

43
A Servant: Christian Ethics

> I speak after the manner of men because of the infirmity of your flesh: for as ye have yielded your members servants to uncleanness and to iniquity unto iniquity; even so now yield your members servants to righteousness unto holiness. For when ye were the servants of sin, ye were free from righteousness. What fruit had ye then in those things whereof ye are now ashamed? for the end of those things is death. But now being made free from sin, and become servants to God, ye have your fruit unto holiness, and the end everlasting life. (Romans 6:19-22)

A review of the context of these verses puts them in clear focus and affirms the nature of Christian ethics—the delightful epitome of a true servant. While it is sadly true that many who profess to be Christians reject this role and "pick and choose" which Bible teaching they will obey and which they will ignore, they cannot do so with Paul's approval. Even this incredible man whom the Holy Spirit used to write approximately thirty per cent of the New Testament consistently referred to himself as the Lord's servant, choosing a word in the language of the day that referred to a slave, not an employee.

Occasionally people fall prey to errant thinking that imputes the active or immediate cause of everything that occurs onto God. The obvious problem with this idea is that it logically blames God for sin, so advocates must creatively find ways to hold to their error but contradict their own logical belief by saying that God causes everything except sin. So is sin not part of "everything"?

A permutation of this excessive view of predestination holds that God effectually and irresistibly causes righteousness but not sin. Advocates of this idea attempt to make every act of faith and obedience the result of a divine decree that rejects any sense of a voluntary act on the part of the obedient believer. Logically this teaching reduces the obedient disciple to something of a robot, mechanistically and irresistibly responding to the divine decree, making even the believer's willingness itself the result of a divine decree.

Paul draws a parallel in our study verses that refutes both of these errant teachings. He reminds the Romans of a time when they were "free from righteousness," certainly not free from the moral laws of God, but free in terms of their cognitive sense of sin and free from any moral inclination to resist it. During this time prior to the work of God's saving grace in them, the Romans quite willingly chose sin over righteousness. They chose it because of their sinful nature. They chose it because of their insatiable appetite for sin. They were not divinely decreed to sin. They were not predestinated by divine ordination to sin. They willing chose sin over righteousness.

Surprisingly Paul draws logical parallels between this past time in the life of the Romans and their present state in the grace of God. He commands that now they be just as insatiable in their pursuit of righteousness as they once were in the pursuit of sin. "...as ye have yielded your members servants to uncleanness and to iniquity unto iniquity" describes the Romans' past attitude toward sin. They did not "yield" to a divine decree in their willing and insatiable choice of sin. They responded to their fallen nature and to their lack of a moral and spiritual conscience toward God. Paul now commands them to do the same thing toward righteousness. In order for Paul's parallel to hold we must consider the motive and character of their sinful actions so as to discover Paul's rather unusual parallel.

"...even so now yield your members servants to righteousness unto holiness." These words describe a personal, voluntary, and cognitive decision to do something—something altogether righteous. "...yield" is in the active voice; it requires a conscious decision by the Roman believers. It does not describe an involuntary response to a divine decree. Further Paul attributes both past sin and present righteousness to a common logical (certainly not moral) choice by the Romans. If we accept that their (our) sins were not the result of an irresistible divine decree, we must accept that their righteous conduct was also not the result of an irresistible divine decree. Otherwise the "as...even so" parallel cannot hold.

The obvious point that Paul makes should be simple to follow. Notice his introduction to this lesson, "*I speak after the manner of men because of the infirmity of your flesh.*" Despite clear teaching to the contrary, at least some of the Roman Christians either came to a different conclusion or they charged Paul with holding to a different view (Romans 3:1-8). If Paul held to the mechanistic view of divine cause that they charged against him in this passage from the third chapter of the letter, he could not write the exhortation now urged upon them in our study verses.

The moral quality of their past conduct and the spiritual and ethical quality of the conduct that Paul now exhorts the Romans to follow with such consistency as to consider themselves "servants" to righteousness are moral opposites. Conscious and voluntary choice is the driving force of our lesson. What motivated the Romans to pursue sin so enthusiastically as to be termed "servants" of sin, literally its slaves? Was it a mechanistic response to a divine decree? No! It was a conscious and voluntary choice to practice that conduct. It was based on their dominant nature at the time, depraved and godless sinners. What distinguishes them now from what they were then? Now they have been born of God. They now possess two natures, one the same nature that drove their former appetites for sin, and one a new spiritual and moral nature that they received in the new birth. It is not automatic or the result of an irresistible divine decree, but the result of cognitive and willing choices that Paul now commands them to make their new spiritual and moral nature the dominant nature in their present conduct.

In the Colossian letter Paul equates these two natures to an "old man" and a "new man" (Colossians 3:5-17). In that context Paul commands the Colossians to put off the "old man" and his deeds, and to put on the "new man" and his deeds. The two passages present a parallel lesson that reveals the necessity of a willing, voluntary, and cognitive choice in our conduct. Neither their former nor their present conduct was the consequence of an irresistible divine decree. Both lifestyles—despite being moral opposites—were the consequence of individual voluntary and conscious choices.

In the context of our study verses from the sixth chapter of Romans Paul has already examined two compromises and rejected them. In the first two verses of the sixth chapter Paul raised the question of a person rationalizing the continued and sadly consistent habit of sinning on the abominable and false premise that in some mystical way the more we sin the more we cause God's grace to abound. In the fifteenth verse of the sixth chapter he raises the question of our rationalizing occasional lapses into sin because "…we are not under the law but under grace." Paul categorically rejects both attitudes toward sin with the strongest negative answer that language could frame, "God forbid!" Our study verses strongly reinforce this consistent ethical principle.

"The devil made me do it" we clearly understand as an inexcusable rationalization for sin. However, Paul rejects "God made me do it" as fully as he rejects the first false premise. His argument to the Romans frames both sinful conduct and righteousness conduct around a conscious, voluntary, and responsible decision in our choice of actions. Paul does not predict or guarantee righteous conduct based on an irresistible divine decree; he bases the Romans' present righteous conduct on their choices, knowingly and willing made.

There are lingering consequences to every decision—every choice—that we make. For example, Paul identifies that the Romans' prior choice of sin only predicted a deeper commitment to more sin, "…iniquity unto iniquity." He distinctly rejects the "Let us sin so that we may have more grace" immoral mindset. His true teaching defines the mirror opposite of that sinful attitude. Equally there are lingering consequences to righteous conduct, "righteousness unto holiness." We predict our future habits, either of sin or of righteousness, by our daily choices in the here and now. Rationalized sin, even the smallest of sins, today lays the foundation for future rationalizations of far greater sins. And habitual practice of righteousness today lays the grounds for future depths in holiness and God-honoring consistency in godly actions.

A servant, literally a slave, was required to obey the commands of his master or face his master's wrath. He was not compelled irresistibly to obey. He might rebel and merely do as little as possible to avoid his master's wrath, or for that matter he might seek opportunity to escape and run away as Onesimus ran away from Philemon. In this analogy of slavery to Christian service Paul urges that the moral choices of our conduct have already been decided by God; He did not consult with us for input before deciding His own moral character. Once we choose to become God's "servants" we are directed to implement God's commandments faithfully, voluntarily, and consistently. Paul framed his teaching in this lesson as a commandment, an exhortation, not as a divine guarantee based on an irresistible divine decree. Paul urges us to be as consistent in our pursuit of righteousness as we were formerly in our pursuit of sin. Only as we understand and accept our role as God's servants can we ever discover the incredible liberty of being God's free men (1 Corinthians 7:22). We discover our incredible liberty in Christ only to the extent that we choose to be His faithful servants.

A balanced view of Biblical discipleship includes the concise and understandable communication of God's instructions to His people through the work of regeneration (God's law written in the heart), the leadership of the Holy Spirit through the believer's conscience, the divinely preserved writings of Scripture, and the preaching of the gospel. Paul's teaching regarding the necessity of a cognitive and voluntary response by us to faith and obedience in no way diminishes these divine influences. Rather his teachings apply all of these witnesses to our conscious minds and inform the right choices that we are commanded to make. None of these responses are described in Scripture as guaranteed or divinely and irresistibly ordained. Scripture teaches that this willing obedience from the heart of the servant is our only correct response to the divine influence. Our conscious and willing obedience is the result of our knowledge of—and response to—these divine influences. Rejection of this willing and voluntary response to the leadership of God irresistibly decreed our righteous acts so "God gets all the credit" is in fact a straw man logical fallacy to the teaching of Scripture that distinctly requires such a willing response.

The stubborn and self-serving attitude of "selective obedience" that so many professing Christians practice in our time is not logically or morally distinct from open rebellion, depicted in Scripture as the equivalent to witchcraft (1 Samuel 15:22-23).

In his farewell address to Israel Joshua commanded the people to put away the idolatrous practices of their former lives and to fear and serve God in truth. Only those people who rejected this commandment to fear and to serve God were given the option to "…choose ye this day whom ye will serve…." (Joshua 24:14-15) In this teaching Joshua revealed the heart of a servant whose mind was set to obey and to honor God his Lord. The conscious and willing decision to serve God settles all other choices for us. We have no desire or need to choose among the endless list of false gods that are available in every culture and every age.

We face similar choices in our own personal discipleship. Will we play the role of the rebel and selectively choose which of God's commandments we will respectfully obey and which of His commandments we will consciously reject and ignore? Or will we embrace the role of a willing servant who knowingly, willingly, and joyfully chooses only to do those things which glorify God? Will we be as consistent in our righteous choices as we formerly were in our sinful choices? Paul charges us to consider nothing less.

44
Wages and a Gift

For the wages of sin is death; but the gift of God is eternal life through Jesus Christ our Lord. (Romans 6:23)

In this verse Paul logically punctuates the points that have claimed his focus through the last several chapters. We often hear Bible teachers quote this verse with no reference to its context whatever. However, in the common reference to the passage as part of the "Romans road" piecemeal roadmap to salvation claimed by advocates of this interpretation, one's salvation relies specifically on following the roadmap. The passage rejects such an interpretation. Does Paul teach that salvation is the result of our reading and following a roadmap? No, he writes that it is the result of a divine gift from God through the Lord Jesus Christ, not through our ability to read and to follow a roadmap? This populist interpretation neglects the most basic point that Paul makes in the verse.

How do you distinguish wages from a gift? Is there a difference between a gift and a proposition? If we earn salvation by something that we do, even if God "pays" us more than our labor deserves, we are forced logically to conclude that salvation and condemnation are both based on the same premise, wages. Paul contradicts this conclusion. The basis for man's final and eternal condemnation is consistently based in Biblical teaching on man's conduct. He earned his just sentence of eternal separation and condemnation from God the righteous Judge. However, Paul categorically distinguishes the process by which we receive eternal life from the basis on which the wicked shall be finally judged. From Paul's specific teaching in this verse, we readily conclude that eternal life comes to us in a manner quite distinct—in fact opposite—from the basis of eternal condemnation. One is the result of conduct, wages earned and deserved. The other is the result of a gift bestowed.

The Greek word translated gift in this passage emphasizes the point that Paul makes.

> a verbal noun from χαρίζομαι (*give*); denoting *what has been given, gift*; (1) as the result of a gracious act of God *gift of grace, favor*

bestowed, benefit, with the meaning varying according to the context:[1]

Many folks who teach salvation by human participation, by our following the "Romans road," redefine the word "gift" as a mere "offer" of salvation that man must accept or reject. This definition of the underlying Greek word refutes such an interpretation. What our friends who teach salvation by following the "Romans road" actually teach from this text is that God sets before the unregenerate sinner a proposition, an offer, but distinctly not a gift as defined by the word that Paul used.

One of my first assignments when I began my secular career in accounting was to compute and process the payroll for my employer. Most of the workers in this firm were paid on an incentive basis. The harder they worked and the more production they completed the more they were paid. When I first received this assignment, a number of these workers challenged my computations of their pay. No doubt they wanted to be sure that I understood the company's policy as it related to their production. As I sat down with them and reasoned through my calculations with them, they soon were comfortable that I understood how to compute their pay correctly. From that time on I seldom had to explain the basis for a pay amount—except when occasionally I really made a computational error, and then I gladly processed the correction.

We correctly associate wages with what a person earns—what he/she works to gain. There is a specific and equitable corollary between the work invested and the wage earned. In this summary verse Paul makes the point clearly that the final sentence of judgment and eternal punishment of the wicked will be based on actual conduct, wages earned and deserved for what they did.

"…but," Paul wants us to understand clearly and without doubt that the basis for man's sentence of condemnation is not the same as the basis on which the righteous shall be taken into eternal and joyful fellowship with God. Paul distinctly puts "wages" and "gift" in

---

[1] Timothy Friberg, Barbara Friberg and Neva F. Miller, vol. 4, *Analytical Lexicon of the Greek New Testament*, Baker's Greek New Testament library (Grand Rapids, Mich.: Baker Books, 2000), 407.

contrast with each other. In this verse they become logical opposites in his reasoning.

The only reasonable conclusion to draw from this contrast leads us to the comforting conclusion that our eternal salvation does not rely on our decisions, on our choices, or on our actions. What we possess in heaven will not be measured by what we did here on earth, but by what our Lord did on our behalf and freely gave to us. Friberg's definition lays the emphasis in the correct place. Our salvation is "the result of a gracious act of God...."

This dialogue, especially viewed as a punctuating summary of Paul's refutation of the false charge laid against him at the beginning of the third chapter, logically addresses that false charge. As he responded to that false charge, Paul covered the broad landscape of Christian theology. For Paul, the whole of Christian truth is interlocked and logically related, not piecemeal links of a chain yet to be constructed by the linking and welding of the pieces together. Paul's perception is that the chain of our eternal salvation is wholly assembled and complete. It does not lack even one contribution from us. It is not an offer or a proposition that we must accept. Friberg's emphasis that the word translated "gift" emphasizes a "gracious act of God" affirms a wholly God-centric view of our eternal salvation, while the "Roman's road" perspective emphasizes a wholly man-centric view of eternal salvation.

When Paul's critics charged that he put too much emphasis on God and divine grace, he accepted their line of reasoning and turned it back against them. If God manages the universe as a cosmic puppeteer, causing or manipulating every event that occurs, then we must reach a startling but logical conclusion regarding man and sin— God, not man, is responsible, so God, not man, should be judged for the presence of sin in the world! The absurdity of such an idea should have shocked Paul's critics into an immediate reconsideration of truth.

As we consider the Roman letter in terms of the criticism leveled against Paul in the third chapter, we can interestingly sum up essentially every teaching regarding man, God, and salvation in terms of Paul's analogy in our study verse of either wage or gift. Here are the errant views that exist, condensed to their logical expression in the wage-gift analogy.

1. Both sin—and its ultimate penalty—and salvation are divinely caused. Therefore both sin and salvation are gifts of God. Paul rejects this idea by the distinction between the two; the punishment for man's sin is a deserved wage, while the enjoyment of eternal life is the result of a divine gift. This errant view leads one to conclude that God is ultimately responsible for both sin and salvation, the core error of the view.
2. Both hell and heaven are the result of what man does. Thus both heaven and hell are the result of wages, what man did to gain either. This error is perhaps the most common error that has historically surfaced in the Christian culture.
3. There is a distinction between sin and its just punishment and salvation, but only in the degree to which one is deserved and the other is not. This error forms the basis for the idea that salvation is a synergistic or cooperative venture in which both man and God must "do their parts" to successfully accomplish the individual's salvation. Advocates of this view explain Paul's analogy of "gift" by merely saying that we must do something in order to gain our salvation, but that God responds to our meager contribution by bestowing far more on us than our effort deserved. Whether we set the equation with God doing ninety nine percent and man doing one percent or with God doing fifty per cent and man doing fifty percent, the logical concept remains. We must make our contribution, and—contingent on our contribution, whatever the percent in the whole salvation equation—God will respond with His contribution.

Paul rejects all of these flawed ideas in favor of a crisp distinction between the two final sentences against mankind on the Day of Judgment. Those who hear the verdict, "Guilty as charged—Depart!" will receive the just consequences of what they did, a true wage earned by their investment and recorded on the "payroll timecard." Those who hear the welcomed, "Come ye blessed of my Father; inherit the kingdom prepared for you..." will enjoy that verdict based wholly on an undeserved and unearned gift, the glorious result of "a gracious act of God." When Jesus used the term "inherit" in the passage mentioned (Matthew 25:34, he taught the same truth that Paul affirmed in Romans 6:23, but with one added feature. Eternity with God is both a divine gift *bestowed* and a divine inheritance *bequeathed*!

45
The Death of Legalism

> Know ye not, brethren, (for I speak to them that know the law,) how that the law hath dominion over a man as long as he liveth? For the woman which hath an husband is bound by the law to her husband so long as he liveth; but if the husband be dead, she is loosed from the law of her husband. So then if, while her husband liveth, she be married to another man, she shall be called an adulteress: but if her husband be dead, she is free from that law; so that she is no adulteress, though she be married to another man. Wherefore, my brethren, ye also are become dead to the law by the body of Christ; that ye should be married to another, even to him who is raised from the dead, that we should bring forth fruit unto God. (Romans 7:1-4)

From the second chapter forward Paul has been reasoning with the Jewish contingency in the Roman church. It is quite likely that the false accusation raised against Paul in the third chapter originated with these people. Before we become too hard on them, we should consider the legalist that thrives within each of us. We did not grow up in Old Testament Judaism, but we grew up with certain deeply ingrained values that follow us through life. When someone (or some circumstance) challenges those values, we immediately and zealously react in defense of our ingrained values. For this reason Paul's introducing the concept of the death of the law would have been incredibly difficult for the Jewish Christians in Rome to embrace. In their minds he was challenging something far more fundamental to them than "motherhood and apple pie." In first century Jewish culture for anyone to question the law of Moses was equivalent to blasphemy. Factually Paul didn't question the Mosaic code's divinely inspired intent, but he distinctly challenged its authority to govern religious life after the death and resurrection of Jesus.

While Paul uses the analogy of marriage and the death of one spouse, this is not the best passage from which to teach the Bible's posture on marital ethics. Paul's purpose here is to expose invalid legalism and an errant use of the Mosaic Law, not marital ethics.

When God introduced His law through Moses, He included ten core moral principles around which the people were to order their lives. Indeed the Mosaic code enlarges and refines those principles, but these Ten Commandments remain at the core of God's moral code. From the strictest interpretation of the Mosaic code marriage was intended for life, though Moses injected a permissive provision for divorce, an allowance which Jesus described as growing out of the "hardness of your hearts." (Matthew 19:8) Interpreting the Mosaic code according to the strict intent in the Ten Commandments, Paul builds his spiritual lesson on the premise that marriage is terminated only by the death of one's spouse. However, upon the death of one's spouse, Paul makes an emphatic point that the surviving spouse is then free from the marriage vow and is also free to marry another person.

What was Paul's point in framing his lesson around this analogy? He states the point in the text, "*Wherefore, my brethren, ye also are become dead to the law by the body of Christ; that ye should be married to another....*" For Paul the death of the Lord Jesus Christ ended the domain of the Mosaic code.

If you want to engage people in an energetic discussion, ask the question, "Are Christians today under the Law?" In the sixth chapter of Romans Paul actually answered the question in a way that many Christians find difficult to accept.

The issue in this context of Scripture is not at all that Christians today are free from the ethics of the Mosaic code, the Ten Commandments, so that they may live life without any ethical constraint. Paul distinctly teaches us in this lesson that the ethical authority of the Mosaic code ended and was replaced by the person of the Lord Jesus Christ. The error of believing that Jesus ended the Ten Commandments, but replaced those commandments with nothing is called antinomianism. The word literally means "against the law," or "without law." Surprisingly some Christians in our time believe that the only binding moral principle to which they must answer is their own sincerity. According to their view, you can believe just about anything you wish—and live just about any way you wish—so long as you do so sincerely. For these people their own conscience becomes the only binding ethics to which they must answer. What about the problem of one believer's sincerity embracing a certain idea, while another sincere believer with equal sincerity embraces the mirror opposite idea? Ask the antinomian Christian this question, and you'll get a rather revealing answer. "What is wrong with that? Christians are not under the law anymore." Logically this idea rejects any fixed moral code in Scripture and replaces Scripture with wholesale relativism.

In terms of the moral principles that God imposes onto all of humanity, the Ten Commandments express a timeless ethical authority. In a very short time a studious Christian can discover that every one of the Ten Commandments is restated as a binding moral code in the New Testament. Neither Jesus nor Paul intended to terminate the Mosaic code and leave future believers free to live with nothing more than their personal sincerity to guide them. Periodically I talk with Mormon missionaries or Jehovah's Witness missionaries who come to my door to talk with me. I have yet to meet one of these people who do not exude sincerity. Are we then to conclude that God is just as pleased with Mormonism or Watch Tower theology as with New Testament teaching? Such an idea can claim no logical or Biblical ground whatever!

When Jesus reminded the disciples in the Sermon on the Mount that He did not come to destroy but to fulfill the Law (Matthew 5:17), He was teaching the same truth that Paul affirmed in our study passage. If Jesus fulfilled the Law, we are now accountable to Him, not merely to our conveniently trained conscience. If you ever encounter a person who claims that conscience alone is the only authority for what they believe and how they act, suggest that they read the Sermon on the Mount (Matthew chapters five through seven). Repeatedly throughout these chapters, Jesus referred to "You have heard..." only to follow up the point with "But I say...." The pattern is unavoidable. The moral framework of the Law was to be replaced by the moral framework of the life of the Lord Jesus Christ.

On the Mount of Transfiguration the three disciples heard a voice from heaven saying, "This is my beloved Son, in whom I am well pleased; hear ye him." (Matthew 17:5) How can we miss the emphasis, "*Hear ye him*"? The voice did not say, "Listen only to your sincere conscience." It emphatically said, "Hear ye him!"

The consistent pattern of Scripture is clear.

1. "But I say...." At the end of the Sermon on the Mount, the disciples "...were astonished at his doctrine: for he taught

them as one having authority, and not as the scribes." (Matthew 7:28-29)
2. "...hear ye him." As Moses and Elijah (the "law and the prophets") were the moral authorities in the Old Testament, even so the life and words of Jesus are the moral authority in the New Testament.
3. *"...ye also are become dead to the law by the body of Christ; that ye should be married to another...."* What ended the ethical supremacy of the Mosaic code over the people of God? Paul affirms that the death—and by implication the resurrection—of Jesus ended the era of the Mosaic Law. Replacing that code now is the Lord Jesus Christ, *"...even to him who is raised from the dead...."*

"... that ye should be married to another, even to him who is raised from the dead, that we should bring forth fruit unto God." Dr. Tom Constable makes a wise observation regarding this verse.

> Every believer not only died with Christ but also arose with Him (6:14). Thus God has joined us to Christ. The phrase "might be joined to another" does not imply that our union is only a possibility. God did unite us with Christ (6:5). The result of our union should be fruit-bearing (cf. John 15:1–6; Gal. 5:23–23).[1]

A. T. Robertson agrees with this point.

> Purpose clause with εἰς τo [*eis to*] and the infinitive. First mention of the saints as wedded to Christ as their Husband occurs in I Cor. 6:13 and Gal. 4:26. See further Eph. 5:22–33. **That we might bring forth fruit unto God** (ἵνα καρποφορησωμεν τῷ θεῷ [*hina karpophorēsōmen tōi theōi*]). He changes the metaphor to that of the tree used in 6:22.[2]

---

[1] Tom Constable, *Tom Constable's Expository Notes on the Bible* (Galaxie Software, 2003; 2003), Ro 7:4.
[2] A.T. Robertson, *Word Pictures in the New Testament*, Vol.V c1932, Vol.VI c1933 by Sunday School Board of the Southern Baptist Convention. (Oak Harbor: Logos Research Systems, 1997), Ro 7:4.

We have briefly examined the underlying principle that rejects legalism as a valid basis for the Christian life, along with antinomianism, whether it appears as "sincerity is sufficient" or any of its other insidious forms. We are now ready to examine the practical implications of this transition to our attitudes and conduct in personal Christian experience.

Jesus' personal moral government of His people is no less specific and binding than the Mosaic code. "…but I say" frames the major outline of the Sermon on the Mount. Before we examine the personal and experiential implications of Jesus' personal moral governance, we should examine what this idea does not mean. Sorry for beginning with the negative, but the prevalence of some of these destructive ideas in our time necessitates their exposure before we can constructively examine the positive implications of our moral accountability to the Lord Jesus Christ.

1. "Jesus has revealed to me that…" is a frighteningly common refrain in contemporary Christianity. When people make such a claim, we need to ask how they know their idea was revealed by Jesus. Perhaps it is merely their personal belief, so they presume that Jesus revealed it to them. There is a flawless test for every claimed "revelation." Peter wrote that the writing of Scripture was performed by the power and working of the Spirit of God. Since God is wholly consistent and immutable, if we discover what the moral concepts of God were in the revelation of Scripture, we may safely conclude that they are exactly the same today as when the Holy Spirit inspired men to write the Scriptures. A major evidence of the supernatural origin of Scripture is that some forty to forty five men contributed to the writing of Scripture over a period of approximately fifteen hundred years; yet there are no contradictions in all of these quite diverse writings. Years ago I was in conversation with a person who frequently claimed "God has revealed to me…" often defending rather unusual ideas behind the claim. I challenged one of the more obvious of these frivolous claims by offering a passage of Scripture that contradicted the idea this person had just presented.

Immediately she responded, "Oh, you are being legalistic." If appealing to Scripture's final authority is being legalistic, I gladly plead guilty as charged! In her comment this person clearly indicated that she viewed her perception of a personal and private "revelation" with more authority than anything written in Scripture. We should set clearly in our minds that no claimed revelation from God will contradict Scripture, so even our supposed "revelations" must be put to the test of Scripture. The fundamental principle involved in this point is rather straightforward for our present study. Jesus' personal moral governance of His people does not occur exclusively through personal or private revelations. Primarily it occurs through a conscientious and ongoing study of Scripture. Paul reminded Timothy of this truth, "Consider what I say; and the Lord give thee understanding in all things." (2 Timothy 2:7) We gain insight into Jesus' personal ethics through Scripture, not through private, personal, and thus non-verifiable "revelations."

2. "Since God has written His law in my mind, if I sincerely think a thing is right, it must be right." This error is akin to the first. Personal sincerity does not supersede Scripture. A person may well be wholly in error and be as sincere as any true believer alive. Once again, the supremacy of Scripture, not one's personal opinion or sincerity, must prevail.

3. "Jesus fulfilled the Law for me, so I don't need to live according to it." This error confuses the imputed righteousness of the Lord Jesus Christ in our redemption with the ethical commands of God to His children. Our legal standing before God in Jesus' impute righteousness in no way diminishes our obligation to live according to God's moral code. Paul affirms this truth, "Nevertheless the foundation of God standeth sure[c], having this seal, The Lord knoweth them that are his. And, Let every one that nameth the name of Christ depart from iniquity." (2 Timothy 2:19) If our legal standing in Jesus' righteousness relieved us of personal

---

[c] sure: or, steady

obligation to live according to God's moral code, Paul could not have written these words.

4. "The Bible has nothing to say about my present situation, so I am free to do whatever I wish to do about it." This error actively seeks to "dumb down" the Bible so that it conclusively says nothing about anything. In over fifty years of studying the Bible and ministry I remain constantly amazed at the incredible enlightenment and relevance of Scripture to my daily life.
5. "My obedience, my personal righteous action, is irresistibly ordained by God, so I don't have to worry about it." This error rejects the clear teaching of Scripture on the role of the believer's will in God's moral government of His people. It reduces personal obedience to a mindless response to irresistible divine power. In this view obedience to God's will is little more than the "obedience" of a molecular chemical reaction or the response of a falling rock to gravity. Most advocates of this view will readily accept responsibility for their sins, but attribute any righteous act to irresistible divine causation.

We could cover any number of similar errant ideas regarding the believer's present moral obligation, but these will suffice to illustrate the point.

Paul's analogy in our study verses confronts us at every decision point of our lives. How do I go about deciding what to do about this question? What do I do about it? In a godly marriage neither partner attempts to manipulate his/her spouse. They live respectfully toward each other, seeking to honor and to please their partner. If we seek to live as if we are truly married to the Lord Jesus Christ, we must face life's decisions with Him and His personal teachings wielding a dominant influence in our decision making processes. "What would Jesus do?" is more than a popular cliché of our time. It is actually quite insightful if we use the question to go to Scripture and learn through Scripture what we can uncover regarding Jesus' ethical teachings.

My wife's family looks back with a certain humor at a time in her youth when her father received his weekly check, and with it a lay off notice. He took his final check to the bank, deposited it, and drove straight to the local Buick dealer where he purchased a new Buick convertible! Needless to say his wife was not happy with the news that night. Had my father-in-law considered his wife's views, he would have never purchased the new car. Scripture teaches us that a married couple should consider their spouse in the things they do and say. Translate this affectionate concern to Paul's analogy in our study passage. If we fulfill the potential and the relational role that he intended, we will consider the Lord Jesus, our "husband" in the analogy, before making decisions, taking action, or uttering words. We will not shamelessly and irresponsibly reinvent Him or His revealed will in Scripture to rationalize our personal appetite.

The "legalist" in each of us often tends to focus the spotlight of the law on others while we remain carefully in the shadows. We will loudly proclaim the faults of others, but become noticeably quiet when others question us about our own faults. This double standard typifies the legalist, making such a person something significantly less than pleasant for those who choose to associate with them. I am convinced that quite often the legalist feels an incredible sense of personal guilt about his/her own failures, but instead of dealing with those failures they busy themselves with the faults of others and carefully work to keep their own faults out of anyone's sight.

This observation leads us to consider the next experiential problem with the legalist. Although they may carefully work to avoid the spotlight, the legalist often struggles with amazing conflict and discouragement, but their legalistic spirit prevents them from confessing their faults and asking others to help them overcome their besetting sins. Therefore the legalist must live a lonely life with his/her faults. As Paul develops this theme later in the chapter, he carefully holds himself, not someone else, up to the legalistic measuring rod of the law. No matter how hard you work, or how much you do, the Law assesses your performance and questions why you didn't do more, or it finds fault with what you did do and questions why you didn't do it better. Legalism is a miserable lifestyle!

It has been my observation that legalistic Christians often become nearly obsessive about "assurance" of their salvation. To hear them speak about their insatiable hunger for assurance, you would think that this was the only topic discussed in all the sixty six books of the Bible.

Sadly, no matter how much the legalist does, at the end of the day he/she struggles with a nagging sense that he/she didn't do enough, lacks the desired assurance, and becomes driven to do more for the primary purpose of gaining more assurance. However, the harder one works with assurance as the primary objective the more discontented he/she will be.

Why this strange phenomenon? It is no mystery at all. Scripture clearly teaches us that true discipleship begins with self-denial, not self-pursuit of assurance. Once we deny self and invest our primary effort in life to the service of others, assurance becomes a peripheral issue, not the primary objective of everything we do. And the beautiful wonder of it all is that the more we invest our lives in the service of others the greater our true assurance! That is exactly the way God designed Biblical discipleship and Biblical self-denial to be. Serve Him by serving others with the least possible emphasis on self, and the blessings of providence and rich assurance flow like an artesian spring in your life. Focus your primary objective on gaining assurance, regardless of what you do, and those same blessings dry up like a drop of water in the desert.

Paul has given us the key to joyful, fulfilling discipleship in this simple analogy. The more we live our life under the perspective that Jesus is our spouse and is involved in everything we do, the more we discover the joys of our relationship with Him. The more we react to disaster by creating another one, be it a new Buick on unemployment or some other equally silly strategy that we invent, the more we will struggle with no joy and with no hope—and with no assurance.

"*...that we should bring forth fruit unto God.*" The fruit that Paul seeks in this lesson is not fruit to self, not stars in our crown—either in this life or in the world to come—not a high mark on the scale of self-assurance, but rather fruit to God. When Jesus introduced the analogy of the vine at the beginning of the fifteenth chapter of John's gospel, He set the proper stage. He, not we, is the owner of the vineyard. We are not even the root of the grape vine. We are a mere branch on the fine. We may choose to bring forth fruit to Him and find the joys of the abundant life described in Scripture, or we may choose to bring forth fruit to ourselves and end up being pruned from His constant supply of blessings. At the end of the day it is both as complex and as simple as that.

The grand summation of this lesson is far easier to grasp that it is to apply to our lives. The life we choose as a legalist is a miserable existence! Why bother? Why choose it? Paul takes us by the hand and gently walks us through a far better way to live, a way that glorifies God and that—as a side-bar issue—also blesses us immensely. His lesson sets the stage for a simple analysis of our life. If you claim to be devotedly married to Jesus, why do live life as if you are married to the Law? What is our answer to this question?

46
How do you Serve God?
The Old Way or the New Way

Wherefore, my brethren, ye also are become dead to the law by the body of Christ; that ye should be married to another, even to him who is raised from the dead, that we should bring forth fruit unto God. For when we were in the flesh, the motions of sins, which were by the law, did work in our members to bring forth fruit unto death. But now we are delivered from the law, that being dead wherein we were held; that we should serve in newness of spirit, and not in the oldness of the letter. (Romans 7:4-6)

From the time Adam grabbed a fig leaf and tried to cover himself and his sin before God humans have attempted to create their own ways either to appease or to please God. Even those of us who believe strongly in the doctrines of God's grace, while zealously rejecting any human contribution to our eternal salvation, are quite easily enticed into a legalistic spirit with which we think we become better Christians or draw ourselves closer to God.

Our study passage reveals two attitudes and avenues of Christian service. Paul describes them as "newness of spirit" and as "oldness of the letter."

If we read the brief description of Paul's and Barnabas' contention with legalists at Antioch (Acts 15:1-2), we might conclude that the legalists were teaching the Arminian view of salvation by works. Given the fact that these folks were members of the Jerusalem church (See Acts 15:24.), it is more likely that they were teaching some form of synergistic worship, a blending of the Mosaic Law and the gospel, as the only true way of Christianity. If they were teaching that circumcision was essential to the new birth or to one's entitlement to heaven, why didn't the letter compiled and sent by the Jerusalem church indicate as much (Acts 15:22-29)? I suggest the likelihood that these false teachers were guilty of attempting to serve God in "oldness of the letter," insidious legalism.

Although the Mosaic code in its entirety is quite extensive, God summarized the ethics of that code in ten life principles, Ten Commandments that were to guide the moral conduct of His people throughout the Old Testament era. Apparently over time the Jewish teachers increasingly came to believe that these simple ten laws were not sufficient to address all the many complexities of life, so they added a rather long list of additional rules, something in excess of six hundred. With the passage of still more time they became anxious over these rules and added some five hundred more rules, calling them "fences." Let me exemplify the legalistic attitude. A caring parent who raises his/her children by the legalistic spirit will continually impose more and more rules on the child. If the child questions the validity of the rules, the parent will defend them with various rationalizations, often injecting "It might lead to...." "It might lead to..." is a dead give-away to the presence of a legalistic attitude. We may have demeaned the Pharisees more than they deserve. No doubt they were sincere and caring people. In most cases the legalist is a sincere and caring person. The problem with pharisaic legalism is not that it is not sincere and caring, but that it is based on a false perception of the Law of God and of human nature.

Let's develop the distinction between a legalistic spirit and a "newness of spirit" attitude of Christian service through an examination of the question of circumcision, the problem in the fifteenth chapter of Acts. The legalists from Jerusalem sincerely believed that no one could fully please God unless they were circumcised "...after the manner of Moses." Not only must you be circumcised, you must be circumcised in a highly specific manner. What was the manner of Moses' circumcision? What does this mean? Moses was circumcised as an adult. Does this mean that circumcision of babies fails to comply with "the manner of Moses"? Must we discover what kind of knife Moses used in his circumcision? During the life of John Gill, the highly respected English Particular Baptist, there was quite a controversy among English Christians regarding the appropriateness of hymn singing in public worship. Some folks rejected all forms of singing, others favored singing only the psalms, and others embraced the singing of contemporary hymns with sound Christian sentiment. One of Gill's members on one occasion complained about the church becoming far too "modern" for her taste. She complained to her pastor John Gill that she wanted only to sing the psalms exactly the way Paul sang them. Gill wisely responded, "Madam if you'll find out exactly how Paul sang them, we'll gladly follow his example." Of course no one seventeen centuries after Paul had any knowledge as to how Paul sang the psalms. The woman's attitude exemplifies the legalistic spirit.

Back to our example of circumcision. It is likely that these same troublemakers who traveled from Jerusalem to Antioch also followed Paul where ever he went preaching the gospel and establishing churches, trying to sow their form of legalistic Christianity as a superior form of Christianity to Paul's way. When Paul wrote to the Galatian churches, rebuking them for abandoning the gospel that he preached to them in favor of the legalistic gospel, which he described as another gospel "Which is not another" of the same quality as the gospel that he preached, he confronted the spirit of legalism head-on. At the close of the Galatian letter, Paul used circumcision to exemplify the new way of worshipping God.

For in Jesus Christ neither circumcision availeth any thing, nor uncircumcision; but faith which worketh by love. (Galatians 5:6)

Paul's point exemplifies the spirit of worshipping God in "newness of spirit" and not in "oldness of the letter." In diametrical contrast to the legalists who invaded Antioch Church and required legalism "after the manner of Moses," Paul tells the Galatian Christians that neither circumcision nor uncircumcision make any difference whatever in the degree to which a person serves God. In other words circumcision is wholly irrelevant to serving God!

Paul introduced a better way for us to serve God, as well as a better way for us to know that we are serving God, faith working by love.

I am convinced that the typical legalist lives with a dreadful lack of trust. Perhaps the legalist doesn't trust his/her own self-control unless "fenced" by endless rules. However, the greater problem of trust the legalist must face is a lack of trust in God. The legalist simply does not trust the New Testament concept of faith working by love. In the place of faith working by love the legalist will insist on faith working by rules and laws.

For Paul faith working by love does not mean faith working by empty headed sincerity apart from—or even contradictory to—the teaching of Scripture. The love with which faith works is the love of—and from—God. It is love that manifests itself in action, not in emotions and sentimentality. If you discover legalistic tendencies in your personality, you should likely read the thirteenth chapter of First Corinthians at least once a week. Especially notice how Paul defined "charity," the same kind of love that Paul intended in Galatians 5:6, in the fourth through the seventh verses of this chapter. Every trait of love that Paul identified in this concise and practical definition of Christian love addresses actions, personal conduct, not sentimentality and emotions. Biblical love, the underlying foundation of Biblical faith at work, manifests itself in actions, not emotions. We may say we love God and His people, but until we treat them with the traits depicted in this passage, we fail to prove our love for them. Only by specific Biblical actions toward others can we prove our Christian love. Notice the manifestation of true Biblical love.

> *Charity suffereth long, and is kind; charity envieth not; charity vaunteth not itself, is not puffed up, Doth not behave itself unseemly, seeketh not her own, is not easily provoked, thinketh no evil; Rejoiceth not in iniquity, but rejoiceth in the truth; Beareth all things, believeth all things, hopeth all things, endureth all things.* (1 Corinthians 13:4-7)

With this passage in mind let's revisit the question in this chapter's title, "How do you serve God?" Do you serve Him through an ever-growing number of rules and "fences" that you build around your life to insulate you from the endless list of "It might lead to…" evils? Do you serve Him by repetitive self-energized and futile efforts to control yourself based on your private set of rules? If so, you live with the dreadful legalist within, and you live with the constant reminder of failed service!

If you energize your faith in God by conduct toward others, specific conduct framed by the kind of actions described in First Corinthians 13:4-7, you realize the joys of a spiritual union and fellowship with the Lord Jesus Christ, "newness of spirit" and not "oldness of the letter."

The legalist will be self-centered and self-obsessed. He/She will constantly seek ways to reassure self that God is pleased with how he/she is living. The believer who lives according to "faith which worketh by love" has forgotten self and invests life in service, winsome and godly Christian service, to others, a life characterized by the joy of being "married to Christ Jesus."

47
Intense Conflict: A Characteristic of Grace

What shall we say then? Is the law sin? God forbid. Nay, I had not known sin, but by the law: for I had not known lust, except the law had said, Thou shalt not covet. But sin, taking occasion by the commandment, wrought in me all manner of concupiscence. For without the law sin was dead. For I was alive without the law once: but when the commandment came, sin revived, and I died. And the commandment, which was ordained to life, I found to be unto death. For sin, taking occasion by the commandment, deceived me, and by it slew me. Wherefore the law is holy, and the commandment holy, and just, and good. Was then that which is good made death unto me? God forbid. But sin, that it might appear sin, working death in me by that which is good; that sin by the commandment might become exceeding sinful. (Romans 7:7-13)

In our last chapter we examined the insidious character of legalism. Given the preponderant victory of grace, it is a logical point to ask why an heir of grace is so vulnerable to legalism. If we were so purified in regeneration that only the mere traces of our old nature (frequently referred to by Paul as our "old man") remain in us, legalism would be defeated before the battle begins.

What Paul describes in these verses is by no means a one-sided struggle. He rather describes a mortal conflict between two powerful though opposite moral forces within. As with so many Biblical truths, balance is essential to our discovery of truth in Scripture. In our study of the internal duel within a regenerate elect we should carefully avoid two unscriptural extreme ideas.

1. The errant idea that the two forces are exact equals. This error lends itself to the Eastern mystical idea of "yin-yang," of two eternal forces that are equal and opposite.
2. The opposite error that in regeneration all of our old nature is eradicated except for a bare vestige or remnant. This error tends toward either the sinless perfection of Pentecostal Holiness ideas, or to the "lordship salvation" of quite recent origin. The first chapter of First John clearly refutes both errors, along with the seventh chapter of Romans, not to

mention many other similar passages throughout the New Testament. Both of these errors inherently foster excessive pride, one by claiming sinless perfection attained by the believer, and the other by claiming near perfection with its inherent arrogant and condescending attitude toward anyone whom its advocates view as having fallen short of their near sinless perfection. The holiness view will somewhat gently make allowance for the struggling believer by asserting that he/she simply has not yet attained "sanctified" status. The lordship salvation error manifests a harsher legalism by questioning that the struggling believer is saved at all. Neither error allows any room in their errant view of a near perfect model family of God for either the struggles of this chapter or the failures of believers that appear throughout the New Testament. One advocate of lordship salvation flippantly rejects any pretense of the "carnal Christian" as being a preposterous and "antinomian" error. To be accurate, neither advocates of these two insidious errors, nor their opponents, seek to justify or glorify sin, nor to denigrate God's moral code. The question at issue is the balanced and correct teaching of Scripture regarding the nature of discipleship. As a matter of Biblical fact, Paul specifically charged the Corinthian church with being "carnal" (1 Corinthians 3:1-5 where he associates "carnal" with their immature status as "babes in Christ" and as being excessively divisive in their schismatic attitude toward various preachers, not as unregenerates who were not born again. Paul further described these people (1 Corinthians 1:2) as "sanctified in Christ Jesus, called to be saints, with all that in every place call upon the name of Jesus Christ our Lord, both theirs and ours...."). I have never heard or read of a preacher or Biblical scholar glorifying the Corinthian church as the model of a faithful local church so the "antinomian" accusation is a classical example of both the straw man and the red herring logical fallacies.

In our study passage Paul draws an informative contrast between a time when he only knew the subtle nuances of God's moral code and character by the teachings of the Mosaic code and a subsequent time when the presence of divine grace (God's law written in his heart as expressed in Romans 2:14-15, as well as a major tenet of God's promised "new covenant" in Jeremiah 31:27-34) revealed and convicted him of *"all manner of concupiscence,"* evil or sinful desires.

Paul raises an interesting question. If God's law written within exposes such embedded sin and the related intense sense of condemnation, is the law then evil? You see, the straw man-red herring accusations of antinomianism so common in our day are not new. *Paul's critics were accusing him of being antinomian!* In the heart of his discussion of the intense struggle within the believer Paul defends the workings of God's law as it exposes sin and convicts the quickened sinner as doing precisely what God intended it to do. God did not institute His law, either in the Old Testament form of the Ten Commandments or in the New Testament form of Scriptural affirmation and the co-testimony of that same law written in the heart of every regenerate elect, to promote arrogant legalism or to give prideful man a platform for boasting in self. He designed it to do exactly what Paul affirms that it did in his own personal experience in this chapter. By exposing sin within as exceedingly sinful, God intended—and uses—His law written in the heart to break self-righteous pride and human arrogance.

Many years ago a "relative-in-law" of mine who held to a distinctly Arminian view of salvation was telling me about an encounter he had with someone who, though quite devoted to his faith, did not agree with my relative's view of salvation by works. After describing an extended session of "Bible verse ping-pong," my relative boastfully described how he concluded the conversation with this person, "Well, there is only one difference between what you believe and what I believe. My sins are forgiven; yours are not." The prideful arrogance of this self-aggrandizing comment surprised and disgusted me. Sadly many professing Christians who claim to hold to the doctrines of grace as taught in the New Testament, corrupted by one of the errors mentioned above, often display similar prideful arrogance as they proclaim anyone who fails to meet their definition of sanctification as being deceived and not saved at all.

I have been amused—and frustrated—over the years at the manner in which various respected commentaries attempt to explain away—

rather than understand and truly explain—this chapter. They ask the question, "Whom was Paul discussing in this chapter?" Following the question they will either attempt to develop the idea that he was describing himself *prior* to his Damascus Road experience, or they will make their case that Paul was describing someone else. The passage clearly explains itself. *Notice the frequency of Paul's use of the personal pronoun in this passage, not to mention also the use of present tense verbs. Paul was describing his present experience as a regenerate elect, living out the conflict between God's law written within and his abiding carnal nature.*

What are we to learn from this lesson? I suggest at least two major themes for our consideration.

1. First the conflict that Paul described affirms that every regenerate elect will experience this conflict. It is an inherent characteristic of a regenerate elect person struggling with the conflicting moral appetites of two opposite natures.
2. Secondly, Paul uses this conflict to help us avoid the unbearable weight of insidious legalism. The regenerate elect who does not understand this conflict, be he inclined toward the holiness view or the lordship salvation view, will struggle to harmonize his/her personal conflict with his/her errant view of salvation and of discipleship. In order to preserve their errant beliefs believers in these errors will increasingly develop harshly legalistic tendencies, or else they will redefine sin in such a way as to boost their false pride in their own inflated sense of personal holiness. In either case they miss the point that Paul makes in this chapter.

Why did God create us "in Christ" through regeneration or the new birth so as to allow this conflict? Paul will end this chapter with a wholly Christ-centric view of himself, not with a self-righteous legalistic view of himself. May we follow his example and learn the truth of his teaching.

48
The Dynamics of Spiritual Conflict

For we know that the law is spiritual: but I am carnal, sold under sin. For that which I do I allow not: for what I would, that do I not; but what I hate, that do I. If then I do that which I would not, I consent unto the law that it is good. Now then it is no more I that do it, but sin that dwelleth in me. For I know that in me (that is, in my flesh,) dwelleth no good thing: for to will is present with me; but how to perform that which is good I find not. For the good that I would I do not: but the evil which I would not, that I do. Now if I do that I would not, it is no more I that do it, but sin that dwelleth in me. I find then a law, that, when I would do good, evil is present with me. (Romans 7:14-21)

As Paul develops the futility of pleasing God by legalism, by perfectly keeping God's law (The law will accept nothing less!), a logical question surfaces. Is God's law then something to be rejected and avoided? Having come from God, the law cannot be so characterized. The problem that Paul surfaces and explains is not an inherent problem with God or with His law, but with a misrepresentation of that law.

For we know that the law is spiritual: but I am carnal, sold under sin. Simply stated, the problem is with us, not with God's law. Here "I" not only refers to Paul, but to all regenerate elect who struggle with the fierce internal conflict between their carnal nature and the law of God written within.

For that which I do I allow not: for what I would, that do I not; but what I hate, that do I. What is Paul's point? He surfaces an intense conflict within. His conscience and his conduct do not always agree. At times he does things that his conscience does not approve—does not "allow." Further at times he desires to do righteously, but fails to perform the good thing that he intended. In fact, at the heart of the matter, according to Paul, there are times when he did the very things that he hated.

This conflict between carnal and spiritual appetites is experienced by every regenerate elect. Sinless perfection is not the true experience of any regenerate elect person, although some folks claim to have developed such a pure state of mind and conduct. A careful examination of their conduct will reveal that they have redefined sin in relationship to their behavior so as to define their personal sins away. Many years ago I visited with a man who boastfully claimed that he had not sinned in around fifteen years. Without thinking too much, I started to probe his conduct, mentioning along the way John's comments about self-deception if we claim that we do not sin (1 John 1:8). As I nudged him in light of this passage, the man began a "slow burn" or increasing anger at my questions. Factually his anger clearly displayed that he just broke an alleged fifteen year record! More factually, he had sinned many times during that fifteen years, but he had carefully redefined sin so as to exempt himself from John's truth.

Often sincere believers who stop distinctly short of any pretense of sinless perfection will so characterize this passage and others that deal with this question so as to minimize any significant conflict in the "true believer." In their minds the spiritual elements of grace have so taken over the life of the believer as to leave only the barest minimum of one's old or sinful nature.

First of all, such a claim stands in rather stark contrast with Paul's depiction of spiritual conflict in this chapter. Further the inference of those who hold to this idea implies—often openly charges—that anyone who claims to experience such fierce conflict is either an inferior Christian or is not even a regenerate person at all. Their false claim in this point charges Paul with their low esteem, for it was his own experience that Paul described in this chapter. Notice the frequency of both the personal pronouns and present tense verbs that appear throughout this chapter.

Now then it is no more I that do it, but sin that dwelleth in me. Paul does not here intend to distance himself from a sense of responsibility for his conduct, nor does he intend to shift the blame for his sins onto God.

Advocates of extreme views of predestination will occasionally represent themselves and their conduct in a form that effectively demonstrates the mirror opposite of this view. Let's examine three views of predestination to see the dynamic of this point.

1. The most radical view of predestination holds that God actively and causatively predestinated everything that occurs, sin included. Factually only a few people hold to this view.

Thank God! This view impugns the righteous character of God by actually charging sin to God and not to man.

2. The second view holds that God orchestrates all events, but only causatively predestinated the good that we do. This view holds that our faith and good works are irresistibly predestinated, or decreed, by God. While this view stops barely short of charging sin to God, it takes predestination distinctly beyond the teaching of Scripture. If God predestinated our faith and good deeds, we would expect to see absolute sinless and pure faith and good works, something that we in fact do not see. Every act of faith and obedience is to some extent mixed, not pure. Does God then predestinate and irresistibly cause imperfect obedience? For example, when Jesus reminded the pleading father that his belief was placed in the balance for his daughter's healing, he responded, "Lord I believe; help thou mine unbelief." (Mark 9:24) At the moment of his strongest belief, this noble and honest man acknowledged the presence to some extent of unbelief within. Surely if God predestinated his belief, it would be whole and full belief, not belief mixed with unbelief? Did God also predestinate the man's partial belief? His unbelief? Scripture repeatedly lays a certain responsibility in active faith and obedience to one's personal willing or voluntary response to God's holy leading in all acts of faith and obedience. Denial of any sense of responsible compliance with God's direction in faith and obedience contradicts the clear teaching of Scripture. Advocates of this idea occasionally claim that only by attributing the whole of their faith and obedience to God, even to the extent of denying any role for their personal response to God's leading, is the only way they can "give God all the glory" for their obedience. Given this view of obedience, I look at the passage before us and wonder. Since Paul specifically stated, "...*it is no more I that do it, but sin that dwelleth in me,*" are we also to deny any element of personal responsibility for the sins that we commit? God forbid such an abominable idea.

3. The New Testament doctrine of predestination attributes our salvation—our final resurrection and our eternal state with

God in heaven to God's causative predestination. Romans 8:29-30 makes this point clearly, along with Ephesians 1:3-5 and 11). Occasionally advocates of one or more of the extreme views of predestination will abandon Scripture and adopt a philosophical view of predestination that reduces it to God's omniscience. These four mentions of the word in Scripture are distinctly and clearly causative, not depictions of God's omniscience. The two other passages where the same Greek work appears in the New Testament have to do with the crucifixion of Jesus and can be understood in a number of ways that do not make God the active and responsible cause of the deeds of the wicked men who tortured and crucified our Lord.

I find then a law, that, when I would do good, evil is present with me. The term "law" can be used in at least two senses. In one sense it is the statement of either proscriptive or prohibitive mandates. In this sense we rightly interpret the Ten Commandments. Some of them specifically proscribe precise positive action, "Thou shalt...." Others specifically prohibit certain sinful conduct, "Thou shalt not...."

The second use of the term "law" explains the way things are, as with scientific laws of chemistry, physics, or mathematics. Newton's "law" does not tell us how we should act. It explains the facts of one particular aspect of the natural world in which we live.

In this statement Paul is using the term "law" in similar fashion to our use of the word when we refer to scientific laws that explain the way things exist. In other words Paul tells us that the intense moral conflict that he has just described is a universal experience within every cognitively aware regenerate elect.

I believe Scripture affirms that one of the distinguishing traits of humans is the ability to know the difference between right and wrong, a sense of moral awareness. This, among other traits, distinguishes humans from animals. The defining difference between a regenerate elect (one of God's chosen vessels of mercy who has been born of God) and an unregenerate (a depraved person void of spiritual life) appears in their mutual appetites. While an unregenerate person has the ability to know the difference between right and wrong, he/she has no appetite for righteousness; in fact such persons loath righteousness and crave sin ("...whose god is their belly..." Philippians 3:19). A regenerate elect person not only knows the difference between right and wrong; such a person also has a deep conviction and longing for righteousness. In other passages Paul refers to our old nature as our "old man," and he refers to our new nature from God as our "new man." Herein is the dynamic of the conflict that Paul presents in our study lesson.

How should we deal with this conflict? How should we make sense of the intense clash? First of all, be aware that only regenerate elect children of God experience such fierce conflict. Never does Scripture depict an unregenerate person as having such an experience. Secondly, Paul clearly instructs us to follow the leading influence of our new and heavenly nature. Carefully study the passage below. I have added bold type to several specific points that appear here in God's inspired teachings to us.

If ye then be risen with Christ, **seek those things which are above,** *where Christ sitteth on the right hand of God.* **Set your affection on things above,** *not on things on the earth. For ye are dead, and your life is hid with Christ in God. When Christ, who is our life, shall appear, then shall ye also appear with him in glory.* **Mortify** *therefore your members which are upon the earth; fornication, uncleanness, inordinate affection, evil concupiscence, and covetousness, which is idolatry: For which things' sake the wrath of God cometh on the children of disobedience: In the which ye also walked some time, when ye lived in them. But* **now ye also put off all these;** *anger, wrath, malice, blasphemy, filthy communication out of your mouth. Lie not one to another,* **seeing that ye have put off the old man with his deeds; And have put on the new man, which is renewed in knowledge after the image of him that created him:** *Where there is neither Greek nor Jew, circumcision nor uncircumcision, Barbarian, Scythian, bond nor free: but Christ is all, and in all.* **Put on therefore, as the elect of God,** *holy and beloved, bowels of mercies, kindness, humbleness of mind, meekness, longsuffering;* **Forbearing one another,** *and forgiving one another, if any man have a quarrel against any: even as Christ forgave you,* **so also do ye.** *And above all these things* **put on charity,** *which is the bond of perfectness. And* **let the peace of God rule in your hearts,** *to the which also ye are called in one body; and* **be ye**

thankful. Let the word of Christ dwell in you richly *in all wisdom; teaching and admonishing one another in psalms and hymns and spiritual songs, singing with grace in your hearts to the Lord.* ***And whatsoever ye do in word or deed, do all in the name of the Lord Jesus, giving thanks to God and the Father by him.*** *(Colossians 3:1-17)*

These are not the words of a man who believed or taught that his faith and obedience are divinely decreed or predestinated.

Warren Wiersbe in one of his works refers to this passage and coins the concise thought, "Put off your **grave clothes** and put on your **grace clothes**." Amen.

49
Two Laws in Conflict

> For I delight in the law of God after the inward man: But I see another law in my members, warring against the law of my mind, and bringing me into captivity to the law of sin which is in my members. O wretched man that I am! who shall deliver me from the body of this death? I thank God through Jesus Christ our Lord. So then with the mind I myself serve the law of God; but with the flesh the law of sin. (Romans 7:22-25)

How do you explain the conflict you experience daily as a child of God? On one side you acknowledge a deep passion for God and for living according to His will. On the other side you realize the presence of intense pressures within, even at times an appealing desire, to ignore the will of God in favor of something that you know is not pleasing to God. Paul explains this conflict in the seventh chapter of Romans, first by honestly confronting the emotions on both sides of the conflict and then by reducing the two sides of the conflict to two "laws." Here Paul uses the term "law" as we think of scientific laws, a statement of fact that explains the nature of things. In basic science studies we learn about the laws of thermodynamics, various "laws" that explain the way gravity works, or the precise manner in which two or more chemicals combine to form new compounds (such as hydrogen and oxygen combining to form water).

Occasionally Bible students lose their touch both with the Bible and with their own nature and either deny the presence of such a conflict or they attempt to redefine it so as to depict it in ways wholly different from Paul's description in this chapter. In so doing they deny both the teaching of Scripture and their own personal experience. Ah, self-deception is the worst form of deception.

How intense—how personal—is this conflict of which Paul writes? First he describes it as two laws, the "law of God after the inward man," and "another law in my members." Next he describes it as a war in which the law in his "members" wars against "the law of God after the inward man." The word translated "warring" is a straightforward word that literally means "**1** to make a military expedition, or take the field, against anyone. **2** to oppose, war against."[1]

The literal idea is that a group of soldiers "take the field" against an opposing army.

Paul further intensifies this idea by stating that the "law in his members" at times "brings me into captivity to the law of sin which is in my members." Not only is Paul involved in an internal struggle of military proportions, but at times the opposing army gains the upper hand and brings his "higher" or spiritual self into captivity; takes him as a prisoner of war.

The idea that after regeneration a mere splinter of one's old sinful nature or self remains is exposed in its utter falsity by these words from Paul. I am convinced that folks who embrace these ideas of near perfect holiness have redefined sin in such a way as to blind themselves to the depth of sin in their own life. In analogy they spray a fog on the mirror of conscience with the design of intentionally blurring the role of conscience against sin within.

O wretched man that I am! who shall deliver me from the body of this death? The internal conflict, the war within, forms the basis for this cry of the soul for deliverance. A minor skirmish will not evoke such a cry from a seasoned soldier! A one-sided clash in which only the rag-tag remnants of a defeated army remain, a "clean-up" operation, will not prompt such a confession.

The visual image suggested by the term "the body of this death" is graphic. Several commentaries link the phrase to a first century practice in which a person convicted of killing another person was severely sentenced for his murder. The dead body of the person he killed was tied to his back and remained there till the murderer himself died. If this analogy was in Paul's mind when he used this phrase, the idea is powerful indeed. The dead body of sins, his old nature, was tied to his spiritual nature and would remain there till Paul died. Only at death would Paul find the full deliverance which he cried out to discover.

While the condition of which Paul writes is desperate and his plea passionate, Paul does not leave us in doubt as to the outcome of this military engagement. Paul sees the end of this conflict and anticipates

---

[1] James Strong, *The Exhaustive Concordance of the Bible : Showing Every Word of the Test of the Common English Version of the Canonical Books, and Every Occurrence of Each Word in Regular Order.*, electronic ed. (Ontario: Woodside Bible Fellowship., 1996), G497.

the final victory. *I thank God through Jesus Christ our Lord.* Paul's perception of victory is not resolved in his self-control, in his own faithful perseverance, or in a one-sided "cleanup operation" in which he ravages the bare remnants of his old nature. He sees the victory in the person of the Lord Jesus Christ.

So then with the mind I myself serve the law of God; but with the flesh the law of sin. Linger long with this thought. Let it soak deep down into your mind. In no way is Paul excusing an unbridled practice of sin. He does not at any time in this chapter characterize himself as the helpless victim of a sinful nature that in any way rationalizes any act of sin, much less a devoted lifestyle of sin. However, he does confront and acknowledge the reality of his present involvement in moral conflict, a conflict that pits his old nature against his new spiritual nature in an intense conflict that he can only accurately represent as a major military campaign.

The old English hymn writer Joseph Hart (1712-1768) captured the essence of this conflict in his poem/hymn.

How strange is the course that a Christian must steer;
How perplexed is the path he must tread!
The hope of his happiness rises from fear,
And his life he receives from the dead.

His fairest pretensions must wholly be waived,
And his best resolutions be crossed;
Nor can he expect to be perfectly saved,
Till he finds himself perfectly lost.

When all this is done, and his heart is assured
Of the total remission of sin,
When his pardon is signed and his peace is procured
From that moment his conflict begins.

We have seen the intensity of the conflict through Paul's eyes and his personal experience. We have discovered ourselves identifying with his description through our own personal sense of conflict. How does this rather surprising and intense passage relate to Paul's opening analogy in which he depicts a marriage, the death of the husband and the wife's liberty—in this case obligation—to marry another man? It is no surprise that both preachers and commentaries often leave the two lessons somewhat disjointed rather than linking them together as they appear in this chapter. Paul used the marriage analogy to introduce this lesson on the internal conflict of the regenerate child of God.

My wife and I have been married for almost forty five years. We occasionally tease that, whatever happens, we'd prefer to die together than for either of us to be left alone without the other. Given our age it is highly unlikely that we have another forty five years to live. Thus I must reason from Scripture and logic, not from personal experience. In the case of the person Paul depicted in his opening analogy the husband has died, and the wife is left alone. She is in fact presently in conflict. Part of her wants to preserve the emotions of love and loyalty to her old husband, and part of her knows that he is dead, but life for her must go on. She is in conflict! Can we miss the fact that conflict forms the common ground between the analogy of the dead husband and Paul's description of his inner struggle?

What are the dominant traits that build a marriage? How does a marriage survive for a lifetime? The emotional "buz" of romantic love will not endure for a lifetime! When the giddy flutter settles into a predictable and steady heartbeat, how does a marriage not only survive, but grow stronger and endure the difficulties that life often brings to the couple? Words such as commitment, loyalty, trust, openness, honesty come to the forefront to paint the image of an enduring marriage. Now ask a professional soldier to describe the traits that define a faithful and honorable soldier. The same words will show up!

Rather than give the spiritual "widow" the option of living any way she wishes, Paul specifically tells her that she needs to form a new lifelong marriage commitment to a new husband, and not just any man she happens to discover, but one specific man. Though she may have memories of her life with the "old man," she is now to acknowledge the obvious fact that he is dead. (Can we miss the analogy of the dead body in Paul's "…who shall deliver me from the body of this death?") Further, she is now to immediately enter into a new "marriage" relationship with the Lord Jesus Christ.

In our daily struggle with our two natures Paul does not give us the option of holding neutral ground and playing one "army" against the other. Nor does he give us the option of switching loyalties so that at one moment we join one army and the next moment we fight for the opposing army. In military terms such conduct would be called treason, and the solider would be arrested and tried! Paul specifically instructs us in our internal conflict between our two natures to take a consistent, lifelong, committed stand with Jesus and our new, spiritual nature.

When shall we finally realize the end of war? When shall we finally see the victory? As long as we live in this life, the conflict will continue. As we move through the various seasons of life, the ground of warfare will shift, but the conflict will go on. Only when we reach the moment of death will the battle end, and the victory shall then be clearly seen.

As we live in the heat of battle, how strong is our loyalty to the "Captain of our salvation?" Are we found constantly standing in formation where He has directed us, ready to hear and obey His commands for engaging the enemy? Do we keep our uniform and equipment in top shape, ready to engage the enemy on the side of the Lord Jesus Christ? When we reach the end of our struggle, will we be able to join Paul as we move into military retirement, saying, "I have fought a good fight, I have finished my course, I have kept the faith"? (2 Timothy 4:7)

Thou therefore endure hardness, as a good soldier of Jesus Christ. (2 Timothy 2:3)

Folks, this verse does not describe a divine guarantee; it presents us with a divine commandment! May it be our life's goal to fulfill, to "retire with honor."

50
Another Law: No Condemnation

> There is therefore now no condemnation to them which are in Christ Jesus, who walk not after the flesh, but after the Spirit. For the law of the Spirit of life in Christ Jesus hath made me free from the law of sin and death. For what the law could not do, in that it was weak through the flesh, God sending his own Son in the likeness of sinful flesh, and for sin, condemned sin in the flesh: That the righteousness of the law might be fulfilled in us, who walk not after the flesh, but after the Spirit. (Romans 8:1-4)

After the conflict and pervasive sense of condemnation in the seventh chapter, the naïve eye would not expect to read the dramatic shift of emphasis to be seen throughout the eighth chapter of Romans. If we were to extend Paul's analogy of marriage with which he opened the seventh chapter, we might look at a dual theme: in the seventh chapter Paul describes life with the "old husband," the law and the general spirit of legalism, while he introduces us to our "new husband" in the eighth chapter. There is a certain appeal to this overview, but the depth of inner conflict in the seventh chapter, coupled with Paul's consistent use of personal pronouns and present tense verbs indicates an even deeper significance.

Early in the dialogue of the seventh chapter it appears that Paul used "law" or equivalent terms to refer to the moral code of the Mosaic Law. As we move into the closing verses of the chapter, he clearly shifts his use of "law" from "proscriptive" to "explanatory." I use the term "proscriptive" in the sense that a moral code either "prescribes" certain conduct by commanding it, or it "proscribes" certain conduct by prohibiting it under threat of penalty upon violation of the code or commandment.

Paul's use of "law" in the closing verses of the seventh chapter more equates to the use of the term "law" in the world of science, as in "Newton's Law." In this sense the word describes factual and predictable events. In this sense "law" explains a "universal" fact that we may predict and expect without exception. Paul's description of a "law" that when he would do good evil was present, his delight in the "law of God after the inward man," and his sense of conflict at the other "law in my members" all exemplify the "scientific law" use of the word.

Now our question regarding the meaning of "law" shifts to the eighth chapter. When Paul tells us in the first verse that *"There is therefore now no condemnation to them which are in Christ Jesus,"* and follows that sentence with a reference to "...the law of the Spirit of life in Christ Jesus..." is he using the term "law" in the sense of a moral code, as in the Mosaic law, or is he using the word in the sense of a scientific—or in this case, a spiritual—principle? Given the context and Paul's use of the word to state factual spiritual principles in the close of the seventh chapter, it is my belief that he continues this use of the word as he opens the eighth chapter.

The question of Paul's intended use of the word "law" is crucial to our interpretation of the opening verses of the eighth chapter. If Paul intends a prescriptive-proscriptive sense of the law, then his qualifying clause, "...who walk not after the flesh, but after the Spirit..." may also be prescriptive-proscriptive. However, if he intended the word "law" to refer to a factual and predictable "universal" spiritual "law," a brief explanation of the way things are in the realm of the Spirit of God and His life-giving work, we should expect the qualifying clause to describe these people rather than direct them.

The fundamental question is quite significant to our theological assessment of Paul's teaching, especially through the remainder of the eighth chapter and his continuation of this teaching into subsequent chapters in the Book of Romans. With only a couple of exceptions—which upon close examination are not really exceptions—every verse in the eighth chapter of Romans begins with a connective word ("For," "That," Because," "So," "And" as just a few examples). Thus Paul will explain in the second verse what he intended in the first verse. *For the law of the Spirit of life in Christ Jesus hath made me free from the law of sin and death.* Now we surface the obvious question and the distinction between the two possible meanings that Paul may have intended in his use of "law" in this context.

Why is there "now no condemnation" to those who are in Christ Jesus? Is it because they practice predestined and near-flawless faith and obedience, the corrupted view of predestined and irresistible perseverance? Or is it because of the life-giving, sin-cleansing work of the Holy Spirit in freeing us from the "law of sin and death"? Paul—I believe—answered the question by his straightforward wording of the second verse.

If our personal walking after the Spirit and not after the flesh explains the absence of present condemnation, then we would expect Paul to go into a concise explanation of how faith and obedience to the commandments of God produce the state of "no condemnation." However, if Paul is referring to the universal law, principle of fact, in which the Holy Spirit gives spiritual, eternal life to every one of God's elect in precisely the same manner, we would expect him to explain this truth rather than leap into a long list of prescriptive-proscriptive rules. (Never get too far away from John 3:8; "...so is **every one** that is born of the Spirit." God's method of salvation is first of all single; He doesn't need several different methods, depending on the age, mental capacity, or geographic or cultural state of the individual. Thus any doctrine of salvation that involves man's action or will for some folks to gain eternal life, while it relies on divine mercy as an exception for others to be saved clearly is not the Biblical method that God designed, and that Jesus explained in His conversation with Nicodemus.) Rather than urge his readers to examine the law of Moses or any other law for that matter, Paul immediately tells us that this life-giving, condemnation eradicating work of God is something which "...*the law could not do*," but it is something that God did accomplish by "...*sending his own Son in the likeness of sinful flesh, and for sin....*"

This wondrous sense of "no condemnation," according to Paul, comes through the harmonious work of the Holy Spirit as He applies the righteous work of the Lord Jesus Christ to each individual elect in regeneration.

Interestingly Paul closes this verse with the same clause that he used in the first verse/sentence in the chapter, "...*who walk not after the flesh, but after the Spirit....*" Never does Paul go into precise details to explain this term. Never does he set artificial hurdles or standards of conduct in the individual regenerated elect. He merely states the principle. They "...*walk not after the flesh, but after the Spirit.*" If the clause defined compliance with a prescriptive-proscriptive moral code in the first instance, it must also apply to a similar code in the second instance. If it rather applies to a statement of universal fact, as with the "laws" of science, in the first instance, it should consistently be interpreted to apply to the same "law" in the second occurrence.

Common Ground

Because of the human tendency to exaggerate the ideas of those with whom we disagree, it is necessary to emphasize some central facts surrounding this lesson. Sadly there are some folks who will readily hurl irresponsible and inaccurate accusations against any and all who disagree with them of being "antinomian" or other ad hominem accusations. Interestingly, it was this same false accusation that Paul's critics hurled against him for teaching the doctrines of grace as he taught them (Go back to the first nine verses of the third chapter of Romans and be sure to notice the accusation they used against Paul and how he categorically rejected it).

While some people exist who are in fact antinomian (opposed to any moral prescription or proscription from God—the relativistic, pseudo-New Age "God loves us too much to impose rules and regulations on us" blasphemy), most Christians agree that God has commanded His children to do certain things, and that He has prohibited them from doing certain other things. I do not question that we honor God by consistently walking after the leading, teaching, and guiding of the Holy Spirit, most often through the study of Scripture and never contradictory to the teaching of Scripture. Nor do I question that God has categorically commanded every one of His regenerate elect children to obey the teachings of Scripture in their daily conduct; "...Let every one that nameth the name of Christ depart from iniquity." (2 Timothy 2:19, KJV) However, the question at hand is this. Is this what Paul intended in these verses, or did he have something else in mind? Based on the verses that explain the first verse, it is my belief that Paul was dealing with a principle of fact, not with the God's commandments and the believer's "perseverance" in faith and obedience. If he had intended the believer's response to the teachings of God or of the gospel, Paul would have explained this "law" in significantly different ways than we see in the verses. His specific explanation corroborates the principle that the emphasis in this context is on the work of the Holy Spirit in regeneration, not on the regenerate elect's subsequent conduct.

Do regenerate elect people conduct themselves differently from the unregenerated and wicked people in the world? To some extent they do, but Paul never develops any kind of minimum performance standards in this context that would justify the arrogant and carnal practice of those who advocate that, unless a person exhibits certain behaviors, he/she is in fact not "really born again at all."

The Greater Truth

Paul's emphasis on God accomplishing in the Incarnation and in the substitutionary death of the Lord Jesus Christ what the "…law could not do…" as he explained the first verse and the amazing fact of "no condemnation" that will permeate the whole eighth chapter of Romans, clearly directs us toward the divine perspective. As God looks upon each one of His beloved children from a legal perspective, He sees in them the perfect obedience of the Lord Jesus Christ. That righteousness, not the regenerate elect's conduct, forms the sole basis from which God now views His elect as void of condemnation and wholly spotless before Him in the imputed righteousness of our Lord Jesus Christ.

If we perceive our present state before God as it factually stands, we must conclude with Paul that "There is therefore now no condemnation…." And if we follow Paul's line of reasoning in this context, we must explain that glorious freedom from condemnation through the work of the Lord Jesus Christ—and that work imputed to us by the Holy Spirit in regeneration—as the exclusive basis for our present standing before God. Later in the chapter (verses twelve through fourteen as just one example) Paul will emphatically teach us the importance of our faithfulness in serving God. However, in these opening verses to the eighth chapter Paul is affirming that our legal, eternal standing with God stands on far more solid ground than our "feelings," our sense of conflict and condemnation as we struggle against our own selves to overcome sin and to practice righteousness. Rather than building his case that our final and eternal standing before God rests on us and on that intense conflict, Paul is affirming that our true standing with God rests on the imputed righteousness of the Lord Jesus Christ, given to us in regeneration experientially through the work of the Holy Spirit.

In the end it is Jesus' perfect obedience to God's Law that gives us righteous standing before God, not how we act or feel. The work of the Holy Spirit in regeneration changes our deepest nature. Although still children of Adam according to the flesh, we are now "A Child of the King" according to the Spirit of God, and that "Child of the King" standing is what Paul affirms in this lesson.

Is this a historical interpretation of this passage? Yes, it is, though many other interpretations exist historically as well. I quote below from the Geneva Bible footnotes[1] to this verse.

> (8:2) A preventing of an objection: seeing that the power of the Spirit is in us is so weakly, how may we gather by this that there is no condemnation for those that have that power? Because, he says, that power of the life-giving Spirit which is so weak in us, is most perfect and most mighty in Christ, and being imputed to us who believe, causes us to be thought of as though there were no relics of corruption and death in us. Therefore until now Paul reasons of remission of sins, and imputation of fulfilling the Law, and also of sanctification which is begun in us: **but now he speaks of the perfect imputation of Christ's manhood, which part was necessarily required for the full appeasing of our consciences: for our sins are destroyed by the blood of Christ, and the guiltiness of our corruption is covered with the imputation of Christ's obedience, and the corruption itself (which the apostle calls sinful sin) is healed in us little by little,** [bold for emphasis] by the gift of sanctification: but yet it is not complete, in that it still lacks another remedy, that is, the perfect sanctification of Christ's own flesh, which is also imputed to us.
>
> **b.** The power and authority of the Spirit, against which is set the tyranny of sin.
>
> **c.** Which kills the old man, and brings the new man to life.
>
> **d.** That is, absolutely and perfectly.

---

[1] Copied from SwordSearcher Bible software.

e. For Christ's sanctification being imputed to us perfects our sanctification which is begun in us.

(8:4) The very substance of the law of God might be fulfilled, or that same which the law requires, that we may be found just before God: for if with our justification there is joined that sanctification which is imputed to us, we are just, according to the perfect form which the Lord requires.

51
Nature vs. Conduct

> For they that are after the flesh do mind the things of the flesh; but they that are after the Spirit the things of the Spirit. For to be carnally minded is death; but to be spiritually minded is life and peace. Because the carnal mind is enmity against God: for it is not subject to the law of God, neither indeed can be. So then they that are in the flesh cannot please God. But ye are not in the flesh, but in the Spirit, if so be that the Spirit of God dwell in you. Now if any man have not the Spirit of Christ, he is none of his. (Romans 8:5-9)

A major debate exists among behavioral scientists regarding the question of "nature versus nurture." One view holds that each individual is born with a strong predisposition toward certain personality traits that follow the person through life. The other view holds that nurture, a sensitive and caring environment, can mold the child much like an expert potter can mold a piece of clay. In human behavior reality likely falls somewhere between these two views. A child is born with certain personality predispositions, but a nurturing environment, especially through the formative years of childhood and youth, will have a significant impact on the child. Probably the dominant view holds to "nurture" over "nature."

It should not be a surprise then to observe that the dominant view of theology in our culture is man-centered, teaching that a sinful individual who has no interest in God can be molded into a conscientious believer by merely exposing the person to a nurturing spiritual gospel environment.

Interestingly the study of Christian apologetics, the study of explaining and defending one's faith, divides along rather parallel lines. One school of apologetics holds to the "evidential" view, the idea that we may convert any human being to Christianity merely by showing the person the convincing and compelling evidence of the facts of Jesus' life, death, and resurrection. The other school, the "presuppositional" view, holds that God must first work grace into the person before he/she will be interested in the gospel or the facts of Jesus' death, burial, and resurrection. Again, I offer a hybrid view of apologetics that falls between these two polarized views. Without question, the first spiritual work, the saving work of regeneration or new birth, must be performed by God in the individual. Following that work of grace, the New Testament model of the gospel follows the evidentiary model with "…many infallible proofs…." (Acts 1:3)

Our study passage provides a compelling insight into these questions, especially in terms of the first work in the individual that changes his/her nature from primary identity with the family of Adam to a primary identity with the family of God.

For they that are after the flesh do mind the things of the flesh; but they that are after the Spirit the things of the Spirit. Based on the verses that follow, I believe that Paul here is defining two distinct natures within the human family. One "family" or group of humans only possess a human or "flesh" nature. The other "family," or group, still possesses their human nature, but they also possess a new, spiritual nature. They now have a nature that is "after the Spirit." Paul uses these two family identities to predict a certain disposition. A person who possesses only the flesh nature will only "mind" the things of their flesh nature. A person who also possesses the regenerated spiritual nature will also "mind" the things of the Spirit of God. The word "mind" here is translated from a first century Greek word that refers to one's mental disposition and related interests.

In the next sentence Paul reinforces this point. *For to be carnally minded is death; but to be spiritually minded is life and peace.* Notice that in both instances Paul refers to "being," not merely to external and observable conduct. He is referring to the deepest inner nature of two classes of humanity. From the external, environmental, racial, and cultural perspective the variety of humans is almost endless. However, from the spiritual perspective of "being," there are only two classes of people. One class is born only of their human parents; their state of "being" is carnal, and their energies are devoted to their carnal interests. The other class is born of their human parents, but they are also born of God; they possess a spiritual nature as well as their human nature, and that spiritual nature explains their interest in spiritual things.

Because the carnal mind is enmity against God: for it is not subject to the law of God, neither indeed can be. So then they that are in the flesh cannot please God. Paul makes—for the dominant contemporary theological mindset—a startling observation. Not only do those who are not born of God work to avoid any kind of spiritual affinity toward God, they in fact cannot do so. They lack the intrinsic ability to do so!

This principle strikes at the root of most theological systems of our time and their man-centric view of salvation. Regardless of their recipe that mixes grace and human action, works, or disposition, most of these ideas require that man take the first step in his new birth. Even some who pay lip service to the doctrines of grace and claim to believe in salvation all of divine grace will find a way to integrate some form of human mindset, human will, or activity into the first work that effects the new birth. They must hear and believe the gospel, or they must "have faith," or they must not only "have faith," but they must prove by their subsequent life that they look to Jesus, not only as their Savior but also as their Lord. In all of these hybrid systems of belief the individual must in some way do something, or believe something, or change his/her mindset for the new birth to occur.

All of these hybrid views contradict the New Testament teaching that our salvation is in some ways similar to God's creation of the material universe. Thus most of these folks in fact hold to some form of "spiritual evolution" in which the fallen—or in most of these systems, not so fallen—sinner merely organizes and effectively uses what already exists within. New Testament teaching affirms that the material universe was "...made of things which do not appear." (Hebrews 11:3) In other words God created the material universe out of nothing as opposed to merely reforming and organizing pre-existing matter. If matter had no existence prior to divine creation, and if our eternal salvation is equated in Scripture with divine creation, how do we explain the requirement in these errant views of salvation that the sinner must either take the first step or in some way cooperate with God to effect his/her spiritual creation? What role could non-existent matter possibly have had in its formation? Likewise what role can a fallen, sinful, "after the flesh," "...carnally minded" sinner have in his spiritual creation? (As only two examples, notice the parallel that Paul draws between the natural and the spiritual creation in 2 Corinthians 5:17 and Ephesians 2:10)

But ye are not in the flesh, but in the Spirit, if so be that the Spirit of God dwell in you. What makes the difference? What single truth identifies one person as "in the flesh" and another person as "in the Spirit"? Is it how they act? Or is it the fact of the indwelling Spirit of God? Paul rejects the superficial, external criteria and comes down decisively for the fact of the indwelling Holy Spirit.

Paul also puts equal emphasis on the other side of this question. *Now if any man have not the Spirit of Christ, he is none of his.* Whether Paul considers the "spiritually minded" or the "carnally minded" person, the presence or absence of the indwelling Holy Spirit is the single deciding factor in his teaching.

Primarily—at least among Baptists—with the appearance of Andrew Fuller and his hybrid "low Calvinism," many folks, even Baptists, have abandoned Paul's simple criteria and have embraced the superficial and external behavior of individuals for their judgment as to whether a person is born again or not. Instead of holding to the historical Baptist view of God's persevering in His grace to preserve His elect so that none shall fall finally away and spend eternity in eternal separation from God, they substitute the external, man-centric view that emphasizes preservation in their own perseverance! A contemporary equivalent to Fuller's Cal-Minian teaching that mixes divine grace and human contribution is Norman Geisler's *Chosen But Free*, a book in which Geisler claims to be "Reformed," but he interprets every passage that he explains in the book in a wholly Arminian perspective.

Factually one human being, however well informed in Biblical teaching, cannot finally and decisively discern the presence or absence of the indwelling Holy Spirit in another individual. The current emphasis on this claimed ability among those who give lip service to the doctrines of grace manifests similar arrogance to the Arminian response to the person that the Arminain believing person cannot convince to embrace his/her views, "There is only one difference between you and me. My sins are forgiven; yours are not." Chuck Swindoll makes an interesting observation that touches this point. We will all be surprised when we get to heaven. Some of us will be surprised to discover that folks whom we expected to be there are not there, while others will be surprised to discover that folks whom they didn't expect to see there are in fact there. The decisive issue of who will be in heaven is not based on external human conduct, but on the work of God within, in Paul's teaching in this passage, the grace of God that changed the nature, the "being" of the individual from "carnally minded" to "spiritually minded." We should be quite happy—not to mention quite content—with the truth that God alone changes human hearts from carnal to spiritual, and He alone possesses the ability to know what lies within each human heart. (John 2:24-25) Why not leave eternal judgment with God where it belongs?

52
A Matter of Life and Death

> And if Christ be in you, the body is dead because of sin; but the Spirit is life because of righteousness. But if the Spirit of him that raised up Jesus from the dead dwell in you, he that raised up Christ from the dead shall also quicken your mortal bodies by his Spirit that dwelleth in you. (Romans 8:10-11)

Our sinful human nature often manifests a sinful focus on the faults of others more than with self. If we sin, our culture looks the other way and even praises us so long as we can get away with it, but if someone whom we dislike sins, and the sin becomes public, we feel wholly justified in harsh judgments and condemnations of that person. Within the Christian community a similar focus often appears in a judgmental emphasis on others. If you happen to meet a Christian in a public place passing out tracts or otherwise trying to "witness" to strangers, do not be surprised if the professing Christian presumes that every person he/she meets is lost, but they have the way to help you get saved. In last week's chapter I quoted what has almost become a cliché in certain Christian circles; when in discussion with a person of a different belief, the judgmental Christian will arrogantly profess, "There is only one difference between you and me; my sins are forgiven, but yours are not."

This same "keep the focus on others" in judgment attitude also appears in more conservative theological circles under the guise of the professing Christian's claim of the profound insight by which he/she seems nearly obsessed with either giving other people assurance of their salvation—or as the case is more often—withholding that assurance and judging the person as not being saved at all. A study of assurance in the New Testament leaves one wondering where these self-appointed judges have any Biblical sense that they possess either such insight into the secrets of other men's hearts, as well as where they claim to find the Biblical authority to put themselves in this role. Scripture affirms that God gives us assurance in the gospel, and especially through the abundant evidences of Jesus' deity and resurrection. Scripture even indicates that as we live in obedience to the teachings of Scripture we may assure our hearts before God

(Likely the experience of personal assurance is the point in this passage; First John 3:18-19), but it seems surprisingly quiet regarding one man standing in the seat of judgment and presuming to have the knowledge and/or ability to give or withhold assurance from others. To this increasingly arrogant and offensive practice I would direct those who presume the role to a simple passage of inspired Scripture, "There is one lawgiver, who is able to save and to destroy: who art thou that judgest another?" (James 4:12)

What is the Biblical criteria for our perception of our spiritual state—of whether we belong to God's family or not? Paul joins a long list of inspired writers in our study passage in his assessment of an internal criteria that exists between God and His own child, not some brand burned in the regenerate elect person's forehead for all to see externally. The single and decisive factor that determines a person's spiritual state is the indwelling Christ. Notice Paul's emphasis in our study verses, *"And if Christ be in you, the body is dead because of sin...."* I may observe certain external evidences of God's grace in you, but the fact of the indwelling Holy Spirit is something I cannot know. That fact is known only to God and to you!

I do not in any way deny that regeneration alters a person's moral compass, and to some extent that incredible change will manifest itself in a person's behavior, but Scripture never makes certain external manifestations the basis for the final judgment. Isn't it intriguing that in Jesus' depiction of the final Day of Judgment even the elect will react with a question?

> *Then shall the righteous answer him, saying, Lord, when saw we thee an hungred, and fed thee? or thirsty, and gave thee drink? When saw we thee a stranger, and took thee in? or naked, and clothed thee? Or when saw we thee sick, or in prison, and came unto thee?* (Matthew 25:37-39, KJV)

If the resurrected righteous on the Last Day ask such a question, should we not ponder the implications for us in the here-and-now?

...the Spirit is life because of righteousness. A single and predictable consequence of the indwelling Spirit of God is the imputed righteousness of the Lord Jesus Christ, the only righteousness that shall enable a fallen sinner to hear the words of Jesus on that Day, "Come ye blessed...."

But if the Spirit of him that raised up Jesus from the dead dwell in you, he that raised up Christ from the dead shall also quicken your mortal bodies by his Spirit that dwelleth in you. Not only does Paul affirm the imputed righteousness of the Lord Jesus Christ in everyone so touched by the indwelling Holy Spirit, he also affirms that person's final destiny. Every person so touched by the Spirit of God shall hear the welcoming voice of the Savior on that Day. Every one so touched by grace shall also experience a transformation of their physical resurrected bodies that is in power and righteousness equivalent to the work of grace that God sent into the soul in regeneration.

The old Particular Baptist John Gill makes a strong point in his explanation of these verses.

> These words are not to be understood as they are by some, of the continued work of sanctification in the heart by the Spirit of God; for regeneration, and not sanctification, is signified by quickening, which quickening occurs when the Spirit of God first takes up his dwelling in the soul; besides, the apostle had spoke of the life of the spirit or soul before; and they are mortal bodies, and not its mortal souls, which are said to be quickened, for these cannot mean the body of sin, or the remains of corruption, as they are said to be, and which are never quickened, nor never can be. To understand the words in such a sense, is not so agreeable to the resurrection of Christ here mentioned; whereas Christ's resurrection is often used as an argument of ours, which is designed here, where the apostle argues from the one to the other.[1]

Gill's point is as relevant in our time as when he wrote the words over two hundred years ago. Paul is not reasoning on our present behavioral sanctification and good works, but rather he is reminding the Romans, and us, of a future work that the indwelling Holy Spirit shall surely complete in us on resurrection day. Our literal bodily resurrection as God's regenerate elect is as assured and certain as the historical fact of Jesus' personal and literal bodily resurrection!

---

[1] Cited from SwordSearcher Bible software.

Let's return to the point made at the beginning. Paul frames these verses in a highly personalized form. Paul repeatedly uses the personal second person pronoun "you" in these verses. He is reminding the Roman Christians of a bedrock truth, a truth that they need in the "here and now" of life. His premise for teaching these people becomes highly personal to them. He fills the role of minister, not judge and jury. His objective is to comfort them with the interlinked truths of the indwelling Holy Spirit and their final joyful resurrection to glory. He in no way presumes to take on the role of dispensing or withholding the blessing of assurance.

Scripture repeatedly teaches us that the preaching of the gospel must be accompanied by the affirmation of the Holy Spirit and His power, both in the man preaching and in the hearers. Without this power a message may be a good lecture, even a true moral lesson quite worthy of believing and practicing, but only when the Holy Spirit directs and seasons a man's words with His power can we say that the gospel has truly been preached. The distinction between a moral lecture and a message in which the gospel was truly preached is not distinguished by the volume or mannerism in the voice of the preacher. Most of us have known people who truly believed that a man is "preaching" only if he chants his words with a certain rhythm or cadence, or in some other way spoke in an unnatural manner. A man may "preach the gospel" in soft conversational tones, or he may need to speak quite loudly so as to be heard by a large gathering of people. He may speak with intense personal conviction and emotions, or he may speak with the quiet and assured tones of a gentle breeze. All of these things are peripheral to the preaching of the gospel. The power of God in the gospel is not controlled or orchestrated by the preacher or the hearers! When a man is truly blessed by God to "preach" the gospel with power from Him, the message transcends both the messenger and the audience. We cannot control or orchestrate this power. Nor can we imitate it!

What Paul is teaching in our lesson takes us to the heart of the gospel. The message of the gospel, affirmed with power by the indwelling Holy Spirit in both the preacher and the hearer, manifests power to convince fallen and sinful—but regenerate—people that they possess title to a family inheritance for all eternity with God. The gospel preached in power declares the family identity of the regenerate elect child with his/her heavenly family, but rest assured, it is the power of God in the gospel, not the personal judgment of the preacher, who conveys this assurance and conviction. That power is life-transforming because it reminds us, regardless of the trials of the moment, that we belong to the King, and that we have an eternal home waiting for us that cannot be taken from us. "What manner of men ought we to be…."

53
Christian Ethics and Life in Christ

> Therefore, brethren, we are debtors, not to the flesh, to live after the flesh. For if ye live after the flesh, ye shall die: but if ye through the Spirit do mortify the deeds of the body, ye shall live. For as many as are led by the Spirit of God, they are the sons of God. (Romans 8:12-14)

Never do we find Scripture leaving Christian conduct in the "optional" category. New Testament teaching consistently affirms that those who have been made alive in Christ have an obligation to manifest that life in their attitudes and actions. In our study passage Paul compares our obligation to godliness with a debt. What happens if you owe a debt and refuse to pay it? You will face the potential of legal action and repossession of the property that secures the debt.

Given the content and structure of the Roman letter, we should not overlook that Paul rejected as "slander" the false accusation of his critics that he taught that divine predestination caused his righteousness (Romans 3:1-9), but he also rejected the opposite theological view that his conduct earned his eternal life. He remained faithfully on solid truth, not allowing any criticism or trial to move him from the balanced truth that had been given to him in revelation. We have that balanced revelation in the Scriptures that Paul wrote.

Our human nature is prone to leaps into extremes when critics press us. If they accuse us of "Error A," either we will immediately brand "Error A" as abominable heresy to evade the criticism or we will stubbornly embrace "Error A" and point the finger back at our critics, blaming them as abominable heretics for their rejection of the error. Paul set our example clearly. The truth of God is not extreme, and no amount of political pressure, criticism, or persecution should divert us from that balanced, healthy truth.

Our chief objective in our study and interpretation of Scripture is constantly to ensure that we follow Scripture and the truth that it teaches, not leading Scripture into private, errant ideas of our own making by perverse and false interpretations of Scripture.

Students of philosophy and of Christian faith use a rather large word to describe a fundamental principle on which people build their ideas. What is your respected source of authority for your ideas? Where do you get your ideas? How reliable in your eyes is your source? Do you have many sources for your ideas or only one? The word is "epistemology." We may readily note and reject the dominant Roman Catholic view of multiple epistemology (not only Scripture but as well, the historical teachings of the church, and the word of the pope), but do we also look to multiple sources for our own epistemology? If we interpret Scripture through our favorite Confession of faith, are we not elevating that confession to the chair of epistemology? If we begin to research the writings of past generations in the faith and start interpreting Scripture according to their teachings, have we not added an alternate source of authority? The problem with multiple sources of epistemology should be obvious but it apparently isn't. Multiple sources of authority seldom fully agree. So when one source of your authority disagrees with another source, which authority will you accept as your final word? If I elevate confessions to the role of epistemological authority, I can find some confession somewhere in history that agrees with my private ideas. If I magnify the writings of past writers, I can eventually find an old writer whose teachings agree with mine. Once a professing Christian leaves the authority of "Sola Scriptura," *of Scripture alone,* not Scripture plus anything else, he/she has left the reliable foundation of truth and will eventually fall into error, error that Scripture rejects.

Let me give you an example. The name of Elder James Oliphant is a highly respected name among Primitive Baptists. The first time I read excerpts from his writings they were brief piecemeal snippets extracted from larger works that he wrote. The pieces extracted left me with a question as to Elder Oliphant's belief regarding predestination. Did he embrace fatalistic determinism? I couldn't tell from the isolated quotes that I was reading. Only years later when I began to read Elder Oliphant's writings, did I realize that he actually opposed fatalistic determinism and wrote against it. His *Thoughts on the Will* is a masterpiece against this error. The people who were quoting brief snippets from him appeared to have intentionally selected these brief quotes to promote the very idea that Elder Oliphant opposed. I would not have known the difference had I not read him more fully. This is the problem with multiple sources of authority. Not only do they inevitably contradict each other, but they are also subject to the reader's interpretation and potential misuse.

Notice Paul's pointed teaching in our study passage. Do not forget that Scripture is to be our exclusive source of authority, not one of several. Paul does not leave the conduct of believers in Christ open to personal choice or human preference. Christian conduct is a debt that every believer owes, first to God and secondarily to his/her fellowman. Paul makes a double point. Once he determines that we owe a debt, he immediately examines the question to know the identity of the one to whom we owe that debt. We owe no debt to our flesh, a word that Paul and other Biblical writers often use to refer to the sinful disposition of our fallen nature.

The only legitimate debt we owe is to live to God according to the leading of the Holy Spirit, a leading that will always direct us to follow the teachings of Scripture. Many groups of professing Christians magnify their private ideas or preferences into a supposed leading of the Holy Spirit, but they seem to have no problem when their claimed divinely informed conduct contradicts Scripture. If you nudge them to follow Scripture alone, they will accuse you of being a "legalist." Since the Holy Spirit inspired the writers of Scripture—and He is God and shares in all the essential and incommunicable attributes of God—He cannot possibly contradict Himself. Thus any claim of Holy Spirit leading that fails to pass the filter of inspired Scripture is de facto not the leading of the Holy Spirit.

Even if we claim that the Holy Spirit is leading us when we fall into error, Paul's criteria of debt will rebuke us. To err and claim that the Holy Spirit is leading us to do so—to borrow Paul's debt analogy—would be the equivalent of writing a check for the wrong amount of money and then sending it to the wrong company at the wrong address, only to claim in self-righteousness that we have actually paid our debt!

For if ye live after the flesh, ye shall die. Good intentions will not satisfy Paul, nor will they satisfy the Holy Spirit. *...but if ye through the Spirit do mortify the deeds of the body, ye shall live.* Paul is writing to believers in Rome, to people who were members of the church in Rome, people whom he has consistently addressed as children of God throughout this letter. He does not here warn them of losing their eternal life, but rather he warns them of the danger of losing the vitality of life by sinful conduct that honors the wrong moral influence in their lives. Actions always impose consequences on the person who acts in a certain manner. Scripture consistently and repeatedly assesses consequences on us based on our personal choices and actions. We cannot practice sin, the equivalent in Paul's analogy of paying our debt to the flesh and not the Spirit, and innocently pretend that we do not face the moral consequences of our sinful choices. We may for a time take advantage of other people's poor moral perceptions or compromised choices, but the final Judge by which we shall be measured is God. He is never deceived!

For as many as are led by the Spirit of God, they are the sons of God. I never grow tired of admiring the precision with which the Holy Spirit directed the writers of Scripture to frame their thoughts and words. John Gill makes the following points regarding this verse.

> Not by the spirit of the world, or of the devil, or by their own spirits: the act of leading ascribed to the Spirit is either in allusion to the leading of blind persons, or such who are in the dark; or rather to the leading of children and teaching them to go; which supposes life in those that are led, and some degree of strength, though a good deal of weakness; and is a display of powerful and efficacious grace, and is always for their good: the Spirit of God leads them from sin, and from a dependence on their own righteousness, in paths they formerly knew not, and in which they should go, in the paths of faith and truth, of righteousness and holiness, and in a right, though sometimes a rough way; he leads them to the person, blood, and righteousness of Christ, and to the fulness of grace in him; into the presence of God, to the house and ordinances of God; into the truths of the Gospel, from one degree of grace to another, and at last to glory; which he does gradually, by little and little he leads them to see the iniquity of their hearts and natures, to lay hold on Christ and salvation by him, into the doctrines of grace, and the love and favour of God, and proportionally to the strength he gives…[1]

---

[1] Copied from the electronic edition of Gill's commentary in SwordSearcher Bible study software.

As Gill observes, the Holy Spirit's leading is precise and predictable. The criteria for knowing that the Holy Spirit is leading, as opposed to our own self-serving motives or desires, will always appear in the consistency of our conduct with inspired Scripture. A private "impression" or "feeling" that goes contradictory to Scripture is no more right than a mystical "burning in the bosom." The Holy Spirit's leading will always lead us to honor His work in Scripture.

The idea that God is "convicting" the unregenerate in a rather incompetent effort to nudge them to save themselves by His powerless moral influence falls distinctly short of Paul's teaching in this verse. Those whom the Holy Spirit thus leads *"...are the sons of God."* The emphasis of this verse finds its fulfillment in regenerate elect whom the Holy Spirit leads to faith and obedience to God. The verse deals with God's moral government of His own children.

Dr. Tom Constable affirms this point.

> Verses 14–17 explain the Spirit's ministry of confirming the reality of the believer's position as a son of God to him or her. Paul believed that the believer who is aware of his or her secure position will be more effective in mortifying his or her flesh...Unlike sin the Spirit does not enslave us. He does not compel or force us to do God's will as slaves of God. Rather He appeals to us to do so as sons of God. [2]

The word that Paul selected to identify the Holy Spirit's leading emphasizes influence or guidance, not coercion or irresistible force.

> **(B)** Metaphorically, to lead, induce, incite, guide (Rom. 2:4, "to repentance"; 1 Cor. 12:2, "even as ye were led," meaning to idolatry, the figure being drawn from pastoral life [cf. Ex. 3:1; Is. 11:6]). Also, to be

---

[2]Tom Constable, *Tom Constable's Expository Notes on the Bible* (Galaxie Software, 2003; 2003), Ro 8:15.
cf (compare, comparison)
[3]Spiros Zodhiates, *The Complete Word Study Dictionary : New Testament*, electronic ed. (Chattanooga, TN: AMG Publishers, 2000, c1992, c1993), G71.

This word is quite distinct from the word that Jesus used in John 6:44 when referring to God's irresistible divine drawing of sinners to Himself in regeneration.

> Our particular concern is with the figur. use in Jn. In Jn. 6:44 Jesus says: οὐδεὶς δύναται ἐλθεῖν πρός με, ἐὰν μὴ ὁ πατὴρ ὁ πέμψας με ἑλκύσῃ αὐτόν, and in 12:32: κἀγὼ ἐὰν ὑψωθῶ ἐκ τῆς γῆς, πάντας ἑλκύσω πρὸς ἐμαυτόν.
> The basic meaning is to "tug" or "draw" (with material obj.: Jn. 18:10; 21:6, 11). In the case of persons (cf. also 3 Macc. 4:7; Ac. 16:19; 21:30; Jm. 2:6) it may mean to "compel"....[4]

Thus Scripture clearly distinguishes the Holy Spirit's effectual and irresistible force in regeneration from His guiding, leading influence in God's moral government of His children in their conduct. God does not drive or drag His own children in obedience! Such would not be obedience at all. It would rather be a form of robotic compliance with a greater force, an action that carries no moral value on the lesser power in the person so moved.

In this way Paul urges us to "pay our debts" to God by a conscious, willing obedience to the leading influence of the Holy Spirit in our lives. In so doing we manifest that we are in fact God's children and that we seek to honor Him with our lives.

We live in a culture that magnifies debt, but sadly it does not always maintain equal value on the payment of the debts that we owe. The media is full of appeals for people to spend money on non-essential goods and services, including offers of supposedly pain-free repayment of the related debt. Economists point out the alarming frequency with which people run up enormous debts for such non-essentials ($50,000 or more is not uncommon for credit card balances). Our nation presently faces a significant mortgage crisis because lenders urged people to buy homes that cost significantly more than they could afford through the use of either "interest only" or even "negative

---

obj. object.
[4]*Theological Dictionary of the New Testament*, Vols. 5-9 Edited by Gerhard Friedrich. Vol. 10 Compiled by Ronald Pitkin., ed. Gerhard Kittel, Geoffrey William Bromiley and Gerhard Friedrich, electronic ed. (Grand Rapids, MI: Eerdmans, 1964-c1976), 2:503.

amortization" loans (a term that means your monthly payment doesn't even cover the interest on your debt, so at the end of the loan period you owe more than you owed at the beginning!).

If you and I compared our Christian life with Paul's analogy of debt, what would be the state of our personal finances? Would we be solvent or bankrupt? Let's work at consistently honoring God by "paying our debts," obviously our literal monetary debts, but more importantly our moral debts to the Holy Spirit to conduct our lives according to His gracious leading.

54
The Spirit of Adoption

> For ye have not received the spirit of bondage again to fear; but ye have received the Spirit of adoption, whereby we cry, Abba, Father. The Spirit itself beareth witness with our spirit, that we are the children of God. (Romans 8:15-16)

What do we have from God now? What shall we have in eternity? Later in this chapter Paul will tell us that we are waiting for the adoption, further explained by him in that setting as "...the redemption of our body." (Romans 8:23) In our study passage before us we learn that we now have the "spirit of adoption." Thus we now have in spirit what we shall have in fact at the Second Coming. Paul's reference to the "redemption of our body" is a clear prediction of our literal bodily resurrection at that time.

How many Christians do you know who go through life, constantly living inside the rigid mold of bondage and fear? They may occasionally talk of their joy in Christ, but their lives manifest far more clearly a dreadful bondage. Many of these folks live in the perpetual prison of deficient assurance. They wrongly focus their pursuit for assurance on their own performance, but, having set their sights too low, they never find sufficient assurance. However well they "perform" their faith, they must face flaws and failures that leave them distinctly short of perfection. If a person looks to his/her own faith and obedience, or "performance," for assurance, anything short of perfection will leave him/her with and equally short assurance. Biblical assurance resides in God, not in human performance.

The same failure can be predicted for those who live their whole life in fear. Fear of failure, fear that someone whom you respect will not approve of you or of something you say or do, fear of the future—the list of potential fears is literally endless. Obsessing over your fears is guaranteed to produce an incredibly miserable life. Who needs it?

Paul sweeps all of these "performance based" marks of ritual, external Christianity away and reminds us that none of them comes from God! Praise God for that revelation!

What has God given us? ...*ye have received the Spirit of adoption, whereby we cry, Abba, Father.* Literally the word "Abba" is not fully translated. A similar word was used in the Aramaic language with reference to one's father. Several points surface in this parallel use of "Father." First of all, the influence that urges a person, regardless of language or culture, to cry out to God from the depth of their being, calling Him "Father," is a divine gift. It grows out of the Spirit of adoption. Paul rejected all the various performance based criteria that advocates of either salvation by works or of extreme perseverance impose on people, and by which they promptly judge people as either saved or not saved. A question that devotees of either of these false systems of belief refuse to answer is "How much must a person do to ensure his/her salvation?" For advocates of salvation by works, the person's degree of faith and obedience serves as a direct corollary to that person's entitlement to heaven. For advocates of extreme perseverance, the person's degree of faith and obedience becomes the badge of identity. If the degree of faith and obedience are deficient, the person has no real "assurance" of their salvation. However, when pressed for specifics, advocates of this errant view either cannot or will not set a precise degree of obedience that a person must meet. Surely if God based our assurance on our performance, He would have been clear and precise in naming the minimum acceptable level of performance on which He would grant assurance.

Some commentators refer to the Aramaic word translated "Abba" as the elemental word of an infant child calling out to his/her father. The word likely conveys far more than mere infant affection.

> "However, we oversentimentalize this word when we refer to it as mere baby talk and translate it into English as 'daddy.' The word *Abba* appears in certain legal texts of the Mishna as a designation used by grown children in claiming the inheritance of their deceased father.[139] As a word of address *Abba* is not so much associated with infancy as it is with intimacy. It is a cry of the heart, not a word spoken calmly with personal detachment and reserve, but a word we 'call' or 'cry out' (*krazo*)...

---

[139] 139. See *Theological Dictionary of the New Testament*, s.v. "abba," by G. Kittel.

"... it would be presumptuous and daring beyond all propriety to address God as *Abba* had Jesus himself not bidden us to do so."[140][1]

It seems quite appropriate in this context to consider the word "Abba" in terms of adult children of God "...claiming the inheritance..." of—in this case their dead but risen and victorious Savior through whom they have full title to their eternal inheritance.

For Paul both of these external criteria fail the final test of divine approval and truth. The single criteria that distinguishes the family of God in his teaching is the indwelling Holy Spirit. Scripture indeed teaches that the indwelling Holy Spirit will make an impact on the life of the regenerate elect person, but Scripture never attributes to that varied impact the weight of the actual work of the Holy Spirit within. God is not so superficial!

So what can we conclude from Paul's teaching here? Simple; if you call out to God from the deep convictions within, that calling evidences the indwelling Holy Spirit.

The Spirit itself beareth witness with our spirit, that we are the children of God. Here Paul defines a "joint testimony" in which the Holy Spirit testifies, along with—and to—our own "spirit" that we are the children of God. One testimony affirms the other and reinforces it. The testimony of God is not to bondage and fear. It is not a harsh and arrogant "critical parent" attitude. Rather it is an affirming assurance to us that we indeed belong to the family of God.

> God has provided the believer with two witnesses to his or her salvation, the Holy Spirit and our human spirit (cf. Deut. 17:6; Matt. 18:16). The former witness is objective in Scripture and subjective (cf. v. 14) while the latter is only subjective.[260]

---

[140] 140. George, pp. 307, 308.
[1] Tom Constable, *Tom Constable's Expository Notes on the Bible* (Galaxie Software, 2003; 2003), Ga 4:6.
[260] 260. Another view is that the Holy Spirit bears witness to God when we pray (v. 15). See Robert N. Wilkin, "Assurance by Inner Witness?" *Grace Evangelical Society News* 8:2 (March-April 1993):2-3. Incidentally, this second reference to "spirit" is the only one in Rom. 8 that is not a reference to the Holy Spirit.

The term "children" identifies our family relationship based on regeneration whereas "sons" stresses our legal standing based on adoption.[2]

What is the distinction between "subjective" and "objective"? "Subjective" refers to our internal and emotional bias as we evaluate various questions. "Objective" refers to more literal and factual foundations that are by definition "free of any bias or prejudice caused by personal feelings.[3]" In a final and literal assessment one's emotions or sentimental bias means nothing whatever. We may delude ourselves and live in our own little dream world—subjectively. However, our emotional or sentimental bias is quite important to us, is it not? Thus by the form of his argument in this lesson Paul addresses both the sentimental and personal issues of God's children, as well as the factual, non-sentimental basis on which that personal conviction rests. Paul gives us the "best of both worlds" in this lesson. God gives His children a personal basis for their hope in Him, an incredibly personal basis, one that Constable observes would be incredibly "...presumptuous and daring beyond all propriety...had Jesus himself not bidden us to do so."

John affirms this same comforting truth.

Behold, what manner of love the Father hath bestowed upon us, that we should be called the sons of God: therefore the world knoweth us not, because it knew him not. (1 John 3:1)

There is nothing whatever within us by nature that gives us either the desire or the basis on which to claim such an intimate fellowship with God. But God in tender grace gives us His indwelling Spirit as an objective witness to our claim. He further alters our internal nature as to give us a subjective sense of Him and of His blessings on us. These two witnesses, one subjective and one objective, bear harmonious testimony to the incredible truth. We—undeserving, sinful creatures that we are by nature—by divine grace are in fact children of God and heirs of heaven. As if that were not sufficient,

---

[2] Tom Constable, *...Expository Notes on the Bible*, Ro 8:16.
[3] Quoted from the online *Encarta Dictionary: English* (North America) dictionary.

God also uses these two joint witnesses to assure us in the here and now that we are God's child and have heaven and eternal joys before us. The basis of this joyful testimony is not personal merit, nor personal actions that "clear the mystical hoop" of the never-defined minimum standard for authentic merit-based assurance. It is rather God's incredible "…manner of love."

55
Joint-Heirs with Christ

> And if children, then heirs; heirs of God, and joint-heirs with Christ; if so be that we suffer with him, that we may be also glorified together. For I reckon that the sufferings of this present time are not worthy to be compared with the glory which shall be revealed in us. (Romans 8:17-18)

Scripture frequently draws the analogy of an inheritance when teaching us about our future with God in eternity. In this passage we are said to be "joint-heirs" with Christ. We share in the richness of his inheritance.

How much shall the heirs of God enjoy in heaven? Shall they enjoy a "basic" heaven on account of their inheritance in Christ, and also enjoy an added richness on account of their faithfulness here in time? This dual concept is rather commonplace among commentaries as well as among contemporary Christians. While offering some excellent points, Dr. Tom Constable indicates his belief in this idea.

> The term "children" identifies our family relationship based on regeneration whereas "sons" stresses our legal standing based on adoption.
> 8:17 Being a child of God makes us His heirs (cf. 1 Pet. 1:3–4). We inherit with Jesus Christ our brother (v. 29). We inherit both sufferings, as His disciples now, and glory, most of which lies in the future (cf. 1 Pet. 4:13). The phrase "if indeed" seeks to render the first class condition in the Greek that in this case we could translate "since." Just as surely as we share His sufferings (Gr. *sumpaschomen*, any sufferings, not just those connected with our bearing witness for Christ) now we will share His glory in the future. This is a reference to the glorification that every believer will experience at the end of his or her life (vv. 18–25). Our glory then will be in proportion to our suffering for His sake as His disciples now (cf. 1 Pet. 4:12–19).
> The New Testament teaches that the amount of inheritance the children of God receive will vary depending on our faithfulness to God (Luke 19:11–27). However, there is no doubt that all Christians are the heirs of God and will inherit glorification as well as many other blessings (cf. 1 Pet. 1:3–12).[261] [1]

There seems to be a rather obvious contradiction in this idea. What determines our degree of blessedness in heaven? Is it what Jesus did for us, or is it what we did? Or is it some combination of both? While I often find Constable to be insightful and helpful, in this case I do not believe he makes the case that he affirms. He merely affirms it without making a case for the idea.

While no doubt all blessings come from God, there are a variety of ideas relative to the character of these blessings. When Paul distinguished between the "wages of sin" and the "gift of God" (Romans 6:23), he made a clear and obvious distinction between the bases for heaven and hell. The people who shall spend eternity in hell separated from God receive their wages, something earned and deserved. However, Paul clearly identified that those who shall spend eternity with God in heaven shall be there due to a divine "gift," not due to wages earned. In that verse Paul didn't indicate that part of the inheritance in heaven shall be a divine gift and another part of it shall be a reward or wages earned. The whole of hell shall be wages earned, but the whole of heaven shall be "the gift of God." Consider the varied ideas relative to conduct here in time and the consequences divinely bestowed.

1. We do good things in time, and we receive the reward for them in eternity, the textbook "salvation by works" idea. We do bad things in time, and we receive the punishment for them in eternity. This view makes heaven and hell equally reliant on man, not God. In this view, be it Arminian or Fulleresque, God did just as much for the saved who shall enjoy heaven as He did for the wicked who shall spend eternity in hell. Therefore, according to this view, one's eternal destiny is wholly determined by the individual, not by God.
2. We do good things in time only because we were ordained irresistibly of God to do them. This is the historical absolute predestination idea; it was far more the dominant idea that

---

[261] 261. For a study of the variable factors in inheriting, see Zane C. Hodges, *The Hungry Inherit*.
[1] Tom Constable, *Tom Constable's Expository Notes on the Bible* (Galaxie Software, 2003; 2003), Ro 8:16-17.

distinguished absolute predestinarians than the occasional predestinarian who went to a greater extreme and attributed even sin to divine predestination. However, as many historical theologians have observed, this idea destroys the fundamental idea of God's moral government. There is no moral government involved in this idea; the believer in this view is merely responding robotically to irresistible divine power. Such a response lacks any moral value whatever. It can be viewed as little more than wholly mechanistic.

3. As children of God already born of God, we do good things in time and receive blessings for them, or we sin in time and receive divine chastening for our sins. This view affirms the Biblical teaching for the family of God.

4. The sinful deeds of the wicked are judged by God on the Day of Judgment, and they shall be justly rewarded, paid their earned wages, by eternal, conscious separation from God in hell.

5. The sinful deeds of God's elect were laid on the Lord Jesus Christ who died for them, paying the divine and just penalty for them in His suffering and death. His spotless righteousness was laid to the elect's account, so that their enjoyment of heaven shall be wholly based on the "gift of God" through the Lord Jesus Christ. This is the Biblical view that Paul affirmed in Romans 6:23.

This passage uses rather interesting language when it introduces suffering into the context. Paul carefully indicates that we "suffer with him." In his commentary on this verse John Gill offers a rather broad and sensible view.

> Christ and his people being one, he the head, and they the members, suffer together; when he suffered, they suffered with him and in him, as their head and representative; and they partake of the virtue and efficacy of his sufferings; and they also suffer afflictions, many of them at least of the same kind with Christ, only with these differences; his were penal evils, theirs not; his were attended with a vast sense of wrath and terror, theirs oftentimes with, joy and comfort; his were meritorious, not so theirs. Moreover, many of their sufferings are for the sake of Christ and his Gospel; on the other hand, by reason of that

> union which is between Christ and believers, he suffers with them, he reckons their afflictions his, and sympathizes with them; and the consideration of this greatly animates and encourages them in their sufferings, and especially when they observe that they shall be "glorified together"; not with his essential glory, nor with his mediatorial glory, but with that glory which his Father has given him for them. There is a glorification of the saints in Christ, and a glorification of them by Christ, and a glorification of them with Christ, which will consist in likeness to him, and in the everlasting vision and enjoyment of him.[2]

Notice Gill's twofold interpretation of suffering in this verse. First, because of our legal union with Christ, when He suffered for our sins, divine justice viewed us as united with Him in that moment. The dual transfer—our sins to Him and His righteousness to our account—was both literal and legal from the divine perspective. Beware any theology that avoids a literal substitutionary relationship between the sins of the elect and the righteousness of Christ. This was perhaps the greatest stumbling block of Andrew Fuller's "efficient-sufficient" error; he would not accept the idea of a literal substitutionary sacrifice in the death of Christ. The literal language of Galatians 3:13 suggests that Christ stepped into the path of the curse that was falling on us, absorbing it wholly so that we would not suffer it.

Secondly, the child of God cannot face suffering in this life alone. Such a thing cannot be! When we suffer here, He suffers with us because of His amazing love for us. But rest assured; His sharing our present suffering is merely the beginning of a far better truth. We shall fully and equally share eternal glory with Him because of His sacrificial death for us. Not only does this truth encourage and comfort us now in the trials of life, but it also anchors our souls in glorious hope of enjoying glory with Him as literally as we suffer now. Hallelujah, what a Savior!

---

[2] Quoted from SwordSearcher Bible software's electronic version of Gill's commentary.

56
Final Things: What do you expect?

For the earnest expectation of the creature waiteth for the manifestation of the sons of God. For the creature was made subject to vanity, not willingly, but by reason of him who hath subjected the same in hope, Because the creature itself also shall be delivered from the bondage of corruption into the glorious liberty of the children of God. For we know that the whole creation groaneth and travaileth in pain together until now. And not only they, but ourselves also, which have the firstfruits of the Spirit, even we ourselves groan within ourselves, waiting for the adoption, to wit, the redemption of our body. (Romans 8:19-23)

Most of us at one time or another have engaged in a "What will heaven be like?" conversation. Typically people take this conversation down one of two paths. The first path claims full ignorance. It professes that we know nothing whatever about heaven, and there is no way to know other than the belief that it will be amazingly good. Advocates of this idea will often quote Paul's words in First Corinthians 2:9, "But as it is written, Eye hath not seen, nor ear heard, neither have entered into the heart of man, the things which God hath prepared for them that love him." Of course Paul was not writing about heaven when he wrote these words, and further in the very next verse he said, "But God hath revealed them unto us by his Spirit…." Thus the person's claim of having no knowledge whatever is immediately contradicted in the next sentence. What Paul is teaching in this context has to do with the unregenerate person's lack of ability to know spiritual things, making Paul's "But God hath revealed them unto us by his Spirit…" comment perfectly logical.

The other path that this conversation often takes is the emotional or sentimental path. Advocates of this path will talk endlessly about how they want to go to heaven to renew their love and fellowship with precious relatives and friends who have died. A rather old hymn in some of our hymnals depicts this sentimental view of heaven with a bit more sentimentality than most of us would consider appropriate. Each verse ends with an "In going there to see…" listing various relatives in order, mother, father, etc., followed by classmates, ending with the final person whom the author of the words wants to see,

"...my Savior." To be bluntly honest, shouldn't the *first person* we want to see when we arrive in heaven be our Lord? As a youth in my faith, I recall a conversation between a couple of older men in the faith. They were discussing personal identity in heaven. Will we know parents, siblings, spouses, and beloved relatives and friends? One of the men mentioned an aunt who raised him, saying, "If I thought I wouldn't know her in heaven, I wouldn't want to go there." This attitude sadly characterizes the sentimental attitude toward heaven.

Scripture rejects both ideas. I believe that Scripture affirms individual identity in heaven. We will not all be a countless multitude of clones with no apparent individuality or identity. However, Scripture also affirms that earthly bonds will not carry over into heaven. Study Jesus' dialogue with the Sadducees regarding the woman who was married to several brothers who each died.

For the earnest expectation of the creature waiteth for the manifestation of the sons of God. Throughout this context the words "creature" and "creation" appear several times. Both words are translated from the same Greek word, so there is not factual or contextual basis on which to distinguish the two words. It is possible, based on Second Peter, third chapter, that Paul's "whole creation" comment here may refer to the whole of the created universe, meaning that the physical universe will be melted down and recreated at the Second Coming. That conclusion, however, falls more in the category of theological development than contextual interpretation.

Strong's exhaustive concordance and lexicon defines "earnest expectation" as "anxious and persistent expectation." Zodhiates illustrates the emphasis of the word,"...Attentive or earnest expectation or looking for, as with the neck stretched out and the head thrust forward...."[1] Only those who have been touched by divine grace and made sensitive by grace of their spiritual state can or will experience such an "earnest expectation."

The "waiting" involved in this passage reminds us that the final epoch in God's incredible and eternal design has not yet been fulfilled. It has indeed begun, but the final chapter has not yet unfolded. That grand event is the theme of this context. Presently we live in the

---

[1]Spiros Zodhiates, *The Complete Word Study Dictionary : New Testament*, electronic ed. (Chattanooga, TN: AMG Publishers, 2000, c1992, c1993), G603.

constant conflict between "vanity" and "hope." In a particular way this conflict integrates with the intense conflict that Paul described in his personal experience in the seventh chapter of Romans.

What are we waiting for? What is yet to come? Paul describes that final day as a time for the "...manifestation of the sons of God." It is rather easy for us to identify some of God's children in this life. Their obvious gentle kindness and devoted faith to their Lord shouts their identity as children of God. There are others who leave us in doubt. We cannot with Biblical authority say that they are either saved or not saved. Many of the errant ideas in contemporary theological circles that attempt to identify every one of God's elect in the here and now demonstrate the vanity of human pride. Advocates of this idea want to know all of God's elect now, so they invent non-Biblical ideas that they can rationalize through which to claim that they can know whether a person is or is not one of God's elect. If we can come to such knowledge now, why would Paul indicate that it will not be known or manifested till a future time and event? Chuck Swindoll makes an interesting observation on this point. We will all discover at least two surprises when we get to heaven. The first surprise is that we will see people there whom we did not expect to be there, and the second surprise is that some folks whom we expected to see there will be absent!

"*...by reason of him who hath subjected the same in hope....*" We live in hope of that day now. Hope as used in Scripture is often misrepresented and misunderstood. It is not mere wishful thinking. Rather it is more akin to the idea in Paul's "earnest expectation" term in this passage. Hope is no better than the reality to which it looks. If we hope for a future and wholly fictional idea, our hope is cruel and empty. Hope takes on value only to the extent to which it grasps a concept of future reality.

What is the future reality in Paul's teaching that makes our present hope in the midst of conflict so invaluable? *Because the creature itself also shall be delivered from the bondage of corruption into the glorious liberty of the children of God.* Be it our physical bodies that shall be transformed in the resurrection, or be it the whole natural created universe, the future is altogether full of incredible treasures for the family of God. Given the contextual reference to the resurrection of our physical bodies, I am a bit more inclined to believe that Paul had the physical literal resurrection in mind when he wrote these thoughts. Based on the third chapter of Second Peter, I am inclined to believe that the whole material universe will be melted down and recreated without the devastating effects of sin that we now see on it. However in this context it appears that Paul is dealing more specifically with the literal resurrection of our bodies.

...waiting for the adoption, to wit, the redemption of our body. In First Corinthians fifteenth chapter Paul deals with the literal bodily resurrection in greater detail than we find anywhere else in Scripture. However, Hosea 13:14 refers to the resurrection in terms of redemption, similar to Paul's use of the term in our study passage.

I will ransom them from the power of the grave; I will redeem them from death: O death, I will be thy plagues; O grave, I will be thy destruction: repentance shall be hid from mine eyes.

When Jesus died for our sins, He paid the price necessary for our "redemption," but He has not yet taken full custody or possession of his full purchase. Paul himself uses this terminology quite clearly.

Which is the earnest of our inheritance until the redemption of the purchased possession, unto the praise of his glory. (Ephesians 1:14)

Notice Paul's careful description of our salvation in financial or "redemption" terms. The "possession" has clearly already been "purchased," but it has not yet been "redeemed." When the trumpet blows and the graves open at the Last Day, Jesus will claim the final segment of what (more accurately "whom") He purchased at Calvary. Not only did He purchase our souls, He also purchased our bodies, giving Him full right to claim what He purchased when He chooses to exercise His legal/fiduciary right to claim what He has purchased.

Our understanding of this amazing transaction, full redemption, lies at the foundation of our Biblical hope. With solid grounds we look forward joyfully and expectantly to that amazing day! "Come quickly Lord Jesus!"

57
Hope: The Interface between the Temporal and the Eternal

> For we are saved by hope: but hope that is seen is not hope: for what a man seeth, why doth he yet hope for? But if we hope for that we see not, then do we with patience wait for it. (Romans 8:24-25)

How do we interface the temporal in our lives—where we live today—with the eternal where we shall live in eternity? If there is no link between the two, what value does anything eternal have for us now? Sadly we sometimes create such a sterile segregation between the two, but Scripture never accepts such a notion. Scripture presents a distinct integration between the temporal and the eternal such that our view of the eternal directly impacts our interaction with—and our reaction to—the temporal events that constantly surround and impact us.

In this context Paul has just completed a focused lesson regarding the final resurrection and the glory that awaits the family of God at the "…redemption of our body." What specific impact should our belief in the final resurrection of our body have on our conduct today? Paul answers this question in our study verses.

In formal argumentation (particularly in the ancient dialectical argumentation in which Paul frames the Roman letter) our study verses fall under the category of an "assertion."[1] Once the writer makes his assertion he then is obligated to add well reasoned "grounds" on which the assertion stands. The remainder of the eighth chapter of Romans will form Paul's grounds for his assertion of hope expressed in these verses. In a logical sense Paul bridges the gap between the first half and the last half of this chapter with these verses. The logical and well reasoned conclusion to his arguments for

---

[1] Actually the form of Paul's argument in the eighth chapter of Romans likely defines the first verse of the chapter as his primary assertion with supporting grounds logically presented throughout the whole chapter. In this more refined structure of Paul's presentation "We are saved by hope" becomes a secondary ground for the primary argument with the supporting grounds that follow affirming hope and thus supporting the primary assertion, "There is therefore now no condemnation to them which are in Christ Jesus.…"

the resurrection is "hope." And the grounds for this hope—actually the grounds for our belief in the resurrection of our body at the end of time—Paul lays out in logical form in the second half of the chapter.

It is sad indeed that radical dispensational teaching has so dominated contemporary Christian teaching as to make the most glorious and assuring truth of Scripture to become the most controversial truth of Scripture. A brief study of historical theology will confirm that modern dispensationalism didn't exist prior to J. N. Darby, Plymouth Brethren, around 1827. Darby's teachings were generally rejected by nineteenth century Christian scholars. Then in the early twentieth century C. I. Scofield published the now-famous Scofield Bible in which he inserted copious notes of his Darby-like views of dispensationalism. Scofield accomplished what Darby failed to do, gain mainstream acceptance of his dispensational views.[2] In more recent years Tim LaHaye (in his *Left Behind* series of "novels") further popularized this view of end times. Today in many Christian circles any form of eschatological teaching is avoided by anyone who dares to reject this extreme and a-historical doctrinal view of the end times. This avoidance of eschatology stands in vivid contrast with the comforting Biblical view of the final end and God's final disposition of all things to His eternal credit and glory.

Rather than saying that final things were so controversial that he preferred merely to avoid teaching on it at all, Paul made these truths the centerpiece of much of his teaching, directly associating it with the death, resurrection, and victorious ascension of our Lord, not with human merit and accomplishment. It is rather fascinating to remind the dispensational believer of John's quite specific description of those who "reign" with Christ through the Biblical thousand years, for his description doesn't remotely relate to the contemporary ideas.

> *And I saw thrones, and they sat upon them, and judgment was given unto them: and I saw the souls of them that were beheaded for the witness of Jesus, and for the word of God, and which had not worshipped the beast, neither his image, neither had received his mark upon their foreheads, or in their hands; and they lived and reigned with Christ a thousand years.*

---

[2] For a critical view of Scofield and his teachings, go to the following web site: http://www.sweetliberty.org/issues/hoax/scofield.htm

(Revelation 20:4) Notice that John describes the souls of martyrs, not the bodies of superior Christians, who were reigning with Christ. Thus unless you die a martyr's death for your faith you have no Biblical authority to expect that you shall participate in this thousand year experience!

For we are saved by hope.... Most contemporary Bible teaching finds no place for Biblical hope. Typically preachers will errantly define hope as "wishful but groundless thinking," and then ridicule the idea. Often these folks will set hope and one's knowledge of personal salvation as diametrical opposites. Paul knows nothing whatever of such a notion. For Paul hope is "...joyful and confident expectation of eternal salvation."[3] More specifically Paul associates his view of hope directly with his expectation of a glorious and literal bodily resurrection at the end of time.

So how are we "...saved by hope"? In this context Paul illustrates the point. We must at times face the intense trials of life, the "...sufferings of this present time." However when we view those sufferings in light of our hope of glory in the end, they are far more easily endured than when we try to deal with them apart from consideration of our future glory. Someone has drawn this contrast. *Do not look at God through your difficulties, but look at your difficulties through God.* What do you see first, your difficulty or God? If you look first at your difficulty before you look to God, your vision of God will be much like looking at the sun through a dense fog.[4] But if you look at God first you will see Him in His glory and grace, fully capable of either delivering you *from* your difficulty or *through* it. Either way you will see God's deliverance and grace more fully than the trial.

... but hope that is seen is not hope: for what a man seeth, why doth he yet hope for? Do not run quickly across this thought. All too often we race through life without pausing to see "*...him who is invisible*" (Hebrews 11:27). In such a panicked rush we wonder why we never discover the

---

[3] James Strong, *The Exhaustive Concordance of the Bible : Showing Every Word of the Test of the Common English Version of the Canonical Books, and Every Occurrence of Each Word in Regular Order.*, electronic ed. (Ontario: Woodside Bible Fellowship., 1996), G1680.
[4] F. B. Meyer uses this analogy in his book, *Abraham*, a spiritual biography of Abraham's life.

deliverance and joys in affliction described in Scripture. Friend, you shall only discover those joys in deliverance by embracing God invisible in your trial, not by ignoring Him!

But if we hope for that we see not, then do we with patience wait for it. We live in a world of the visible. We struggle with things that we cannot see. Even when those things surround us their lack of form and visible image bothers us. Stop to consider how many forces in nature constantly impact our lives, in most cases things that are incredibly beneficial; gravity, electricity, light (Light is invisible, but it manifests our whole world to our visual senses), wind, not to mention the whole world of chemical reactions and processes by which our natural bodies live and function. In addition we live with many invisible things that are detrimental to us (If you have reached at least your "middle age" status, you likely have regular discussions with your physician about the cholesterol factors in your body or perhaps your blood pressure's inclination to rise to an unhealthy degree. How effective would your life be if you chose to ignore anything that you could not see? You likely wouldn't live for twenty four hours!

If we shift from our physical existence to our spiritual existence, we are confronted there too with a near endless array of invisible factors and forces. Have you "seen" faith" or "grace" recently? You've seen the fruit of their action, but you haven't seen them. For that matter neither have you seen "hope."

In this setting Paul urges us to incorporate "hope" into our view of life as we live it. He assures us that hope will "save" us. No, he is not discussing our going to heaven when we die, so he is not dealing with our eternal salvation. Yet he uses the word "saved." Hmm, it appears that Paul believes in more than one "salvation" or deliverance. So should we!

A godly consideration of the invisible things of God in our daily life will transform the way we live life and deal with the many trials and difficulties that we face. Indeed Paul's words are true to reality. "...we are saved by hope"! As Paul develops his thoughts in this lesson, he affirms that the thing we "hope" for is a reality. It is not a groundless wishful desire; it is the most comforting reality of our life! Regardless of the pain and difficulties you face in this life, nothing in this life's experience is "*...worthy to be compared with the glory which shall be revealed in us*" (Romans 8:18). Victory is certain; joys are assured!

58
The Holy Spirit: Our Holy Helper

> Likewise the Spirit also helpeth our infirmities: for we know not what we should pray for as we ought: but the Spirit itself maketh intercession for us with groanings which cannot be uttered. And he that searcheth the hearts knoweth what is the mind of the Spirit, because he maketh intercession for the saints according to the will of God. (Romans 8:26-27)

The connective words at the beginning of almost every verse in the eighth chapter of Romans suggests a tight logical sequence in Paul's reasoning through this chapter. In our last study we examined the role of hope in helping us bridge the gap between us and God, between the temporal and the eternal. Paul's introduction of his next point with "Likewise" incorporates prayer into that list of spiritual abilities or traits that God has given us to help us "connect" with Him and with His ways. "Also" in the first clause of the verse provides additional integration of this verse with Paul's prior thoughts.

Likewise the Spirit also helpeth our infirmities.... Paul does not say that the Holy Spirit gave us those infirmities, nor does he indicate that the Holy Spirit manipulates or orchestrates our infirmities; he rather acknowledges the reality of our infirmities before encouraging us with the good news of the Holy Spirit's role in helping us deal with them.

This passage raises many questions. In the Sermon on the Mount Jesus gave us a model prayer. On other occasions the disciples asked Him to teach them to pray, and He responded with various instructive lessons; for example, the parable of the importunate widow. So, given these multiple teachings from Jesus, how are we to explain Paul's comment, "*...for we know not what we should pray for as we ought...*'? It appears that Jesus fully covered both the "what" and the "how" in His teachings. I suggest that the answer lies in the application of Jesus' teachings to our personal lives, especially to our moments of weakness. If we are walking in strong faith and close fellowship with God, prayer flows like an artesian spring. When we stumble or falter in our spiritual walk, prayer becomes more difficult. You are willing to confront the simple truth that you—even you—have some personal infirmities, weaknesses, are you not? Lord deliver us all from those pretentious "perfect" Christians who, according to their description of themselves, never stumble, falter, or even struggle with the slightest weakness! Scripture indeed deals with people in the first century who had such an opinion of themselves, but they were never numbered with Jesus and His disciples.

To the question, how do we reconcile these tension points between what Jesus taught the disciples and Paul's acknowledgement of weakness, infirmities, within the believer regarding appropriate prayer? When you face major decisions in your life, do you always know God's will? Do you always know whether you should accept that job offer that will uproot your family and move you across the country? Do you make an offer to buy that new home or decide to "fix up" the old one where you now live? What is God's will for you, not only in the major decisions of life, but in the day to day choices you make? The model prayer instructs us to pray for God's will to be done in earth as in heaven. But if you are not sure about what God's will is in a particular matter, how do you pray for it? I suggest that these kinds of issues drive to the heart of Paul's teaching in this lesson. Rather than rebuking us for not knowing the intimate details of God's will, Paul encourages our prayers and our fellowship with God in these verses.

At the moment of your faltering stumble in faith, your momentary slip into temptation, your stubborn unbelief at God's promises, that very moment when the "accuser of our brethren" hurls your own weakness in your face and taunts you with your own failures; ah, that is the moment when this lesson becomes the most precious to our spiritual health. I cherish the simple statement that the angel gave the disciples when He instructed them to meet Jesus in Galilee after His initial appearances to them around Jerusalem after His resurrection, *"But go your way, tell his disciples and Peter that he goeth before you into Galilee: there shall ye see him, as he said unto you"* (Mark 16:7).

Can we miss the obvious point--*and Peter*? Do not allow Peter in his discouraged state to walk away from his faith. Be sure to remind Peter that the resurrected Christ expects to see him there too! We live in a sad age for historical Biblical Christianity. Instead of perpetuating the nurturing Biblical teaching to the weak and the struggling Christians, professional Christian teachers and preachers sadly often use scare tactics to frighten the weak and the struggling back into the fold. "If you die in this state, you may lose your salvation," or "If you backslide, it means that you were never really saved at all." Such fear-based intimidating attitudes are sadly commonplace in churches today. Where is the angelic gospel that reminds the struggling faltering disciple that his/her risen Lord expects to see him/her among the saints? Someone has said that the Lord's church is not a "sanctuary for the sanctimonious, but a hospital for sin-sick sinners." Amen!

I suggest that the twenty seventh verse adds even more evidence of God's gracious inclination to His struggling and less-than-perfect children. *And he that searcheth the hearts knoweth what is the mind of the Spirit, because he maketh intercession for the saints according to the will of God.* In the twenty sixth verse the Holy Spirit is providing assistance to our prayers, particularly to our prayers in our moments of weakness. In the twenty seventh verse we see, not the Holy Spirit, but Jesus—resurrected and seated in His glory—who perfectly knows what the Holy Spirit is doing with us. While the Holy Spirit is assisting us in our faltering prayers, Jesus in His intercessory role in heaven is working in full cooperation with the Father to answer our prayers according to the will of God.

Occasionally—sometimes far too often—we hear a non-Biblical model of God presented in terms of our sins and our relationship with God. God the Father is depicted as the stern, harsh, and impartial Judge on the bench. Jesus is depicted more accurately as our attorney, or Advocate, our Intercessor. And the Holy Spirit is depicted as in some mystical way trying to bridge the gap between Father and Son. Wrong! Wrong! Wrong! Scripture depicts the Trinity in full harmony and in full cooperation, all loving God's elect, all working in perfect harmony to secure their ultimate and final good. In this passage we see this role in terms of the Holy Spirit, now functioning as our "Comforter," encouraging us in our infirmities to "Hang in there" and to stay in close fellowship with God through abiding prayer. We see Jesus in synchronous intercession with the Spirit simultaneously pleading our case with the Father. And we see the Father joyfully answering their petition in our best interest. Do not overlook the simple closing of the twenty seventh verse, "…according to the will of God."

Sometimes, especially in long flowing contexts that are rich with multiple truths, we become too bogged down in the details of the immediate lesson to sense the "big picture," the greater flow and function of the lesson in its whole. Given the breadth of this chapter, we might easily fall into this mindset as we read and study through the chapter. How does this lesson fit into the greater flow of Paul's reasoning in this chapter?

First of all, we need to understand that the entire Roman letter forms a cohesive single message from Paul to the Roman Christians. This chapter does not exist in an isolation chamber. Errors were growing among the Roman believers that would, if allowed to mature, have destroyed their faith. Paul confronts those errors and writes his most theological letter to them.

Some commentators refer to the Roman letter as Paul's "systematic theology" text. The major error, surfaced by Paul in the third chapter, challenged the very character of God. Does God orchestrate, perhaps even cause, sin so that by our sins He will gain greater glory? Paul categorically rejects such an abominable notion in the first nine verses of the third chapter. He then develops the true character of God in both our salvation and in our walk of faith through the following chapters. In the seventh chapter he confronts our internal conflict, the abiding internal struggle that every cognizant believer in Christ realizes, but often struggles to resolve.

And now in the eighth chapter Paul begins to tighten his reasoning that will bring us to a grand conclusion. *"There is therefore now no condemnation to them that are in Christ Jesus..."* becomes Paul's primary thesis, the logical assertion that becomes the essential pivot for all other issues between God and us. Everything else becomes futile and even irrelevant if we stand condemned before God! Paul goes to the heart of this matter systematically throughout the eighth chapter. "Cliché Christians" rightly, but often sadly in a rather superficial manner, point out that this chapter begins with "...no condemnation" and ends with "...no separation." How can this be? How can God deal with our sins, our weaknesses, and yet accomplish this incredible feat? This chapter walks us through the details of glorious truth to answer this question.

As with Paul's initial surfacing of the problem in the third chapter, so here in the eighth chapter, he builds a solid and systematic basis from which we may acknowledge the holiness and glory of God and yet stand securely on God's work in our hope of salvation, of final and consummate glory. Does God need and thus use—if not cause—our sins to accomplish His ultimate glory? No! That precise point is what

Paul's accusers hurled at him in the third chapter, and that abominable error is what Paul unequivocally rejected in his response to them in the third chapter! He will not contradict himself now in the eighth chapter.

Do not overlook the fact that Paul quoted Psalm 51:4 in Romans 3:4.

> *Against thee, thee only, have I sinned, and done this evil in thy sight: that thou mightest be justified when thou speakest, and be clear when thou judgest.* (Psalm 51:4, KJV)

> *God forbid: yea, let God be true, but every man a liar; as it is written, That thou mightest be justified in thy sayings, and mightest overcome when thou art judged.* (Romans 3:4, KJV)

...that thou mightest be justified... does not refer to David, but to God Himself. Fallen sinful man accuses God, but God will not so compromise Himself as to leave any question regarding the falseness of the abominable accusation. The faithful disciple, even the fallen, compromised disciple will not charge his own sins upon God!

Can we miss the incredibly obvious point? Paul in our study verses specifically addresses our moments of weakness, of infirmity. When Paul quoted an Old Testament passage in Romans 3:4 to strike at the heart of the blasphemous false charge against him, he quoted a passage from David's prayer of confession to God for his sin with Bathsheba, *David's moment of weakness*. Paul insightfully uses David's most obvious sin to illustrate his utter rejection of the charge made against him by his accusers.

God didn't cause David to sin with Bathsheba, nor did God orchestrate the sin to accomplish His glory (Paul's reasoning in Romans 3:1-8 is not sanctified double-speak, but tightly reasoned teaching that rejects any notion of divine manipulation of or reliance on sin for His glory). God used David's own conscience (Read Psalm 32 in this light), and Nathan's accusation to convict David and to lead him to repentance. God confronted and convicted David for his sin. God in goodness (Romans 2:4) lead David to repentance. God mercifully forgave David the sin. But God in no way gained greater glory due to David's sin. Rather this black moment in David's life dishonored both David and God.

The Roman letter forms a single theological fabric, and Paul's tightly reasoned teaching in the eighth chapter pulls all the pieces together into a single harmonious whole. In this chapter, as in the third chapter, Paul will not depict God as a cosmic schemer, a diabolical schizophrenic being who secretly manipulates good and evil similarly to the eastern mystical yin-yang teaching. This mystical teaching was nicely clothed with a pretense of respectability in the Star Wars movie series where the "Force" is consistently depicted as having a "light side" and a "dark side." Scripture rejects such a view of God.

> *But he is in one mind, and who can turn him? and what his soul desireth, even that he doeth.* (Job 23:13, KJV)

We may rest fully assured from the consistent testimony of Scripture that everything that God does grows out of His consistent, righteous, and holy nature, His "mind."

Pivotal to Paul's integration of all the pieces of his teaching is this verse.

> *And if Christ be in you, the body is dead because of sin; but the Spirit is life because of righteousness.* (Romans 8:10, KJV)

Paul didn't say that the Spirit gives life, but, more fundamental to his teaching here he tells us that the Spirit *is* life because of righteousness. We also notice that he did not attempt to defend the error of which he was accused, that the Spirit relied on our sins to accomplish His purpose.

Consider this thought relative to David's experience, as we noted from the third chapter of Romans. David had no awareness that he needed to put up his guard against lust. He didn't even know it would be a problem that day, but the Holy Spirit did. What was David's failure on that sad day in his life? He became too focused on himself. "I" need a day off. "I" have been working too hard. Had David remained faithful to his soldiers and to the serious business of being king of God's nation, he would never have fallen prey to this temptation. So what is the lesson for us? We need to stay busy with the simple day to day activities of life, ensuring that we face them and make decisions that please God. Then when the major issues confront us, we have the aid of the Holy Spirit to help us.

How does the Holy Spirit help our infirmities? He does so through hope, connecting us to God and to the bright future that awaits us according to God's eternal purpose. And hope steps in to assist us in our weaknesses. Standing alone, we are wholly vulnerable to our "Achilles heal," our besetting sins. Sometimes we don't even know what that weakness is, but the Holy Spirit knows, and, if we remain faithful in what we do know to God's teachings, the Holy Spirit steps into our lives to help us with those areas of weakness. Do you think you could even "…lay aside every weight, and the sin which doth so easily beset us" apart from the help of the Holy Spirit? He will not lay aside the weight or deliver us from the besetting sin, but He does provide us with the help necessary to enable us to do so.

In this chapter Paul confronts the heart of the false accusation and refuted its foundations. If Paul had believed what his accusers claimed, he would have to make the case that the Holy Spirit relied on our infirmities to accomplish God's greater good. Rather than affirm this idea, Paul refutes it. The role of the Holy Spirit in David's life was to convict and to rebuke him for his sin, gently leading him to repentance.

That is the same role the Holy Spirit fills in our lives. He does not cause us to sin. He does not rely on our sin to accomplish a mystical greater good. He lives within us and constantly exercises His influence on us to make those small daily decisions for right. Then when those "blind-side" trials or temptations come our way from Satan (not from the "dark side" of God!) the Holy Spirit lives within and leads us to overcome our own weaknesses. Notice Paul's emphasis, "…the Spirit is life *because of righteousness.*" Never will Paul so much as hint that the Holy Spirit orchestrates the dark side of life against the light side to accomplish His will. Paul was not an eastern mystic; he was a devoted follower of the Lord Jesus Christ!

In this key verse Paul affirms what he has been teaching throughout the Roman letter. The indwelling Holy Spirit makes a dramatic and pervasive change in our nature at the new birth. He writes His law in our hearts in indelible ink, not in disappearing ink that shows up on some occasions and becomes invisible at other times. The indwelling Spirit is a permanent element of our regenerate life, not a coming and going force. His influence—His abiding influence—in residence urges, convicts, and empowers us to avoid sin and to pursue righteousness in the "walk of faith." Even in our own inherent areas of weakness—especially in those areas—He abides to strengthen us against our greatest weakness so that, even there we may overcome our own infirmities and conquer our sins. "...because of righteousness," the Holy Spirit's exclusive domain is righteousness. He is righteous. He constantly works in us to guide us into righteousness.

The Biblical pattern that explains the working of sin in us consistently presents a progression of sins, the lesser being either permitted or rationalized so that they grow progressively into greater sins. That principle was true for David, and it is equally true for us. If we ignore the Holy Spirit's guiding light and continue to pursue our "besetting sins," we will inevitably advance to greater, more serious sins. He is the "anointing" that abides with us (1 John 2:27). We may sin ignorantly, but the ignorance will be what Scripture cryptically refers to as "willful ignorance," not a deficiency in His work in us. His work consistently urges us to righteousness, even against our besetting sins. At every step He uses two major strategies in His assistance. First he uses "hope" to help us make decisions and live life from an eternal perspective. He leads us to live life from a perspective of "resurrection ethics." Secondly, He constantly assures us that we do not face anything, even our greatest personal weaknesses or besetting sins, alone. He reminds us that He is ever present, always abiding in us and available to help us make the right choices and walk the "walk of faith."

From regeneration to "resurrection ethics" and our "walk of faith," the Holy Spirit "abides" with us constantly (Take the time to study the fourteenth, fifteenth, and sixteenth chapters of John's gospel and Jesus' repeated emphasis to the bewildered disciples that He would send the Holy Spirit as their abiding "Comforter" of the same power, kind, and quality that He personally afforded them during His time with them). He provides His help to our fleshly or carnal weaknesses. Only in this way can believers in Christ succeed in their fight of faith, their conflict with their own fleshly disposition that Paul confronted in himself as an example in Romans the seventh chapter. Through every conflict and every trial of life, we have the ever-present ministry of the Holy Spirit, instilling hope where there is no hope from our human perspective, adding His strength to our weakness where we fully expect to fail because of that personal weakness. It is for this reason that true Christianity must rise above the level of the individual self, or it is no real Christianity at all. May we ever live in sensitive awareness of that greater Life within us that overcomes!

We believe that our eternal salvation is by God's grace. This lesson from Paul helps us to apply that grace to our feet so that we show that grace in both conversation and conduct (Colossians 4:6).

59
Who? What? How?
Things that Work for our Good—
Things that do not

> And we know that all things work together for good to them that love God, to them who are the called according to his purpose. (Romans 8:28)

It seems that Satan often works his greatest diligence to neutralize the most crucial truths, doctrines, and passages set forth in Scripture. If that be the case, we might readily conclude that this verse is one of the most central passages in the Bible for the comfort and instruction of God's children. It is also sadly true that, when people become engaged in controversy, they become most narrow in their perspective and seek ways to contradict their counterparts in controversy more than seeking for the truth of the passage. Thus it is necessary for us to study some of the historical controversies surrounding this verse before we address its contextual teaching and its vital significance to the family of God.

Let's examine some of the major interpretations of this verse that have surfaced through history.

1. The London Confession of Faith of 1689 offers the following comment on God's "decrees." "God hath decreed in Himself from all eternity, by the most wise and holy counsel of His own will, freely and unchangeably, all things whatsoever come to pass; yet so as thereby is God neither the author of sin, nor hath fellowship with any therein; nor is violence offered to the will of the creature, nor yet is the liberty or contingency of second causes taken away, but rather established, in which appears His wisdom in disposing all things, and power and faithfulness in accomplishing His decree.
2. Although God knoweth whatsoever may or can come to pass upon all supposed conditions, yet hath He not decreed anything, because He foresaw it as future, or as that which would come to pass upon such conditions.

3. In 1900 a rather significant group of Primitive Baptists met in Fulton, Kentucky to discuss the major doctrinal beliefs of historical Baptists. They agreed to begin with the London Confession and to add footnotes to explain their understanding and to address various changes in the English language where they believed it had affected the general understanding of the London Confession. Their primary footnote to this section of the Confession reads as follows: "This clearly distinguishes between God's attitude to sin and His attitude and relation to holiness. A failure to make this distinction has been a fruitful source of division and distress of our holy cause, and a failure to so distinguish between God's permissive and overruling decree of sin and His causative decree of holiness will ever cause distress and confusion among our people. This distinction is expressed in the last clause of Section 4 of Chapter V.: "Which also He most wisely and powerfully boundeth and otherwise ordereth and governeth in a manifold dispensation to His most holy ends; yet so as the sinfulness of their acts proceedeth only from the creatures and not from God.", etc. Chapter VI., last part of Section 1: "Satan using the subtlety of the serpent to seduce Eve, then by her seducing Adam, who without any compulsion did willfully transgress the law of their creation and the command given unto them in eating the forbidden fruit, which God was pleased, according to His wise and holy counsel, to permit, having purposed to order it to His own glory." We believe that God is perfect in wisdom and knowledge, knowing all things both good and evil from the beginning that would take place in time. That He is a Perfect Sovereign over all things, and that He absolutely and causatively predestinated all His works of creation and eternal salvation of His elect."

4. In the appendix of the Fulton document the following appears:
"For God to foresee that man will yield to influences of a secondary nature does not imply that God moves man to sin, but only that He is the Permitter of sin. Webster defines "permit", to suffer, without giving authority". We use it in the

sense of "not hinder". Section 3 they say: "Others being left to act in their sins to their just condemnation, to the praise of His glorious justice." If they had believed that God moves men to sin, they would not have said, "being left to act in their sins," etc. We insist that we should not use language implying that God's attitude to sin is the same as His attitude to holiness, for this tends to destroy the distinction between right and wrong. The expression, "unlimited predestination of all things", seems to convey the idea that God's purpose concerning sin is as unlimited and as unrestricted as it is concerning holiness; and if so, then God's decree concerning sin would be causative, since it is causative concerning holiness, and this view would destroy all distinction between right and wrong. Chapter XVI., Section 2: "These good works, done in obedience to God's commandments, are the fruits and evidences of a true and lively faith; and by them believers manifest their thankfulness, strengthen their assurance, edify their brethren, adorn the profession of the gospel, stop the mouths of the adversaries, and glorify God," etc.

Section 3: "Their ability to do good works is not at all of themselves, but wholly from the Spirit of Christ; and that they may be enabled thereto, besides the graces they have already received, there is necessary an actual influence of the same Holy Spirit to work in them to will and to do of His good pleasure; yet are they not hereupon to grow negligent, as if they were not bound to perform any duty unless upon a special motion of the Spirit," etc. They do neglect, not being forced in duty irresistibly. We believe the Scriptures teach that there is a time salvation received by the heirs of God distinct from eternal salvation, which does depend upon their obedience. The people of God receive their rewards for obedience in this life only. We believe that the ability of the Christian is the unconditional gift of God.

The emphasis the Fulton elders placed on the believer's will in acts of obedience, coupled with their comment regarding two salvations in the final paragraph quoted above, is quite revealing as to the theological perspective that these men held. First of all, they categorically rejected the notion that God predestinated sin, either directly or indirectly. Secondly, they equally rejected the notion that God unconditionally and irresistibly predestinated the believer's acts of faith and obedience.

Does anyone really believe that God predestinated sin? Indeed they do! I recently ran across a web discussion among a group of men who hold to what is commonly identified as "absolute predestination of all things" in which the writer quoted the first portion of Romans 6:17, "But God be thanked, that ye were the servants of sin...." This is as much of the verse as the writer quoted. Wholly void of the remainder of the verse or of any contextual analysis, the writer then drew two conclusions; 1) Paul affirmed that God predestinated sin, and 2) Paul thanked God that He did so. Both conclusions reveal an abysmal neglect in the writer to interpret Scripture by Scripture and to interpret Scripture in its inspired context. The basis for Paul's thankfulness was that the Romans had now "...obeyed from the heart that form of doctrine which was delivered you," not that God predestinated sin. Many commentaries make this same point. For example, Albert Barnes presents his thoughts.

> The *sense* of this passage is plain. The *ground* of the thanksgiving was not that they had been the slaves of sin; but it is, that notwithstanding this, or although they had been thus, yet that they were now obedient. To give thanks to God that men were sinners, would contradict the whole spirit of this argument, and of the Bible. But to give thanks that *although* men had been sinners, yet that now they had become obedient that is, *that great sinners had become converted*--is in entire accordance with the spirit of the Bible, and with propriety. The word *although* or *whereas*, understood here, expresses the sense, "But thanks unto God, that *whereas* ye were the servants of sin," etc. Christians should thank God that they themselves, though once great sinners, have become converted; and when others who are great sinners are converted, they should praise him.[1]

---

[1] From Barnes' commentary, quoted from the electronic edition in SwordSearcher Bible software.

More common among absolute predestinarians is the idea that "God predestinates all things that come to pass, yet God is not the cause of sin." This comment is non-sensical at best! Is sin a "thing" or is it not a "thing"? In a debate with Elder Ariel West, a Primitive Baptist, Elder R. W. Rhodes, an absolute predestinarian, made this comment.

> There is no doubt in my mind that Hitler doesn't know that he is fulfilling the purpose of God.

When Elder West challenged this statement, Elder Rhodes responded in his next speech as follows:

> I say, my friends, that all of this trouble must come or the Scriptures will be broken, and Jesus said, also, "the Scriptures cannot be broken." They must be fulfilled. I say, if there is one single ounce of this trouble-and this included Hitler-and God knows, my friends, if I had that scamp in my hands, with as little grip as I have, I could squeeze his neck in two. Yes, I could do that. But I want to tell you, brethren and sisters, he has brought the greatest trouble the world has ever known. Is the world not in the greatest trouble today it has ever been in? And yet, my friends, the righteous, and holy, and sinless, the Almighty, and powerful God decreed and spoke by his prophet that there shall be a time of trouble such as was not since man was upon the earth. I tell you-my brethren, would you have any confidence in Almighty God if He said that a thing shall be and it failed to come to pass? I say that I wouldn't have any confidence in Him. No, sir, not even if God said, "He shall save His people from their sins," and then not do it. There wouldn't be much comfort in His words for you. But He says, "I will," concerning everything-concerning all things that come to pass, just exactly like God purposed it and as He predestinated it. I am not afraid of the word "predestination." I am here to do my dead level best and carry my point with me on foreknowledge, and he will not stay with me on that.[2]

---

[2] This debate took place in El Dorado, Arkansas in 1943.

I find it amazing; the manner in which Elder Rhodes coupled passages wholly unrelated to support his extreme view that—of all men—Adolph Hitler with all of his atrocities was doing the will of God. "...the scripture cannot be broken" in its context hardly addresses the abominable sins of Adolph Hitler!

I offer these quotes as a mere sample of the manner in which absolute predestinarians will use "double-speak" to say that God causes all things, but He doesn't cause sin, and yet they will in substance repeatedly affirm that God does in fact cause sin. Consistency is not one of their stronger traits! A man cannot say that God causes every thing that occurs, even to the blowing of a grain of sand in the Sahara Desert or the falling of a single drop of rainfall, but "...he doesn't cause sin." The whole argument is nonsensical, not to mention the manner in which it blasphemes the holy character of God.

Occasionally advocates of the absolute predestinarian view will defend their view based on a claim that the manner in which God can predestinate all things and yet not cause sin is "a mystery." First of all, ***implicit in this claim is the argument from silence, which is in fact no argument at all.*** The New Testament's use of "mystery" clearly contradicts this idea of mystery associated with the aberrant claims of absolute predestinarians. Let's examine the passages where this word appears in the New Testament.

> And he said, Unto you it is given to know the mysteries of the kingdom of God: but to others in parables; that seeing they might not see, and hearing they might not understand. (Luke 8:10)

> But we speak the wisdom of God in a mystery, even the hidden wisdom, which God ordained before the world unto our glory. (1 Corinthians 2:7)

> Behold, I shew you a mystery; We shall not all sleep, but we shall all be changed. (1 Corinthians 15:51)

Notice that these three passages use "mystery," not in terms of an unknown or contradictory "hidden truth," but in terms of *something that has been revealed to the saints.* It was hidden from past generations, or from the unsaved, but it is known by the saints. Never does Scripture use the word "mystery" to mask a contradiction that it never explains elsewhere.

Next we should note that God consistently distances Himself from any form or appearance of sin. He never so much as implies that in some mystical way He is using, manipulating, or orchestrating sin for a greater good. Consider just three passages that clearly affirm this point.

> *And they built the high places of Baal, which are in the valley of the son of Hinnom, to cause their sons and their daughters to pass through the fire unto Molech; which I commanded them not, neither came it into my mind, that they should do this abomination, to cause Judah to sin.* (Jeremiah 32:35)

> *For God is not the author of confusion, but of peace, as in all churches of the saints.* (1 Corinthians 14:33)

> *For all that is in the world, the lust of the flesh, and the lust of the eyes, and the pride of life, is not of the Father, but is of the world.* (1 John 2:16)

In no place does Scripture ever use "mystery" to impute to God the cause of sin or any other act that contradicts His essential nature. In fact as these passages consistently reveal God disassociates Himself from any appearance of sin.

Given the wording of the London Confession quoted above, it seems clear that the compilers of this Confession intended to leave no doubt as to their rejection of the idea that God causes sin, as well as the idea that He irresistibly and unconditionally predestinated every good thing that we think or do. Notice the following excerpt from the quote above, "…*yet so as thereby is God neither the author of sin, nor hath fellowship with any therein; nor is violence offered to the will of the creature, nor yet is the liberty or contingency of second causes taken away, but rather established*.…" If the writers of the Confession believed that God predestinates all of our faith and good works irresistibly and unconditionally, their comments regarding no "…violence offered to the will of the creature" and their reference to the existence of "…the liberty or contingency of second causes…" would have no meaning at all. Had this excessive view of predestination been their intent—their belief—they would have omitted any reference to the will of the creature and the "contingency of second causes."

When a person affirms that God causes every event that occurs to "work together for good," beware. If he maintains consistency with his statement, he will inevitably end up making God the cause of sin, either directly or indirectly.

Regardless of their dominant theological bent, many sincere Christians will rather thoughtlessly quote Romans 8:28 when faced with calamity and seeking to comfort those most directly harmed by it. I recall from my childhood hearing a Pentecostal Holiness preacher reading this verse to a bereaved family whose teenage son had just been killed in an automobile accident. He wouldn't have dared to preach to his congregation what he tried to teach this grieving family in their distress!

In the first eight verses of the third chapter in Romans Paul rejected an accusation made against him that he held to such a view. He will not in the eighth chapter revert to the very belief that he rejected and labeled as a slanderous false report against him in the third chapter. If you read the first eight verses of the third chapter and see confusing double-speak, slow down and read it again. Paul is dealing with the heretical error that claims that God caused or mysteriously manipulates sin so He could receive greater glory because of it.

As we proceed, we will examine the internal conditions or qualifiers in this verse that prima facie refute the absolute predestinarian views named above, as well as examine both the theological and experiential truths that overflow with comfort to the family of God as we face the trials of life under the banner of the faith once and for all time delivered to the saints.

The "Five Things"

We have examined the absolute predestinarian views of this verse—actually two of them; one that holds that literally everything that occurs is divinely and irresistibly predestinated and the other that holds that every act of faith and obedience is divinely and irresistibly predestinated (the more popular view historically among absolute predestinarians). Now, we shall examine what is sometimes referred to as the "five things" view of the verse. The "five things" view links Romans 8:28 with the two following verses.

For whom he did foreknow, he also did predestinate to be conformed to the image of his Son, that he might be the firstborn among many brethren. Moreover whom he did predestinate, them he also called: and whom he called, them he also justified: and whom he justified, them he also glorified. (Romans 8:29-30)

The "five things" view distinctly holds a strong advantage over the prior view in that it relies on the immediate context for its interpretation instead of pouring mystical meaning into "all things" that neither appears in the context nor in the general teachings of Scripture.

In addition to the contextual link of adjacent verses this view builds on the connective "For" that begins Verse twenty nine. Further in the flowing context of this chapter the precise term "all things" appears in another verse. In fact "thing," "things," and "all things" appear prominently in the verses following this lesson.

What shall we then say to these things? If God be for us, who can be against us? He that spared not his own Son, but delivered him up for us all, how shall he not with him also freely give us all things? Who shall lay any thing to the charge of God's elect? It is God that justifieth. (Romans 8:31-33)

What shall we then say to these things? It would be difficult to make a contextual case that "these things" does not refer to the five things previously named in verses twenty nine and thirty.

He that spared not his own Son, but delivered him up for us all, how shall he not with him also freely give us all things? (Romans 8:32) In this verse Paul specifically identifies a category of "all things," the same precise term used in Verse twenty eight, with "things" that work together for our good.

Who shall lay any thing to the charge of God's elect? (Romans 8:33) The clear implication in this verse appeals to a broad scope of "things," all of which are laid to the charge of God's elect by their adversary, clearly not something that "works together" for their good.

And finally Paul will close this lesson with yet another reference to "things."

> *Nay, in all these things we are more than conquerors through him that loved us. For I am persuaded, that neither death, nor life, nor angels, nor principalities, nor powers, nor things present, nor things to come, Nor height, nor depth, nor any other creature, shall be able to separate us from the love of God, which is in Christ Jesus our Lord. (Romans 8:39)*

Can there be any doubt that whatever God bequeathed us through the substitutionary, sin-atoning death of our Lord truly "works together" for our good?

Paul lists the major categories of "things" that Satan attempts to bring against God's elect with the amazing conclusion, "*Nay, in all these things we are more than conquerors through him that loved us."*

Now we have the information before us to examine this lesson in its context within Paul's message to the Roman believers. It is my belief that Paul has developed two distinct lists, two separate categories of "things" in this context. One list of "things" was purchased for us by the death of our Lord on our behalf. The other "things" are orchestrated by Satan "against" us, not for us or for our good. In the closing verses of this chapter Paul will list the major categories of "things" in this list, concluding that none of "all these things" can separate us from the love of God which is in Christ Jesus our Lord.

It seems highly reasonably that, if Paul lists the "all these things" that Satan hurls against us in his futile attempt to separate us from God's love which is in Christ Jesus our Lord, he would also innumerate the "things" that work together for our good—verses twenty nine and thirty. Thus in the greater context of the eighth chapter of Romans we discover two lists, one highlighted by five things, all of God and so designed and intertwined that one "thing" irrevocably links to the other, and the other highlighted by a list of representative "things" that Satan orchestrates to separate us from God's love.

Many advocates of the "five things" view appeal to the *past tense verbs* in the list, even glorification, as indication that Paul is relating these five things to the eternal covenant of grace. Even though in terms of actual events, the calling of some of God's elect is yet future, and the glorification of all the elect is yet future, awaiting the Day of Resurrection, the fact of these "things" is as certain as if they'd already occurred because they are provided in God's covenant of grace. Another evidence of the eternal covenant basis for these five things is the manner in which they are intertwined. If you are included in one of them, you cannot be excluded from the remaining four! The "whom" included in God's foreknowing is the same exact "whom" included in glorification.

Critics of the doctrines of grace occasionally protest that "foreknowledge" in this passage relates to God's incommunicable attribute of omniscience. Omniscience is a noun and refers to a divine attribute, but "foreknow" in this lesson is a verb and relates to something specific that God did. To "know" is often used in the King James Bible to refer to intimate and exclusive love. (Amos 3:2 for example; it is not remotely sensible to interpret this passage as simply referring to divine omniscience, for if that were the case, the clear implication is that God didn't "know" any of the other families of the earth)

It is altogether reasonable—I believe correct—to interpret God's foreknowing in Romans 8:29 as equivalent to God's unique and exclusive, sacrificial love for all of His elect, a love from which Paul asserts in this context that we cannot be separated. If we cannot be separated from God's love by "all these things" which Satan orchestrates against us, then we are assured of being blessed in the final glorification that shall become an eternal reality at the Last Day.

A beautiful and comforting reference to God's eternal covenant appears in David's dying words.

> *Although my house be not so with God; yet he hath made with me an everlasting covenant, ordered in all things, and sure: for this is all my salvation, and all my desire, although he make it not to grow.* (2 Samuel 23:5)

In the verses immediately preceding this passage David described a perfect day, no clouds, no smog, "…clear shining after rain." His opening clause in the verse above draws a sad contrast between

David's house and the perfect day. David's "house" was marred by sin. It displayed the glaring cloud of adultery and murder from the Bathsheba affair. It displayed the dark cloud of a distracted and at times partial father whose children despised each other and committed atrocious sins against God and each other. But when David looked at his standing in God's everlasting covenant, he saw no clouds. Praise God, he saw no sin clouds whatever! He saw the perfect day that God's elect only enjoy through the sacrificial atonement of our Lord Jesus Christ. Yes, that sacrifice covered the sins of God's elect prior to its occurrence in time as fully as it covers our sins (Romans 3:5).

David further confesses that "...this is all my salvation, and all my desire...." David didn't view his salvation as a synergistic effort between God and him. All of his salvation rested on God and God's everlasting covenant!

This lesson ends with a rather surprising note, "...although he make it not to grow." God's covenant was not framed as an open ended "offer" of salvation to the folks who would cooperate with its terms and conditions. It was made with a specific people, chosen by God out of His grace and not out of their merit. The ratification of that covenant was not between God and man, but within the Triune God alone. Notice Abraham's vision of the ratified covenant (Genesis 15:8-17). Abraham lies in a slumbering stupor on the sidelines, but the light and glory of God alone walked united back and forth between the divided carcasses of the covenant animals. Abraham, like David—and like you and I—was the blessed beneficiary of the covenant, but God was the exclusive signatory to the covenant. Abraham, the Chaldean, clearly understood the implications of this covenant, precisely the form of Chaldean covenants. It was binding!

Next, we shall examine the language and the incredible comforts of Romans 8:28 as set forth in Paul's inspired language within that verse. Once you see the profound comfort of the lesson (It rests on what we have here examined.) you will understand why Satan works so hard to confuse it.

Two Lists, Not One

In the closing verses of the eighth chapter of Romans Paul draws a contrast of sorts between two lists. In order to understand our study verse in its context we need to examine these two lists. Let's start with the second list. Paul introduces this list in the thirty fifth verse, *"Who shall separate us from the love of Christ? shall tribulation, or distress, or persecution, or famine, or nakedness, or peril, or sword?"* (Romans 8:35). The list includes the following:

1. Tribulation.
2. Distress.
3. Persecution.
4. Famine.
5. Nakedness.
6. Peril.
7. Sword.

He then expands this list in the closing verses of the chapter, *"For I am persuaded, that neither death, nor life, nor angels, nor principalities, nor powers, nor things present, nor things to come, Nor height, nor depth, nor any other creature, shall be able to separate us from the love of God, which is in Christ Jesus our Lord"* (Romans 8:38-39). Notice the expanded content.

1. Death.
2. Life.
3. Angels.
4. Principalities.
5. Powers.
6. Things present.
7. Things to come.
8. Height.
9. Depth.
10. Any other creature.

Paul's settled conclusion is that none of these things "…shall be able to separate us from the love of God, which is in Christ Jesus our Lord." Although Paul structures this list in a highly inclusive form, we might name specific "things" not mentioned in the list, though they likely are included in one of the categories mentioned.

Every item in the two versions of this list has a common goal by its instigator Satan, to separate us from the "…love of God, which is in Christ Jesus our Lord." Praise God, Paul's settled conclusion is that both the instigator and his list shall fail in their sinister objective. We shall not—cannot—be separated from the love of God in our Lord Jesus Christ.

The first list Paul sets in a contra-position to this diabolical list. It appears in these words, "*For whom he did foreknow, he also did predestinate to be conformed to the image of his Son, that he might be the firstborn among many brethren. Moreover whom he did predestinate, them he also called: and whom he called, them he also justified: and whom he justified, them he also glorified*" (Romans 8:29-30). Thus the first list contains the following:

1. He foreknew.... Foreknowledge is not equivalent with the divine attribute of omniscience; it appears in verb form and refers to something God did, not to something He is. Paul's thesis is that these five things together manifest God's love toward us, ensuring eternal life with Him—that we shall never be separated from His love.
2. He predestinated.
3. He called.
4. He justified.
5. He glorified.

Notice that each of these verbs is associated with a personal pronoun, confining the function of the verb's action to people, not events; "whom...." Secondly, notice that each of the verbs appears in the past tense, not the present or the future tense.

As with the second list in the passage, this list is not necessarily all-inclusive, but it is distinctly representative of a greater comprehensive list, a list of every provision in the eternal covenant of grace.

Clearly we can conclude that the ultimate objective of the items in this list is to keep God's elect safe in "...the love of God, which is in Christ Jesus our Lord," or, stated negatively, to prevent us from being separated from His love.

How do we gain protection in these "things"? Paul tells us.

He that spared not his own Son, but delivered him up for us all, how shall he not with him also freely give us all things? (Romans 8:32)

We do not gain the benefit of these items, these "things," by our works, by our faith, or by anything else in us. We receive the divine enrichment of them through the sacrificial death of our Lord Jesus Christ. The Father did not "spare" His own Son, but rather "delivered him up for us all."

It is my belief that the "these things" in Romans 8:31 refers to this list of "things" given to us by our loving and merciful Father specifically through the sacrificial death of our Lord Jesus Christ. Before leaving this context, we shall examine the experiential or practical dimension of the passage as fully as we now examine the theological or doctrinal aspects of it.

There can be no contextual or reasonable basis on which the serious Bible student can or should confuse these two distinct lists, one from God and one from the archenemy of both God and His elect. Here is the mark of the true distinction between them: in Verse 32 Paul posed a question; *"He that spared not his own Son…how shall he not with him freely give us all things?"*

Did Jesus die so that we would have the Adolph Hitlers or the Saddam Husseins of this world? Did Jesus die so that we would have "9/11"? Did Jesus die so that we would receive Virginia Tech? Did Jesus die so that we would receive cancer, birth defects, and enticing temptations? If Jesus had not died, would our world be void of these things? Surely no serious Bible student would dare to make such a preposterous point! To do so is to assert that sin is a free gift from God that we receive in Christ Jesus. How then can anyone attempt to force the "all things" of Romans 8:28 into an interpretation that implies such an idea?

In context Paul uses "things" or "all things" with reference to both of these lists. A simple analysis of the context is possible with one question as we examine each appearance of "things" throughout this context. "Which list is Paul referring to when he uses 'things' in this sentence?" Clearly his intent is to draw a contrast between the two lists, their source and their objective. The two lists are set in diametrical opposition against each other.

Once we identify the unique character of these two lists, especially the categorical distinction between them, the next question should be obvious. When Paul introduces "all things" in Romans 8:28, to which list does he refer? We cannot either Biblically or rationally say that the list of satanic devices intended to separate us from the love of God "work together" for our good. However, there is no difficulty in concluding that the first list of "things" mentioned by Paul are all of God and all indeed "work together" for our good.

God's eternal covenant of grace is a comprehensive covenant that provides for everything the elect of God need to ensure—to guarantee—their eternal security in Christ. Consider its description in David's dying words. Before he mentioned God's covenant, David described a cloudless day, a day with perfect weather, "…clear shining after rain." Then he introduced his reliance on God's covenant.

> *Although my house be not so with God; yet he hath made with me an everlasting covenant, ordered in all things, and sure: for this is all my salvation, and all my desire, although he make it not to grow.* (2 Samuel 23:5)

This covenant is neither temporary nor temporal; it is "everlasting." It is not partial or piecemeal; it is "ordered in all things." It is not provisional or open to revision or failure; it is "sure." It did not provide a loose framework in which David could comply with terms and save himself; it included full provision for his salvation, "all my salvation." As he waved goodbye to this world and all things in it, David comfortably looked forward to the joys of that covenant's provisions; "all my desire." And finally, this covenant was not subject to revision; God made it "not to grow." Human contracts often grow out of near endless negotiations between the parties and include an ever-growing list of exceptions, qualifications, and provisions. God unilaterally framed this covenant and gave it to David—and to every one of His beloved elect. No one has ever discovered a missing provision, a poorly written clause, or a deficiency. It has never grown with added after-thoughts, nor shall it ever so grow.

Next, we will examine the words and grammatical form of Romans 8:28, laying the foundation for both the theological truth that we have examined in this and the last chapter and the practical-experiential truth that we shall then be able to develop and examine in coming chapters. Scripture generally—and Paul rather consistently—builds rock-solid foundations of theological or doctrinal truth, and then builds practical truth on that theological foundation. We are now ready to examine the practical implications of this passage.

Grammatical Assessment

Having examined the context and various aspects of this verse, we now turn to a more detailed grammatical examination of the verse. Before we can reach a proper interpretation of any passage, we must faithfully examine what the verse says, not recreate the verse in our corrupted image to make it say what we want it to say. Often advocates of various errant views of this verse almost shamelessly rewrite it to say what they wish it said, but not at all what it does say. For example, some advocates simply reject Paul's categorical statement that the workings of this verse refer to "...them that love God" and replace that concise affirmation with a wholly different meaning, "...them that God loves." These two expressions are not at all the same in their meaning.

By beginning the sentence with "And..." Paul is connecting what he writes here with what he has already stated. This verse should never be viewed or interpreted as if it stands alone in a sterilized isolation chamber, a sadly common approach to it. It must be interpreted within the tightly reasoned and flowing context in which it appears.

We Know

"...we know." The word translated "know" means perception or perceptive knowledge. What Paul will state is something that both Paul and the Romans not only could, but did in fact perceive. It was not a controversial, mystical, or philosophical idea that only a few folks could grasp. I offer three possible explanations of this sense of perceptual knowledge.

1. Paul generalized the point. In this context Paul is being anything but general or non-specific in his reasoning. To unexpectedly shift from a specific and tightly reasoned flow of thought to a generalization more smacks of sophistry than of credible and accurate reasoning through connected facts to a reasoned and logical conclusion.

2. Paul knows his audience and thus knows personally that they know what he will assert here. This conclusion is possible but highly unlikely since Paul had never visited Rome or this church before. Further it appears throughout the Roman letter that Paul is addressing a controversy within the Roman church involving the scope of divine predestination or decrees (Romans 3:1-8). Thus it would be illogical and a sign of weak reasoning for him to assume as fact points that lay at the heart of the controversy.
3. Paul makes this statement—draws this conclusion—based on specific information that he provided in the body of his letter to the church at Rome. He has already shown in the letter how that loving God by doing good works and walking by faith (the Abraham example) and by repentance (The David example) result in hope (Romans 5:1-5; 8:24-25), hope that predicts good results. In effect these attitudes and behaviors in God's regenerate elect "work together" for their good.

The third explanation more clearly follows the flow of information and reasoning that we see in the Roman letter. It also is comfortably compatible with Paul's concept of "perceptual" knowledge than either of the other explanations. We can readily grasp this concept without straining our own imagination or compromising the moral character of God.

Thayer's New Testament Greek lexicon references this verse with this explanation of "know;"..."so far as the sense is concerned, equivalent to *it is well known, acknowledged....*"[3]

Work Together

"...work together;" the word translated "work together" appears in four other New Testament passages. I quote them here for your review with the words translated in bold type.

*And they went forth, and preached every where, the Lord **working with** them, and confirming the word with signs following. Amen.* (Mark 16:20)

---

[3] Quoted from Thayer as presented in BibleWorks Bible software.

*That ye submit yourselves unto such, and to every one that **helpeth with us**, and laboureth.* (1 Corinthians 16:16)

*We then, as **workers together with** him, beseech you also that ye receive not the grace of God in vain.* (2 Corinthians 6:1)

*Seest thou how faith **wrought with his works**, and by works was faith made perfect?* (James 2:22)

In each of these verses we see either God or godly people cooperating in simple, straightforward activities for a godly outcome. In no instance do we see good and evil mystically cooperating for an equally mystical greater good. If the word is used so consistently in every other appearance in the New Testament, we have no reasonable warrant to redefine it in Romans 8:28. In each of these cases, I also observe, the conclusion is readily perceptible. It requires no philosophical mysticism to understand its meaning.

Them that Love God

"…to them that love God." As noted above, there is no warrant whatever to ignore this language and effectively reject the KJV translation, retranslating the phrase into "…to them whom God loves." When reasoning with friends of Arminian persuasion, we will occasionally quote Psalm 5:5 to prove that God does not in fact love every human being, "The foolish shall not stand in thy sight: thou hatest all workers of iniquity." Predictably our Arminian friends will attempt to retranslate this verse into "…thou hatest the **works** of iniquity." Their abuse of textual authority we reject as inexcusable, and rightly so. For the same reason we have no warrant whatever to presume to retranslate Romans 8:28 from "…them that love God" into a distinctly different meaning, "…them that God loves."

What does Paul mean with this term, "…them that love God"? Whatever his intent, he gives no basis whatever for anyone to conclude that all things work together for good to anyone other than the people described in this term.

In this verse the verb "love" appears in the Greek present tense, active voice, and it is a Greek participle. Let's look at the definition of each part of speech.

> **Present tense.** The present tense represents a simple statement of fact or reality viewed as occurring in actual time. In most cases this corresponds directly with the English present tense.
> Some phrases which might be rendered as past tense in English will often occur in the present tense in Greek. These are termed "historical presents," and such occurrences dramatize the event described as if the reader were there watching the event occur. Some English translations render such historical presents in the English past tense, while others permit the tense to remain in the present.[4]
>
> **Active voice.** The active voice represents the subject as the doer or performer of the action. e.g., in the sentence, "The boy hit the ball," the boy performs the action.[5]
>
> **Participle.** The Greek participle corresponds for the most part to the English participle, reflecting "-ing" or "-ed" being suffixed to the basic verb form. The participle can be used either like a verb or a noun, as in English, and thus is often termed a "verbal noun."[6]

In the simplest possible terms, based on this straightforward grammatical information, Paul is stating that the conclusion he reaches in this verse is specifically confined to people who are presently, actively, loving God. There is no basis whatever to draw a broad general conclusion that the implications of the verse apply to all of

---

[4] Larry Pierce, *Tense Voice Mood.* (Ontario: Woodside Bible Fellowship.), TVM5774.
[5] Larry Pierce, *Tense Voice Mood.* (Ontario: Woodside Bible Fellowship.), TVM5784.
[6] Larry Pierce, *Tense Voice Mood.* (Ontario: Woodside Bible Fellowship.), TVM5796.

humanity, to all whom God loves regardless of their present conduct, or to all events that occur.

The verb translated "love" in this verse is precisely defined in Scripture; we need not consult an original language lexicon to understand its meaning.

> *Charity suffereth long, and is kind; charity envieth not; charity vaunteth not itself, is not puffed up, Doth not behave itself unseemly, seeketh not her own, is not easily provoked, thinketh no evil; Rejoiceth not in iniquity, but rejoiceth in the truth; Beareth all things, believeth all things, hopeth all things, endureth all things.* (1 Corinthians 13:4-7)

Our Western cultural concept of "love" as an emotion is altogether non-Biblical. Biblical "love" is a verb and describes how we act, not how we feel! Thus Paul is stating that when we are actively, presently loving God as shown by our faith and actions, whatever he intends with "all things" will perceptively be working for our good. He makes no assertion whatever that anything will "work together" for our good at any other time or when we are conducting ourselves in any manner other that as he asserts in the verse as our loving God.

For Good

"…for good…." Again I quote Thayer from *BibleWorks* Bible software. "…When used of love to a master, God or Christ, the word involves the idea of affectionate reverence, prompt obedience, grateful recognition of benefits received: Matt. 6:24; 22:37; Rom. 8:28…." This definition is wholly compatible with Paul's reference to "work together" as the word is used in the four other passages in the New Testament. When we walk by faith in the midst of life's trials, showing "affectionate reverence, prompt obedience, and grateful recognition of benefits received" from a loving and gracious Father, we may face our trials with the assurance of God's presence, grace, and blessings showered upon us. If we allow life's difficulties to turn us bitter, we have no reason whatever from this or any other passage to expect anything to work out well for us!

"…for good…." What is the good to which Paul refers in this verse? Is it a vague mystical "good" that in some way grows out of tragedies and human depravity? This view builds more on sophistry than on sound hermeneutics. Look at the flowing context of Romans the eighth chapter. The concern at the beginning of the chapter deals with condemnation. The grand conclusion at the end of the chapter addresses the surety of our standing in Christ—no separation. Interestingly the word translated "For" that begins Romans 8:29 is defined as "Because" in most New Testament Greek lexicons. Libronix Bible software (formerly known as Logos Software) includes two quite detailed original language resources. *OpenText.org Clauses* identifies "And we know…" as the primary clause and "For whom he did foreknow…" as the secondary clause in the extended sentence, clearly linking Paul's reasoning in verses twenty nine and thirty with his teaching in verse twenty eight. *New Testament Clausal Outlines* interprets the sentence in the same manner.

Paul's intent in verse twenty eight appears to be highly intertwined with the five principles of the two following verses. However, the point of verse twenty eight deals with our experiential perspective of these verses, not with God's operation of them. In other words we come to "know" the value of these truths and to enjoy their comfort through the walk of faith, particularly faith in our seasons of trial. However, the objective reality of these five principles are secure whether we come to the knowledge of them or not.

Paul's intent is to teach us to apply these principles to our experiences in life so that we may enjoy being "…saved by hope" (Romans 8:24-25). The ultimate good to which Paul refers then is that in the midst of our greatest trials we may recall God's eternal purpose for us and in us and find the specific comfort to which he alludes in verse eighteen, "*For I reckon that the sufferings of this present time are not worthy to be compared with the glory which shall be revealed in us.*" In this way Paul does in Romans 8:28-30 precisely what he does throughout his writings. He builds our experiential knowledge and spiritual joy on the solid foundation of doctrine, of what God has done, is doing, and will do for us.

All Things

And finally, we now visit the question of "all things." Given the two lists that Paul frames in this context and his careful distinction of one list, aimed by its framer and instigator to cause us grief and to separate us from God's love in our Lord Jesus Christ, and the other list categorically framed by God to ensure that we shall neither suffer condemnation nor be finally separated from the love of God in Christ, how are we to interpret "all things" in this context?

In an earlier chapter I indicated that neither list is framed so as to be on its surface wholly comprehensive, but that rather both lists are representative of a larger list. While the second list clearly intends to refer to any and all devices or events that Satan uses in his stubborn attempts to separate us from God's love, I believe the first list (Romans 8:29-30) refers to the covenant of grace with its ultimate objective of purchasing and keeping all of God's chosen vessels of mercy in God's love and safe-keeping. Romans 8:29 begins with "For" in the KJV; the word effectively adds verses 29-30 to Romans 8:28 with a "because" explanation.

I offer two verses that corroborate the point that I believe Paul is making in Romans 8:28.

Blessed be the God and Father of our Lord Jesus Christ, who hath blessed us with all spiritual blessings in heavenly places in Christ: According as he hath chosen us in him before the foundation of the world, that we should be holy and without blame before him in love: Having predestinated us unto the adoption of children by Jesus Christ to himself, according to the good pleasure of his will, To the praise of the glory of his grace, wherein he hath made us accepted in the beloved. (Ephesians 1:3-6)

Grace and peace be multiplied unto you through the knowledge of God, and of Jesus our Lord, According as his divine power hath given unto us all things that pertain unto life and godliness, through the knowledge of him that hath called us to glory and virtue: Whereby are given unto us exceeding great and precious promises: that by these ye might be partakers of the divine nature, having escaped the corruption that is in the world through lust. (2 Peter 1:2-4)

In Paul's own words from the first chapter of Ephesians we enjoy "…all spiritual blessings in heavenly places in Christ" and this enjoyment is "according" to God's election, to the provisions of the covenant of grace.

In Peter's words God's "divine power" has given us "…all things that pertain unto life and godliness…."

Both passages affirm that everything we enjoy that is good comes as a gracious blessing from God. Both passages categorically define or restrict the "things" in question; Paul restricts them to "spiritual blessings in heavenly places," and Peter restricts them as things that "pertain" to both life *and* godliness. Neither inspired writer makes any reference whatever to the evil events of Satan or of his list of strategies aimed at the destruction of our faith and our separation from God. Our spiritual blessings in heavenly places, all things that pertain to life and godliness both flow to us as a result of God's eternal purpose in the covenant of grace. To borrow from our context, being saved by hope, the joyful experience of God's secure provisions for us in Christ as we experience the trials of life, is in keeping with God's incredible love and with His provisions of grace for us in Christ. "...faith which worketh by love..." (Galatians 5:6) is a principle of God's blessings to His regenerate elect in time based on their applying faith to their lives and loving God in the midst of their trials. These temporal blessings are quite in harmony with the provisions of the covenant of grace, but they are not irresistible and effectual. Rather, God's provision for these blessings affirms a contingency on our applying them to our lives as we encounter trials and difficulties.

Neither of these two passages indicates in any way that these blessings are bestowed apart from our walk of faith. In fact Peter goes into significant detail to explain how that we presently enjoy the blessings referenced above only as we make our faith fruitful by adding seven principle virtues to our faith. (2 Peter 1:5-11) Paul similarly qualifies these spiritual blessings that we receive "...in heavenly places in Christ" by later in the chapter affirming "...That we should be to the praise of his glory, who first trusted in Christ" (Ephesians 1:12).

Neither of these passages in any way implies that our eternal destiny is contingent on our making our faith fruitful or our trusting in Christ. In fact both passages affirm that these actions relate to the already-saved, the regenerate elect of God who respond to God's grace with—to borrow Thayer's words—"...affectionate reverence, prompt obedience, grateful recognition of benefits received."

As God included in His covenant with Abraham both conditional and unconditional promises, even so the eternal covenant of grace includes both unconditional and conditional promises and provisions.

First, God gives us life in our Lord Jesus Christ. Then He uses His law written in our hearts, the teachings of Scripture, and the preaching of the gospel, to instruct us in faith and obedience. Our obedience is not the result of an irresistible divine decree, but rather the synergistic outcome of the divine leading through the Holy Spirit and God's law written within, and our conscious, willing, and informed decisions to follow God and to walk by faith. In this obedience God "works with" us and in us, but He does not robotically manipulate us to faith and good works.

Thus in the flowing context of Scripture, the eighth chapter of Romans and elsewhere, we see the initial work of God's grace redeeming and regenerating us, as well as the regenerated hearts of God's elect consciously responding—not robotically being manipulated—to God's instructions to faith and good works. In Romans 8:28 Paul affirms what we find throughout Scripture. When we are consciously, actively, and presently loving God, as shown by our faith—and its inevitable fruit, hope in the face of trials—and good works, divine providence protects and blesses us for good. Specifically the good that we receive in this instance is assurance that nothing can separate us from Him that loved us (Romans 8:38-39); which effectively eliminates the despairing thought in the midst of tribulations that God counts us merely as sheep for the slaughter (Romans 8:36). This assurance comforts us in the reality that we are more than conquerors (Romans 8:37) and gives glory to God in the midst of tribulations (Romans 5:1-5). Far from mystical, this is the tangible good to which Paul refers in Romans 8:28. When we refuse to consciously, actively love God, we face the righteous consequences of our sins, and nothing works for our good!

Personal Examples

Paul's glorious truth in this chapter reaches its zenith in these verses. The five eternal principles of God's saving grace revealed in Romans 8:29-30 will without question or doubt ensure the eternal "good" of every one of God's elect, as the saying goes, "from grace to glory." Yet to the extent that we come to the knowledge of them and "love God" in our daily conduct, these five things and all that they entail will give us this incredible joy in tribulation, this salvation by hope in the midst of every ordeal so that we may find *the joy and comfort* of that eternal "good" in the here and now. Five years ago this very month I learned that I had cancer. For almost a month I struggled with paralyzing fear. My first cognitive thought as I awoke from surgery was, as if displayed in bright lights on the top of a mountain, "God is *good.*" All of the fear that had tortured me for the weeks leading up to this event melted. Whatever I faced, I now understood that God would not leave me alone. He would stand by me and comfort me through it all. That amazing comfort in trials is the life-changing truth that Paul seeks to teach us in Romans 8:28. No, he in no way intends that our eternal state is contingent on anything that we think or do. We are eternally secured by grace through the death of Christ (Romans 8:32), but if and when we apply these truths to our ordeals in life we come to understand the temporal good that he intends in Romans 8:28. Neither our faith and obedience nor our comfort in afflictions is divinely or robotically predestinated; our joy in affliction only occurs to the extent that we understand and apply these glorious truths to our life as we face our trials.

We see this interaction clearly in Paul's two Old Testament personal examples in the Roman letter, Abraham and David. In the case of Abraham a strong faith that believes in God and believes His promise, despite incredible odds against those promises, God blesses and leads us with goodness and grace—"things" work together for our good. In the case of David on the rooftop with an entrenched case of the "wandering eye and the lusting heart," we see the mirror opposite outcome. When David lusted after Bathsheba and orchestrated Uriah's murder, he was not loving the Lord! And this episode did not work together for his good! In fact God told him that he would live with the consequences of that sin for the remainder of his life.

Perhaps not in every case, but often wise men have observed that, when a person starts affirming that every evil, sinful event is in some way divinely caused or orchestrated for a mystical good, he has either just committed an atrocious sin, or he is planning to do so. Regardless of this prediction, nothing about this explanation of Romans 8:28 in any way praises the glory of God in Christ (Ephesians 1:12).

Life will bring its crosses, its trials, and its difficulties. We shall not avoid them for long. However, this passage wonderfully comforts us with the interaction of faith, hope, and godly conduct—actively, presently loving God—God will stand by us as we stand faithfully with

Him through them. Do not overlook the interaction of the conscious, obedient, faithful heart in Biblical "justification by faith."

> *Therefore being justified by faith, we have peace with God through our Lord Jesus Christ: By whom also we have access by faith into this grace wherein we stand, and rejoice in hope of the glory of God. And not only so, but we glory in tribulations also: knowing that tribulation worketh patience; And patience, experience; and experience, hope: And hope maketh not ashamed; because the love of God is shed abroad in our hearts by the Holy Ghost which is given unto us.* (Romans 5:1-5)

Study this lesson in conjunction with Paul's assertion/conclusion in Romans 8:24-25. When we keep faith as our constant companion through our trials, however intense they be, the ultimate outcome of the trial will be hope that "…maketh not ashamed; because the love of God is shed abroad in our hearts by the Holy Ghost which is given unto us." This passage from the fifth chapter affirms the same precise truth that we find in Romans 8:28.

May God lead us to the deep spiritual comforts and truths of this passage—and away from the controversial muddy waters that so often stir it.

60
God's Five-Step Plan: Eternity to Eternity

> For whom he did foreknow, he also did predestinate to be conformed to the image of his Son, that he might be the firstborn among many brethren. Moreover whom he did predestinate, them he also called: and whom he called, them he also justified: and whom he justified, them he also glorified. (Romans 8:29-30)

This lesson links with Verse twenty eight with Paul's use of "For" or "Because" at the beginning of this verse. In the twenty eighth verse Paul is dealing with the comfort we draw from God's eternal purpose and work based on our knowledge of that truth, "And we know…." In verses twenty nine and thirty Paul makes no reference to the contingency or conditionality of our knowledge. He goes to the heart of God's eternal truth that stands based solely on God's purpose and power. "We know" often prefaces our thoughts and observations. In the human experience sometimes we start with a "We know" but must regroup when at a later date we discover that we *didn't know* what we thought we knew. In this context Paul assures us that our comfort in the gospel is based on fact, fact affirmed by God in Scripture. Thus if we embrace the truth of the gospel regarding these eternal principles, we will never need to "relearn" what we thought we knew. This knowledge will stand the test of time.

Paul condenses God's eternal covenant of grace to five relevant principles that he names in this passage. As with our study of Romans 8:28, here too we need to briefly examine major errant views before we affirm the full and glorious truths that Paul teaches us here.

Whom—not What

The first point to be observed is rather simple, so its belief by anyone seems altogether incredible. Both in our English language and in New Testament Greek manuscripts/language, the consistent emphasis that Paul lays on all five of these principles relates to people, not to "things" or events. Paul does not write, "For *what* he did foreknow, he also did predestinate…." Rather he wrote, "For *whom* he did foreknow…." The personal pronoun emphatically appears in association with each of the five principles named in these two verses.

Thus any attempt to interpret this passage so as to embrace the idea that God included events and actions of men in these verses rejects the most basic grammatical construction of the lesson.

Occasionally folks who attempt to embrace this errant view will ask, "Well, don't you believe that God's omniscience includes the actions of men?" I believe that God's omniscience embraces all thoughts, actions, and deeds that ever occur, but God's divine and incommunicable attributes are not the topic of Paul's lesson here. Paul is discussing God's *acts, not His attributes*. The five things in this list of God's eternal purpose and work all appear in verb form, not noun form. They inform us as to what God did, not who He is.

Predestination—not Perseverance

The next point to be observed in this study relates to God's predestination, specifically in this passage of people, not events.

A common error regarding Paul's teaching on predestination attempts make it a statement about predestinated perseverance by linking this passage with Second Corinthians 3:18.

> *But we all, with open face beholding as in a glass the glory of the Lord, are changed into the same image from glory to glory, even as by the Spirit of the Lord.*

The only connection between these two passages is the word "image." Otherwise the two passages appear in different letters, written by Paul to two quite different churches with quite distinct issues and problems. Further the passage in Second Corinthians includes a specific human conditionality; our transformation into the "image" of our Lord is contingent on our looking into the mirror, "…glass," so that we constantly see the image that we are exhorted to become, the moral and spiritual likeness of our Lord Jesus Christ. If we do not look into the reflective mirror of Scripture and the gospel that teaches those Scriptures, we shall be just like the first century Jews who refused—who in fact spurned—to see the image of God Incarnate in the Lord Jesus Christ. Like their earlier counterparts under Moses, when they saw His glory, *they sought consciously not to look at the glory.* In the context of 2 Corinthians 3 Paul draws this comparison and concludes that these folks succeed in not seeing His glory or of being transformed by it. Their eyes are darkened and blinded by conscious and willful rejection of the very glory that they should seek in their lives. Nothing in the context of Second Corinthians 3:18 even hints at unconditional divine predestination! Nothing at all! To link this verse with Romans 8:29-30 is a sad example of faulty hermeneutics that chases an individual word rather than following the correct teaching of Paul as directed by the Holy Spirit. We could as properly equate Judas Iscariot's suicide with Jesus' crucifixion because the word "hanged" appears in both contexts!

Inherent in the faulty attempt to connect these quite dissimilar passages is an excessive and imbalanced view of Scripture that confuses predestination with perseverance. This view incorrectly focuses the historical doctrine of perseverance away from God who "perseveres" in His eternal purpose to "preserve" His elect without the loss of one and onto the faith and obedience of the regenerate elect. It then seeks to affirm that all acts of faith and obedience are divinely predestined so that our faith and obedience are as effectually and irresistibly predestinated as our eternal destiny.

While we should rightly respect and appreciate many of the noble accomplishments of the Reformers, our acceptance of truth should begin and end with Scripture, not with Scripture plus the Reformers or any other group of men for that matter. In this work I will not devote the time necessary to distinguish between the teachings of the Reformers themselves and their would-be followers today. Our focus needs to remain steadfastly on Scripture and the teachings of Scripture. If we follow this simple strategy, we readily discover that every appearance of any form of the word "persevere" in the New Testament appears in the context of exhortations to prayer and faithfulness—never in the context of God's preservation of His elect so that none shall be eternally lost. Scripture describes God's keeping His elect from eternal loss, the historical doctrine of "perseverance," with such words as "preserve" or "kept" not "persevere" (Jude 1:1; 1 Peter 1:5). Do we wish to follow the language of Scripture or the language of subsequent theologians who were uninspired men subject, just like you and me, to error? When Scripture uses a form of the word "persevere," it always teaches us to remain faithful in our service to God. In these passages Scripture tells us what we should do through exhortation and/or admonition, not what God has predestinated that we will irresistibly and effectually do.[1] Never—never—does Scripture use this word in reference to divine predestination. When Scripture teaches us the truth regarding God's exclusive work in preserving His elect from final or eternal ruin, it uses words that relate to "preserve" with consistent clarity. We should follow Scripture!

The Antinomian Straw Man

Beginning at least with Andrew Fuller (around 1792), theologians who object to this Biblical distinction between divine preservation and the exhortation to regenerate elect people to persevere in their faith, prayers, and good works, will quickly and frequently label any and all who disagree with them as being "antinomian," a word that suggests a sinful, careless, even licentious attitude toward the regenerate elect's ethical responsibility to obey and to serve God in every aspect of his/her life. Frequently in our day a new work will appear in which the author singles out the antinomian straw man and argues that anyone who fails to teach as they teach is "antinomian."

At its heart this argument also commits the "horns of the dilemma" fallacy. This logical fallacy creates two opposite views, and demands that one's only position is an either-or choice between the two. In fact there may be any number of views and/or choices, not just the two set up in the fallacy. The Fulleresque idea that we must either agree with his "duty-faith" and related errors or be "antinomian" ignores the solid Biblical truth of faith which works by love (Galatians 5:6). The theological legalist who must include some element of human activity in the salvation equation appears to have an intense distrust of this Biblical principle, if not a regrettable ignorance of it. In this person's mind there are apparently only two options, legalistic perseverance (Either you persevere or you "…aren't really saved at all") or antinomianism.

Hidden behind this straw man is a rather dangerous and insidious error. Dr. Tom Constable observes this error as it relates to both the contemporary error of "lordship salvation" and the contemporary,

---

[1] Ephesians 6:18 as an example; Paul admonishes us to "persevere" in prayer and supplication for all saints. In this context he makes no reference, even remotely to divinely predestinated conduct.

perverted and extreme view of "perseverance." "Lordship salvation" teaches that unless and until Jesus is "Lord" of your life, meaning that you are actively walking by faith in good works, He cannot be your Savior. A marriage of this idea with the Biblical doctrine of election blends precisely with Fuller's notions of "duty-faith" and the necessity for a person to embrace the gospel in order to gain the new birth. Advocates of these two ideas must resort to predestined belief and obedience to ensure that all the elect will hear the gospel, believe it, and obey it. Thus by blending an errant doctrine with Biblical teaching we end up with "predestinated perseverance." Although this is a rather lengthy quote from Dr. Tom Constable, it contains invaluable points that deserve your serious consideration.[2] i

Constable (professor of theology at Dallas Theological Seminary, hardly a Primitive Baptist) rightly observes that "lordship salvation" effectively "front loads" salvation by grace with the necessity of works, and the contemporary errant view of perseverance "back loads" salvation with a similar necessity for works. Constable also insightfully observes that advocates of one of these errors typically also embrace the other error. Thus those who embrace these errors effectively both "front load" and "back load" the truth of salvation by grace alone with works. The hair split offered by advocates of both views that works do not contribute to salvation, but that anyone who is "really saved" will perform such works does not effectively avoid Constable's "front load—back load" exposure. Based on the historical consequences of Fuller's teachings, within a very few generations the folks who today are indoctrinated in either lordship salvation or human-centric perseverance will embrace some form or Arminian salvation by human effort.[3]

---

[2]Tom Constable, *Tom Constable's Expository Notes on the Bible* (Galaxie Software, 2003; 2003), Ro 4:4.)

[3] As an example of this theological drift, consider that Fuller introduced his "duty-faith" error against what he described in his Particular Baptist ancestors as "the cesspool of high Calvinism" in 1792. Only forty years later our Primitive Baptist ancestors in the faith rejected this theological drift in 1832, wisely and correctly observing that the effects of Fuller's errors opened the door to full Arminian theology. Those of us who grew up in the deep south of this country in the mid-twentieth century can appreciate that Southern Baptists in that era were far more Arminian in their theology than grace-centered or "Calvinistic." It is my personal belief that, unless the contemporary Southern Baptist Founders Movement gets in touch with the pre-Fuller doctrines of grace, they too within a few generations will

The view that transforms divine predestination into human-centric perseverance through the artificial association of Romans 8:29-30 with 2 Corinthians 3:18 must necessarily interpret the work of predestination in Romans 8:29-30 as something that occurs experientially in the regenerate elect here in time. Stop and consider for a moment the other four items that appear in Paul's list. Are they all merely experiential to the regenerate elect? Is Paul really dealing primarily in these verses with our experiential perspective, or is he dealing with God's objective work of saving grace?

If Paul intended to teach the doctrine of "predestinated perseverance," either in this lesson or in any of his other teachings, we should consistently find the evidence of this doctrine in the lives of people in Scripture to support the doctrine. I will list just a few Biblical examples that either refute the idea of predestinated perseverance, or else they indicate that predestination did a really poor job in controlling these people since they hardly persevered at all.

1. ***Abraham!*** No one would remotely consider saying that Abraham wasn't really saved at all. However, based on Genesis 25:5-6, we see the last record of Abraham's life prior to the account of his death. The text reveals that he resorted to concubines and even had children by them in his later years. Perseverance? Predestinated?

2. ***Lot.*** If I read the account of Lot's life in the Book of Genesis, I like him in the beginning, but I intensely dislike him in the end. The last historical reference to Lot (Genesis 19:30-38) reports his shameful drunken incest with his two daughters, hardly an example of "predestinated perseverance"[4]

---

revert back to mid-twentieth century Southern Baptist Arminian theology. Were Fuller to have lived in our day, he would likely have described himself as a "moderate" Calvinist, likely a "four-point Calvinist." Fullerite Calvinists struggle with at least one of the five major points of Calvinistic theology, most often the doctrine of limited atonement—just as Fuller did in his "sufficient-efficient" theological gymnastics. They occasionally—often—also struggle with "effectual calling," confusing the direct, immediate work of the Holy Spirit in regeneration with the call of the gospel, making the gospel at the least an instrument in effecting the new birth. Others working their way toward Fullerite Calvinism will exaggerate the effects of the gospel, concluding that every regenerate elect will certainly be brought by divine predestination to believe in the gospel if he/she hears it.

! His life seems more a sad example of confused priorities and incredibly bad choices. He chose his land based apparently on appearance and without consideration that it lay adjacent to Sodom and Gomorrah. At first he merely "pitched his tent" toward Sodom. Then he moved into town. And finally he was "elected to the City Council;" he stood in the city gate with the respected leaders of the city. If I judged a person's eternal state based on their supposed predestinated perseverance, I'd have to judge Lot as hell-bound for sure. However, in the New Testament Peter under the inspiration of the Holy Spirit draws a different conclusion regarding him (2 Peter 2:7-8; Peter refers to him as a "just man" who was vexed with the filthly "conversation," a likely reference to the dominant lifestyle, not mere spoken words).

3. *Jonah.* Jesus uses Jonah's experience with the "whale" or "great fish" and his preaching in highly commendable ways. Yet how do we see Jonah at the close of his book? He is sulking against God for forgiving the Ninevites, hardly the expected image of a man whose conduct was the consequence of "predestinated perseverance."

4. *Gideon.* In the eighth chapter of Judges we read that in his old age Gideon made an "ephod" and encouraged the people to worship it. Further we read that he "had many wives." Is this dual conduct the result of "predestinated perseverance"? Yet we find Gideon's name in the list of the heroes of faith in Hebrews 11:32. Would God place the name of an unregenerate who had no faith in this context? Dare anyone claim that Gideon's final chapter of life exemplifies "predestinated perseverance"?

5. *Samson* died with a bare hint at regained glory, but it was his utter lack of self-control, a habit that appears throughout his life, that lead him to the deplorable state of shame which set the stage for his death. Samson also appears in Hebrews 11:32.

---

[4] Advocates of this errant view will occasionally substitute "decreed" perseverance for "predestinated perseverance," but their intent effectively is precisely the same as "predestinated perseverance."

6. ***The rich young man*** (Mark 10:17-31). Although this young man appealed to Jesus for answers to his questions, he refused to change his lifestyle when Jesus directed it because "...he had great possessions." Here we have a young man whose final appearance in Scripture is described as "...went away grieved: for he had great possessions." Yet in the immediately prior verse (Mark 10:21) we read the specific words "Then Jesus beholding him loved him...." If Jesus loved him, surely he was one of God's elect. Yet his final appearance in Scripture is that he walked away from Jesus, the greatest teacher and preacher who ever lived, having rejected Jesus' message and having refused to repent and make Jesus "Lord of his life." Occasionally advocates of "predestinated perseverance" will appeal to the possibility that he later repented and persevered in obedience to Jesus' command to him. However, this idea builds on an argument from silence. Advocates of the view must go wholly outside Scripture and presume their view in order to prove their view. Argument from silence is no argument of credible weight.

We could examine any number of similar examples throughout Scripture, but these should more than suffice to make the point. If God predestinated the perseverance of His elect so that they will "advance in holiness" as they grow older, how do we explain these and the many other similar examples from Scripture? Were the inspired writers of Scripture "antinomian"? Isn't this absurdity the heart of Paul's rejection of antinomianism in Romans 3:1-8? Of course such a notion is absurd. Our conclusion then must be to reject the errant view of predestinated perseverance, not only from our passage in the eighth chapter of Romans, but as well from any support anywhere in Scripture.

If Paul intended these verses and these five principles to be primarily experiential to the regenerate elect, how are we to view divine foreknowledge and divine glorification from a temporal, experiential perspective? If one of these principles is correctly viewed from the temporal, experiential perspective, then all of them must be viewed in the same way.

In the next chapter we shall examine the interlinked truths of these five principles and their foundational posture to our secure position in the surety-ship of Jesus' atoning and substitutionary death for our sins—and for our eternal standing with God in glory.

Eternity to Eternity
Consistent Truth

Often as we study Scripture we neglect one of the safest methods of assuring ourselves of a lesson's intended meaning when the Holy Spirit inspired its writing. As we ponder various possible interpretations, we should examine the full and contextual implications of the lesson. As presented in its context, does this lesson either say too much or too little for our proposed interpretation? If the lesson says either too little or too much, we need to eliminate this view from our mind and seek an interpretation that harmonizes with the passage. This rule is especially helpful with our study lesson. For example, the common Arminian view of this passage reduces "foreknew" to the divine attribute of omniscience. However, if this view is correct, the person who holds this view must embrace universal salvation, for all who are included in foreknowledge are also included in all of the four remaining acts of God, including being glorified. None who were foreknown drop out of the number of those whom God glorified.

The Pronoun Question

The pronoun that connects all five acts of God in these two verses appears in our English King James Bible consistently as "whom," a personal pronoun specifically referring to people. The Greek word translated "whom" in these verses is rather consistently identified by New Testament Greek scholars as being a relative pronoun. It takes on the identity of its antecedent. A relative pronoun must be identified with its antecedent before we can rightly determine its intent. Why did the King James (and most other) translators choose the personal pronoun form in our English language instead of an impersonal form such as "what" or "which"? Apparently their analysis of the passage identified the antecedent of the pronoun in these two verses with "…who are the called according to his purpose" in Romans 8:28. Inanimate "things" or events do not love God; nor are they "called according to his purpose."

When a Bible teacher ignores the word form "whom" in these verses and attempts to make a case for "what," referring these five divine and integrated actions to actions of men rather than to people whom God chose in Christ, they reject the translation and presume to become their own Bible translators. Despite the occasional difficulties of the unique dialect of the English language in which the King James translation appears, it has remained since its appearance as one of—if not—the most respected literal translations of the Bible ever to appear in the English language[5]. I have used the King James translation for all of my life and expect to use it to my end. I have no desire or intent to retranslate it, either in the case of these two verses or elsewhere. Typically when a man starts chasing ways to "correct" the Bible, it is because he has embraced an errant idea not supported by the Bible. We are to be faithful students of God's word, not correctors of it!

Who are the "Whom"?

By the unique syntax of these two verses we must conclude that the same "whom" included in the divine act of foreknowing are the same "whom" still included in "...glorified" at the end of the sequence.

The comforting truth of these two verses affirms precisely what Jesus said during His personal time on earth.

> *All that the Father giveth me shall come to me; and him that cometh to me I will in no wise cast out. For I came down from heaven, not to do mine own will, but the will of him that sent me. And this is the Father's will which hath sent me, that of all which he hath given me I should lose nothing, but should raise it up again at the last day.* (John 6:37-39, KJV)

---

[5] As a matter of interest, the same personal pronoun form "whom" appears in the New King James and in the New American translations of the Bible. The King James and these two translations are viewed as the three most literal translations of the Bible available in our language, even to this day. Other "Bibles" are distinctly less literal and more discolored by interpretations and the theological opinions of their editors and publishers. There are multiple reasons for Primitive Baptists to retain the King James as their preferred and respected translation. This question lies outside the scope of this work, but the literal devotion of the King James translators in their translation of the word "whom" in these two verses stands on solid Biblical scholarship.

From the Father's gift (eternity "past" when the Father "foreknew" and chose His elect in Christ, giving them to Him) to His "...raising them up again at the last day," His final act of glorifying them, the number of people involved here, as in Romans 8:29-30, remains a fixed constant. It does not change even by one person.

Old Christian writers and old confessions of faith often use the word "perseverance of the saints" to refer to this Biblical truth. In the language of that day and in the context of their use of the word "perseverance" the theological intent was clearly that God "perseveres" in His grace and in His eternal purpose to preserve every one of His elect to the final redemptive act of resurrection and glorification at the Last Day. Occasionally contemporary Bible teachers will refer to the historical use of this word and "morph" the Biblical doctrine of divine preservation into a human-centric doctrine of progressive sanctification. Among the Primitive Baptists, Elder James Oliphant wrote a concise work on this question, *The Final Perseverance of the Saints*. I have provided in endnote a lengthy quote from this work to confirm Elder Oliphant's intent with the term. Clearly it had to do with God's preserving work, not with the believer's progressive sanctification.[ii] Without question Scripture teaches that every person whom God has redeemed by grace should "...grow in grace, and in the knowledge of our Lord and Saviour Jesus Christ" (2 Peter 3:18). However, this Biblical teaching appears as a divine admonition to God's regenerate elect, not as a divine, irresistible, effectual, and predestinated act.

Many years ago I was talking with a woman who was raised by a Primitive Baptist mother, but she had grown away from her childhood training. She had attended the church where I preached on this particular Sunday morning, and I was preaching on these two verses that day. As I touched the word "predestinate," I noticed distinct negative body language in this woman. She simply heard the word and likely drew the common conclusion of contemporary superficial Christians (typically the idea of fatalism; of God predestinating everything that occurs). A preacher should always carefully watch his audience. In fact many messages are communicated from the pew to the pulpit! If a man preaches while looking at the walls, ceiling, and floors of the auditorium, he misses these very important messages that the audience is sending to him. When I noticed this woman's reaction, without calling attention to her, I simply interacted with the fact that most contemporary Christians have a sadly errant view of the word "predestination." I appealed to the passage (Romans 8:29) and asked the question, "Based on this passage from Scripture, what does predestination really mean? It does not refer to what wicked people do; it refers to what God has purposed for every one of His chosen people at the Last Day. When the trumpet blows and the dead are raised, do you object to being resurrected in the '…image of his Son that he might be the firstborn among many brethren'? That, my friends, is what Bible predestination is about!" This woman's countenance immediately changed from rejection to joy; joyful tears began streaming down her cheeks. The amazing joy of Biblical truth far excels all the hair-splitting errant philosophies and sophistries that men occasionally take to the Bible in their vain attempts to legitimize their errors.

God's eternal work, purposed and accomplished in the Lord Jesus Christ, ensures that Jesus' words (John 6:37-39) are true. You—and everyone whom He chose in Christ before He created this universe—shall be resurrected at the Last Day in His glorious and sinless image to spend eternity with Him. This truth is the foundation on which Paul concludes that all "…the sufferings of this present time are not worthy to be compared with the glory which shall be revealed in us" (Romans 8:18). This truth affirms that God shall never look upon one of His beloved children as "…sheep for the slaughter" (Romans 8:36). This truth affirms the major theme of the eighth chapter of Romans; divine grace that removes sin's condemnation from us will faithfully complete its purpose so that nothing that men and demons may do "…shall separate us from the love of God, which is in Christ Jesus our Lord" (Romans 8:39) Hallelujah! What a Savior!

Endnotes

[i i] "Advocates of lordship salvation effectively add works to faith when they make commitment to Jesus Christ necessary for salvation. One astute writer has observed that this "front loading" of the gospel with works is "paving the road back to Rome."[121] Some lordship salvation advocates believe that an unbeliever only has to be willing to submit to Christ's lordship. However this is only changing the human work from submitting to being willing to submit.

One lordship salvation advocate wrote that to exclude submission to Christ's lordship from the gospel message amounts to antinomianism.[122] Later he defined antinomianism as follows.

"*antinomianism:* the idea that behavior is unrelated to faith, or that Christians are not bound by any moral law. Antinomianism radically separates justification and sanctification, making practical holiness elective."[123]

...Another subtile [sic] modern form of works salvation often accompanies an incorrect interpretation of the biblical doctrine of perseverance. This view says that if a professing Christian does not continue in the faith and in holiness all his or her life, allowing for occasional lapses, he or she was not a true believer. This view "back loads" the gospel with works. Faithfulness to the Lord thus becomes a condition for salvation. This incorrect interpretation of perseverance usually goes hand in hand with lordship salvation.

Some who hold these views try to get away from their connection with works by saying that it is God who produces submission and or sanctification in the believer, not the believer himself.[125] (Emphasis mine; Holder) Nonetheless it is the professing Christian whom God holds responsible for his or her choices, not Himself.

"Indeed, every command to the believer implies the necessity of his involvement as part of the process [of sanctification]."[126]

Constable's reference to some who hold to the view that it is "…God who produces submission and or sanctification in the believer…" is a direct reference to what I have labeled in this chapter "predestinated perseverance." This view effectively attributes all the causative impetus for every act of faith and obedience to divine predestination with no weight whatever laid to the obedient believer's "involvement," as Constable describes the process. Advocates of this view make divine predestination the **only** effectual and irresistible cause of perseverance. In this view even the believer's will is merely responding to irresistible and effectual divine predestination. Such a view rejects every passage in the Bible that builds God's promise of blessings on obedience, as well as the passages that warn of God's righteous judgments against His people for their acts of rebellion and disobedience. Of the 1595 appearances of the word "if" in the Bible, most of them in some way refer to God's exhortations of "conditionality" in which either He promises blessings or judgments, conditioned on our willing and cognitive choices to obey or to disobey His commandments. This view of "predestinated perseverance" must rely eventually on the premise of divine robotic causation that Paul confronted and rejected in Romans 3:1-8.

(References contained in Constable's quote: [121] 121. Earl Radmacher, "First Response to 'Faith According to the Apostle James' by John F. MacArthur, Jr.," *Journal of the Evangelical Society* 33:1 (March 1990):40.

[122] 122. John MacArthur, *Faith Works*, p. 94.

[123] 123. Ibid., p. 259, cf. pp. 94-98.

[125] 125. E.g., MacArthur, pp. 100–101.

[126] 126. Charles C. Ryrie, *So Great Salvation*, p. 152.)

[ii] Who can calmly reflect upon these plain declarations of God's word, and yet believe that all was left in uncertainty respecting our final salvation? If he bore our sins in his own body, and put them away by the sacrifice of himself, and by this one

offering perfected forever them that are sanctified, what can hinder our final salvation? Sin cannot, for it was borne and put away by Christ, and we were thus perfected forever by his one offering. "Moreover, Christ hath once suffered for sins, the just for the unjust, that he might bring us to God." {1Pe 3:18}. Will he fail in his undertaking? If Jesus suffered for our sins, shall we have to suffer for them a second time? Does divine justice require two penalties for the same sins? "If God be for us, who can be against us." {Ro 8:31}. Who has the temerity to answer the apostle's challenge? "For whom he did foreknow, he also did predestinate to be conformed to the image of his Son, that he might be the first born among many brethren. Moreover, whom he did predestinate, them he also called, and whom he called, them he also justified, and whom he justified, them he also glorified." {Ro 8:29-30}. No wonder the apostle challenges any one to show who it is that can be against us, for with God on our side, the final victory will be ours.

Some regard the suffering of the Son of God as only conditional satisfaction to the divine law, and hold that faith, or belief, is the prime and all important condition. But what are we to believe as the conditions? Shall we say that the condition of salvation is the belief that Christ is the Son of God? But this the devils believe, and tremble, and even made public confession of their belief, see {Mt 8:29}. Certainly such belief and confession cannot be a condition of salvation, unless we say that the devils have a chance to be saved. But, say others, we must believe that Jesus is our Savior, and that this is the condition upon which we are to be saved. But how can a person believe that Jesus is his Savior, if it be not a fact until he has believed it? Are sinners required to believe that which is not true until they have believed it? But, say some, they are required to believe, as a condition of salvation, that Christ died for them on the cross. But how can they believe that Christ actually died for them, if it be true that he died for them on conditions to be performed by them? If this is the scheme of salvation, they cannot believe that he really died for them until after they have believed it. For it is not a fact until they have performed the condition by believing it, for that is necessary to make it a fact.

If such belief is the condition upon which it becomes true that he died for sinners, then they will have to believe that to be true, in order to make it true. But others say they must believe that Christ did bear their sins on the cross, and put them away by his death and suffering. But how can they make that a fact now, by believing it? If he bore their sins in his own body on the cross eighteen hundred years ago, why do they have to believe it now, to make it a fact? How can they make what occurred eighteen hundred years ago true now, by believing it?

61
All Things or All Things?

> What shall we then say to these things? If God be for us, who can be against us? He that spared not his own Son, but delivered him up for us all, how shall he not with him also freely give us all things? Who shall lay any thing to the charge of God's elect? It is God that justifieth. Who is he that condemneth? It is Christ that died, yea rather, that is risen again, who is even at the right hand of God, who also maketh intercession for us. (Romans 8:31-34)

As we have examined the verses leading up to this lesson, we noted the historical variation of interpretations related to these verses, especially those views that relate to "all things" as first mentioned in the twenty eighth verse. Sadly many of these views interpret that verse as if it existed in a vacuum, wholly apart from its tightly reasoned and logical context. Exegetical accuracy often rightly observes that "A text without its context is a pretext." We can extract any verse from its inspired context and impose any number of contrived or philosophical views onto it, but we can only discover the correct interpretation through careful and faithful study of the lesson in its contextual setting in the Bible.

This chapter examines four verses that follow immediately upon Paul's assertions in Romans 8:28-30, verses that present his inspired conclusions from the points that he made in those verses. "What shall we then say to these things?" sets the stage for Paul to tell us by the direction of the Holy Spirit the ultimate "meaning" of those verses and what his inspired reasoning through them should lead us to conclude. Is Paul's motive in this context a design to assert the absolute sovereignty of God, the general conclusion of many advocates of the idea that "all things" in Romans 8:28 refers to every event in human history? "If God doesn't control every event in human history, then He isn't really sovereign" is the typical rationalization made by advocates of this view. Despite this excessively broad generalization, most advocates of this view will quickly evade the clear implications of the statement by asserting that they do not believe that God causes sin. Then, based on their own reasoning, do they deny God's absolute sovereignty over sin? A false perspective of a passage will lead to false conclusions, often conclusions that border on the absurd, but always ideas that expose the fallacy of the view. A reasonable implication of this errant view of "all things" would be this statement, "If God doesn't control sin, then He isn't really sovereign," meaning that God must cause every sin, or we must deny His true sovereignty! Herein the absurdity of the error appears most clearly.

In the context of Romans the eighth chapter, though on occasion Paul may indirectly deal with divine sovereignty, his primary objective, stated at the beginning and the end of the chapter, explores our standing with God through the Lord Jesus Christ, not divine sovereignty. Throughout the chapter Paul introduces various issues and truths that affirm his opening assertion, "There is therefore now no condemnation to them which are in Christ Jesus...." When we listen to a musical score, especially a classical number, we are trained to hear the "major movements" in the number and to observe how the composer transitioned from one movement to the next. In Scripture we should consider that the Holy Spirit has both composed the "number" and is serving as the conductor when He directed some forty to forty five men to write the sixty six "movements" of our Bible. Let's identify just a few of the major movements of truth within the eighth chapter of Romans.

1. **8:1;** opening and therefore foundational theme. There is no condemnation to those who are identified by their being "...in Christ Jesus."
2. **8:2-4;** first and most crucial point that explains this amazing assertion. God transferred the legal debt of our sins onto Jesus, and now transfers the legal merit of His sinless life and atonement onto us, His chosen people.
3. **8:5-15;** moral or ethical implications of this new standing in Christ. In the new birth God conveys to us experientially (Legally He conveyed it at Calvary) the benefits of what Jesus did for us. This work alters our most basic nature. It so identifies us with the Lord Jesus Christ as to relieve our obligation to legalism, not with a vacuum of antinomianism, but with the higher obligation of a living "marriage" relationship to the Lord Jesus Christ (Romans 7:1-4), a relationship that leaves us no longer in debt "...to the flesh, to live after the flesh." Our interpretation of "flesh" here is

critical to our understanding of Paul's point. Neither Jewish nor Gentile Christians in the church at Rome were flirting with antinomianism, though some who were highly critical of Paul accused him of this error (Romans 3:1-8). Rather, based on Paul's discussion in the seventh chapter of his personal internal conflict between legalism (his old and dead "husband") and the new life of Christian liberty in Christ (the true "husband" whom we should live to faithfully "…till death do us ***NOT PART***"), I suggest that Paul's primary thought with this term "flesh" in Romans 8:12 refers to any form of legalism that fails to embrace the Lord Jesus Christ as the primary basis for our standing with God. Some legalist in our time use human performance, the essential trait of all legalism, as the basis for one's new birth and eternal standing. Other legalists in our time hold strongly to the doctrines of grace, but teach legalism no less fiercely than those who teach eternal salvation by works, will affirm a different form of legalism either as one's "assurance of salvation" or as the ultimate litmus test to determine if "you are really saved or not." It is for these reasons that Dr. Tom Constable (quoted in an earlier chapter of this work) made the point that lordship salvation "frontloads" salvation by grace with works, and that a human-centric view of perseverance (not God's preservation of His elect) "backloads" salvation by grace with works. Regardless of one's theological perspective, legalism justifies its existence by creating and maintaining a "debt to the flesh," the precise point that Paul rejects in Romans 8:12. The Biblical alternative to all forms of legalism is "…faith which worketh by love" (Galatians 5:6). At the heart of the matter all legalists by building their theology on legalism acknowledge that they do not trust nor believe that faith can effectively work by love!

4. **8:16-17;** our true assurance comes from God and not from our own legalistic "performance." "…faith which worketh by love" is sharply contrasted with imprisoning legalism that requires us to view ourselves as "…debtors to the flesh, to live after the flesh," (8:12), the precise lifestyle that Paul described in the seventh chapter of Romans through the failed

and torturous ordeal of trying to live up to the expectations of legalism.
5. **8:18-23;** living life in a constant awareness of what God has done for us will lead us to anticipate the Second Coming and our literal, bodily resurrection, the ultimate defeat and disgrace of Satan and of sin in Christ.
6. **8:24-25;** "resurrection living" gives us the joys of our salvation in the "here and now."
7. **8:26-27;** both in the Holy Spirit's integral work of assisting us in our prayers and in the intercession of our Lord Jesus Christ, pleading His work as the full and eternal satisfaction for our sins, our view of living a God-honoring life anchors in "…faith which worketh by love," not in a debt to any form of imprisoning legalism.

Thus Paul effectively sets the stage throughout both the seventh and eighth chapters of Romans to lead us to a Christ-centric view of our standing in Christ and of our victorious, joyful, and liberating Christian living in the here and now. This Christ-centric view stands opposed to a human-centric view of our spiritual standing in either of its typical forms: 1) Arminian theology that teaches various forms of salvation by human works, or 2) various unresolved and unbiblical views of salvation by grace that consistently fail to shed the human-centric errant view of legalism through either frontloaded lordship salvation or back-loaded human-centric perseverance.

Contextually when Paul then introduces the verses that we have recently examined, he is explaining the divine basis for our ultimate victory over sin and our secure standing with God, the point that he made at the beginning of the chapter.

When Paul writes *"What shall we then say to these things?"* to what "things" is he referring? If we adopt a contextual view of Romans 8:28-30 that reconciles the "all things" of Verse twenty eight with the "five things" of verses 29-30, this question and Paul's subsequent conclusions present us with no problems. If we embrace the indiscriminant view of "all things" mentioned above and throughout this study, then we face a major challenge. Is Paul referring to everything that occurs in our fallen world, or is he referring only to certain things that occur in our fallen world? And how are we to distinguish those things based on the context?

If we embrace the errant view of "all things" in the twenty eighth verse, we face a still greater dilemma in Romans 8:32. If "all things" are contingent on the death of Christ, Paul's specific point in Verse thirty two—if we only receive them because of His atoning work—are we to seriously conclude that the Holocaust, 9/11, and the recent Virginia Tech insanity, as well as all other acts of human sin and depravity were secured for us by the death of Christ? This is the logical, if absurd, conclusion of an errant view of "all things" in Romans 8:28. In 8:32 Paul chose the same precise words to refer to everything that we receive exclusively through the Lord Jesus Christ. If we are supposedly compelled by some mysterious, but never contextually stated, reason to conclude that "all things" in Romans 8:28 must necessarily refer to all events in human history, on what hermeneutical basis are we to change Paul's definition of the term in Romans 8:32 where he used precisely the same term? Otherwise, since Paul attributes "all things" in Romans 8:32 to the death and intercession of our Lord Jesus Christ, how are we to explain the absurd, illogical, and non-Biblical conclusion that Jesus' death and intercession are directly responsible for the Holocaust, 9/11, Virginia Tech, and every other travesty of human depravity and the general ordeals of "life under the sun"? Such are the illogical and unnecessary trappings of an errant and non-contextual interpretation of "all things" in Romans 8:28.

Rather than chase such absurdities, let's follow Paul and examine his reasoning in these verses.

What shall we then say to these things? If God be for us, who can be against us? (Romans 8:31)

What is the logical implication of God having fore-loved (the correct view of "foreknow" in this context), predestinated, called, justified and glorified us? In having done so God is obviously *for us*. Who then can successfully oppose our standing with him? **Here is the logical conclusion in Paul's own inspired words:**

> *He that spared not his own Son, but delivered him up for us all, how shall he not with him also freely give us all things?* (Romans 8:32)

Having sacrificed Christ to assure our salvation thru his fore-love, predestination, calling, justification, and glorification, it is not reasonable to presume that God will withhold any of the qualities or characteristics of these five things. Rather, having paid such a great price to accomplish His purpose in these things, it is reasonable to believe that **all the blessings and benefits produced by these five elements of our salvation are also given by his grace and mercy.** In context, these include faith which works by love, and hope that Paul says saves us in 8:24-25. Specifically, these are the products of the five things. Our love, the integral trait of active Biblical faith, is based on God's fore-love and appears as a quality of the new birth. Faith is also a quality bestowed in regeneration (Galatians 5:22-23) and is based on functional principles of justification and glorification. As we view life from God's eternal perspective, we live in the comfort of our present justification and our certain future glorification.

> *Who shall lay any thing to the charge of God's elect? It is God that justifieth.* (Romans 8:33)

Who can make any charge—by any claim—that any of God's elect are not saved? If God is for us, who can successfully oppose our standing in His sight, since He is the Judge and He has declared our innocence? Later as Paul concludes this chapter, he will provide us with a comprehensive list of charges—things—that we might think could separate us from the love of God in our Lord Jesus Christ. However, as he ticks off the items on that list, he concludes that none of them can—or shall in fact—separate us from God's love. Interestingly, if first century Christian Jews and Gentiles had embraced the erroneous interpretation of justification by faith as (in Constable's terms) a frontloaded works-for-salvation system, "You must believe and accept Jesus to be saved," or else a back-loaded works-for-salvation system which implies, "Only those few who persevere through faith in Christ are saved," the scenario would have played out something like this:

Christian Jews at Rome would have claimed that any Gentile believer who failed to embrace some form of legalism was "...not really saved." Likewise Gentile Christians would have claimed that Jewish believers who embraced legalism instead of "...faith which worketh by love" were "...not really saved." To some extent this scenario may have existed, but Paul and the other apostles, along with the Jerusalem church, distinctly rejected it (Acts fifteenth chapter), rather than embrace it.

Who is he that condemneth? It is Christ that died, yea rather, that is risen again, who is even at the right hand of God, who also maketh intercession for us. (Romans 8:34)

What Christian Jew can reasonably condemn any elect Gentile to eternal separation from God because he is not circumcised and does not follow Mosaic—or any other form of—legalism? We are justified by Christ. He successfully atoned for our sins as indicated by his resurrection, and is even now making intercession on our behalf (both for our eternal standing and for God's providential mercies for our temporal blessings in the here and now). Conversely, in context of chapters nine, ten, and eleven, it is similarly unreasonable for Gentile Christians to pronounce condemnation against elect Jews who ignorantly seek to establish their own righteousness by the law and have not submitted themselves to God's righteousness in Christ, in whom their justification is also effectually accomplished by his shed blood.

Notice that Peter makes precisely the same point that Paul has made in our Romans context.

According as his divine power hath given unto us all things that pertain unto life and godliness, through the knowledge of him that hath called us to glory and virtue: Whereby are given unto us exceeding great and precious promises: that by these ye might be partakers of the divine nature, having escaped the corruption that is in the world through lust. (2 Peter 1:3-4)

God gives us "...all things that pertain unto life and godliness," not all things that grow out of "life under the sun," or all things that occur due to the sinful state of the present world. Following these verses

Peter directs his readers to make their faith fruitful by adding seven key virtues to it. He never indicates that God predestined their fruitful faith, but he rather teaches that God's work of grace in us provides the motive and the inclination, and we are to use the blessings that God has endowed to produce a fruitful faith, one that "...worketh by love" and avoids empty and barren pretensions.

The "all things" of Romans 8:28 are things that grow out of and directly relate to the five things named in Romans 8:29-30, or as Peter frames the same thought, "...his divine power hath given unto us ***all things* that pertain** unto life and godliness...." If in the essential work of grace depicted in the five things of Romans 8:29-30, God demonstrates that He is "for us" and that none can therefore be successfully against us in the final analysis of eternal things, Paul emphatically affirms that all related things, things accrued to our account by the atoning death and present intercession of our Lord Jesus Christ, are equally provided to us and will work for our good. The temporal realization of these blessings occurs only as—and to the degree to which—we actively and presently love God in our daily activities. Isn't that precisely what Paul stated in Romans 8:28? Isn't that what Peter affirmed in the above quote? Our eternal end is secure in Christ alone. If God has so secured our eternal standing and destiny, why should we for a moment doubt or question that He will provide us with the riches of heaven to meet our needs and to enrich our lives in the here and now?

Never throughout the eighth chapter of Romans does Paul sidestep his stated and primary objective, to remind us of our secure standing in Christ, justified—not condemned, and eternally finally united with—not separated from our beloved Savior.

Truly indeed; God's grace is amazing!

62
Who's Behind the Who?

> Who shall separate us from the love of Christ? shall tribulation, or distress, or persecution, or famine, or nakedness, or peril, or sword? As it is written, For thy sake we are killed all the day long; we are accounted as sheep for the slaughter. Nay, in all these things we are more than conquerors through him that loved us. For I am persuaded, that neither death, nor life, nor angels, nor principalities, nor powers, nor things present, nor things to come, Nor height, nor depth, nor any other creature, shall be able to separate us from the love of God, which is in Christ Jesus our Lord. (Romans 8:35-39)

No, I have not decided to write a new version of Dr. Seus! However, the question in this chapter's title goes to the heart of what we have been studying for the last several chapters and, to some extent, throughout our study of Paul's Roman letter.

First, notice that Paul did not ask the question, "What shall separate us...." Rather he asked the question, "**Who** shall separate us...." Do not overlook this subtle but rather significant point. While Paul develops a comprehensive list of "things," he understands that people are the instigators of these things. We could correctly review Paul's list and ask, "Shall the people who instigate tribulation, distress, persecution, famine, nakedness, peril, or sword separate us from the love of Christ?" The form of Paul's question requires a negative answer, "No, neither these people nor what they do shall separate us from the love of Christ."

If we revisit the primary source of the controversy that Paul addresses in the first eight verses of the third chapter of this letter, or if we revisit the verses that we've studied earlier in the eighth chapter, especially from the twenty-eighth verse forward, the significance of "Who" becomes apparent. If in fact God is causing both the "who" and the "what" in our present list for some mystical purpose or the function of a "secret will," then we must conclude that God is behind the "who." And if we conclude that God is behind the "who" of this list, we cannot logically avoid the obvious conclusion that God is not merely manipulating or orchestrating sin, but that He in fact is its cause. Thus we return to the logical and self-contradictory absurdity of the errant doctrine, "God causes everything, but He doesn't cause sin."

Advocates of this errant view often demonstrate incredible skill at logical fallacies. Sometimes I think they wrote the book on logical fallacies. To avoid the consequences of their own error, they have historically used the "horns of dilemma" logical fallacy to defend their errant view, "If you don't accept my view that God causes everything, you are a deist who believes in an absentee god who created the universe and vacated any governance whatever of it or of what goes on in it. The "horns of dilemma" logical fallacy" falsely asserts that there is no other view to be considered. Either you must accept the fallacious view, or you must accept the mirror opposite absurdity. Scripture rejects both views and affirms the righteous character of God; it exonerates Him of any culpability in the operation of both sin and of sinful men and demons, as well as affirming God's wise and righteous providential involvement in the affairs of men. De facto most thoughtful and studious Christians reject both errant views, extreme predestination and deism, and bear loud and convincing testimony to the fact that other views exist, views that far more accurately interpret the teaching of Scripture regarding both God's rejection and judgment against sin—and sinners—and His kind providential involvement in the lives of His children. When a person is reduced to defending his/her view by resorting to logical fallacies, the depth of his/her errant view and the implication of its utter lack of Biblical grounds and Biblical defensibility should be transparent to the thoughtful Bible student. Scripture defends itself, so correct Biblical interpretations will defend themselves without the necessity to use logical fallacies to affirm them.

Both people and demons who hate God will ever work in every way they can to either separate us from the love of Christ, or, failing in that objective, will deceptively use every ploy they can muster to create deceitful illusions in us that we are separated from His love, even though we in fact are not so separated from His love. This evil strategy does not originate with God! It originates from both God's and our arch-enemy, Satan and his minions.

In the context of this lesson Paul repeatedly juxtaposes God against Satan and all his forces. Emphatically Paul reminds us that it is God who—

1. Is "for us" (8:31)
2. "...spared not his own Son, but delivered him up for us all..." (8:32).
3. Through the work of Christ, "...freely gives us all things..." (8:32).
4. "...justifieth. Who is he that condemneth?" (8:32-33).
5. Through Christ, "...died...is risen...is even at the right hand of God...maketh intercession for us..." (8:34).

If, after going to such lengths in our support and defense, God diabolically employs Satan as His agent to orchestrate the people and actions mentioned in our present list, we discover an incredible degree of inexcusable duplicity in God Himself!

If in fact God is "behind the who" of this lesson, we cannot avoid the logical conclusion; we are living the theological equivalent of a new episode of "Star Wars" in which we discover that the "Force" is characterized by both a "light side" and a "dark side."[1] However entertaining, Star Wars religion is a nicely revamped version of fatalistic Eastern Mystical religion in which "yin" and "Yang," good and evil, are eternally counterbalanced against each other. Thus the dark or evil, sinful side of life in this sci-fi view of God is no less an integral part of God than His good side. My friend, this is not the Biblical view of God! It is abominable to the Biblical view. "But he is in **one mind**, and who can turn him? and what his soul desireth, even that he doeth." (Job 23:13, KJV) God is not characterized by double-minded moral duplicity!

Deuteronomy 29:29 affirms that God has not revealed all things to us, but it does not affirm that God operates from the dual—and often contradictory—perspectives of both good and evil.

The secret things belong unto the LORD our God: but those things which are revealed belong unto us and to our children for ever, that we may do all the words of this law. (Deuteronomy 29:29, KJV)

---

[1] In his article at the end of *Hassell's History* Elder Gilbert Beebe, one of the original "absolute predestinarians" among Primitive Baptists, does exactly this. He draws a parallel between the "mystery of godliness" and the "mystery of iniquity," asserting that God is as fully involved in one as in the other!

Further, the absurdity of using this passage to affirm a supposed Gnostic inner knowledge of God's secret will by which we may mystically reconcile God being holy and yet either causing or orchestrating all sinful activities of men and demons in order to accomplish some unspecified (mystical) good should be obvious to the reader. If such "secret things" belong to God while we can only function with "...those things which are revealed..." how can we build our primary theological foundation on a premise that we do not know, on a hidden "truth" that does not belong to us? And even more central to the point, how can we use this passage to rationalize glaring moral contradictions onto God under the presumption that God's "secret will" involves moral contradictions to His "revealed will"? Moses did not write that God had a mystical "secret will." Rather he simply asserted the obvious fact that we cannot know everything about God or His will. However, Moses wrote nothing to so much as hint that anything in those "secret things" in any way contradicts what God has revealed to us. Such a reckless use of this verse in fact offers no real basis whatever to the idea that God in any way is morally confused or contradicted. Nor does it in any way justify the often elaborate and involved defense of errant doctrine based on a presumed private revelation of "God's secret will" to the person making the errant allegation. If God has revealed this "secret will" to them, it is no longer a "secret will." And if He has not revealed it to them, they have no grounds on which to build their errant doctrines.

A thorough contextual reading of Deuteronomy 29 will in fact disprove the "secret will" interpretation of this verse altogether. Moses is dealing quite directly with sinful conduct among his people. In Deuteronomy 29:18-19 he addresses the sinful abomination of an Israelite whose heart departs from God. This person, though in utter rebellion to God, may display a nicely convincing exterior to other people, but he cannot deceive God! Moses develops the point that, despite this wicked person blessing himself despite his sinful departure from God, God knows about the sin and will bring it to judgment. In context "secret things" refers, not to secret things that God is doing, but to secret things that men do. They are secret to us. We cannot know or see them, but we can rest assured that God knows and will judge them righteously. Moses' point, "...those things which are revealed…" especially his conclusion, "…that we may do all the words of this law," rounds out the contextual point. If a person openly breaks God's law, righteous people who see and understand that departure, are charged by God to deal with the sin according to God's law. However, when people sin in secret and we do not know about it, we may rest confidently that God will judge those sins righteously.

[2] The quote below from John Gill's commentary on Deuteronomy 29:29 affirms this interpretation.

> "The Jews generally interpret this and what follows of the sins of men, and punishment for them, and, particularly, idolatry; take Aben Ezra's sense instead of many, 'he that commits idolatry secretly, his punishment is by the hand of heaven (from God immediately); he that commits it openly, it lies upon us and upon our children to do as is written in the law….'"

Rabbai Rashi, a predecessor of Aben Ezra, one of the most frequently quoted Jewish scholars by Gill, offers this commentary to the verse, a strong affirmation of Gill's statement that the "Jews generally interpret this verse…of the sins of men, and punishment for them…."

> ***The hidden things belong to the Lord, our God*** Now, you might object [to God, saying]: "But what can we do? You punish the entire community because of the sinful thoughts of an individual, as Scripture says, 'Perhaps there is among you a man…' (verse 17 above), and after this, Scripture continues, 'Seeing the plagues of that land [and the diseases with which the Lord struck it]' (verse 21) [which seems to indicate that for the sinful thought of even one individual, the whole land would be struck down with plagues and diseases]. But surely no man can know the secret thoughts of his fellow [that we could somehow prevent this collective punishment!" In answer to this, God says:] "I will not punish you for the hidden things!" [I.e.,] because "[The hidden things] belong to the Lord, our God," and He will exact punishment upon that particular individual [who sins in secret]. However, "the revealed things apply to us and to our children" [that is, we are responsible for detecting the sins committed openly in our community, and] to eradicate any evil among us. And if we do not execute judgment upon these [open transgressions, over which we do have control,], then the whole community will be punished [because they would be remiss in their responsibility]. There is a dot placed over [each letter of] the words iÈðáÌ åìÌÀàÈðÅðÀåÅðáÌ here, to teach us homiletically that even for open sins [which were not brought to judgment, God] did not punish the whole community-until Israel crossed the Jordan. For then, they accepted upon themselves the oath at Mount Gerizim and Mount Ebal, and thereby [formally] became responsible for one another (***Sanh.*** 43b). [When dots are placed over letters of the Torah, this denotes an exclusion of some sort. In our context, our Rabbis teach us that the exclusion refers to the period prior to the crossing of the Jordan.]

God does not hold us accountable for sins in others of which we have no knowledge. In the New Testament—in fact earlier in the Roman letter—Paul makes this same exact point, "...In the day when ***God shall judge the secrets*** of men by Jesus Christ according to my gospel." (Romans 2:16, KJV) Thus this verse in fact offers no grounds whatever for anyone to claim that God possesses or operates from a "secret will," especially a secret will that either contradicts or even imposes moral tension against His "revealed will."[2]

The most obvious truth of our lesson from the eighth chapter of Romans throughout appears in the diametrical opposite, not mystically cooperative, roles that God and Satan fill in our lives. God and Satan are not secret partners orchestrating both evil and good for our good! They are archenemies, one bent on our safe and secure deliverance, and the other bent on either separating us from the love of Christ or, failing in that objective, deceiving us into thinking we have been so separated from Christ's love.

Paul's grammatical and logical juxtaposing men or demons and their sinful deeds against God's holiness and His righteous defense and protection of His chosen people further refutes the notion of divinely caused or orchestrated sin. God consistently stands opposed to both sin and sinners who attempt to separate His beloved and chosen people from their loving God. Further his grammatical structure in this lesson demands a negative response. In addition to the grammatical requirement for a negative answer, Paul begins the next "movement" in this theological masterpiece with an affirmation of the point, "Nay...."

Given Paul's incredible development of these profound truths, we may joyfully sing "Safe in the Arms of Jesus" with confident joy in our ultimate victory over sin and sin's diabolical instigator—Satan, not God!

63
No Separation: God's Commitment

> Who shall separate us from the love of Christ? shall tribulation, or distress, or persecution, or famine, or nakedness, or peril, or sword? As it is written, For thy sake we are killed all the day long; we are accounted as sheep for the slaughter. Nay, in all these things we are more than conquerors through him that loved us. For I am persuaded, that neither death, nor life, nor angels, nor principalities, nor powers, nor things present, nor things to come, Nor height, nor depth, nor any other creature, shall be able to separate us from the love of God, which is in Christ Jesus our Lord. (Romans 8:35-39)

Can a person who has been born again lose his/her salvation?" This question is sure to prompt lively discussion in most Christian circles in our day. Despite various errant nuances of related theology, I am grateful that a growing number of contemporary Christians speak up on the right side of this issue, supporting their belief with such passages as the verses now before us.

"Fact versus faith" presents us with an interesting corollary, not only regarding this doctrine and passage, but throughout our study of Scripture. If I believe a lie to be the truth, my belief itself is in fact a lie. If I believe an error to be true, my belief is equally an error. No faith, or no belief, can rise above the factual basis of its object. My belief is no better than the factual reality of its object.

As an example of "fact versus faith," I offer this illustration. In my fifty plus years as a minister, I have often preached funerals or at other times preached to people who were not Primitive Baptists and who did not know about our beliefs of Biblical teaching. Perhaps at the time they reacted fairly positively, even indicated a desire to visit our church to hear more of this gospel. However, in many cases these folks never visited our church. In other cases many of us on occasion either preach to or otherwise interact with people from various religious groups or views that we would generally classify as holding to significant error, and the person remains entrenched in his/her errant views. What effect did their indoctrination in that error have on their reaction to our preaching or conversation? If a person's eternal security relies on that person's perception of faith, and not on the fact of God's work of grace, then anyone who believes an errant gospel and thus believes in "another gospel" (Galatians 1:6-10) that often inherently preaches another Jesus is doomed to eternal ruin. However, if their eternal standing with God relies on the heart and work of God, not their personal perception of that work, this same person's eternal state may be altogether secure, despite their present state of theological confusion. Later in this chapter we will examine a New Testament example of this precise question.

In our study verses Paul takes us behind and beyond our faith to a fundamental fact that stands at the heart of his whole Romans eighth chapter teaching. *"For I am persuaded..."* defines Paul's profound study and conclusion of this question. A. T. Robertson equates Paul's choice of the word with "I stand convinced..."

> "I stand convinced." The items mentioned are those that people dread (life, death, supernatural powers, above, below, any creature to cover any omissions).[1]

In his commentary Albert Barnes observes—

> *For I am persuaded.* I have a strong and unwavering confidence. Latin Vulgate, "I am certain." The expression here implies unwavering certainty.[2]

Add to the meaning of the word chosen the fact that Paul wrote these words under the inspiration of the Holy Spirit and you see the depth of Paul's conviction regarding this truth. For Paul this question transcended the idea of a polite discussion of a point on which sincere Christians disagree. It was a central truth—a thought-out and settled conviction—that he would not compromise! It should be no less for us.

We could call this list of things "Satan's list," for it covers the major things that he uses to discourage God's children, even to convince them that they have in fact been separated from God's love.

---

[1] A.T. Robertson, *Word Pictures in the New Testament*, Vol.V c1932, Vol.VI c1933 by Sunday School Board of the Southern Baptist Convention. (Oak Harbor: Logos Research Systems, 1997), Ro 8:38.
[2] Copied from the electronic version of Barnes' commentary in SwordSearcher Bible software.

While Paul doesn't list everything that Satan might use in his diabolical schemes, he expands the scope of his conclusion from the specific items to the comprehensive, all-inclusive by his injection of the phrase "...*nor any other creature*...."

Our secure standing in God's love is not based on our belief of that truth or our understanding of that inseparable bond between God's love and us, but on God's heart and work that created and sustains that inseparable and undefeatable love. Paul refers to false teachers, exemplified by Hymenaeus and Philetus, who taught the abominable error that the resurrection was already past. (Could this be an aberrant version of the contemporary view of "Rapture" theology and its companion "Left Behind" madness of our own time?) Like the advocates of most effective errors in doctrine, these men were winsome and convincing in their promotion of their errors, so much so that Paul complains that they "...overthrow the faith of some." Notice Paul didn't go into the contemporary judgmental errors such as "Well, you know, if they were overthrown in their faith, it is obvious that their faith wasn't real in the first place. Therefore, they weren't really children of God anyway. They were just pretenders." He tells us that these folks had faith and that these smooth and convincing men overthrew their faith and convinced them of an abominable error. (2 Timothy 2:16-19)

Consider the implications of this lesson from Second Timothy. If Hymenaeus and Philetus were correct, the Second Coming and the final resurrection had occurred, and all the people still alive at the time had missed out on the event! Paul, Timothy, Hymenaeus, Philetus, and those sincere but deceived sheep were all living after the event and thus were not participants in the event! In our time the dominant eschatological view of Scripture (eschatological referring to the doctrines dealing with end times) is Darby, Scofield, LaHaye dispensationalism. This contemporary theology began in 1827 with J. N. Darby and Plymouth Brethren. It never existed before Darby! It is distinctly a different belief from historical millennialism. If it is true, the Lord's people and church lived in ignorance of it for eighteen hundred years before Darby introduced it. It is easy to excite people that this glorious event is imminent and to encourage them that they might be included in it. It is quite a different thing to teach folks that the event has already occurred, and we were left out! That is the essence of the error these men taught—and taught so effectively that they convinced sincere believers that they were right.

Now let's overlay this theological error and its effects on sincere sheep who fell under the "canker" of such teaching (2 Timothy 2:17). Can Hymenaeus and Philetus or their cankerous error "…separate us from the love of God, which is in Christ Jesus our Lord"? We need not speculate. Paul answered the question for us in our study verses at the close of the eighth chapter of Romans. The eternal security of God's chosen people does not stand in the accuracy of our belief or in the orthodoxy of our ideas. This principle applies even to Christians of other faith that promote or follow a perverted gospel (Galatians 1:6), even when they hear the true gospel and do not respond favorably. Nor is it reliant on—or destroyed by—the effects of false teachers. The eternal security of God's chosen people stands secure in the surety-ship of the work and person of our Lord Jesus Christ. Paul affirms this truth by his language in our study passage, "…which is *in* Christ Jesus our Lord."

Based on Paul's concise teaching in this context (Romans 8:33-34), God "…justifieth…" and Jesus performed the work necessary for the eternal security—and surety—of His chosen people. Thus no creature can add new terms or conditions to the divine equation of salvation. Even the contemporary inclination of "front loading" or "back loading" the question of salvation with our perceived requirements violates Paul's point here. God is the exclusive designer in the work of our eternal salvation, the Lord Jesus Christ is the exclusive Cause, and the Holy Spirit is the exclusive agent.

Paul further affirmed this fact in the context of his teaching in Second Timothy.

> *Nevertheless the foundation of God standeth sure, having this seal, The Lord knoweth them that are his. And, Let every one that nameth the name of Christ depart from iniquity.* (2 Timothy 2:19, KJV)

Paul in no way implies that we know who is and who is not the Lord's children, but he leaves no doubt about his inspired conviction that God knows His own, and that false teachers, however smooth and effective, cannot separate even one of God's chosen vessels of mercy from His love.

Beginning at least with Andrew Fuller, anyone who holds to Paul's view of divine grace is liable to the false accusation, "You are an antinomian." In fact this tactic didn't begin with Fuller; it began with Paul's critics (Romans 3:1-8). Paul refused to budge in his view of divine grace, but he equally rejected the antinomian charge as a slanderous error. Paul's holding of divine grace as God's exclusive force—and agency—in the salvation of the elect in no way diminished his strong and consistent teaching that grace motivates, rather than discourages, godly living. Notice his emphasis on this point in his concluding summary from the verses in Second Timothy, "*Let every one that nameth the name of Christ depart from iniquity.*" He didn't allege that God decreed or predestinated that everyone who names the name of Christ would depart from iniquity. Rather he framed the point as an exhortation, "Let...." A. T. Robertson indicates that this word appears in the active voice and the imperative mood. In both English and New Testament Greek the active voice "...represents the action as accomplished by the subject of the verb."[3] The imperative mood is used to issue a command to do something, not a description of something being done to you. Paul clearly instructs Timothy and us to incorporate exhortations to godly conduct and attitudes into our most theological teachings. No one who teaches Biblical truth will affirm the doctrines of grace and then pretend that any sin committed by the individual is "no big deal." Nor will anyone who teaches the Biblical truth of grace make eternal saving, keeping grace contingent on the individual's conduct. God's grace changes our nature in regeneration, including our will and our moral inclinations and abilities. Once grace has changed us we are subject to the commandments of Scripture to actively, willingly, energetically, and voluntarily engage our lives in service to God, beginning with a decisive departure from the habits of sin.

As in Paul's day, if you hold to a full and balanced view of God's grace, some will accuse you of being a fatalist. Others will accuse you of being antinomian. Rather than retreat from the truths that he taught because of these criticisms and false charges, Paul held to his course and affirmed the truth of God's grace on all points throughout the Roman letter. In the heat of conflict it is always easy for sincere people

---

[3] Quoted from the Zodhiates Study Bible's "Grammatical Annotations."

to jump to extreme views in their opposition to error. Scripture demands that we hold to God's balanced truth, refusing to allow extremes and error of any kind to affect the glorious truth of God's revealed truths to us in the faith, the body of truth, which He "once and for all time" delivered to the saints in the body of Scripture. Our confidence in the comforting doctrine of "no separation" from God's love stands on solid rock. Praise God!

www.ingramcontent.com/pod-product-compliance
Lightning Source LLC
Chambersburg PA
CBHW020941230426
43666CB00005B/110